The Crisis of Indian Planning

The Royal Institute of International Affairs is an unofficial body which promotes the scientific study of international questions and does not express opinions of its own. The opinions expressed in this publication are the responsibility of the authors.

The Institute gratefully acknowledges the comments and suggestions of the following who read the manuscript on behalf of the Research Committee: Ian M. D. Little, Professor W. H. Morris-Jones. and Andrew Shonfield.

The Crisis
of Indian Planning

ECONOMIC PLANNING IN THE 1960s

Edited by

Paul Streeten and Michael Lipton

Issued under the auspices of the
Royal Institute of International Affairs

OXFORD UNIVERSITY PRESS

LONDON NEW YORK TORONTO

BOMBAY

1968

Oxford University Press, Ely House, London W1.

GLASGOW NEW YORK TORONTO MELBOURNE WELLINGTON
CAPE TOWN SALISBURY IBADAN NAIROBI LUSAKA ADDIS ABABA
BOMBAY CALCUTTA MADRAS KARACHI LAHORE DACCA
KUALA LUMPUR HONG KONG TOKYO

Printed in Northern Ireland at the Universities Press, Belfast.

Contents

Abbreviations   vi

Indian Administrative Units   vii

1. Introduction: Two Types of Planning *Michael Lipton and Paul Streeten*   3

THE POLITICAL BACKGROUND

2. Power Shifts and Regional Balances *A. H. Hanson*   19

ECONOMIC SECTORS

3. Targets and Investment in Industry *James Mirrlees*   63
4. Strategy for Agriculture: Urban Bias and Rural Planning *Michael Lipton*   83
5. Economic Overheads: Co-ordination and Pricing *J. M. Healey*   149
6. The Case of Energy Investment *E. A. G. Robinson*   173

THE HUMAN FACTOR

7. Investment in Human Capital *David Ovens*   187
8. Population Control: Aims and Policies *Robert Cassen*   251
9. Social Anthropology: Its Contribution to Planning *David Pocock*   271

EXTERNAL CONSTRAINTS

10. Foreign Trade: A Commodity Study *Sidney Wells*   293
11. Aid to India *Paul Streeten and Roger Hill*   323
12. Planning and Defence *K. Subrahmanyam*   351

Statistical Appendix *Roger Hill*   379
Glossary   395
Index   397

ABBREVIATIONS

AID   Agency for International Development (US Govt.)
ARC   Administrative Reform Commission
B.   *Bulletin*
BDO   Block Development Officer
CEO   Chief Executive Officer
DMK   Dravida Munetra Kazagan
4DO   *Fourth Plan Draft Outline*
HYVP   High Yielding Varieties Programme
IAAP   Intensive Agricultural Areas Programme
IADP   Intensive Agricultural District Programme
IAS   Indian Administrative Service
IBRD   International Bank for Reconstruction and Development (World Bank)
IDA   International Development Association (part of IBRD)
IMF   International Monetary Fund
ITI   Industrial Training Institute
J.   *Journal*
MFB   *Material & Financial Balances*
MLA   Member of the Legislative Assembly
MVPE   Marginal Value Product Equalization
NCAER   National Council for Applied Economic Research
NCC   National Cadet Corps
NDC   National Development Council
NPC   National Planning Council
OECD   Organization for Economic Co-operation & Development
PL 480, 665   Public Law 480, 665 of the US
PPD   Perspective Planning Division
Q.   *Quarterly*
VLW   Village Level Worker

Note: Throughout the text quotations not otherwise attributed are from Planning Commission, *Fourth Five-Year Plan: A Draft Outline* (1966).

The terms 'pre-devaluation' and 'post-devaluation' refer to the Indian devaluation of 1966. All calculations in sterling terms are at the rate prevailing before sterling devaluation in 1967, i.e. roughly 1 pre-devaluation rupee = 1s.6d., and 1 post-devaluation rupee = 1s. in terms of British currency before October 1967.

ADMINISTRATIVE UNITS

(An approximation of a system that varies from State to State and is in the process of change.)

Village — (300–2000 people). Elected Village Panchayat. Administrators: 1 village level worker, 1 revenue collector for 3–7 villages. Responsible to BDO.

Block — (20–30 villages). Elected Panchayat Samiti. Administrators: 1 Block Development Officer (BDO); about 5 technical officers.

District — (2–30 Blocks). Indirectly elected Zilla Parishad. Administrators: 1 Chief Executive Officer (CEO) + Revenue Collector. Both are members of Indian Administrative Service (IAS) and have substantial staffs.

State — (typically 15–30 districts). State Parliament. Members of Legislative Assembly (MLA). State Ministries and civil services (partly IAS).

Union of India —
President
Lok Sabha (contains Cabinet)
Rajya Sabha
} Parliament
Central Ministries and IAS staff
Planning Commission

Introduction

1

Two Types of Planning*

MICHAEL LIPTON AND PAUL STREETEN

1. THE FALMER CONFERENCE

In April 1967 some forty British and Indian academics, businessmen, journalists, and professional planners and administrators met at Sussex University to consider the state of Indian planning. The Conference was jointly sponsored by the Royal Institute of International Affairs, the Institute of Development Studies, and the University of Sussex. Four days of discussion, and subsequent events in India, led to a revision of all the papers submitted to the Conference, often so drastic that little remained but the titles, which are listed on p. v. Yet some critics may view the revision as insufficient and the conference as misconceived. For papers and conference alike, while covering several aspects of Indian political economy and social anthropology, took as their starting point a doubtful document: the Draft Outline of India's Fourth Five-Year Plan.

2. WHY THE DRAFT FOURTH PLAN?

The Draft Fourth Plan has been neither disowned nor made official by the Government of India. Since the Plan was published in August 1966, events seem to have made it defunct, and its predictions (a doubling of the growth rate of commodity production from the Third Plan period, and the diversion of 30 per cent of all extra income to saving) excessively optimistic. The 1966 harvest was as bad as its disastrous predecessor. Congress lost eight of India's seventeen States at or soon after the 1967 election. Many

* We gratefully acknowledge comments on this introduction from V. K. Ramaswami of the Indian Ministry of Finance, and helpful and detailed comments on the whole book from I. M. D. Little, W. Morris-Jones, and Andrew Shonfield. We also thank the Indian High Commission, especially the Economic Minister, Mr K. S. Raghupathi, for their most helpful co-operation in providing facts and documents for what they well realized would be a critical work; the U.K. Ministry of Overseas Development, for paying the fares of our Indian guests; and Miss Bridget Martyn and Miss Hermia Oliver of Chatham House, for patient and careful editorial work. We are indebted to Mr Tarlok Singh for valuable comments.

3

observers allege a decline in both prestige and morale at the Planning Commission and a reduction in the weight attached to long-term planning. Certainly, between June 1966, when the Draft was published, and mid-1967, the Planning Commission lost some of its Ministerial members (though not the Prime Minister or the Finance Minister) and some of its formal powers (though not those it was ever able to exercise effectively). Planning has been based on three successive Annual Plans, related to the Draft Fourth Plan in a rather loose and informal way, if at all. So why discuss Indian planning on the basis of a dead document?

Several replies are possible. First, the Draft Outline contains, as the Annual Plans do not, an attempt to formulate a consistent development strategy, and to estimate its measurable consequences. Second, therefore, the projects in the Draft have great survival power. True, officials deny that the Annual Plans are a phased execution of the Draft Outline, which has not been approved by Parliament, and which can scarcely be the basis for the final Fourth Plan, to appear in 1969 after three years without long-term planning. But the Annual Plan projects, and the ratios between sectoral targets, must rely on the roughly consistent strategy and data of the Draft; perhaps for this reason, by Spring 1968 Dr Gadgil and Pitambar Pant had done much to re-establish the policy-making role of the Planning Commission. Third, the Draft at least *mentions* almost every aspect of Indian planning. We cannot cover them all; finance, for instance, is barely touched on, though most conferees thought that the planners' hopes for private saving, taxation, and aid were too rosy. But at least the Draft Fourth Plan *allows* each author to discuss the relevant issues within a framework that is both roughly consistent and semi-official.

But the Draft Fourth Plan is more than a conveniently recent point of reference for an academic discussion. Many of the projects on which it is based are being built now, as part of the Annual Plans. These projects were submitted by Central and State Government Departments and by the Planning Commission itself. The Perspective Planning Division has checked consistency in a much more systematic and revealing way, for the period 1966–76, than ever before; the Division's *Material and Financial Balances*[1] are the

---

[1] Planning Commission (Perspective Planning Division), *Draft Fourth Plan, Material and Financial Balances* (*MFB*) *1964–65, 1970–71, and 1975–76* (1966). Planning Commission, *Fourth Five-Year Plan, A Draft Outline* (*4DO*) (1966).

fullest and clearest available account of the past and projected impact of planning on India, and without the Draft Fourth Plan they are meaningless. Further, however power shifts in India, the Draft Fourth Plan (or its putative successor, the Plan itself) holds the stage as the only official blueprint for investment, employment, and output in India to 1971. It embodies the official account of success and failure to date, and the official philosophy of planning. The account is franker than ever before. The philosophy, largely unchanged on equality and regional balance, is transformed when it comes to the role of price incentives, and modified on the vital question of priority and strategy for agriculture.

The Draft Plan is thus the central document in the running crisis of Indian planning. This is analysed by Hanson on pp. 19–60. Optimists view it as a short-run crisis. They point to the Third Plan's bad luck—two droughts and two wars. Pessimists see the failure of the Third Plan as marking the virtual collapse of political authority over India's economy. They see federalism rampant as non-Congress States abolish taxes, Congress weak at the Centre and defeated or faction-ridden in the States, and over-optimistic projections by planners who are unable to raise taxes or aid (or to improve the efficiency with which they are used) to anything like the extent their plans require.

The Conference considered the realism and consistency of the Draft Fourth Plan in order to decide what, if anything, is wrong. Critics of the Draft Plan often merely extend the time needed to achieve its objectives; indeed, both the starting and the terminal date of the Fourth Plan have already been advanced by three years. But the strategy remains unaffected, and it is on the strategy, expressed in the key *ratios* and *sequences* as opposed to targets and dates, that this book concentrates. Relations between inputs and outputs, balances and consistency within and among economic sectors, trend rates of growth—these, rather than exact quantities and years, are our main concern.

3. REALISM AND PERFORMANCE

Most people doubt the realism of the targets for 1970–1. Under-fulfilment has been too frequent, improved rates of return on capital and higher tax yields relied on too often, extra capacity from projects 'in the pipeline' from the last Plan too recurrent a hope for the claims of greater accuracy this time to sound fully convincing.

Several papers suggest both that the planners' output projections require more inputs than they admit, and that even the admitted input requirements will not be forthcoming (see below, p. 72). Yet all this is less damning than it sounds. This is not because the Plan is mere drum-beating to create political enthusiasm; exhortations to do the impossible would become counter-productive.

Indian planning is better than it seems, not because it does not mean what it says, but because it must be compared with achievements elsewhere and possibilities in India. Some critics seem to compare it with a completely comprehensive, consistent, and optimal plan in Utopia. British economic planners, after their experience with the 1965 'National Plan', are in no state to criticize India for optimism, exhortation, or inconsistency. All three are leading features of India's plans, partly because a plan must reconcile sectional, departmental, and regional claims with economic efficiency. Planners cannot lose sight of the need to rally diverse interests, to mobilize public support, and to maintain political stability. The pursuit of the aims of efficient planning has to be seen against these requirements.

Thus the ambiguities of the successive plans do not justify the cataclysmic view of Indian disintegration presented above (p. 5), and discussed more fully by Hanson (pp. 19–60). Indeed the extreme pessimism after the 1965–6 harvest is no more useful to analysis than the extreme optimism generated by the good harvest of 1967. By the standards of most underdeveloped[2] and some developed countries, Indian planning is technically efficient, administratively competent, and sober in its predictions. Nor was its performance, at least till the monsoon disasters of 1965 and 1966, unimpressive. According to the planners

In aggregate terms, India's national income increased by about 69 per cent (at 1960–61 prices) between 1950–51 and 1964–65 or at a compound rate of 3·8 per cent per year .... Even in agriculture ... the rate of growth has been about 3 per cent per annum (compound) as against an average rate of less than $\frac{1}{2}$ per cent in the previous decades.[3]

---

[2] For a comparison between planning in India and Pakistan, see Edward S. Mason, *Economic Development in India and Pakistan*, Harvard University Center for International Affairs, Occasional Papers in International Affairs, no. 13, Sept. 1966. Pakistan received some $2\frac{1}{2}$ times as much aid per head as India during the period of the Third Indian Plan.

[3] *4DO*, pp. 7–8. These estimates are approximately confirmed by OECD., *National Accounts of Less Developed Countries*, Development Centre (Prelim. Feb. 1967), p. 55.

4. CRITIQUE OF INDIAN PLANNING

Yet none of the contributions to this book accepts the view that India's crises of 1965–7—food deficiency, inflation, foreign exchange scarcity, and industrial slack all at once—are merely the result of short-run bad luck. A fundamental line of criticism emerges from this book. It avers that Indian planners rely too much on bad data; that consequently they over-emphasize the big aggregates of heterogeneous items,[4] and neglect detailed and concrete analysis of social and economic microcosms; that such deficiencies have probably meant too much outlay on the more easily measurable sectors, and too little (and too wasteful) outlay in education and agriculture, where detailed field research is needed to predict responses to expenditures, and that (both as cause and as effect of this imbalance) planners know too little about the rates of return on many of their most important proposed schemes.

This relates to India's short-run problems too. If the expected rates of return on projects in various sectors are not known, then the *response* of such rates to drought or inadequate aid cannot even be guessed. Intelligent short-run response requires contingency planning well in advance of a crisis, so that costs can be minimized when the crisis occurs. Intelligent long-run planning requires investment criteria, so that we know what (and whether) we are maximizing. Neither contingency plans nor investment criteria make sense if we are completely in the dark about rates of return in key sectors. This criticism applies to British planning as much as to Indian, but it matters more in India, because its plans are commitments to action, and because India, being poor, can less afford waste.

5. TWO TYPES OF PLANNING

The *Material and Financial Balances* may project and reconcile aggregates with great sophistication, but studies to select projects and plan for sectors are still rudimentary. Macro-economic planning, at which India excels, reconciles demand, supply, and trade projections for things like total food, steel, or even gross output. It also covers supply and demand of main categories of manpower. In

[4] Not only the familiar butts like 'total investment', 'capital', and 'employment', but many less obvious aggregates are much less homogeneous than is often supposed. 'Rice output' comprises several varieties, harvested under many different climatic and soil conditions, and at various times and places; this suggests that projections must be considerably disaggregated.

such matters the advance from the 1955 'Plan Frame'[5] has been
enormous. Yet even here there are huge gaps, and they suggest the
heterogeneous reality of the social and economic microcosms that
the aggregates conceal.

Consider the fact that one cannot get a plain answer to the
question: are the investment data in the Plans gross or net of
depreciation? Probably they are an uneasy amalgam of the two:
net in industry where they add up a number of cost estimates of
public projects, gross in agriculture where the rate of replacement
is hard to estimate. But this key question, to which different answers
might halve or double India's savings requirements, is left open.
This is because its resolution would require fact-grubbing on a small
and undistinguished scale.

Small-scale planning, at the level of village and project, barely
exists in India. It would require estimates, for main types of plan
project (and alternative ways of doing them), of (1) rate of return
to the operators of the project itself; (2) external effects on output
and costs for other operators, and on costs and benefits of consumers;
(3) distribution of income and of costs implied by (1) and (2); (4)
division of such income among various consumption, saving, and
import uses; and ideally (5) the rates of return on the uses under
(4). These estimates cannot be confined to projects in the public
sector; the best balance of investment between public and private
sectors (financed from a fixed pool of aid and saving) cannot be
decided without comparing the rates of return. Nor can project
analysis be confined to investment. 'Public consumption' that
eliminates roundworm among harvest labourers, or 'private consumption' that feeds ill-nourished and apathetic workers better, will
affect output too.

The lack of small-scale, local analysis and planning is the real
cause of the concentration of planning (even in a fairly dirigiste
economy like India's) on public investment aggregates. Such
concentration produces the incorrect belief that maximum investment
produces maximum growth and that there is always a conflict between
equality (which is thought to reduce aggregate investment) and
growth. If planners disaggregated and looked at the composition
of investment and the yield on outlay, they would find it difficult to
persist in such beliefs. The emphasis on investment also encourages

[5] P. C. Mahalanobis, *Draft Recommendations for the Formulation of the Second
Five Year Plan 1956–61* (Planning Commission, 1955).

the view that there is a fixed relationship between investment and extra output, thereby diverting attention from ways of better utilization of existing plant and equipment. Healey (pp. 168–9), Mirrlees (p. 81), and Lipton (p. 107) suggest that the projections for improved capital utilization contain a good deal of wishful thinking. Improved utilization depends not only on more careful project planning, execution, and management, but also on more detailed study of the area between project planning and aggregate planning, because much under-utilization is due to imbalances between sectors.

The concentration on big aggregates like physical investment has led to some neglect of human factors in economic development. The rates of return to various types of change in education, nutrition, or power-structure are very hard to assess at all; as is shown by Ovens (pp. 188–9), Lipton (p. 111), and Pocock (p. 273), hardly any assessment is even attempted. Without a great deal of work at local level—for specific projects in specific environments—it is impossible to use such assessments in project selection.

Worse still, planners cannot judge how far any given Plan measures up to stipulated investment criteria, unless micro-planning has got at least as far as stage (2) above. Stage (1) has just been reached, nominally at least, by some public overhead sectors (see Healey's discussion on pp. 165–71), which are now to stipulate 11 per cent rates of return on new investment. But it is not clear whether higher levels of efficiency or higher prices are to achieve this; if the latter, private industrial profits and hence reinvestment are likely to fall. Thus stage (2) analysis is essential to assess the effects of overhead policies on growth rates; but no such analysis is attempted by the planners.

The sort of conflict between investment criteria that requires microcosmic planning for rational discussion is well exemplified by the problem of industrial location. The claims of the States, and democratic pressures for the dispersal of influence, point to the erection of numerous small plants in many districts. The need to create employment also appears to militate against large-scale, modern, capital-intensive plant.[6] On the other hand, competitive

[6] However, P. N. Dhar and H. F. Lydall, *The Role of Small Enterprises in Economic Development* (Asia Publishing House, 1961), show that most small enterprises have higher ratios of labour *and of capital* to output than large-scale enterprises.

2

exports require maximum economic efficiency and thus modern, large-scale plant. Export promotion, by enabling India to afford imports that break industrial bottlenecks, may itself raise employment levels. Without information on the headings (1)–(5) above, at the level of the project and the locality, the choice will be made in the dark.

The great importance of this sort of small-scale information, and the relative irrelevance of aggregate investment criteria, may be seen by looking at the practical implications for India of the classic conflict of investment theory: the balance between high-yield projects and high-saving projects,[7] or, very crudely, between agriculture and heavy industry. The shorter the period over which growth is to be maximized, the more will planners try to select the group of projects with the highest ratio of current output to capital; projects where equipment is itself very productive, or else makes bottleneck-breaking outputs that greatly raise the yield from other equipment. The longer the planners' perspective, the more will they emphasize projects with high ratios of saving to income yielded: projects in the public sector, or with a high profit/wage ratio, or urban and thus taxable. The balance of priorities between agriculture and industry (pp. 63–64, below) still owes much to a rather self-defeating victory of very long perspectives over immediate needs.

6. THE STRATEGY OF THE FOURTH PLAN

Is India aiming at rapid or at self-sustaining growth? It is a cruel choice. If it is quickly to become independent of aid, it will aim at self-sustaining growth. India will then concentrate its investments (even if the yield is very low) on 'machines to make machines', supplementing initially low domestic savings with as much aid as possible; it will thereby hope to build up the 'basic' capacity (generally in the saving sectors, with high profit/wage ratios) that will finance investment without aid later. That was the strategy of the Second Plan. But the experience of the Third Plan suggested

---

[7] W. Galenson and H. Leibenstein, 'Investment Criteria, Productivity and Economic Growth,' *Q. J. Econ.* 1955; A. K. Sen, *Choice of Techniques* (Oxford, 1963). In an open economy, the conflict can be eased by a surplus of imports, permitting a country to invest more than it saves, and allowing the balance to be tilted towards low-yield, high-saving projects. India has now hardly any reserves to finance such a surplus and the prospects of aid are made gloomy by the growing burden of debt (pp. 327–37 below). The conflict is thus more acute than ever.

that the strategy was too long-term, too vulnerable to shortfalls in aid and excesses of political pressure, and above all too sensitive to food scarcity and consequent inflation. This last weighs especially heavily because of the unsure future of US food aid.

In the Draft Fourth Plan, and even more in the three Annual Plans into which it has so far been transformed, there is greater emphasis on *rapid* growth. Quick-yielding projects are being preferred within each economic sector. Of course, in default of microcosmic planning, too little is known about just what projects really do produce quick results. In any case, roads, light industry, and improved seeds have been favoured at the expense of railways, heavy industry, and community development.

This shift of emphasis is induced partly by rapid population growth, and the long period required for family planning to make an impact on birthrates (as analysed by Cassen on pp. 252–4). If population is growing by $2\frac{1}{2}$ per cent per year, and the political claims discussed by Hanson (pp. 26–35) have to be appeased with consumer goods, the scope for 'basic' investment is reduced. Probably rightly, therefore, long-run yields and reinvestment rates are being sacrificed to attain rapid short-run results. The sacrifice imparts special urgency to family planning; Cassen suggests (p. 261) that it yields fifteen times as much as other forms of planned investment.

In the short-run, India's political state makes this shift of policy, from self-sustaining growth towards rapid growth, almost unavoidable. Many participants at the Conference would have gone further, accepting a smaller Plan (and a marginal savings ratio lower than the Draft's optimistic 30 per cent) and redirecting public outlay to family planning, foodgrains, and adult technical education. That would leave steel and heavy industry for later. This is less of an ideological dispute than it appears. If we believe that India's prospects of aid are better (say) in 1968–72 than in 1973–7, then the revised Fourth Plan should include more basic industries and fewer high-yield projects than if we believe the opposite. Thus the strategy of the Plan depends critically on the assumed time-profile of aid to India.

7. EXTERNAL CONSTRAINTS ON PLANNING

Subrahmanyam shows (pp. 374–5) that defence expenditures involve less diversion of foreign exchange resources than is generally believed. Defence is an external constraint only in a special sense: that it is exogenous to the planning process. Some participants thought it was too exogenous, that more might be done to co-ordinate defence and development planning. However, it became clear that (1) the resources released by a politically plausible settlement with Pakistan would be rather small and not automatically devoted to development investment, (2) the armed forces, being concentrated in sparsely populated border areas, cannot be much used for developmental purposes, (3) the material requirements of defence are less of a drain on fully-utilized factories producing developmental outputs than is usually believed.

It remains true that the upper limits to developmental investment are set by the availability of the surplus of production over consumption; what defence absorbs of this surplus is lost to development. This remains true even if the Army draws entirely on men who would otherwise have been idle. Politicians inevitably concentrate on the political costs of border compromises; it would be worth calculating their economic benefits too.

To relieve the foreign exchange constraint, the most obvious ways are to import less or to export more. The devaluation of June 1966 was one of many signs that the Indian Government is relying increasingly on price incentives, reducing the burden on the administration of direct controls. The export incentives could be amplified by improving Indian marketing—much emphasized at the Conference. Unfortunately, the devaluation of the rupee itself will not stimulate much new demand for Indian jute or tea exports (nor is it clear that India could meet such a demand). And Indian firms cannot respond to devaluation by big cuts in raw material imports; nor would it help India's industrial development if they did. On p. 294 Dr Wells suggests that policy has shifted from import substitution towards export promotion. That shift was encouraged by the success of exports in the Third Plan, but also by the obvious dislocation caused by shortages of development imports. Unfortunately, the absence of microcosmic planning prevents the planners from estimating the imports saved (or exports generated) by specific projects in specific areas.

India has hardly any reserves of foreign exchange. If she is to finance development by a temporary import surplus, inflows of capital are essential. At the Conference some participants pointed to adverse effects from capital flows into India. Some of these effects, such as that of surplus food disposal in reducing food prices and hence incentives to farmers, applied in particular to aid. Others related to the effect of *any* capital inflow in permitting imports—indistinguishable in the aggregate statistics from machinery and maintenance imports—which are used to cater for the luxury demands resulting from the unequal income distributions. Worse still, some inflows, especially of private investment managed by expatriate or Indian élites, can lead to the payment of incomes spent in a way that encourages wasteful luxury spending. Aid may also have detrimental effects on domestic efforts to mobilize private and public savings.

But the dispute amongst participants over the size of aid that India should seek was partly a difference over timing, partly a matter of strategy ('show you can do without aid and you will get it') and, in any case, did not stand in the way of agreement on India's need for debt relief. Most of India's aid receipts in 1968–74 must go straight back to the donors to repay former 'aid' loans—with interest. The rescheduling of such repayments, discussed by Streeten and Hill (pp. 323–49 below), is thus one way of giving aid to India. In any event the uncertainty of aid—the fact that Indian planners could not assume a definite quantity of aid over the ensuring Plan period—exemplified a recurrent theme of the conference: the need to deal with short-run risks if long-run strategy is to be pursued successfully.

8. THE PROBLEM OF RISK

The risks of aid are largely a fortuitous result of the donors' national budgeting, contracting, and electoral procedures. The case for *more* aid to India, on almost any criteria, is made by Streeten and Hill (p. 339); but the *assurance* of $900 mn a year for five years would be worth more to India than an average of $1,000 mn yearly over that period, if this average were liable to large and unpredictable fluctuations. Such an assurance would also be cheaper for donors. With the World Bank's new emphasis on non-project aid to Plans as a whole, such arrangements should become acceptable to the consortium of donor countries that supplies over 90 per cent of aid to India.

The need for the State (not just the individual) to take account of risk was a recurrent theme at the Conference. Healey (pp. 151–72) and Robinson (pp. 173–83) point out that there is an asymmetry of risks with regard to overhead capital. Admittedly it is expensive to build 5 per cent too much rail capacity everywhere, but it is much more expensive to be caught with 5 per cent too little; production is disrupted, capacity elsewhere is wasted, and men are thrown out of work. Lipton suggests (p. 112) that if agricultural extension (and incentives) persuade people to adopt a good but risky policy, droughts may destroy confidence in Government advisers.

The possibility that things may not turn out as planned is not an argument for less ambitious planning. It does point to the case for holding various forms of reserves—and for contingency planning. This is a much abused term. To say that, if aid and savings are 10 per cent below target, then all investment and output targets will be cut by 10 per cent, is a very crude and inefficient form of contingency plan. Unfortunately the linear assumptions on which Indian aggregate planning is based render such a procedure as tempting as it is easy.

In general, three policies exist to deal with risk. Firstly, growth and investment can be concentrated in low-risk areas and projects, e.g. by putting farm improvements where there is ample water; this is not always inegalitarian, though the sacrifice of output may be large. Secondly, investment can be concentrated on projects that directly reduce variability of yield from other capital; irrigation is the most familiar example. Finally, one can hold bigger reserves of the outputs normally yielded by risky projects, e.g. foodgrains. All these policies involve some sacrifice of current production, compared with the policy of ignoring risk and selecting the group of projects that maximizes total output in a typical year. The optimal balance among the three ways to deal with risk is a problem to be assessed in each sector. Such assessment urgently requires the microcosmic planning suggested on pp. 7–10. Until we know what rate of return to expect on a project, we cannot estimate how the rate will be affected by various forms of risk.

9. HOW BIG A PLAN?

At an early stage of public discussions about the Fourth Plan, a growth rate of $7\frac{1}{2}$ per cent yearly was advocated in many quarters. Yet, as we have said, most participants thought the output targets of the Draft Plan—which seeks growth of $5\frac{1}{2}$ per cent per year—were too optimistic. Neither aid nor savings appear likely to reach the amounts needed to buy the investment goods required; and these goods, even if India could afford them, seem unlikely to produce the outputs planned for.

People who believe the Draft Plan is too big argue that straining for impossible targets will produce bottlenecks and breakdowns, and that more will be achieved with a more modest programme, making flexible provision for unexpected windfalls; the Second Pakistan Plan is their model here.[8] Compared with a modest and flexible set of targets, a plan precariously balanced on a series of optimistic projections of *complementary* requirements—investment finance (aid and domestic savings), low capital/output ratios, export opportunities, the pace of import substitution, the growth of necessary skills—will yield less output, and waste more of the *other* efforts, if any single one fails. On the other hand, it was argued that an ambitious plan, serving as a target and trimmed if necessary, would produce more than an initially modest plan. A climber may get higher by failing to reach the top of Mt Everest than by successfully scaling Mont Blanc.

In much of this introduction, we have been forced into the terminology of the planners. We speak of 'the Plan' being too big or too small, when we mean the investment programme—or even the public investment programme. Yet a plan for development must cover both 'productive consumption' and incentives to the private sector. Hanson shows (pp. 36–37) that much of the ideology of mass enthusiasm and 'planning from below' is out of place in a democratic Indian framework, but it remains true that the Plan must harness the will and energy of hundreds of millions of individuals. There is plenty of evidence that the planners are becoming better disposed to incentives and price policies as instruments of planning. As yet, there is little sign that they see the various components of investment and current spending, private as well as public, as the proper subject of a plan—to be managed with a balance of direction, permission, and incentive. Micro-analysis will have broken through into planning, and India will be some way through its troubles, when planners regard 'the size of the Plan' as the meaningless concept it really is.

[8] See, however, E. Mason.

The Political Background

2

Power Shifts and Regional Balances

A. H. HANSON

1. MAKING THE PLAN

As the preparation of the Draft Fourth Plan was not accompanied by any review of India's planning philosophy, it did not involve a fundamental reconsideration of objectives. Essentially, the Fourth Plan was regarded as a logical continuation of the Third and Second. Long-term planning objectives and a strategy to reach them had been hammered out during the discussions that preceded the publication of the Second Plan, and neither the Government nor the Planning Commission wished to re-open the debate. The most important questions confronting the planners, therefore, were (*a*) what rate of growth was feasible during the course of the next planning period, and (*b*) what changes in the layout of available resources were necessary in order to correct the distortions and imbalances that the Third Plan was displaying.

The perspective remained a self-generating economy, free from dependence on foreign assistance, capable of providing employment for all job-seekers at a living wage, increasingly egalitarian in wealth and income distribution, and increasingly reliant on public and co-operative, as distinct from private, enterprise. Hence the un-expressed slogan of the Draft Plan was: 'Much the same as before, only more and better'. Inevitably, such a plan tended, as one of the leading officials of the Commission said, to look 'somewhat humdrum'. This appearance was reinforced by the nature of the corrections that circumstances forced the planners to make, viz. a greater emphasis on programmes designed to increase agricultural production, a better utilization of existing industrial capacity, and a heavier concentration on quick-yielding projects.

The maintenance of objectives and continuation of strategies were accompanied by a repetition of the formulation procedures that had been used for the Second and Third Plans. There was the same sequence of plan frame, draft memorandum, and draft outline; the same dialogue between Commission and Cabinet, with periodical interjections by the National Development Council (NDC); the same use of working parties; the same efforts to bring about a happy marriage between central plan and state plans; a similar degree of consultation with interest groups and independent experts; and yet another chase after the will-o-the-wisp of 'planning from below'.

Preparatory work began in May 1962, with a meeting of Permanent Secretaries. Simultaneously the Perspective Planning Division (PPD) of the Planning Commission began preparing a long-term study intended to provide guidance similar to that provided by Mahalanobis's 'Plan Frame' of 1955[1] and Pitambar Pant's *Dimensional Hypotheses concerning the Third Five Year Plan* of 1958. At about the same time the first working groups were established—for steel, coal, power, heavy engineering, basic chemicals, fertilizers, transport, and technical education.

By the autumn, the PPD had produced its *Perspective of Development, 1961–76—Implications of Planning for a Minimum Level of Living*. This recommended a total Fourth Plan outlay of Rs 243,300 mn of which Rs 164,150 mn were to be in the public sector. An indication of the possible dimensions of the plan thereby became available to the working groups. These continued to be established until May 1963, when they were instructed to produce preliminary reports (with tentative targets) by December, and final reports by March 1964. In July 1963 the Commission began a series of meetings to consider objectives and strategy; in September the State Governments were asked to establish their own working parties; and in November the NDC was informed of all these arrangements and of the progress that had been made.

Meanwhile, the PPD had been continuing studies which culminated in April 1964 with *Notes on Perspective of Development—India: 1960–1 to 1975–6*. To ensure even the poorest classes in India Rs 20 per person per month by 1975–6 (i.e. at the end of the Fifth Plan), the PPD sought to raise the overall annual rate of growth for the period 1961–76 to 7 per cent—'by no means an unattainable objective'. Equipped with this further guidance, the Commission in the following month held a 'full' meeting (i.e. with ministerial members in attendance) to consider broad issues of policy.

---

[1] P. C. Mahalanobis, *Draft Recommendations for the Formulation of the Second Five Year Plan 1956–61* (Planning Commission, 1955).

In August parliament began to take an interest in these pro-
ceedings, through the appointment of four groups to consider the
preliminary sectoral papers prepared by the Commission's technical
divisions and the proposals contained in the interim reports of the
working groups. In the same month, members of the Commission
met the Prime Minister (Lal Bahadur Shastri) individually to explain
the various sectoral proposals. This was a preliminary to another
full meeting of the Commission in the following month, to consider
the total size and pattern of the plan. By the end of September,
after examination of working group reports and consultation with
Union ministries, the Commission was able to submit to the Cabinet
a paper, *Size and Pattern of Investment in the Fourth Five-Year Plan.*
In October the Draft Memorandum appeared, providing for a plan
with a total outlay[2] of Rs 215,000–225,000 mn (1963–4) prices. It
was submitted successively to the Cabinet (14 Oct.), the Advisory
Committee on Economic Policy (23 Oct.), the NDC (27–28 Oct.),
and the Informal Consultative Committee of Members of Parliament
(4, 9, and 22 Dec., and 20 Feb. 1965). At the suggestion of the Prime
Minister, the NDC established five committees (Resources; Agriculture and Irrigation; Industry, Power and Transport; Social
Services; and Development of Hill Areas) to 'go into and advise on
policy issues relating to programmes in the respective sectors of the
Fourth Plan'.

Following the general approval given to the Draft Memorandum
by the NDC, the State Governments were asked to submit their own
memoranda by 1 January 1965. To guide them in their work, they
were provided with a 'very tentative distribution of outlays' between
States and Centre, divided into Agriculture, Irrigation, Power,
Small Industry, Organized Industry, Transport and Communications, Social Services, and Miscellaneous, and were advised to
regard a total outlay at twice the Third Plan level as an upper
limit.

Meanwhile, the NDC committees were at work, and detailed
programmes and projects were being discussed in the Central
Ministries. Fourth Plan programmes and projects were also, at the
request of the Commission, brought into the States' 1965–6 annual
planning exercise as 'proposals for advance action'. In formulating
such proposals, with the assistance of their working parties, the
States were asked to give particular attention to '(i) measures for

[2] Public investment, public current-development outlay, and private investment.

accelerating implementation of projects already under execution with a view to making their output or benefits available in the early years of the Fourth Plan,' and '(ii) training of personnel, surveys and investigations, preparation of project studies, and preliminary steps for new projects whose benefits are required in the first half of the Fourth Plan'.

All this work, punctuated by a further full meeting of the Commission to consider progress (18 Jan.), continued into 1965, when it became supplemented by the deliberations of the newly created National Planning Council (NPC). This was composed of the whole-time members of the Commission and seventeen expert, 'non-official' members; its purpose was to enable a 'small body of specialists' to 'work in close and continuous association with the Planning Commission'. At its first meeting, on 22 April, it established twelve study groups 'for detailed consideration of selected problems relating to various sectors of development'.

By the summer of 1965 the Commission was in a position to revise its Draft Memorandum proposals, taking into consideration the criticisms and recommendations it had received from Central Ministries, States, the Parliamentary Committee, and the committees of the NDC and the NPC. By this time, too, it was becoming evident that proposals for the Fourth Plan would need modification in the light of a Third Plan shortfall even more serious than predicted in the *Mid-Term Appraisal* of November 1964. Accordingly, a revised plan, with a total outlay of Rs 215,000 mn (at 1963–4 prices) was embodied in *Fourth Five-Year Plan—Resources, Outlays and Programmes*.

The presentation of this document to the NDC in September 1965 coincided with the outbreak of hostilities between India and Pakistan, and the accompanying suspension of foreign aid. The NDC, after discussion of a perfunctoriness fully understandable under the circumstances, agreed to the proposed total outlay, but authorized the Prime Minister (Mr Shastri) 'to re-orient, alter or amend the Plan as necessary to meet the emergent situation and safeguard the country's security and long-term interests'.

The Prime Minister then asked the Commission 'to undertake studies in order to determine the changes that were needed to be made in the programmes proposed for the Fourth Plan to ensure that the requirements for both defence and development were met, as far as possible'. This meant doing much of the work all over again. Already behind schedule, the Commission could not possibly have the final plan ready on time. Further delay was imposed by the decision to formulate the Annual Plan for 1966–7 (the first year of the Fourth Plan) in advance of the Draft Outline. The need for this re-scheduling (which involved concentration on immediate targets at the expense of more distant ones) was underlined by the serious setback in agricultural production, with its concomitant rise in prices and increase in non-plan expenditure. Accordingly, the Commission sent circulars to the Central Ministries and State Governments, urging the utmost economy and maximum resource mobilization, and appealing for 'special emphasis on quick-yielding schemes for raising agricultural and industrial production', and for 'an all-out effort to maximize the use of existing capacity or potential created in all sectors of the economy, particularly industry, irrigation and power, and to augment facilities at existing establishments and institutions in preference to the setting up of new ones'.

Thus guided, the Central Ministries and State Governments formulated their proposals, which the Commission, through discussions during November and December 1965, attempted to bring within the compass of a 'financial ceiling of Rs 20,800 mn or nearabout'. On 7 April 1966 the Annual Plan for 1966–7 was laid on the table of both Houses of Parliament.

Work on the Draft Outline was further disrupted by the devaluation of the rupee on 6 June 1966, which 'brought about a major change in the economic situation necessitating a complete re-examination of Plan resources, priorities and outlays'. Presented in August, the draft proposed a plan with a total outlay of Rs 237,500 mn at 1966 (post-devaluation) prices, which involved a considerable reduction in the physical programmes envisaged in the document of September 1965, and an even bigger one in those set out in the Draft Memorandum. At the time of writing (Sept. 1967) the final version of the Fourth Plan is still not ready.[3] This process of formulating the Fourth Plan was not substantially different from that employed for the two previous plans. To follow its stages, however, usefully

---

[3] Documentary sources used in compiling the above account: *4DO; Notes on Perspective of Development, India* (Apr. 1964); *Memorandum on the Fourth Five-Year Plan* (Oct. 1964); *Fourth Five-Year Plan—Resources, Outlays and Programmes* (Sept. 1965); *A Review of Important Activities and Studies 1965–6* (Apr. 1966); *National Development Council: Summary Records of the Twenty-First Meeting* (27, 28 Oct. 1964); *NIC Summary Records of the Twenty-Second and Twenty-Third Meetings* (5, 6 Sept. 1965, and 20, 21 Aug. 1966, mimeo.).

stresses the fact that the Commission makes a serious and prolonged effort to ensure that a plan is both realistic and widely accepted as such. Far from sitting in its ivory tower and attempting to impose the results of its econometric calculations on those charged with implementation, it enlists the participation of many organs of government, and takes advice from a wide variety of unofficial sources. Therefore, unsatisfactory results cannot, at least *prima facie*, be attributed to a failure to consult, to promote independent studies, and to strive for agreement.

The only 'interest' that may have some justification in alleging that it has not been invited to make its full contribution is private industry; this may be partly its own fault, since it has shown little enthusiasm for the Development Councils, which could play, but so far have failed to play, a significant role in the formulation process. But there are remnants of the belief that private enterprise is an unruly horse which must be made to obey. So far, the Commission has not responded to J. R. D. Tata's demand[4] for a 'French' system of planning, emphasizing *commissions de modernisation* in which the private sector is strongly represented. On the other hand, there is considerable exaggeration in Mr Patwant Singh's allegation that outlay for the private sector in the Fourth Plan was 'decided without any prior consultation with the spokesmen of private industry'.[5]

In some respects the consultative process was improved. The NDC, for instance, appears to have played a somewhat larger part. Critics of it can still allege that it does no more than give 'perfunctory consent to the plans prepared by the Commission, its scrutiny being a mere ritual that is gone through at infrequent intervals'.[6] The *Summary Records* of its meetings provide some support for this judgment—but by appointing the five committees of October 1964 it displayed an unusual interest in detailed plan programmes.

We know that these committees met and reported, but as their reports have not been published we cannot say whether they made more than a marginal contribution to plan formulation. Nor can we say much about the role of the new advisory body, the NPC, which was not constituted until February 1965. Some importance may be

[4] J. R. D. Tata, Address to the Central Advisory Council of Industries, *Economic Times* (13 Aug. 1965).
[5] Patwant Singh, *India and the Future of Asia* (London, 1966), p. 53.
[6] N. S. Jagannathan, 'Face-Lift for Planning Commission', *Hindustan Times*, 3 May 1967.

attached, however, to the inclusion in this Council of three men from the private sector and of one trade unionist.

Delay and interruption were the source of the main divergences from previous formulating exercises. The hostilities with Pakistan, the crop failures, and the devaluation of the rupee prolonged gestation to such an extent that when the Draft Outline appeared, more than four years after the Commission had set the planning process in motion, the original calculations seemed to date from another epoch. Hence many voices (although, as far as one knows, none within the Commission) were raised in favour of scrapping the whole exercise and starting again on a more realistic basis. The planners, however, displayed their usual persistence—or obstinacy, as some choose to call it—and succeeded in producing a draft which could at least claim conformity with the objectives, strategy, and pace of advance worked out by the PPD in its *Notes* of April 1964.

Throughout the formulation process, the guiding hand of this most prestigious of the Commission's divisions was much in evidence—more so than in the formulation of the Second and Third Plans. Its studies were circulated to all concerned, and it was given representation on nearly all the working groups, for which it 'provided a set of sectoral projections derived from a common set of assumptions regarding the growth of income, consumption and investment, the composition of final demand, balance of payments, and other relevant aspects'.[7] As these groups were more numerous than before (a total of 43 with 75 sub-groups), the co-ordination thus provided by officials with special responsibility for looking at the plan as a whole in the light of a long-term projection must have been particularly valuable.

However, the important role played by these econometric wizards, with their esoteric 'value added' and 'material balances' tables, reinforced the suspicion of many administrators, industrialists, and politicians that the Commission was giving too much thought to the hypothetical shape of the economy in 1976, and too little to its urgent current problems. I do not endorse this view, but merely note that it was widespread and seems to have had some impact on informed public opinion. What really emerges from a reading of the successive documents is that there was a tendency in the Commission to treat the *Notes on Perspective of Development* (as the Mahalanobis *Draft Recommendations* and the Pant *Dimensional*

[7] Planning Commission, *Review of Important Activities and Studies* (1965), p. 5.

3

Hypotheses had been treated in the previous planning exercises) as holy writ, from which deviations could be made only with great reluctance and special justification. Here the Commission may perhaps be accused of over-deference to the theoretical brilliance of its Head of Perspective Planning.

2. PRESSURE ON THE PLANNERS

The techniques of planning that the Commission employs, which involve wide consultation and extensive publicity, provide opportunities for the effective exertion of a variety of organized pressures. This is advantageous to the extent that the pressures can be absorbed, or that the people exerting them can be persuaded to accept compromises. It is disadvantageous to the extent that the Commission is compelled to diverge from economic rationality, to raise hopes doomed to frustration, and to seek fictitious 'agreement' by the use of the familiar 'on-the-one-hand-but-on-the-other' formula. Both the advantages and disadvantages, however, are the essence of any planning in a political order based on conciliation.

Without having full information about what pressures were exerted, how they expressed themselves, and with what results, one may safely say that the situation was not *substantially* different from that prevailing when the Third Plan was being prepared. Attitudes towards planning among the various political parties and voluntary associations had become more or less routine. The difficulties arising from Chinese aggression and the conflict with Pakistan may have hardened them; on the other hand the immediate threat to India's security, together with the political uncertainties following the death of Nehru and the absorption of the energies of many public men in non-economic issues such as the linguistic struggle, had the effect of diverting attention from the planning process itself. Central Ministries, working parties, and States all displayed the familiar tendency to inflate their demands far beyond the limits of realism, overestimating the availability of both resources and administrative capacity, in the hope that thereby the final result of the bargaining process would be as favourable as possible to themselves. There was nothing new in all this, and the unshakeable mandarins of the Planning Commission had plenty of experience in coping with it.

As far as the ministries and working parties are concerned, the manner in which the various bargains were fixed is difficult to document. With the States we are in a slightly better position, since they stake out their claims semi-publicly at NDC meetings, the *Summary Records* of which are printed 'for official use only'.

As is usual at NDC meetings, most State Chief Ministers demanded, if only for the record, greater emphasis on programmes and projects that would win them electoral support, particularly in the rural areas. Specific demands varied from State to State, but rural drinking water, rural housing, and village approach roads were generally regarded as winners, closely followed by irrigation, water, and electricity. Bhaktavatsalam of Madras, at the 1966 NDC meeting, referred most openly to the electoral advantages of giving satisfaction to such demands. (The elections were only six months ahead, and in Madras the Congress was already being hard pressed by the DMK.) Free meals for schoolchildren, the distribution of textbooks and uniforms, and the provision of housing sites for the poor in rural areas were the main examples he used of 'programmes . . . which had a widely beneficial impact on the countryside'. Larger outlays for them should be provided at the expense of other programmes 'which did not have the same degree of appeal'. The current view among the people, he alleged, was that the plan was only a prelude to new measures of taxation. Hence, unless the plan document 'made some specific reference to these projects and held out some prospect of their early fulfilment, it would fail to touch the hearts of the people'. Moreover, if 'at this stage the States were to recast their Plans and in the process axe the very programmes on which the hearts of the people were set, considerable discontent was bound to be generated'. Nijalingappa of Mysore, supporting, demanded more efforts to implement Congress's last election manifesto, which promised every village a school, an approach road, and a well for drinking water.

In some respects, the Chief Ministers were pushing at an open door. In the Annual Plan, published in March 1966, provision had been made, within a reduced outlay on power, for increased expenditure on rural electrification;[8] and the allocation for 'Health and Water Supply' was to be cut at the expense of health, to such an extent that water supply expenditure could register a slight increase.[9]

[8] Planning Commission, *Annual Plan 1966–7* (1966), pp. 48–50.   [9] Ibid. p. 77.

On the other hand, housing and construction was cut from Rs 33.560 mn (anticipated 1965–6 expenditure) to Rs 24·060 mn, while education was slashed from Rs 180·130 mn to Rs 98·380 mn.[10] The Commission and the Central Government, while not neglectful of the demands of the States, were apparently attempting to select from their 'immediate benefit' those projects likely to make the greatest contribution to economic growth.

On such matters there was, as might be expected, considerable unanimity among the representatives of the State Governments. There was also a general demand for more decentralization of the planning process. This was usually presented as a contribution to efficiency; but its main aim was to give the State Governments more elbow-room to cater for the 'felt needs' of the people. Here again, at the 1966 meeting, Bhaktavatsalam gave clearest expression to a point of view which commanded widespread support. After deploring the proposal to reduce the States' share in public outlay from 53·4 per cent in the Third Plan to 49 per cent in the Fourth, he demanded that the list of centrally-sponsored (as distinct from centrally assisted)[11] schemes should be curtailed, and that the States' programmes should receive their central assistance as block loans and grants 'tied only in respect of select high priority sectors like agricultural production or power'. 'With a greater freedom and flexibility in implementation of their plans,' he said, 'the States could respond more adequately and quickly to felt local needs and show better results in mobilisation of resources'. K. Brahmanandra

---

[10] Ibid. pp. 70, 88.
[11] A centrally-sponsored scheme is sponsored by a central ministry and executed by the State Government under that ministry's technical guidance and supervision. Financial assistance for such a scheme is additional to the assistance provided in respect of the State's own plan. Payment is made to the State on the basis of reported expenditure on each individual scheme. The criteria supposed to be used for deciding which schemes should be sponsored, rather than assisted, are as follows: (1) they should relate to demonstrations, pilot projects, surveys, and research; (2) they should have a regional or inter-state character; (3) they should have an all-India as well as a local significance. Ministries have disregarded these criteria, with the result that central sponsorship, which reduces the role of the State to that of a mere executive (and financially irresponsible) agency, has made rapid headway. In the Third Plan, as originally approved, centrally-sponsored schemes were scheduled to absorb 13·4 per cent of total central assistance to the States; in the Fourth Plan, they are tentatively scheduled to absorb 27.8 per cent. Although the States do not like them in principle, they accept them with alacrity, being unable to resist the financial bait. Some are departmental fads. There is even a scheme for the air-conditioning of mortuaries.

Reddy of Andhra also advocated such decentralization, 'in order to generate the necessary enthusiasm in the rural section of the people'. Naik of Maharashtra asked simply that 'the central assistance proposed in the Fourth Plan should be increased', because 'the real impact on the masses could be created by the State plan rather than by the central plan'.

Such demands are not new; nor are accusations that the Commission wishes to curtail the States' plans in order to expand the Central plan, and exercises excessive control over State plan expenditures. There is some substance in both charges;[12] but obviously the degree and kind of decentralization of economic decision-making in a federal or quasi-federal country, where planning is 'concurrent' (the joint responsibility of Centre and States), cannot be determined solely by reference to the people's alleged 'felt needs'. Much depends on the relative administrative capacities of the States and the Centre. In estimating these, one must consider the inherent disadvantages of remote control. Much also depends on resource scarcities and on the extent to which the Centre believes that the coherence of the plan is bound up with rigid insistence on certain priorities.

The most important factor of all, however, is the political strength of the States *vis-à-vis* the Centre. This has been increasing; as a result of the election of February 1967 it will probably increase further. One will watch with interest, therefore, how far the Centre, despite the extreme tightness of resources, is constrained to satisfy the demands of the States' representatives at the NDC meeting of 1966.

The Draft Outline does not deal specifically with the division of responsibilities for implementation between States and Centre. It indicates, however, that discussions continue 'about the classification of Centrally sponsored and State Plan schemes', and it 'explains'

[12] Although there is little substance to the excessive control charge nowadays, except in respect of centrally sponsored schemes. For assisted schemes, grants are in theory tied to heads of development, and in some cases to groups within the heads, but in practice a State will rarely find much difficulty in switching appropriations since at the end of the annual plan, the patterned central resources which it has lost through its indiscipline will be made good by a miscellaneous development loan. The fact that the grant is replaced by a loan is no deterrent, since the service charges are usually covered by further loans from the Centre. Some States may be deterred by the complexities of these crazy financial arrangements, but most of them know their way around. See below, p. 157.

much of the 'differential step up between the Centre and States by the fact that the former has a larger import component, the cost of which in rupee terms has gone up as a result of devaluation'. Extra expenditure on 'felt needs', such as 'irrigation, power, village and small industries, technical education and water supply . . . may be considered, it warns, only 'if the States are in a position to raise resources additional to what have been envisaged in the present estimates' (p. 45). Thus, predictably, it throws the ball back to the States themselves. This should be seen against a background of the State Ministers' expressions of dismay, at the 1966 meeting, at being asked to raise the additional taxation and make the economies in current expenditure required for the fulfilment of the plan as it stood.

On plan priorities and the allocation of responsibilities, the States can sometimes unite against the Centre. On the principles governing the division among themselves of total central assistance, as on the location of central projects, they are at odds with one another. At the 1966 NDC meeting, each State Minister advocated a 'principle' which would bring his own State maximum advantage. Sen of West Bengal, as Chief Minister of one of the most advanced States, made the surprising claim that 'disparities in development in respect of social services' had been 'almost removed', except in areas like Nagaland and Kashmir, and held that, as a consequence, 90 per cent of assistance should be on a population basis and only 10 per cent on the basis of 'special needs'. For obvious reasons, Sadiq of Jammu and Kashmir disagreed that population could provide a 'satisfactory criterion', and argued that other factors 'like backwardness' should be considered. For even more obvious reasons, he was supported in this view by Reddiar of Pondicherry. Nijalingappa of Mysore argued that assistance to a state should be based on 'need and capacity and what it deserved', while Naik of Maharashtra considered that it should be determined *ad hoc*, after consultation with the State Government concerned. Chaliha of Assam tried a little gentle political blackmail by asking the NDC 'to appreciate that the frontier areas of the country had certain peculiar problems and that unless these problems were tackled properly and in time serious complications might arise'. Both Dharma Vira, the Governor of Punjab, and Naik of Maharashtra expressed themselves on the allied subject of the location of Central Government projects. The former alleged 'gross imbalance'; the latter held that location should be based on 'technical feasibility and national interest and other technical and financial considerations and not on political considerations'—each on the reasonable supposition that the application of such criteria would favour his own State.

As allocations to individual States in the Fourth Plan are not yet known, it is impossible to say what effect, if any, such representations have had on the Central Government and the Planning Commission. The allocation process has always been a balancing act, in which political considerations have been weighed against those of economic rationality; the act becomes more delicate as each State develops independent political consciousness. Nevertheless, their inevitable disunity on this issue gives the Centre some freedom of action and an ability to 'divide and rule'. (The States' only escape would be to declare independence of the Union and to take control of all the revenues that the Centre now collects within their borders—an unlikely course which, though less disadvantageous to some States than to others, would be perilous for all.) So far, the Commission has shown marked diplomatic skill in dealing with the problem. Wisely, it has refused to lay down firm and unambiguous principles of allocation,[13] thereby giving itself maximum freedom in State-by-State negotiations. In this field, as possibly in others, the much-criticized 'on-the-one-hand-on-the-other' line of approach has its advantages. Probably, if such negotiations remain the responsibility of the Commission, it will continue to listen to the advocates of the various 'principles' without irrevocably adopting any of them.

All these views had been expressed at previous NDC meetings, and therefore came as no surprise to the Commission. At the 1966 meeting, however, other things were said which must have sounded more ominous. H. K. Desai of Gujarat, typical of several States's representatives, feared that a plan as big as the one proposed, because it would prove impracticable, was likely to reinforce an already general scepticism. Bhaktavatsalam of Madras said that 'in the last two or three years, due to the failure of agricultural production, rise in prices and growing dependence on external aid, there had been a measure of disillusion with the Plan'. The Prime Minister (Indira Gandhi) herself admitted that 'there was a certain amount of cynicism in the public'. The actual and prospective rise in prices had

---

[13] For explanations of the criteria which it claims to use, see *Third Five-Year Plan*, p. 153; Planning Commission, *Economic Development in Different Regions of India* (1962), p. 3; A. H. Hanson, *The Process of Planning* (London, 1966), pp. 315–16.

not, H. K. Desai considered, been fully taken into account by the planners; they had also underestimated the likely increase in non-plan expenditure, and hence overestimated the surplus accruing from revenues.

Here the NDC was anticipating the widespread scepticism that greeted the long-delayed publication of the Draft Outline. If the newspapers and journals in any way reflect Indian public opinion, it would seem that the only noise made by the descent of this large document into the political arena was a dull thud. A thorough survey of press reactions, undertaken by the Public Opinion Analysis Unit of the Planning Commission, admitted that the 'overwhelming majority of opinion in the English and Language (i.e. Indian language) Press [was] critical of the size of the Draft Plan'. Editorials contended that a big plan would 'create chain reactions such as additional taxation, deficit financing, inflation etc.', and criticized as 'unrealistic' the planners' assumptions about 'anticipated foreign aid, surplus from current Budgets of the Central and State Governments and contributions from the public undertakings'. Despite a welcome for the stress on agriculture and on family planning, and a recognition that the Commission's targets in all fields represented worthy aims, there was also a widely expressed belief that the 'implementation machinery', being characterized by 'widespread corruption, wastage and inefficiency', was 'neither capable of mobilising the resources nor of implementing the Plan programmes'.[14] Even allowing for the habitual editorial sourness of Indian newspapers, such a welcome is far from satisfactory.

Subsequently, the Draft Outline underwent attack by India's two outstanding business leaders, G. D. Birla and J. R. D. Tata, severely by the former, more moderately by the latter. Birla, in a highly propagandist and rather untidy speech to the Engineering Association of India, used a simple process of extrapolation to predict failure.

Now, what is the achievement of our planning here? Let us analyse our records. The First Plan was just a totalling up of various projects undertaken by the Government of that time. The Second Plan was something modest. The Third Plan—a real venture—completely failed, and the Fourth Plan, over which most of you are excited, . . . I am sure cannot be

---

[14] Public Opinion Analysis Unit, Press Information Bureau, *An Analysis of Press and Public Opinion on Draft Outline of the Fourth Five-Year Plan*, no. P/9/4/66/ Gen. Series 2, Pt A/B (mimeo), p. 1.

implemented. We have not got the resources. I do not have to go into the figures—20,000 and 24,000 and all sorts of things. I think this is all rubbish. This plan, as it is prepared, is mostly for the purpose of election. This Plan could not be implemented. We have not got the resources.[15]

There is no real argument here, and the passage would hardly be worth quoting if it did not reflect what many people were thinking. Tata, as one might expect, was more constructive. His major criticisms were directed at lack of focus, excessive reliance on physical controls, and continued emphasis on slow-maturing, capital-intensive and inflation-creating projects.

What we require [he said] is not a plan that will repeat past mistakes in its formulation or implementation. We need a plan that is more selective and less comprehensive, that will concentrate our limited financial and administrative resources on the achievement of top priority targets. We need a plan that relies more on incentives than on controls .... We need a more thorough evaluating machinery built into the Planning Commission which will go to make an annual plan assessment more purposive and the plans more realistic.[16]

'Business' has always been critical of India's plans—more critical, perhaps, than it would have been if the Commission had involved it more closely in their formulation. While, for the most part, refraining from any condemnation of planning as such (in view of the manifest advantages it has derived from the planned expansion of infra-structural services), it freely expresses its dislike of the planners' 'doctrinaire' emphasis on the public sector, their predilection for enforcing priorities through strict controls, their advocacy of higher taxation, and their alleged preference for sticks rather than carrots. Some representatives of the private sector, inspired by the writings of Professors Friedman and Bauer and the propaganda put out by the Forum for Free Enterprise, have even accused the Commission of soviet-type methods and totalitarian ambitions.[17] There is nothing new, therefore, in these criticisms of the Draft Outline.

The Government and the Commission, however, may have to pay more attention to these attacks than previously, for several reasons. First, the crisis that has overtaken India's plans gives business the

---

[15] S. Birla, 'Bad Planning, Bad Fiscal Policy Root Cause of Economic Failure', *Economic Times*, 14 Feb. 1967.

[16] 'The Implementation of Plans', *Economic Times*, 5 Feb. 1967.

[17] P. T. Bauer, *Indian Economic Policy and Development* (London, 1961); A. D. Shroff, *Planning and Finance in India* (London, 1966); P. Singh, *India and the Future of Asia*, ch. 4, 'The Anatomy of a Developing Economy'.

offensive and puts the planners on the defensive. Second, the cautious relaxation of controls during the last few years represents a trend, difficult to reverse, towards the acceptance of the business case. Third, the 'socialist pattern' slogan, employed to justify most of the policies that business dislikes, has lost whatever magic it ever had. Above all, the Aid India Consortium, which provides most of the assistance on which India relies for the achievement of her economic targets, has leaned towards the private sector. Therefore, in the absence of strong countervailing forces—which are not, at present, very evident—one may expect to see 'right-wing' modifications of the Draft Outline, either before it undergoes its transformation into the Fourth Five-Year Plan or, more probably, during implementation.

Press reactions, business reactions, and even party reactions to the Draft Outline are insufficient indications of that amorphous entity, public opinion. A better indication could conceivably have been provided by the election of February 1967. Birla, as we have seen, alleged that the Draft Outline was no more than a plank in Congress's platform. It is unlikely that the Congress bosses placed much reliance on it as such; if they did, they must have been cruelly undeceived. One cannot say much about the election issues until a scholarly study of them has appeared, but planning did not seem prominent among them. Research will probably support the journalist who, on the eve of the first round of polling, wrote:

In the General Elections this time there are no all-India issues as such—there are only all-India grievances centering on rising prices, which are creating countrywide privation and unrest. Foreign policy, defence, socialism, and self-reliance are not even major talking points in these elections. The people are more concerned about food shortage, inflation, parochialism, indiscipline and the general atmosphere of violence which has created such a vaguely negative atmosphere in the country.[18]

Certainly, if the 'condition of the people' was really as predominant as that statement suggests, the decline in support for Congress implied a vote of no confidence in Congress's capacity to plan the economy. This is serious if the successful implementation of the plan depends, as the Commission says it does, on 'mass understanding, mass support and mass involvement' (p. 33). One must therefore inquire, firstly, how far the Commission, as the Congress Government's planning agency, bears responsibility for the prevalent

[18] *Times of India*, 15 Feb. 1967.

scepticism; secondly, how far this scepticism is likely to affect the prospects of plan fulfilment.

3. PLANNING ORTHODOXIES

The Commission can all too easily be made a scapegoat. Much of the responsibility for the present crisis of Indian planning rests with what Mohan Lal Sukhadia, Chief Minister of Rajasthan, succinctly called 'two foreign aggressions and three bad weathers'. Much is also due to the insufficiency of foreign assistance in quantity, predictability, and type. For none of these causes of shortfall is the Commission responsible—although it might have done more to foresee them and provide against them.

Moreover, in present circumstances, the Commission gets little of the credit for the massive advances registered by the Indian economy since 1951, which it proudly catalogues in the first chapter of the Draft Outline. Admittedly, it is a moot point how far these may be attributed to planning as such, or as the Commission conceives it; but it is nonsensical to argue, as Birla does (with curiously Rostovian overtones) that India's economic progress is the product of a 'spontaneity' which the planners have done their best to stifle.[19]

Nevertheless, it can be argued[20] that during the last sixteen years the Commission has developed a collection of orthodoxies which have become less and less relevant to India's socio-economic situation and less and less helpful to the cause of planned growth. Reading the succession of Five-Year Plans, one develops a suspicion that much of the time the Commission is engaged in ritual bowing before idols whose clay feet are becoming ever more obvious. These idols, of course, have not been constructed by the Commission itself; they are the work of its political masters. Arguably the Commission, as a body of servants, must make due obeisance and dutifully work within a political philosophy including the socialist pattern, economic equality, planning from below, *panchayati raj*, and the Industrial Policy Resolution of 1956. But the Commission is not just a body of

[19] Birla, 'The whole world has progressed and willy-nilly, due to world events and progress all over the world, we too are dragged towards the path of progress. We would have progressed much more, had the Government been more practical, had the initiative been given to millions instead of to a few'.

[20] As in Hanson, *Process of Planning*, particularly ch. 8.

servants; it is a highly political organization, and, in any case, since it presumably accords top priority to maximum economic growth, it might be expected to subject this collection of interlinked shibboleths and panaceas to continuous critical examination. This it has failed to do; hence, in part, the accusations of lack of realism, and the decline in its reputation as the 'philosophy' that it has helped to construct appears to decline in relevance.

Again, one must not exaggerate. The Commission is not entirely lacking in adaptability. The Draft Outline contains plenty of evidence, documented in the other contributions to this symposium, of its capacity to respond to a changing situation. But its response, being constricted by its own orthodoxies, is usually slow and belated and, for the same reason, its ability to discover or accept new ideas and approaches is limited. This can be seen from the history of rural decentralization during the last twelve years.

As early as 1955 it became clear, from the reports submitted by the Programme Evaluation Organization, that the Community Projects, which had the increase in agricultural production as one of their major objectives, were not going well.[21] Obsessed by the prevalent 'grass-roots' doctrines, the Planning Commission recommended, the Balvantray Mehta Committee elaborated,[22] and the authorities accepted the remedy of replacing bureaucracy by democracy, in the form of *panchayati raj*. Anyone with knowledge of the realities of village life and of local politics could have predicted that, whatever virtues *panchayati raj* might have as a means of political 'socialization', it would not, at least immediately, do much to promote the economic development of the rural areas.[23] For example, A. D. Gorwala expressed his doubts thus:

A Village panchayat does not work well. It performs its simple duties most inadequately. But a committee of representatives of village panchayats must do splendidly. Let us call it a "Taluka Samiti", give it

[21] See particularly Planning Commission, Programme Evaluation Organization, 3rd, 4th, 5th, and 6th *Evaluation Reports*.

[22] Committee on Plan Projects, Team for the Study of Community Projects and National Extension Service, *Report* (1957).

[23] The most comprehensive of the many explanations why *panchayati raj* failed as an *economic* specific is Ilchman: 'Democratic Decentralisation and Planning in Rural India' (Dec. 1964, unpubl. London Ph.D thesis). C. Potter produces figures which suggest that, in Rajasthan at least, its effect on economic growth was sharply negative. (See his Bureaucratic Change in India, in R. J. D. Braibanti, ed., *Asian Bureaucratic Systems Emergent from the British Imperial Tradition* (Durham, N.C., 1966), particularly pp. 187–208.)

ample powers, repeat the sacred charm of democratic decentralisation and all will be well.[24]

Panchayati raj, however, fitted the orthodox ideas of collectivism, democracy, and equality. Hence the new institutions were to be introduced as rapidly and widely as possible, and given responsibility for the Community Projects which, started in 1952, now covered most of the country. Yet, while officialdom was making enormous efforts to equip every block with its *panchayat samiti* and every district with its *zilla parishad*, critics continued to insist not only that 'grass-roots' democracy would not work in the way envisaged, but that the services designed to improve agricultural production should be directed towards (*a*) those farmers who showed signs of entre-preneurial initiative and (*b*) those districts where topography, ecology, hydrography, and society were conducive to rapid progress.

This view, vigorously urged by the Ford Foundation,[25] was responsible, first, for the inclusion of the intensive 'pilot projects' in the Third Plan, and then for the inauguration of the IADPs. Whether the latter have been well devised and located, and whether the concentration of agricultural inputs will be more successful than their dispersal, are questions which cannot as yet be answered. All one can say is that the new strategy looks more realistic than the old. The point, however, is that it has had to make its way against a great deal of prejudice based upon near-superstitious respect for the Holy Trinity of 'collectivism, democracy and equality'.

Idol-worship of this kind is now less fashionable. The death of Nehru, whose greatness was always somewhat diminished by his enthusiasm for ideologically-inspired panaceas, gave it a severe blow; and experience of its fruits has given it an even harder one. The abandonment of idols, however, is difficult and dangerous; respect for public opinion, desire for political self-preservation, and pride in consistency dictate that one should back slowly away from them rather than attempt to topple them over. For the Planning Commission, the process is particularly tricky. It was Nehru who

---

[24] A. D. Gorwala, *The Mysore Administration: Some Observations and Recommendations* (Bangalore Govt. Press, 1958), pp. 75–76.

[25] Agricultural Production Team sponsored by Ford Foundation, *Report on India's Food Crisis and Steps to Meet It*, Ministry of Food and Agriculture (1959), esp. pp. 5, 19.

created, inspired, and guided the Commission and defended it from its many enemies. Now that it has to defend *itself*, it sees danger in openly admitting mistakes—hence the unyielding attitude, slightly desperate but obstinately poker-faced, which many foreign observers have noted as currently characteristic of some of the Commission's leading officials. Naturally, therefore, many of the old orthodoxies, with their accompanying unrealities, continue to grace the pages of the Draft Outline.

Perhaps the clearest example is to be found in the section on co-operation, a 'form of organisation of economic activity . . . crucial . . . in the achievement of the social objectives of Indian Planning' (p. 150). Now co-operation, particularly when brought to the people from above, is not an easy way of organizing economic activities. Both public enterprise and private enterprise avoid many of the problems that beset this pig-in-the-middle. For success, it demands mutual loyalties very difficult to establish in a community stratified into castes and ridden by factions, and a far-sightedness comparatively rare among poverty-stricken illiterates and semi-literates. One might imagine, therefore, that the Commission would encourage co-operative forms of organization only where (*a*) the minimum conditions for success were present or could be quickly brought about, or (*b*) there was no alternative form of organization likely to do better, as in the provision of rural credit. In co-operative farming, the Commission has learnt by experience. It pays lip-service to the Nagpur Resolution by demanding that the co-operative farm 'should be looked upon as an important element in schemes for achieving new advances in agriculture' (p. 144), but it does not provide much money for co-operative farming (p. 152).

Where certain other forms of co-operation are concerned, however, it would seem that the Commission has yet to learn its lesson. Despite the prevalent malfunctioning and high death-rate of rural credit co-operatives (which might indicate consolidation and concentration on the intensive areas rather than rapid over-all advance) it proposes that, by the end of the Fourth Plan, the coverage of these societies should increase from 33 per cent of the rural population (1965) to 75 per cent, and their membership from 24 mn (1964) to 45 mn (p. 136). This target, which looks unrealistic (particularly as the increase in membership was only 7 mn between 1961 and 1964), might be justified as a means of getting the peasant out of the hands of the rural moneylender, if the formation of credit co-operatives is the only practicable method of doing so. But what are we to make of the demand for 'progressive reorganisation on co-operative lines' of agricultural processing plants 'which are at present privately owned' (p. 142), or of the suggestion that forest labour co-operatives shall 'progressively take over from the contractors the exploitation of forests, e.g. felling of trees, conversion into logs, firewood, and charcoal and their transport and sale as well as collection, processing and disposal of minor forest products' (p. 147–8)? Has the Commission any evidence that the co-operative entrepreneur will generally do better than the private entrepreneur in these important fields of economic endeavour? Instead of being presented with such evidence, we are assured that co-operation, far from being 'merely a form of economic organisation', has 'deep social and ethical values and is intended to lead to a new and better way of life' (p. 150). This may be true, but it does not indicate why co-operation should be promoted in a particular field, in a particular way, and at a particular pace. Apparently, the co-operative principle is one of the remaining idols.

Again, one must avoid exaggeration. The 'co-operative' chapter of the Draft Outline is one of the most woolly. Many of the other chapters show a new realism. The treatment of community development and *panchayati raj*, though unimpeachably orthodox, is so perfunctory as to suggest that the Commission no longer places any great reliance on these institutions for the implementation of its programmes.[26] Parts of the chapter on 'Village and Small Scale Industries' are also refreshing. Worship of the small scale is a peculiarly Gandhian idolatry which has been responsible for some of the weakest and woolliest formulations of policy in previous plans. Here it is recognized that small, labour-intensive units are desirable only in industries where 'a large size of operation and a high degree of mechanisation have no decided advantage'. In other words, the small unit has to justify itself on economic grounds. The process of justification, says the Commission, requires the 'systematic identification' of fields and processes where 'smaller units of operation and less capital-intensive methods' are economically viable (p. 240).

The form of idolatry most deleterious to rational and coherent

---

[26] *4DO*, p. 212–14. The 3rd Plan provided an outlay for 'community development and panchayats' of Rs 3,220 mn (1961 prices) (*Third Five-Year Plan*, p. 332). The Draft 4th Plan provides Rs 2,600 mn (1966 post-devaluation prices) (*4DO*, p. 48).

planning is the belief, which the Commission still appears to hold, in the Power of the Word. This belief takes two forms, conceptually distinct but practically interconnected. The first is confidence in the validity of the Bellman's dictum—'what I tell you three times is true'. Once a target, however unrealistic, has been selected, it is regarded as at least half-way towards realization. How else can one explain the persistence with which the Commission, in setting its sights, gives itself the benefit of every possible doubt? Optimism is the occupational disease of planners, and one is never surprised when some little back-room planning bureau in a Ruritanian-type country comes up with a comically inflated projection of growth. But one *is* surprised when planners as knowledgeable, experienced, sophisticated, and prestigious as the Indians do the same—particularly when the failures of their past exercises in this *genre* are available for contemplation.[27] Yet the practice of setting 'minimum' objectives, realizable—if at all—only on the supposition that the most favourable possible combination of circumstances actually materializes, is as evident in the Draft Outline of the Fourth Plan as it was in previous planning documents.

Nowhere is this clearer than in the programme for raising financial resources (*4DO*, ch. 4). The outlay of Rs 160,000 mn 'envisaged for the public sector programmes' depends on achieving 'anticipated increases in production and national income during the Fourth Plan period'—which itself depends on successful progress in resource mobilization. Also required are 'effective steps . . . to reduce tax evasion and tax avoidance through improvements in the machinery of tax collection and to recover the arrears in respect of taxation and other payments due to Government under non-tax heads'. A third requirement is the avoidance, 'except in special circumstances', of subsidies and waivers of interest on Government loans. Fourth, 'it is anticipated' that in public enterprise 'there will be effective utilisation of available capacity, strict economy in operating expenses, minimisation of inventory holdings and prevention of leakages in revenue'. Fifth, 'in the public as in the private sector, price increases induced by policy decisions of the Government to curtail imports, to generate surpluses for exports or to reduce consumption for other reasons, will have to be absorbed by wage and salary earners as by other sections of the people'. Sixth, the yield of

[27] A. H. Hanson, chs 5 and 6.

market borrowings and small savings must reflect not only 'trend increases' but 'special programmes of popularisation and intensification of collections'. Seventh, the increase in 'non-developmental expenditure' must be cut by 'very special efforts' to $3\frac{1}{2}$ per cent yearly, as against the 5 per cent originally estimated. Eighth, economic policies—and particularly fiscal policies—designed to realize all this must also place 'constraints on accumulation of property and wealth in the hands of private individuals to narrow down disparities in economic status and power'. Ninth, 'additional agricultural taxation by way of surcharges on land revenue, higher irrigation charges, surcharges on commercial crops and so forth', which *some* States have been levying 'in a modest way' ('modest' because of the strong resistance of the cultivators) must be stepped up. Though the pages on which these *desiderata* are listed are ambiguous, Table 3 on page 80 suggests that even their full achievement will leave a gap of Rs 18,000 mn to be raised by 'further measures to be adopted in the remaining period of the Fourth Plan', i.e. from 1967 to 1971 (pp. 80–89).

Although conditions for the realization of *some* of these nine objectives may be favourable, they will not be favourable for them all. Quantification in these areas is difficult, but it may be reasonably conjectured that the improvement envisaged over the whole field of resource mobilization would require very favourable socio-political and administrative developments and a gread deal of luck. The programme for resource mobilization, therefore, is as much an act of faith as an exercise of reason. It may be good exhortation, but it is not good planning. It shows excessive belief in the Power of the Word.

The second form taken by this belief is the persistent suggestion that, if the right words are spoken to the right people at the right time, 'the masses' can be mobilized for plan fulfilment. Apparently, despite the prevailing scepticism, mass mobilization is possible if only the people can be convinced that the plan represents their 'real will'. Indeed, such mobilization is sometimes regarded as a *sine qua non* of success. Early in the process of plan formulation, the PPD, justifying its programme for a big acceleration in the rate of development during the decade 1966–76, wrote:

This is certainly a difficult task, but as subsequent analysis shows, it is by no means an unattainable objective. Development of this magnitude does not seem to raise any insuperable difficulties whether of organisational

4

capacity, finance or balance of payments, provided we approach the problems in a scientific spirit, with a boldness of vision, and determined action, *backed by the national will and the united effort of the people*.[28]

In the second chapter of the Draft Outline, 'Self-Reliance and Perspective of Development', there is much more in the same vein. 'Constraints which loom large in the immediate present', we are told, 'tend to diminish or even disappear, given timely decisions and prompt action in the present, and *a deliberate strengthening of the national will towards social and economic growth*'. The perspective itself, continue the planners, 'can ... be an active element in accelerating the process of economic growth *by the effect it has on national will* for the reduction and elimination of constraints based on current attitudes to consumption, savings, work, *swadeshi*, and exports'. There must be '*mass understanding, mass support, and mass involvement*'. This, as the planners themselves say, necessarily involves psychological transformations of the deepest kind. 'Attitudes and behaviour patterns ... have to undergo as much of a fundamental change as they do when a country gets engaged in war'. Specifically, there has to be 'a change in the attitude of the well-to-do sections of the community towards consumption ... a change in the public attitude towards taxation', 'a general willingness to put up with the reduced availabilities caused by the imperative claim of exports on the domestic output of exportable commodities'—and even a movement of public opinion 'in favour of common educational facilities in place of the current trend of going in for private schools with differential advantages for the higher income groups'! (pp. 27, 33, 36–38).[29]

All this might be dismissed as speech day stuff—a hortatory exercise which no-one is expected to take seriously but which the Commission, as the creature of that greatest of exhorters, Jawaharlal Nehru, feels that it must for decency's sake perform. To some extent it is just this; no-one imagines that the Commission *really* relies, to any significant extent, on 'mass understanding, mass support and mass involvement' for the realization of its objectives. Only in a 'mobilization' type of polity, where the central authorities enjoy a monopoly of the means of propaganda and the services of a disciplined, ideologically-oriented party as a transmission-belt, can

[28] *Notes on Perspective of Development* (Apr. 1964), p. 2. Author's italics.
[29] Author's italics.

these mass phenomena be made to appear. Even then, the circumstances have to be exceptional if the widely-reported 'enthusiasm' is to contain a substantial element of the genuine and spontaneous, as distinct from the simulated. The Soviet Union in the 1930s is, of course, the *locus classicus* of this approach to planning, and it is significant that for Nehru, the *guru* of the Planning Commission, Russia's experience during these years—which, like most 'leftists' of the 1930s, he seriously misunderstood and misinterpreted—seemed of immense importance.

Throughout the remainder of his life, Nehru dreamed of combining economic mobilization with political conciliation, a soviet economy with a western polity. Encouraged by advisers such as Solomon Trone and P. C. Mahalanobis, he never entirely lost sight of this delusive vision. But, as time went on, he became less and less inclined to regard mobilization as a strategic concept with immediate practical applicability; and one may be certain that the more tough-minded members and officials of the Commission such as S. R. Sen or the late S. G. Barve have been even less tempted to treat it as such. They know that public enthusiasm for—or rather satisfaction with—a plan is *post hoc*, proportionate to successful accomplishment. In a multi-party democracy, where criticism of the government is rampant and contradictory purposes find free expression, it cannot become a significant *means* of accomplishment. If people are to be induced to work 'for' the plan, they must be provided with individual and group incentives of the most material and specific kind. To a considerable extent, therefore, one can dismiss the faded phrases about mass mobilization in the second chapter of the Draft Outline as window-dressing.

But not entirely. The impact of such phrases on their audience may be minimal—which offers no cause for rejoicing. Their impact on those who habitually use them may be highly deleterious. For the use of this kind of language—which is scattered over the pages of the Draft Outline and not merely concentrated in the second chapter—induces habits of thought incompatible with the stern realism that a planner should cultivate. In particular, it encourages an already strong tendency to plan beyond the limits of likely resources, in the vague hope that the various gaps will be filled as a result of extra effort, induced by the shining vision of a better life for all. Significantly, in all the plans, the planners have used their most hortatory expressions where the cracks in their projected structures are most obvious.

The effect on public opinion of this verbal papering-over is almost certainly the opposite of what is intended. The literate and well-informed people who read the plans, or the newspaper accounts of them, are *not* stimulated to greater effort. Habitually on the look-out, as Indians tend to be, for spots on every sun, they are confirmed in their scepticism. Hence the attempt to mobilize has the effect of de-mobilizing.

The Commission, then, cannot be entirely acquitted of responsibility for the poor reception of the Draft Outline. But does this reception really matter? How far will public scepticism affect plan fulfilment?

Perhaps the Draft Outline, whatever its virtues as an economic projection, cannot succeed because it does not carry conviction with those to whom it is principally addressed, i.e. the educated Indian public. Their scepticism, serious enough in itself, may trickle down among the uneducated and semi-educated, creating universal disbelief. However, particularly in a pluralistic polity, the efficacy of a plan depends on its capacity to enlist the economic ambitions of individuals and groups, rather than on its popular appeal as an exercise in building a new social order. If so, lack of support *as such* will not kill a plan. Widespread scepticism about stated targets may be compatible with economically motivated behaviour which, *in toto*, will achieve them. Will the plan enable the authorities, as they try to implement it, to induce the required behaviour?

The answer must be speculative, but one can point to certain aspects of plan implementation where scepticism about the viability of the planners' projections will surely have a negative effect. First, one must remember, in talking about motivations, that the primary responsibility for implementation is with the public authorities themselves. If, therefore, the plan is unconvincing to the Central Ministries, State Governments, public enterprises, and all executive authorities down to grass-roots level, it is unlikely that implementation will be fast, vigorous, or imaginative. Second, some of the scepticism reflects a view that, because such a big plan demands stringent mobilization of resources, particularly for the public sector, the motivations that it offers individuals and groups *cannot* be adequate. Third, if persons with responsibilities for economic decisions are convinced that the plan is not going to succeed, they will take decisions accordingly, and their decisions will make their pessimism self-fulfilling (see below, p. 53).

One can therefore say that if a plan gets a bad reception, this is *prima facie* evidence of something wrong with it. In India today, the prevalent belief that the Fourth Plan is too big probably means that it *is* too big. This belief, and the associated lack of confidence, have been accentuated by the series of 'scalings down' which, between 1962 and 1966, have been forced on a reluctant Commission. Each new figure has been presented as the irreducible minimum; each time, the Commission has emphasized that the latest cuts constitute a case of *reculer pour mieux sauter*, and that today's smaller effort will require correspondingly more effort tomorrow to attain 'irreducible' perspective targets for 1975–6. The idea that less growth today can produce more savings tomorrow is so unconvincing that one sometimes feels that the Commission is merely whistling to keep its courage up; while the *succession* of irreducible minima induces sceptics to ask whether the planners can provide *any* firm and reliable guide to policy. In the end, and at the extreme, planning itself comes to be written off as 'dead as the dodo'. One then has to ask whether the existing strategies of planning are themselves sound. Has not the time come for the Commission to look again at these strategies, with fresh and unprejudiced eyes?

4. THE PLANNING COMMISSION: PRESTIGE, STATUS, AND POWERS

Perhaps the Commission itself needs a spring-clean. Certainly something must be done if it is to restore its lost prestige. Confidence in the Commission has waned with the growth of scepticism about the usefulness of its product. Today, it is a popular target of abuse. How far, and in what respects, is the criticism justified? What can the Indian Government now do to meet the critics' case?

The critics allege that the Commission occupies an anomalous position in the governmental structure; that although outside the constitution, owing its origin to a mere Cabinet resolution establishing it as an advisory body, it has nevertheless become an executive body of enormous power, an *alter ego* of the Cabinet, showing a persistent and increasing concern with administrative matters outside its province, and supporting its pretensions by equipping itself with an excessively large bureaucratic apparatus. A source of administrative overlapping, duplication, and dispute, these empire-building proclivities are also seen as one of the reasons why the Commission's distinctive advisory duties have been unsatisfactorily performed. Its usefulness as an aid to policy formation, the critics continue, has been further undermined by the inclusion among its members of ministers. These, who include the Prime Minister and Minister of Finance, now outnumber the expert members. As a consequence, the advice given by the Commission to the Government, which ought to be as objective as possible, is held to be biased towards current government policy and excessively influenced by the ideology of the ruling party. Further, the prestige of the Commission, and its financial sanctions in the so-called negotiations with the States, are considered to have diluted the federal element in India's constitution. The States appear before the Commission as suppliants, not as partners in a joint planning endeavour. The consequent tension is alleged to have produced a degree of centralization which is not only hostile to the spirit of the constitution but incompatible with effective planning. The remedies proposed are (1) to deprive the Commission of its executive powers and to insist on its purely advisory status; (2) to reduce its proliferating divisions, sections, and associated bodies; and (3) to eliminate its ministerial, non-expert members.[30]

Defenders of the Commission, while recognizing that these criticisms have some force, have argued that the Commission's high-powered status has imparted a drive to Indian planning that it would not otherwise have possessed. Ministerial membership has facilitated a fruitful dialogue between politicians and experts, and has given the former a sense of commitment to plan priorities. As for federalism, if the activities of the Commission have enhanced the powers of the Centre at the expense of those of the States, this is a necessary consequence of the decision to have an all-India plan and a useful check to those fissiparous tendencies which, particularly since the creation of linguistic States, threaten to pull the Indian federation apart.

For a long time, despite the distinction of such critics as Gadgil and Chanda, and the prestige of others, such as the Estimates

[30] For a fuller account of these criticisms, with reference to their authorship, see ch. 3 of Hanson, *Process of Planning*; also A. Chanda, *Federalism in India* (London, 1965), ch. 8.

Committee of the Lok Sabha, the Commission had the better of this argument. So long as it could credibly point to the comparative success of its plans, it could resist changes in its status, powers, and composition; so long as Nehru was there to defend it, it could afford to treat its critics as more of a nuisance than a menace. But the situation has radically changed. Indian planning is in a state of crisis, for which the Commission—rightly or wrongly—is getting much of the blame; and since Nehru died the prestige that it once derived from its intimate association with him has disappeared.

Moreover, as so often happens with an organization when circumstances turn against it, the Commission has lost some of its former self-confidence and cohesion. This may be partly due to the personal style of its Deputy Chairman, Asoka Mehta.[31] His predecessor, Gulzarilal Nanda, had no obvious qualifications for the job. A politician grown elderly in the service of Congress, he was not conspicuous for drive or originality, while his respect for *sadhus* and habit of consulting astrologers did not enhance his influence among his better educated and more secular associates. But Nanda had been a member of the Commission (with one short break) since its establishment, and its Deputy Chairman since 1953. He possessed experience and had acquired the ability to provide liaison between his political colleagues and the experts. Mehta, who took over the Deputy Chairmanship at the end of 1963, just when the process of formulating the Fourth Plan was getting under way, is a man of different stamp. Formerly leader of the Praja Socialist Party, he is very much the intellectual and ideologist. Neither a true expert nor a successful and influential politician, he suffers from a certain isolation, which is reinforced by a somewhat brooding and introspective manner. How far he is consulted by the Government before important economic decisions are taken is not certain; presumably, as Minister of Planning, he makes his views known. Certainly he sometimes omits to consult his colleagues and subordinates, preferring to play a lone hand.

Of these colleagues, there are now only two,[32] M. S. Thacker and Tarlok Singh[33] (both non-ministerial members), with long experience

---

[31] Subsequently replaced by D. R. Gadgil.

[32] More precisely, three; but P. C. Mahalanobis, who has been a *de facto* member since 1955 and a *de jure* one since 1959, is elderly, lives away from Delhi, and hence rarely attends.

[33] Both have subsequently left the Commission, as a consequence of its reorganization in the autumn of 1967.

of the Commission, and at least one of them is less than happy about his situation. Two other non-ministerial appointees, V. K. R. V. Rao, the distinguished economist, and the late S. G. Barve, who had enjoyed a successful period of ministerial responsibility for finance and planning in Maharashtra, resigned to participate in the elections of February 1967. At a time, therefore, when the Commission is most in need of experienced and talented members, it appears to be worse equipped in this respect than ever before.

This alarming personnel situation is partly responsible for a lack of creative thought emanating from Yojana Bhavan. Even the *Economic and Political Weekly*, no anti-planning journal, accuses the Commission of 'intellectual bankruptcy'.[34] Partly responsible are the over-long domination of the organization by its ministerial members, and the tendency for its planning philosophy to harden into an inflexible orthodoxy. An important countervailing force has been the ability of the Commission to retain the services and the loyalties of such distinguished secretarial officials and heads of divisions as Pitambar Pant,[35] S. R. Sen, and K. S. Krishnaswami. But the only division to sustain its reputation is the PPD under Pant's brilliant and virtually independent leadership; and even this reputation is slightly bogus, based as much on superstitious veneration for mathematics as on appreciation of what the PPD is doing (which, by and large, has greater long-run than short-run significance).

Therefore, once India's new Central Government has settled down and taken the measure of its tasks, it will make considerable changes in both the process of planning and the personnel and organization of the Planning Commission. Some of these changes may well be forecast by the report on the Commission by the Administrative Reforms Commission (ARC), to which, at the time of writing, the Government is giving consideration. Central to the ARC's proposals is upgrading of the NDC, 'visualised as the supreme political body giving broad guidance relating to national planning'. As the representatives of the States have an overwhelming majority on this body, this 'supremacy' would subject the whole planning process to the principle of 'cooperative federalism', thereby institutionalizing the shift in the balance of political power from the Centre to the

---

[34] *Economic Weekly, Ann. no.* (Feb. 1967) (Bombay), p. 90.
[35] Now, as a result of the recent reorganization, promoted to membership of the Commission.

States. Such a change is considered by a recent commentator, N. S. Jagannathan, to be 'irresistible because of the changes in the political configuration of the country after the general election'.

It is no longer possible [he continues] for the planners or the Central Government to assume automatic consent for any plan that they may draw. Mr Asoka Mehta is no doubt right in saying that no Chief Minister is opposed to planning; but notions about the contents of the plan, especially as they affect the interests of his own State, may differ from Chief Minister to Chief Minister, and these may not coincide with those of the Planning Commission or of the Central Government. These differences are not a new factor in planning, but reconciling them will be far more difficult now. There is, therefore, no escape, from the political point of view, from planning becoming, in the modish jargon of the times 'indicative' rather than 'imperative'.[36]

A corollary of this proposal—capable, nevertheless, of standing on its own—is the suggestion, also made by the ARC, that the Commission should be 'minister-free'. Reduced to the status of a purely technocratic body, it would thereby be enabled, presumably within the framework of the broad policies sent down to it by the NDC, to submit independent alternative proposals to its political masters, who would assess them, also quite independently, for political feasibility. Thus the present overlapping of roles between the Commission and the Union Cabinet would be brought to an end, and together with it the 'unhealthy' practice whereby the Union Cabinet ascertains the Commission's views on major issues of current economic policy—a practice which, the ARC believes, has prevented the Commission from giving adequate attention to its proper duties.

If these proposals are accepted *in toto*, the critics of the present status and functioning of the Commission will have won a complete victory, and the case for a strong planning organization, as presented among others by Albert Waterston,[37] will have been lost. Powerful only to the extent that it can exercise persuasion, the Commission will be confined to preparing perspective plans, five-year plans, and annual plans, and evaluating plan performance.

However, the Government will hardly swallow the ARC's doctrine

---

[36] 'Face-Lift for Planning Commission', *Hindustan Times*, 3 May 1967.
[37] A. Waterston, *Development Planning*; *Lessons of Experience* (London, 1966) pt ii. See also Hanson, pp. 66–75.

whole.[38] 'Having built the planning machinery so laboriously over the years', writes the author of a recent newspaper report, 'the Government is in no mood to reduce it to the level of a research organization'.[39] Even among the members of the ARC itself, there appear to be doubts about a complete de-politicization of the Commission; for the ARC's study team was of the opinion, not persuasive to the main body, that the Prime Minister should continue as the Commission's chairman, to provide an effective link between Commission and Government, and to ensure that its advice did not fall upon deaf ears. Commentators will doubtless continue to debate whether additional links are required, such as that provided by the Finance Minister; while the suggestion that the Planning Ministry should be abolished, because a purely advisory body cannot have direct responsibility to the legislature, will certainly be challenged.[40]

For political reasons, some re-organization is inevitable; but re-organization as such, particularly along the lines which have been suggested, may merely restore some temporary public confidence in the planning organization. Re-organization has all too frequently been presented in India as a panacea, and there is a persistent tendency to argue that if something is not going well organizational deficiencies must take the blame. Yet, when such deficiencies are removed, the diseases for which they were blamed often remain as virulent as ever. The proposed reorganization of the Planning Commission appeals to devotees of administrative logic and of root-and-branch reform. In this case they may be right; but much depends on whether devotion to the idea of a national plan has now

---

[38] It did not. The reorganized Commission (Sept. 1967), although predominantly 'expert', includes both the Prime Minister and the Finance Minister. Moreover, other ministers may be invited to attend meetings at the discretion of the Prime Minister, who remains Chairman. Appointed as full-time members are Dr D. R. Gadgil (Deputy-Chairman), Dr B. D. Nag Chaudhuri, Mr Pitambar Pant, Mr B. Venkatappiah, and Mr B. Ventataraman. Apart from the two ministerial members, the only remaining part-timer is Professor Mahalanobis. At the first meeting of the new Commission, Mrs Gandhi announced that, although the 1951 terms of reference would remain unchanged, the Commission would henceforth concentrate on plan formulation and evaluation and avoid 'executive functions' (*Hindustan Standard*, Calcutta and London, 6 Sept. 1967).

[39] Ibid. 9 May 1967.

[40] So far (Sept. 1967) the Government has resisted pressure to appoint another Planning Minister. Dr Gadgil, however, is reported as expecting 'the appointment of a Minister of State attached to the Prime Minister to provide the liaison between the Commission and the Government' (*Hindustan Times*, 6 Sept. 1967).

become sufficiently deep-rooted, at all levels, to survive the reduction of the Commission to the status of an advisory bureau and its replacement, as a decision-taking centre, by a National Development Council which, hitherto, has shown little capacity either to reach meaningful agreements or to exercise effective authority.

One cannot discuss re-organization, therefore, purely as a question of administrative reconstruction. The Indian Government has to decide, not which planning organization is administratively ideal, but which is most feasible in a political context that makes the old type of planning increasingly difficult to operate. Indeed, it must go further, and ask if planning itself, 'old' or 'new', is still possible, in view of the way that India's socio-political situation is developing. It is to these very speculative questions that we will turn in the last section of this chapter.

5. AFTER THE 1967 ELECTION: THE
FUTURE OF INDIAN PLANNING

Let us start, as Viscount Wavell used to do when preparing for his tortuous discussions with the Indian political leaders, with the 'worst possible case': the Selig Harrison syndrome.[41] This postulates that Congress breaks up into a chaos of irreconcilable factions; the States, under variously constituted governments, assert their independence of the Centre; meanwhile, throughout the country, casteism and communalism go on the rampage. In fact, the 'dominant party' pattern, which has given India's political life its coherence, disintegrates, and there is no emergent alternative pattern to replace it. In view of the extreme difficulty of judging the direction in which Indian history is moving, this cannot be ruled out; indeed, it represents one of the alternative extrapolations of existing trends. But, almost certainly, the threat that it embodies is not immediate. If there is to be a descent into a chaos of this kind, it is more likely to take the form of a gradual roll than of a sudden drop; and a roll can be arrested, if sufficiently strong countervailing forces are mobilized. In any case, if chaos is really the prospect, any discussion of planning becomes futile, since planning will become impossible.

Almost as bad would be a disintegration of the Indian Union, during which power passes to groups of States, each group retaining

[41] S. Harrison, *India: The most dangerous decades* (Princeton University Press, 1960).

or re-establishing governmental coherence on a democratic, authori-tarian, or totalitarian basis. Provided disagreements among the new units did not provoke mutual conflict or foreign intervention, planning would remain possible—though not for India as a whole. While the advantages of all-India planning would be lost, at least some of the successor-states would be large enough, and equipped with sufficient resources, to frame reasonably satisfactory plans for the development of their own economies. If, however, the new State boundaries followed the old, there would obviously be some States, such as Assam and Rajasthan, whose very economic survival would be in jeopardy. Moreover, there would be a decline, everywhere, in the efficiency of economic planning, as a result of the shortage of competent planners and an exacerbation of existing administrative weaknesses at the State level. These evils could be minimized if the split-up resulted in the creation of a small number of comparatively large and economically viable units, reflecting either the north-south dichotomy or the zonal groups. Even greater advantage would accrue from the preservation of a 'Centre', federal or confederal, responsible for defence, foreign policy, currency, and long-distance transport and communications. Here again, however, we are confronted with remote possibilities; to discuss planning in such a situation is to approach the limits of the speculative.

We may also, for somewhat different reasons, dismiss the possi-bility of a 'take-over' by the communists or by the military. As the strength of the communists is local rather than national, any communist accession to unrestricted power is likely to be local too, and is at present conceivable only in the context of a disintegration of the Union. As for a military take-over, this appears to be discussed in civilian circles rather than prepared in military ones—although soldiers rarely advertise their intention to organize a coup. In either case the planning process would continue—and might even become more effective—but would have to adapt to unforeseeable changes in the political environment.

For practical purposes, therefore, one must assume a continuation of the political trends of the post-Nehru period—trends sharply registered and considerably reinforced by the elections of February 1967. These may be briefly summarized as (*a*) erosion of Congress dominance, particularly in the States; (*b*) a shift in the balance of power from Delhi to the State capitals; and (*c*) an increase in political fluidity, evidenced not only by the greater difficulty of forming stable governments, but by the growing articulation and articulateness of interest and attitude groups old (e.g. caste) and new (e.g. trade and profession).

Yet to people like Selig Harrison these are precisely the trends that point towards disintegration. Their assumption is that, in any under-developed economy with pitifully few goods to share among a growing number of increasingly exigent claimants, the preservation of a democratic consensus becomes less and less possible. Such circumstances indeed hamper the functioning of democratic (and federal) institutions. All too easily a vicious circle can come into motion: the shortage of goods undermines democratic consensus; that causes a reduction in the effectiveness of government; that weakens its capacity to promote economic development; and the weakening of government's capacity to promote economic development increases the shortage of goods.

On the other hand, India may still possess the capacity to break this vicious circle. It has social and political assets rare in under-developed countries: a comparatively sophisticated political leadership which, despite the apparent violence of its internal feuds, in the last resort has the will to keep the fissiparous and anomic forces in check, and has displayed a remarkable capacity to do so; a people which, particularly in the rural areas, has shown—and will probably continue to show—extraordinary patience; a comparatively long experience (beginning with the Montagu–Chelmsford Reforms) of democratic self-government, and an affection for it which cannot be explained merely by the absence of a viable alternative; and a corps of top-level administrators whose prestige, training, and intelligence facilitate the translation of political promises into concrete benefits, to the extent that resources permit.

These assets however, cannot be realized without a conscious effort to develop what Almond calls 'a bargaining culture in the key roles of the political system—in the political parties, in the bureaucracy, and among the interest groups . . .' Although the elements of such a 'bargaining culture' are already present—for, indeed, bargaining is inseparable from political democracy—there also exists, among the country's leading groups, a certain 'lack of an appreciation of the specifically political aspects of development'.

The Indian governmental and bureaucratic elites, overwhelmed by the problems of economic development and the scarcity of resources available to them, inevitably acquire a technocratic and anti-political frame of mind. Particularistic groups of whatever kind are denied legitimacy. As a consequence, interest groups either become captives of the government and bureaucracy and lose much of their followings or are alienated from the political system.[42]

The elections of February 1967 have emphasized that alienation rather than captivity is the clear and present danger. It can be lessened only by a political leadership prepared to give closer attention 'to the facts of local and state political power which affect the implementation of policy'.[43]

In India there is still a widespread illusion that successful economic development by itself is capable of establishing sufficient consensus for the satisfactory functioning of democratic institutions. Some planners even argue that if India can emerge from her current crisis and resume her forward march,[44] however haltingly, rising expectations can be prevented from seeking satisfaction outside the limits of the present political order. By now, however, we know that rapid economic development, like complete economic stagnation, is politically destabilizing. For the élite, the major political advantage of development over stagnation is that development provides resources which can be used for restabilization. But these have to be consciously deployed; they do not operate automatically. Whatever the rate of growth, therefore, a deliberate effort has to be made to satisfy, accommodate, or divert into harmless channels the demands of both groups and regions. Can the Indian élites, for all the assets they possess, acquire sufficient of these qualities in time for them to become effective? Does the bargaining process itself demand departures from economic rationality serious enough to

---

[42] G. Almond, in Foreword to M. Weiner, *The Politics of Scarcity* (Chicago, 1962).

[43] Weiner, p. 239.

[44] Some of them are optimistic about this, believing that the seriousness of the economic crisis has been exaggerated and that India is on the eve of an agricultural breakthrough, largely as a result of the favourable response of the farmers to newly-developed varieties of high-yielding seed. The Draft Outline itself, in its chapter on agriculture, refers encouragingly to 'the breakthrough in the matter of seeds and the change in the attitude of the Indian cultivator towards chemical fertilizers' (p. 175). Tarlok Singh, in a contribution to a seminar discussion at the Indian Institute of Public Administration, made the same point, and suggested that the main problem was to get the right inputs to the right cultivators at the right time—a problem of administration which, although difficult enough, is simple compared with the one that was previously regarded as crucial: that of inducing the cultivator to change his attitudes and extend his horizons.

impede growth and thus destroy the very resources that provide the most significant of the bargaining counters?

Neither question can be answered. What is important is that they are being persistently asked, in India itself. There is growing recognition that *if* effective economic planning is to be accommodated with federal democracy, a new basis for consensus must be sought. Whether the search keeps pace with a goal which, of its very nature, is constantly receding depends overwhelmingly on what happens to Congress—still the only party capable of providing India with overall political leadership.[45]

For planning, the 'new consensus' approach has unavoidable consequences. First, there will be a general, probably cautious move from the command towards the indicative style. This has already begun, and its possible implications for planning organization have been brought out by the ARC report.

Firstly, the Planning Commission, citadel of the 'old style', will almost certainly be reduced in size and powers. Composed predominantly of non-political experts, it will cease to be a second cabinet, and become purely technical and advisory. This virtual abolition of 'Nehru's Commission' is to my mind *saeva necessitas;* the Commission, as at present organized, emanated from a type of political leadership that no longer exists.

Secondly, in the formulation of both quinquennial and annual plans, there will probably be wider and more intensive consultation with organized interests. Consultation is already prominent, but from now on certain groups, such as organized industry, are likely to be listened to more closely, and the bargaining aspect of consultation will become more prominent.[46] This will probably increase the acceptability of the plans at the expense of their rationality.

[45] Many have hoped that, having shed a number of dissident elements, Congress would emerge from its electoral near-catastrophe chastened, reunited, and determined to do better in future. One cannot say, as yet, whether these hopes are likely to be fulfilled. As was to be expected, the new Congress government at the Centre began with some rather bad fumbles, and the rapid disintegration of the Congress governments in Harayana and Uttar Pradesh, as a result of floor-crossing, seemed ominous; but the revival of the party's self-confidence in Rajasthan and the election, by an overwhelming majority, of Congress's presidential candidate (despite an unprecedented campaign of vilification by the Hindu communalists) at least temporarily restored the hopes of the persistent optimists.

[46] There has been some demand, so far resisted by the Government, to give representation to 'persons qualified to speak for the private sector' on the National Development Council (see editorial in *Statesman*, 19 July 1967).

Thirdly, with the curtailment of the quasi-executive powers of the Commission, greater freedom in plan implementation will be accorded to (or taken by) Central Ministries, State Governments, and other executive agencies. This *may* mean that the plans are executed with greater dynamism; it will certainly mean that they are executed with less discipline.

Fourthly, broad planning decisions will no longer be the responsibility of the Planning Commission or even the Central Government; they will emerge from bargaining between Centre and States. If the NDC is to be effective for this purpose, it must become less a mere forum and more a decision-taking agency. To function thus, it will need to add to its members the more important Central Ministers with economic responsibilities, and to create some kind of permanent secretariat. The probable consequence of its new role will be that national planning strategy will be less influenced by a centrally-promoted ideology and more by the various objectives of the States.

Fifthly, within the limits of resources allocated by the Centre, the States will formulate their plans more independently and with less regard for the national interest. The central plan will therefore become more a summation of State plans than at present. This will compel the States to strengthen their own planning machines and give them a greater enthusiasm for plan fulfilment, but will make genuine *national* planning more difficult.

If such planning is to work, co-operation between the States and the Centre (and where possible among the States) is crucial. How far, under the new post-electoral dispensation, is such co-operation likely to be achieved? The election of 1967 is not necessarily a watershed in Centre-State relationships; it may merely reinforce pre-election tendencies. If so, the relationships that prevailed when the Fourth Plan was being formulated may be used in evidence. These suggest that the so-called centrifugal forces are weaker than is sometimes imagined. The States gave free expression to their individual and collective grievances, but no more than usual. Indeed, the discussions recorded in the *Summary Records* for 1964, 1965, and 1966 seem mild-mannered after those of the 1950s. This impression is confirmed by a statement, made to me by a high official of the Commission, that negotiations with the States about the size and shape of the Fourth Plan were smoother than comparable negotiations for previous plans.

Possibly comparative peace has reigned only because the States have concluded that planning discussions do not matter; but this is unlikely, for though a State may not take planning as such very seriously, it is anxious enough to get its share—and preferably more than its share—of centrally-allocated resources, without which it could barely meet current expenditures. Moreover, the States, although persistently complaining of being tied to centrally-devised schemes with fixed patterns of expenditure, have enjoyed a degree of *de facto* freedom often difficult to distinguish from licence. For, in practice, the Centre could enforce neither the fixed patterns nor the agreed distribution of expenditure. Having been promised the money, States do almost what they like, confident that whatever they may thereby lose in specific project grants will be made up at the end of the annual exercise by way of 'miscellaneous development loans'. Through the issue of these the Centre has become a party to the States' circumvention of planning priorities. Even now, therefore, central discipline is more vexatious than restrictive.[47] Admittedly, the Commission and the Central Ministries perpetually nag the States and attempt (harmfully) to exercise remote control over their administrative behaviour; but, except to the extent that dependence on Central funds restrains the States from abuses on a scale that might provoke cessation of supply, they enjoy a freedom in respect of the lay-out of their total approved plan expenditure which makes their periodical complaints about being the 'slaves' of the Commission look a little odd.

The States know that no more revenue can be made over to them, since such major revenue-raisers as income tax, corporation tax, and excises *must* be centrally controlled so long as India remains a united country. Indeed, the States would be embarrassed at having to levy heavy imposts for which the Centre now gets the odium. All they can reasonably ask, by way of further relaxation, is that the 'patterns' of expenditure be abandoned, that the centrally-sponsored scheme be less freely used, and that they be guaranteed receipt of a given quantum of resources (other than those they already receive through the Finance Commission's statutory awards) on a five-yearly instead of on an annual basis. These demands are likely to be accepted by the ARC, if current reports of its discussions are reliable.

Has all this been radically changed by the fact that, since the

[47] See above, p. 29 n. 12.

election, Congress is no longer the ruling party in half the States? Will not this intolerably exacerbate Centre-State relations, making coherent, all-India planning impossible? I doubt whether the situation has changed as radically as some people imagine.

The worst feature is not the ousting of Congress Governments, but the prospect that in the non-Congress States, apart from Kerala and Madras, stable governments will prove difficult to form. In conditions of governmental instability, economic development rarely receives high priority; such conditions, moreover, encourage the kinds of demagogy and opportunism which are bound to complicate Centre-State relations. Unfortunately, many State governments— including some key ones—are opportunistic alliances of parties with little in common. This makes the achievement of stability a daunting task. Admittedly, weak State Governments might enhance the authority of the Centre; but this hypothetical advantage is out- weighed by the inefficiency of such governments as instruments of economic planning.

If, however, reasonable political stability can be established in the non-Congress States, the blow to Congress could, on balance, benefit Centre-State relations in formulating and implementing economic plans. First, there is the advantage of greater openness. Decisions after frank negotiation between the representatives of different parties are more likely to be recognized as bargains, to be faithfully observed, than decisions after bickering between people owing nominal allegiance to the same party. Moreover, the influence exerted on the Centre by a State Government with an independent party base may well be recognized as more legitimate than that exerted by a State Government which can employ the threat of swinging a large bloc of votes in the national counsels of the party that enjoys power at both levels.

Possibly, while the Centre controls most of the investment funds—as it is bound to do, so long as the Union remains—non- Congress Governments in the States will be on their best behaviour, for fear that they may be discriminated against. The record of the eariler Communist Government in Kerala, which behaved very co-operatively in discussions about plan allocations, suggests that this may sometimes be the case. This same Government, far more readily than its Congress predecessors, could agree with the repre- sentatives of neighbouring Madras, then a Congress State, to the use of inter-State river water and other controversial matters.

Perhaps more important is the improvement of the States' own planning which, other things being equal, could ensue from their probable increase in independence. Although accusations of 'Planning Commission dictatorship' are greatly exaggerated, there *has* been excessive centralization. While encouraging the States—mostly in vain—to improve their planning machinery, the Commission has tried to do too much of their planning for them, with all the disadvantages of remote control. This has made for passivity among the State authorities. 'Why should we bother with planning when the Commission is doing the job for us?' was a question put to me by a high State official. Yet although the *apparatus* of control has developed formidably, the actual control has been rather feeble, because of the impracticability of applying effective financial sanctions.[48] Thus both the Commission and the States have had the worst of both worlds. If, therefore, the Centre is now compelled, by political *force majeure* if not from more rational motives, to clear away the bureaucratic encumbrances upon its planning relations with the States, and to concentrate its controls on key points, something will have been achieved. Given greater responsibility, the States may in time become more responsible. They might even give the Commission the satisfaction of seeing them develop adequate planning machines of their own.

Whether these potential advantages are realized depends on factors too numerous to catalogue and impossible to arrange in order of importance. Prominent among them, however, are two that depend on human will and intelligence rather than on objective circumstances. The first is the readiness of the centre to renounce 'big stick' policies (which are in any case abandoned, as Myron Weiner has emphasized, as soon as there is real opposition) and to recognize both the reality and the necessity of the bargaining relationship. The second is the capacity of the new and untried State politicians to renounce demagogy and face reality. Probably the Centre has learnt its lesson, and there are some signs that State politicians are beginning to learn theirs. Little further has been heard of the threats made by some newly installed non-Congress Governments, in the flush of victory, to monopolize revenues generated locally, unless they got a fairer deal from the Centre. At a meeting of State Chief Ministers, which agreed to maintain the existing food zones, Orissa's Chief Minister, whose party, Swatantra,

[48] See above, p. 57.

favours free trade, accepted the arrangement with the words: 'Theory is one thing, but practically there is no escape from single-state zones'.[49] It is said, moreover, that in West Bengal quite a number of Communist Members of the Legislative Assembly (MLAS) have been converted to the incentive value of high food prices. These swallows do not make a summer, but they are encouraging.

So the political outlook for planning is not entirely black, though the prospects of fulfilling the Fourth Plan as at present conceived are dim. If disintegration does not set in, and if India succeeds in avoiding the horrifying discouragement of widespread famine, we can expect a period of concentration on a series of one-year emergency plans, which will probably claim to be more closely-related to the Draft Outline (or to the final plan, when it appears), than they really are.[50] If these, with foreign aid, restore some stability to the economic situation, interest in long-term planning, which at present strikes most people as an exercise in unbridled imagination, will revive. But planning, whether long-term or short-term, can never be quite the same again.

[49] Inder Malhotra, *Guardian* (10 Apr. 1967).

[50] The newly-reorganized Commission has taken a decision to this effect. Work on the Fourth Plan has been deferred and priority given to the preparation of the annual plan for 1968–9. Asked whether the 1968–9 annual plan would 'have some connection with the Draft Fourth Outline', Professor Gadgil replied: 'The Draft Outline is a draft. It has not been accepted by the NDC. How can this be connected with something which has not been accepted?' *Hindustan Standard*, 6 Sept. 1967.

Economic Sectors

3

Targets and Investment in Industry

JAMES MIRRLEES

1. ORGANIZED INDUSTRY IN ECONOMIC DEVELOPMENT

IN India, as in many other underdeveloped countries, organized industry has been the main location of capital accumulation during the period of deliberate economic development. By 'organized industry' we mean the production that is undertaken in relatively large-scale plants. Even in the proposals for the Draft Fourth Plan, investment in organized industry is as great as investment in all other sectors taken together: although the emphasis has been somewhat muted as compared with the previous two plans. This capital investment is poured into projects that have a much higher productivity per man employed than does production in agriculture, services, or unorganized industry.

In India a large part of the production of the organized sector is investment goods, to be used in further expansion of the industrial sector and of the economy as a whole; a little is exported, but most of the rest of industrial production consists of consumer goods for the domestic market. Income generated by the organized sector has been growing much faster than production in the rest of the economy.

Many arguments can be put forward to justify this pattern of economic development. In the process of capital accumulation, so it may be argued, certain capital-intensive, or large-scale sectors producing non-importable commodities—the prime examples being railway transport and electricity—are bound to grow. Again, it is argued that India cannot, at reasonable cost, expand her exports rapidly; and that as a consequence expanded production of fertilizers, dams, railways, textiles, and buildings require some domestic production of the necessary capital goods and inter-mediates. The response of the agricultural sector to investment may be slow and uncertain. The most promising source of saving to finance development may be the profits of the organized sector.

63

Many of these arguments turn on export possibilities, or on the potential of the agricultural sector—questions that would take us too far from the main topics of this paper. Other elements of the case for an industrial emphasis will be examined below. It certainly appears that, in a broad sense, industrialization remains the policy of the Indian Planning Commission, as reflected in the Draft Fourth Plan. It is tempting to conclude from the poor results of the Third Plan period that radical changes in policy are required. Yet the experience of the Third Plan has done little to gainsay the arguments for dual development that we have listed.

The present chapter is concerned mainly to explain the pattern of industrial development proposed in the Draft Outline of the Fourth Five-Year Plan. Examination of the proposals is largely concerned with the asking of questions rather than with attempts to give answers; the latter would depend on extensive calculations and on information which is not available to the author. But some attempt is made to assess the realism of the Planning Commission's intentions and predictions. We begin by placing the industrialization in the context of the proposed Fourth Plan as a whole. An attempt is then made to disentangle, from the available documents,[1] the main features of the planned and anticipated investment during the period, and the increases in output that are expected. We take the opportunity to comment on the feasibility of the Draft Outline plans. Even granted the feasibility of a plan, there might be much better feasible plans. Admittedly, this is a hard question to settle. I content myself with discussing two of the more appealing criticisms that may be made of the kind of industrialization programme that the Planning Commission has suggested; namely, that there is too little attention to India's comparative advantage, and there is too great a concentration on the production of consumer goods for

---

[1] In preparing this paper, I have relied primarily on two documents: *4DO* and *MFB*.

The latter document gives a detailed statistical background to the plan. The figures in it do not, however, correspond exactly to the aggregate figures finally arrived at for the Draft Fourth Plan. Very roughly, we can say that *MFB* assumes that targets would be achieved six months sooner than is supposed in *4DO*. It has been impossible, too, to get figures on the different aspects of the plan in a consistent set of prices. In the tables below, sometimes 1961 prices are used, sometimes 1966 (post-devaluation) prices.

I have been very much helped also by some very interesting discussions that I have had with friends in the Planning Commission and Ministry of Finance. But they are in no way responsible for what is written here.

those with relatively high incomes. Having given only weak and modified support to these criticisms, I turn to certain very important consequences of the plans in the form proposed. In a country like India, the nature of the goods produced by industry is no more important than the use of the incomes generated by it. We must therefore, though briefly, consider the new jobs that will be created by the intended investment, and the extent to which the additional production is likely to be available for further investment.

It is now very unlikely that the Fourth Plan, when one is eventually agreed, will correspond closely to the Draft Outline. But if industrial investment is merely slowed down, rather than changed drastically in composition, the following analysis will continue to be relevant. And in any case, as a study of a development programme that has at one time been thought to be feasible, it may throw some light on the problems of the Indian economy.

2. THE PLAN IN OUTLINE

The intentions of the Draft Fourth Plan can be seen most simply in terms of the usual national expenditure aggregates, as shown in Tables 1 and 1a. In Table 1 comparison is made between the final year of the Plan period and 1964–5, a more normal year than 1965–6, which suffered from war and weather. In Table 1a, figures for 1970–1 are shown at post-devaluation prices; and it is possible to

TABLE 1

National Expenditure (1964–5 and 1970–1)
(Rs '000 mn, 1961 prices)

	1964–5	*1970–1*	*Increase (per cent)*
Private consumption	147·5	191·4	30
Public consumption	20·0	31·8	59
Gross capital formation	29·0	49·4	69
Excess of imports of goods & services over exports of goods & services	5·2	2·5	
Gross domestic product at market prices	191·3	270·1	41

Source: MFB, p. 141.

obtain a breakdown of the balance of trade between exports and imports for the period covered by the plan itself.

TABLE 1A

National Expenditure (1965–6 and 1970–1)
(Rs '000 mn, 1965–6 prices)

	1965–6	1970–1	Increase (per cent)
Private consumption	180·2	262·4	46
Public consumption	25·6	33·7	32
Gross capital formation	35·0	64·7	88
Exports of goods & services	8·1	19·3	138
Total demand	248·9	380·1	
Imports of goods & services	13·9	23·5	69
Gross domestic product at market prices	235·0	356·6	51

Note: 1970–1 figures are at post-devaluation prices.
Sources: MFB, p. 115: *4DO*, ch. 5. Some of the figures have been slightly adjusted.

No information is available about the probable distribution of consumption among income groups. The growth in aggregate consumption may therefore be taken as an index of the immediate benefits to be provided by the Plan. In the six years beginning 1964–5, consumption per head was intended to increase by 14 per cent. One may well wonder whether, at this stage of development, that is not a generous allowance. Certainly the planners cannot be accused of a harshly restrictive attitude to current consumption. From a long-term point of view, the increase in gross investment may be taken as an index of virtue. If a 9 per cent per annum increase in gross investment can be achieved, as hoped, over the six-year period, that will indeed be impressive. A large proportion, 63 per cent, is intended to take place in the public sector.

The increase in the value of exports shown in Table 1A appears dramatic; but it is considerably exaggerated because of the devaluation of the rupee by 36·5 per cent during 1966. Even allowing for the devaluation, the forecast of export growth is ambitious, especially in the light of past stagnation of exports. The ambition is understandable. The annual rate of foreign assistance (net of interest and repayments) is to fall during the plan. Indeed it is intended to eliminate country-to-country aid entirely during the Sixth Plan. An outsider may regret the aim, but must admit that it is understandable and may be necessary. Doubt remains even as to the level of assistance that may be expected during the current Plan. There is considerable uncertainty about the amount of foreign exchange that will be available during the Fourth Plan period, and the assumptions made in the Draft Fourth Plan are definitely optimistic. If these hopes are confounded, many of the programmes will have to be delayed or changed, particularly the investment plans for organized industry.

Yet imports are expected to increase rather faster than national income. In that sense at least, the aim of the plan is not maximum import substitution. It is nevertheless true that industrial expansion is, as we shall see, to take place on many fronts, and the proposed export growth is expected mainly from traditional lines of Indian export.

It is difficult to avoid the impression that the industrial programmes of the Draft Fourth Plan would suffer severely from any cuts in the foreign exchange available; and it might be unwise of India to risk so much. But in the remainder of the chapter we shall accept the targets of the Draft Fourth Plan in this area, and restrict ourselves to the problem of industrialization within these constraints.

3. THE PROPOSALS FOR INDUSTRIAL DEVELOPMENT

One need only compare the rate of growth of capital formation with the rate of growth of imports in the Draft Fourth Plan to realize the probable importance of industrial development in the Plan. Table 2 shows the Perspective Planning Division's estimates of the growth of the different sectors of the economy. These estimates are, of course, a mixture of proposed Government action and forecast of private (and public) sector response.

It will be seen that organized industry is expected to grow at nearly 12 per cent per annum during the six years from 1964/5 to 1970/1, despite the slow growth in the first year of the period. This is a rate of growth considerably greater than the achievement of the Third Plan period, though comparable to the targets of the

Third Plan. It is claimed, however, that a considerable backlog of Third Plan projects is expected to mature in the early years of the Fourth Plan.

The intention of this rapid growth is to build up the capacity of the economy to make its own capital goods, and so substitute home production for imports. A detailed analysis of the proposed industrial growth is shown in Table 3.

TABLE 2

National Income by Industrial Origin
(Rs '000 mn 1960–1 prices)

	1964–5	*1970–1*	*Increase (per cent)*
Agriculture	75·1	92·9	24
Mining	1·9	3·7	95
Small enterprises (including transport)	12·9	18·7	45
Construction	3·9	6·2	59
Commerce, communications & services	52·0	72·2	39
Organized industry (including railways)	22·3	42·7	91
Net domestic product at factor cost	168·2	236·3	40

Source: MFB, p. 9.

Chemicals, iron and steel, and machinery and engineering are to more than treble in size in six years. The production of electricity is to expand by nearly as much. The enormous expansion in engineering and machinery is the most remarkable feature of this programme. It is intended, for example, to supply the entire domestic demand for turbo-generators and power boilers by the early years of the Fifth Plan. By 1970–1 over 50 per cent of the metallurgical equipment for new steel plants is likely to be supplied indigenously (p. 267). It is hoped to be able to provide most of the plant and machinery for installing two new fertilizer plants a year from the beginning of the Fifth Plan period. The programme is remarkable not only for the extent of the expansion envisaged, but

TABLE 3

Net Value Added in Organized Industry
(*Rs '000 mn 1960–1 prices*)

	1964–5	1970–1	1975–6
Food products	1·4	1·9	2·6
Textiles, footwear, &c.	3·4	5·2	7·3
Chemicals & chemical products	1·1	3·6	6·5
of which: fertilizers	(0·1)	(0·8)	(1·5)
Machinery & engineering	3·0	9·6	16·6
Iron & steel	1·2	3·6	6·0
Other metals & metal products	0·3	0·9	1·6
Non-metallic minerals (cement, oil, &c.)	0·7	1·9	3·1
Electricity generation	1·2	3·3	5·4
Railways	4·5	6·9	not given say 10·0.
Others, & adjustment for coverage	5·5	8·8	12·6
Total	22·3	45·7	71·7

Note: The aggregate figure for value added by organized industry in this table is larger than that given in Table 2. In Table 2 it is assumed that the targets initially assumed for 1970–1 will be achieved with a lag of 6 months. The breakdown given in the present table is not available on the modified assumptions.

Source: MFB, sect. I.

also for the range of production proposed: machine tools, precision instruments, electronic equipment, electric motors, as well as many kinds of consumer durables.

The estimates for investment expenditure in the Fourth Plan period are shown in Table 4 on page 70.

The increase in output during the Plan period will result in part from investments undertaken before the beginning of the period, and a considerable proportion of these investments will yield output increases only after 1971. For that reason alone, it is a little hard to relate the investment outlays given in the Plan to the proposed increases in value added. In any case, not all the categories correspond neatly with one another. It is probable, to take only one example, that some of the increased value added resulting from the

TABLE 4

Investment Outlays in the Fourth Plan
(Rs '000 mn, 1966 prices)

	Public sector	Private sector
Machinery & engineering	3·5	4·5
Iron & steel	16·2	)3·8
Other metals	3·3	)
Non-metallic minerals & mining	8·1	)16·0
Miscellaneous	1·6	)
Fertilizers & pesticides	2·7	2·2
Electricity	20·3	0·5
Railways	20·9	—
Total	76·6	27·0
Small scale industry	2·3	3·2
Other industry, &c.	30·3	38·3
Agriculture & irrigation	25·4	9·0
Grand total	135·1	80·5

Source: 4DO, chs. 3, 14, 15 (some adjustments made to achieve consistency).

proposed investment in fertilizers would be classified under 'chemicals' in Table 3.

We should naturally expect that the investment required for a unit increase in the output of the main intermediates—steel, electricity, and railway transport—would be considerably greater than that required for the production of final goods, whether consumer goods or capital goods. The differences between these two kinds of industry as shown in Tables 3 and 4 are indeed remarkable. Assuming that the average lag between the capital expenditure and the increase in output is between one and two years in metals, electricity, and railways, it seems that roughly 10 mn 1966 Rs of capital expenditure is required in these industries for every additional 1 mn 1960–1 Rs of output. On the other hand, the most striking increase of all, the increased output of the machinery and engineering sector, to be accomplished at a rate of between 6 and 7 thousand mn 1960–1 Rs in a five-year period, is associated with capital investment during the

Five-Year Plan period of only 8 thousand mn 1966 Rs. The investment cost per unit increase in output is almost ten times as great as
this in the production of the main intermediates.

4. THE REALISM OF THE PROPOSALS

It is possible to suggest several reasons for this striking diversity
of capital coefficients. First, it is suggested that there is at present
considerable excess capacity in the machinery and engineering
sectors. But this can do little to modify our calculations. The
rather imperfect evidence on the relation between installed capacity
and output in 1964–5 does not suggest a proportion of unutilized
capacity in the machinery and engineering industries at that date
considerably greater than in other sectors; and even if it did, the
capacity of the sector in 1964–5 must still have been small in relation
to the vast expansion contemplated. Nor was the backlog of
uncompleted investment in the sector so great at the beginning of
the Fourth Plan period that the backlog we must expect at the end
of that period is unlikely to exceed it. We must conclude that extremely productive investment in this sector is an implicit assumption
of the Draft proposals.

It might be supposed, then, that investment in the engineering
industries simply is much less capital-intensive than investment in,
say, steel. Yet we can see from Table 5 that productivity per man

TABLE 5

Capital, Employment, and Output in Certain Industries, 1963
(Rs mn)

	Productive Capital	Persons Employed (000)	Value Added	Value Added per Man
Iron & steel	9,470	260	1,298	5,000
Electric light & power	6,502	135	630	4,700
Railroad equipment	739	168	541	3,200
Machinery, except electrical	1,346	138	539	3,900
Electrical machinery	1,451	108	494	4,600

Source: Min. of Finance, Dept. of Economic Affairs, *India Pocket Book
of Information 1966*, Table 6.5.

has in the past been little different among the industries we are considering. (Wage rates have not varied much among these industries either.) It seems, therefore, that if existing relative prices provide any guide to the relative value of production in these different industries, India is very unwise to be contemplating investing in steel, say, at all. But this would be too hasty a conclusion.

TABLE 5A

Employment and Output in Railways, 1963–4

Average of persons employed at beginning & end of 1963–4	1,246,000
Value added in 1963–4 (National Income originating)	Rs 4,900 mn
Value added per man	Rs 3,900

Source: Central Statistical Org., *Statistical Abstract of the Indian Union, 1965.* Tables 14 and 100a.

We must conclude, in fact, both that the Planning Commission estimates are probably over-optimistic, and that the prices of intermediate goods (produced mainly in the public sector) are low relative to industrial prices in general. Table 5 certainly suggests capital-output ratios considerably higher than the incremental capital-output ratios implicit in the Planning Commission's estimates. More thorough studies of capital coefficients[2] suggest that in the machinery and engineering industries the capital cost per unit of additional value added averages about two. This is to be compared with the coefficient implicit in Tables 3 and 4 of less than one (when one allows for the substantial increase in prices between 1961 and 1966). There is no suggestion that the *kind* of expansion contemplated for the engineering industries is such as to require abnormally small investment. It is hard to see why import-substitution in the capital-goods industries is thought to be so cheap.

The conclusion that the prices of intermediate goods are unreasonably low is at least as important. It affects both production decisions and the generation of saving in the economy. We shall return to both these effects.

Meanwhile, let us remark that, their prices being artificially low, the contribution of the intermediate products to the national

[2] A. S. Manne and A. Rudra, 'A Consistency model of India's Fourth Plan', *Sankhya*, series B, vol. 27, pts 1 and 2 (Calcutta, 1965).

product will be greater than it seems from Table 3. And, whatever increases in investment in the engineering industries should perhaps be made, the large-scale capital expenditures in steel, electricity, and railways will continue to loom large in India's development budgets. The long gestation periods of investment projects in these industries will also continue to be an important feature of India's economic development.

During the Third Plan the lengthening of these gestation periods in steel, fertilizers, electricity, and other fields—at least as compared with expectations—was notorious. Some of the delays must be put down to ill luck—unforeseen changes in technique, labour troubles, delays in getting the necessary foreign assistance, or in getting the assistance on acceptable terms. Yet similar causes of delay are likely to occur during the Fourth Plan, and it seems virtually certain that some projects will mature more slowly than might be hoped. One may inquire whether the programmes of the Draft Fourth Plan have allowed for such delays, and for other 'unforeseen' costs. The Draft Fourth Plan does not sound optimistic, but it does not sound realistic either:

Construction works have to be completed in time if the physical outputs are to be realised. Yet, in the light of past experience, there can be little doubt that unless considerable economies in design and construction are achieved and there is marked reduction in the cost of materials and increase in efficiency in the construction industry as a whole, it will not be possible to accomplish the physical tasks envisaged in the Fourth Plan within the financial outlays provided (p. 159).

It may be added that if delays begin to occur, there is no certainty that the outputs can be obtained at *any* reasonable cost at the time originally hoped for. Elsewhere, the Draft Outline indicates that actual investment costs are likely to be higher than the figures given in the document (p. 42) and reduces the estimated increase in national income to allow for 'delays . . . and other unforeseen developments' (p. 61).

This means that the prospects offered by the Draft Fourth Plan are available only on condition that efficiency and organization are improved (and on condition that the desired aid is available when wanted). Plans may try to provide a coldly realistic appraisal of possibilities: assuming that the planners will do their best, but everyone else will do only what is most likely. Or a plan document may try to show what is possible if everyone does his best—even if such a concerted effort is objectively unlikely. The Fourth Plan, like the Second and Third Plans, is essentially of the second kind. The Draft Outline asks:

Can this perspective be realised or is it merely a matter of setting the sights high in order to urge the nation to greater effort? The answer depends upon what will be done by the people. (P. 29.)

When assessing the realism of the Plan it is perhaps appropriate to bear in mind the kind of projections that the planners, implicitly, intend. Certainly it is hard to regard the programme of industrialization as in all respects a realistic prediction.

5. ARE THERE BETTER ALTERNATIVES?

It is risky to attempt to assess the feasibility of a plan. It is much harder to determine, on any superficial examination of the evidence, whether on its own assumptions the pattern of investment has been well chosen. I shall content myself with considering the most obvious lines of criticism that the proposals in the Draft Fourth Plan invite. Above all, many economists will suspect that the Plan pays only lip-service to comparative advantage.

Critics will argue that the massive expansion in the production of capital goods (like machinery) and inputs required for their production (like steel), and the production of other industrial commodities (like electricity) is the result of an unwise reluctance to purchase industrial goods from abroad now and in the future. They will claim that India could obtain more of the consumer goods that it wants, now and in the future, if it would aim the expansion of production at export markets, and use the proceeds to purchase the desired consumer goods, or—in the case of non-tradable commodities like electricity and housing—the main inputs required.

The evidence we have already obtained, that investment in engineering is expected to be much more profitable than investment in steel, seems to offer strong support for this view. But we should not be misled. The risks and costs associated with rapid export expansion seem to be considerable. In any case, transport, marketing, and tariff costs add up to give developing countries a substantial encouragement to substitute for imports rather than expand exports. In the particular case of India, export growth has been poor in the past, and only partly as a result of production bottlenecks. Certainly it ought to be possible to expand exports more rapidly, and substantial encouragement may be called for. But all this is already implicit in the Plan's export targets. It would be very hard to find evidence that India should rely on a faster growth of exports than that which is presently assumed.

The foreign exchange earnings from India's exports scarcely cover the current demand for raw materials and capital replacements dictated by the existing industrial structure; the demands arising from new investment have to be covered by foreign assistance. It is not surprising that India is planning to reduce the import content of its industrial inputs.

There are some grounds for suspicion on the other hand, that Indian industry could be even more provident in its use of foreign exchange. Prices in the Indian economy are a very long way from accurately reflecting relative marginal costs. We have already noticed that the prices of the large public-sector intermediates are too low. Since prices do have some influence on production decisions, the use of steel, electricity, and transport is being encouraged. No doubt this is inadvertence; but capacity is built to meet the expected demand and it is perhaps forgotten that expected demand depends upon present prices. Although these goods are made in India, their production costs India the foreign exchange that is spent on the capital, and that could have been saved by the labour if it had worked elsewhere. The Government may be able in particular cases to persuade and bully individual producers into using inputs less costly in foreign exchange: but they cannot hope to notice all the opportunities, nor can they expect to be insensitive to the importunate. Would so much steel be used in construction if building contractors were made to pay a price that correctly represented the costs of inputs used in the production of steel? Would so much electricity be used in homes if domestic users paid its value in import-competing industries? We cannot answer such detailed questions; we can only wonder what guarantee there is that the questions have been posed.

To summarize, there is little ground for thinking that India is wrong to emphasize heavy industry in its development plans. There are grounds for thinking that too little attention has been paid to the small, marginal decisions, which in aggregate may have a very considerable effect on the demand for, and allocation of, foreign exchange.

There is another kind of argument to which I should like to devote some attention. This is a criticism, not of the way in which particular demands for consumer goods are and will be met, but of the kinds of consumer goods that will be supplied. Too much weight, it might be argued, is given to the production of consumer durables, residential housing, sophisticated clothing, soap, cars, and so on. It is true that a substantial part of the increase in production of consumer goods, in the current and later Plans, consists of commodities that, in some sense, are less essential. But it is a mistake to criticize the production strategy of the Plan for intending to meet the pattern of demand that will be generated by the Government's fiscal and social policies. One may regret that some people have high real incomes: one has no reason to regret that, having high real incomes, they spend them on motor cars and television sets instead of on food. One ought to criticize the Government of India for rationing motor cars instead of taxing them, since the absence of a tax amounts to a subsidy to those who buy motor cars. But if, for good reasons or bad, high real incomes are an unavoidable part of the Indian economy, it is best to provide the consumer goods that these high real incomes demand.

If the Plans concentrated on the production of food, while the Ministry of Finance allowed large incomes to multiply, there would be no guarantee that the poor would get the food; and in any case, producers would find ways of producing the non-food consumption goods that would be demanded by high-income consumers. One will not eliminate the high incomes by trying to make machine tools instead of refrigerators; by leaving the high incomes one makes such plans impossibly difficult to carry out. Professor K. N. Raj has pointed out[3] that during the Third Plan period there has been some tendency for the production of industrial consumer goods to come closer to the targets than has happened in the case of capital goods. Thus there is a case for bringing the plans for production and the demands generated by the incomes people are allowed into closer harmony. Ideally, if one wants more investment—as surely one does—consumption will have to be cut by appropriate taxation. Otherwise, if the extent of taxation is not to be increased, consumer demands will have to be satisfied; the appropriate question to ask is whether these demands are being satisfied in the way that is cheapest to the economy as a whole.

[3] K. N. Raj, *India, Pakistan and China*, Delhi School of Economics (1966).

Arguments of very much the same kind are often used to criticize the allocation of investment between organized industry and other sectors of the economy, particularly agriculture. Much as I should like to discuss these issues, I have restrained myself; this chapter is concerned primarily with the allocations within industry.

6. THE GROWTH OF INDUSTRIAL EMPLOYMENT

Until the last few paragraphs, we have concentrated our attention on the pattern of production proposed by the Draft Fourth Plan. In a world where the distribution of incomes was perfect, we should not have to consider any other aspect of the investment plans. In India, the distribution of incomes is far from perfect, and it is of the first importance to predict who will gain from any particular investment programme. The investment projects to be established during the period 1966–70 will provide employment in the organized sector, so increasing the number of households who depend upon industrial wages. They will establish a flow of profits, some of which will be spent upon consumption, some of which will be saved. In the classical theory of dual development, such savings are a major generator of growth, while the new employment is the chief way in which the benefits of industrialization are distributed to the population at large. In India, neither the new saving nor the new employment is yet very large; and there are reasons for thinking that both ought to be larger, particularly the flow of profits.

The brief chapter on employment in the Draft Outline gives very little information that can be used to assess the probable amount of employment to be generated in organized industry. It speaks of a 23 mn addition to the total labour force during the Fourth Plan period, and an increase of 14 mn in job opportunities outside agriculture. We may get some impression of the probable increase in employment in organized industry from the increase in value added to be achieved during the Plan. If value added per man employed is about Rs 3,500 in 1960–1 prices (it is perhaps now a little more), the increase in employment between 1964–5 and 1970–1 implied by Table 3 is less than 7 mn. This is likely, on present plans, to be a considerable overestimate. During the Third Plan, value added in organized industry grew much more rapidly than employment in these sectors; and there is no evidence that value added per man is now likely to decrease. Although small increases in employment by the organized sector can be contemplated with relative equanimity in the early years of development, it is depressing that the employment increase during the Fourth Plan cannot, on current targets, be much greater than during the Third.

If average real earnings of industrial labour in 1960–1 prices is now about Rs 1,200 (it may well be lower), the increase in the industrial wage bill during these six years is to be less than Rs 8,000 mn.

TABLE 6

Real Wages in India, 1948–1964

(Rs 1949 prices)

Year	Average Earnings in Industry	Consumer Price Index	Real Earnings
1948	883	97	910
1949	986	100	990
1950	959	101	950
1951	1,036	105	990
1952	1,112	103	1,080
1953	1,111	106	1,050
1954	1,111	101	1,100
1955	1,174	96	1,220
1956	1,187	105	1,130
1957	1,234	111	1,110
1958	1,285	116	1,110
1959	1,310	121	1,080
1960	1,385	124	1,120
1961	1,414	126	1,120
1962	1,465	130	1,130
1963	1,479	134	1,100
1964	1,475	152	910

Note: The samples on which these statistics are based are rather unsatisfactory, and the figures should consequently be treated with caution.

Source: Min. of Finance, 'Average Earnings': *Pocket Book of Economic Information*, Table 2,5; Consumer Price Index: Table 11,1; Real Earnings: 2nd col. divided by 3rd col.

Thus only a small part of the Rs 44,000 mn increase in private consumption (Table 1) is to be provided through increases in the wage bill of organized industry. The wage bill would be a bit larger if real wage rates were likely to increase. This would hardly be desirable, since industrial wage-earners are already a relatively high-income group, and in any case an increase in their wages would be, to a considerable extent, at the expense of saving. Fortunately, as Table 6 shows, real earnings have shown no tendency to rise in the last ten years. The Draft Fourth Plan guardedly suggests the need for continued discipline, and it seems unlikely that real earnings will start rising now.

It will be realized, then, that the contribution of industrial development to current consumption is relatively small, and that it benefits the lowest income groups only in a rather expensive way, by offering them an additional relatively small number of highly paid jobs. In this respect investment in organized industry compares poorly with investment in agriculture. The great advantage of investment in industry, on the other hand, is that a large part of the profits it generates—which are in any case rather large—is available for further reinvestment.

7. PROFITS AND SAVINGS IN INDUSTRY

The increase in profits generated in organized industry, after allowing for salaries, should be well over Rs 12,000 mn, if the investment programmes are carried out as proposed. The gross figure would be much larger. Thus profits will certainly be rising faster than investment, and saving out of profits can make a substantial contribution to the increased saving required—through taxes, public enterprise surpluses, corporate retentions, and household savings. It can be argued that more saving could be created by increasing taxes on profits; but since this is not a matter of industrial policy as such, we shall not explore the possibility. On the other hand, the savings generated by the public sector profits are very much influenced by the price policy of public enterprises; we must now consider this important aspect of industrial policy again.

We have seen already that the profitability of steel, electricity, and—to some extent—railway transport is low. The same could be said of fertilizers. No doubt some past investment decisions have been in error, and there may well be room to reduce current costs in these industries. But the profits being made are also the result of the pricing policy that has been followed. Electricity is a good example of the problems, and is referred to several times in the Draft Fourth Plan. It has now been agreed that electricity prices should be set sufficiently high to ensure a rate of return of 11 per cent (including excise duty). The Venkataraman Committee[4] recommended that this return should be achieved within three to five years; but the authors of the Draft Outline are concerned at the slow progress being made (p. 86). The Draft Outline also urges that other public sector enterprises should raise their prices (or reduce their costs) sufficiently 'to get a rate of return of not less than 11 to 12 per cent on capital employed' (ibid). Progress in achieving revised pricing policies is impeded by the usual political pressures, accentuated by the consciousness of inflation.

It should be emphasized that this is an argument for getting prices raised primarily as a means of obtaining government revenue. Undoubtedly Indian economic development is held back by the reluctance, or inability, of the Government to raise taxes; but there are some areas where it would seem to be particularly easy to raise further revenue, above all on the output of public sector industries. I have remarked earlier that higher prices in these industries would probably improve production decisions in other sectors, both on investment and on current input. Higher prices would also allow more use of the price mechanism as a means of allocating commodities, so saving scarce administrative skills for better employments. I now want to go further. In almost all public sector industries it is desirable that prices should be set so high as to make a higher rate of profit on capital than is obtained in other sectors of the economy, since additional profits accruing to the public sector are entirely saved—or at least there is no reason why they should not be. The greatest advantage of the public ownership of industry is lost if public wealth makes an inadequate profit, and subsidizes the earnings of private wealth instead. The Draft Fourth Plan is right to emphasize the need for revising prices upwards. It could have been wished that the policy changes required had been spelt out in more detail.

Certainly the profits of organized industry should be financing more than half of gross capital formation by the end of the Fourth Plan. This is a prime justification for India's policy of industrialization, since political arrangements have left agriculture so lightly taxed. It cannot be too strongly emphasized that the role of the industrial sector as a producer of profits needs constant deliberate encouragement.

[4] *4DO*, p. 230.

8. CONCLUSIONS

The Fourth Plan, as it appears in the Draft Outline, follows closely the intentions of earlier plans. I have argued that it is a portrayal of a development of the Indian economy that would only be possible if everyone in the Indian economy acted more or less as the Planning Commission would like them to. If this is indeed the intention of the document, the case for the policies it proposes is rather weakened by such unrealism. The programmes for the development of organized industry do seem, at least in parts, to make very optimistic assumptions about production possibilities. At any rate, the progress in industrialization that is proposed depends, if it is to be undertaken successfully, on reforms in project administration and price policy, on success in obtaining foreign exchange through exports and aid, on widespread success in cutting costs and eliminating delays, and on strong fiscal policies. In fact, if the plan is pursued in this form, the industrial targets are all too likely to be achieved more slowly than the Draft Outline suggests: and if that were not so, the investment cost would almost certainly be greater than the controllers of the fiscal purse are likely to allow.

Since the growth in industrial employment that we can expect from these programmes is in any case small, slower growth of organized industry would not have a very serious effect on the distribution of consumption within the economy. Slower growth would however sharply reduce the savings generated in the sector. This might even be so serious that the fiscal problem would be enhanced rather than eased by slower growth in the industrial sector.

In this chapter I have attempted to portray the Draft Fourth Outline proposals in a series of summary tables, and to comment on the most obvious possible criticisms of them. I have argued that the emphasis on heavy industry may well be right, and that in any case there is insufficient evidence to suggest the contrary. I have suggested that the highly imperfect pricing policies followed in India may have prevented producers and planners from finding numerous better ways of using the available foreign exchange. I have provided arguments to support the continued production of industrial consumer goods.

It is to be expected that an economist should complain that the Planning Commission has given insufficient attention to production alternatives. Yet one cannot point to any alternative programme that is obviously better and feasible; nor can one point to many other planning organizations that do consider a wide range of alternatives. The plan that we have in the Draft Fourth Plan is supported by careful checks on the balance of supply and demand for the major industrial commodities.[5] There is reason to expect that, if the Plan is followed, industrial growth should be more coherent than in the past, even if it must be slower than the optimistic forecasts suggest. At least India has some right to hope that industrialization can proceed more rapidly in this Plan that it did in the last.

[5] *MFB*, sects 2 and 3.

4

Strategy for Agriculture:
Urban Bias and Rural Planning*

MICHAEL LIPTON

1. THE ARGUMENT

A PARADOX lies at the heart of Indian agriculture. Few resources
are allocated to it; rightly, it is set ambitious targets; demonstrably,
the resources are not very likely to reach the targets; yet the potential
yield from extra resources is high. Agriculture's planned share of
investment is lower in 1966–71 than in any previous plan period
(paras 5–9). Yet extra investment would produce more in agriculture
than elsewhere (paras 10–18). Moreover, the short-run targets for
Indian agricultural growth, while roughly commensurate with
requirements, are very ambitious; past trends, which the planners
have interpreted somewhat hopefully, do not suggest that the proposed inputs can approach these targets (paras 19–31). These doubts
are deepened by the structure of incentives, which has led to an
uneconomic diversion of scarce manpower from villages to cities, to
under-utilization of farm resources, and to a composition of agricultural efforts unduly concentrated on big farmers and cash crops
(paras 32–44).

2. Low agricultural inputs might yield more output than past
experience would suggest, if better use were made of the inputs, or
if they improved in quality. In some respects (though not in the
emphasis on animal husbandry) the restructuring of agricultural
outlays aims at such improvements (paras 45–48). Principally,

* I owe much to written comments by Robert Cassen, Sir John Crawford, Dr
Meghnad Desai, Prof. Len Joy, I. M. D. Little, Dr James Mirrlees, Sir Penderel
Moon, Hermia Oliver, Dr Ashok Parikh, Andrew Shonfield, Prof. Paul Streeten,
Krishnaswami Subrahmanyam, and Daniel Thorner, and to verbal comments by
Prof. K. N. Raj, Prof. E. A. G. Robinson, and Maurice Zinkin. Many of them
disagree at several points with my conclusions, and responsibility for the paper is
entirely mine.

however, the central paradox—low outlays, necessarily ambitious targets, high yield of potential outlays—is to be resolved by an improved *location* of farm inputs: the Intensive Agricultural Areas Programme (IAAP). Unfortunately, IAAP rests on a doubtful view of peasant behaviour in conditions of risk, and on an urban image of 'the progressive farmer'; the past record, too, casts doubt on the hopes for IAAP (paras 49–69).

3. Even if IAAP is the best policy, the wrong areas may have been selected (paras 70–74), and the human problem of implementation underestimated (paras 75–80). This is partly due to the planners' tendency to see agriculture in terms of big aggregates; this is also illustrated by the treatment of land reform (paras 81–87) and co-operative credit (paras 88–91). Here, as in the case of social services (paras 91–95), the effect of outlays on farm output—the rate of return over cost—is not estimated, so that the real efforts and achievements of Indian planning are not concentrated on the most fruitful projects or places. In land reform, rural credit, and social services, the big improvements (past and proposed) do not suffice to explain the huge rise in the yield of direct farm investment expected by the planners for 1966–71. The paradox still stands.

4. The small amount and the persistently unsatisfactory composition of agricultural outlay suggest that the planners are somewhat remote from the nature and needs of village India, and rely on big aggregates rather than local studies. This is strange, for India's planners fully accept the abstract case for agricultural priority, and are as intelligent and honest as any planners in the world. The suggested explanation is *urban bias* in the Indian system of economic reward, political power, education, and intellectual preference. This urban bias is echoed in the unconscious assumptions of the planners themselves (paras 96–106). Thus they tend to neglect the balance of power within villages, and to discuss rural attitudes and behaviour in a rather general and unrealistic way (paras 107–18). The drift of inputs to big farmers is directly linked to their place in the *urban* power-structure (paras 119–21). Policies on employment and nutrition, both of which have tended to worsen both resource use and rural–urban inequality, are typical consequences of the 'grand alliance' of big farmers, urban employers, and industrial employees (paras 122–25). Unless the planners can break free of such pressures, and of the counterpart in their own minds, neither the research nor the action required to achieve sustained agricultural progress in

India will be forthcoming. The drought of 1965–6 did not create urban bias; the good harvest of 1967 will not destroy it.

2. THE FALLING SHARE OF AGRICULTURE

5. 'Highest priority for agriculture' is the core of Indian planning until 1970.[1] To attain self-sufficiency in food, 'we are not sparing any resources or efforts'.[2]

Yet agriculture's planned share of public development outlay[3] is lower than the share proposed in any previous Indian plan or Draft Outline. Table 1 also shows that desired reductions in total plan outlays have usually been achieved by cutting the share of agriculture, and that the share of actual outlays going to agriculture has been even less than planned. It might therefore be suspected that the reduced share of outlays for agriculture reflects greater realism on implementation. However, the share of planned agricultural outlay devoted to major irrigation is smaller than ever before;[4] since such schemes are less difficult to implement than most others, agriculture is likely to fall even further behind its planned share of public development outlays than in earlier plans.

6. The distinction between public 'investment' and 'current' development outlay is obscure; and the projection of private investment is a rough estimate rather than a plan. Discussion of plan allocations, therefore, should probably concentrate on public development outlay, as in Table 1. Investment plans, however, tell the same story. Of *public investment*, agriculture's planned share was 20·9 per cent in the Second Plan, 22·4 per cent in the Third, and only 18·7 per cent for 1966–70. Of projected *total investment*, agriculture was to get 20·3 per cent in the Third Plan and only 16·1 per cent in 1966–70.[5] Real planned *private investment* in

---

[1] Asoka Mehta, 'The Challenges of the Fourth Plan', *India 1966: Ann. Rev.* (London, 1967), p. 2, subtitle.

[2] Ibid. p. 5. See also *4DO*, p. 30: 'To begin with, and claiming the highest priority, is the programme for increasing agricultural production. Necessary financial outlays have been provided'.

[3] In this paper, outlays for 'agriculture' include the following plan categories: agriculture, forestry, fishing, community development, co-operation, and irrigation.

[4] See Table 3 below. Moreover, emphasis has been placed on field channels, extension of earlier works, &c.; items very hard to control, and hence subject to a big 'implementation gap' (*4DO*, p. 218).

[5] Planning Commission, *Second Five-Year Plan* (1956), p. 56; *4DO*, pp. 42–43.

TABLE 1

Planned Public Development Outlay

Percentage share devoted to:	First Five-Year Plan, 1950/1–1955/6					Second, 1956/7–1960/1					Third, 1961/2–1965/6			Fourth, 1966/7–1970/1	
	Draft Outline	Plan	Revised Plan	'Adjusted' Plan	Realized	Draft Outline	Plan	Plan (1st Revision)	Plan (2nd Revision)	Realized	Draft Outline	Plan	Likely Realization	Memorandum	Draft Outline
Agriculture, community development, co-operation	12·8	17·4	15·8	14·9	14·8	11·8	11·8	11·8	11·3	11·5		14·2	12·8	15·4	15·1
Irrigation			16·8			9·5	10·1				23·1				6·0 (a)
Flood control										9·1		8·7	7·6	6·4	
Power	30·2	27·2	11·3	7·2	29·1	9·2	8·9	17·9	18·2	9·7	12·8	13·5	14·6	12·5	12·7

(a) Falls to 5·9 if Tenugat Dam (for Bokaro steel plant) is excluded.
Sources: Hanson, *The Process of Planning*, pp. 110, 134, 205; likely realization of 3rd Plan, and 4DO, p. 43; Fourth Plan Memorandum from Economist Intelligence Unit, *Annual Supplement to Quarterly Economic Reviews of India and Nepal, 1966* (1966), p. 17.

agriculture in 1966–70 is to *fall* by 25–30 per cent from its planned Third Plan level; so that the declining scope for new major irrigation does not mean a big planned expansion of private tubewells, as it did in Pakistan. Total real planned agricultural investment, public and private, is to rise by only 3·7 per cent—as against 53–63 per cent for organized industry and minerals.[6]

7. The contrast between words and planned deeds seems harsh. There are three arguments designed to show that agriculture's true share for 1966–70 is more than it appears to be. First, agricultural investment has a relatively low import content; thus devaluation in June 1966 may have cut the real value of planned outlays in agriculture less than in other sectors, so that an allocation of 21 per cent to agriculture means a bigger emphasis on that sector *after* devaluation than an identical share would have meant *before* it (p. 43). The effect is real but small. Devaluation cut the values of planned agricultural outlays by 2·8 per cent through direct effects on import prices, and of planned total outlays by 5·3 per cent.[7] Since inflation gets transmitted among sectors, and since most private investors had to pay scarcity prices rather than official prices for imports even before devaluation, the relative 'benefit' accruing to agriculture will be even smaller than these figures suggest.

8. Secondly, a much bigger share of non-agricultural investment than in previous plans might be directed towards agricultural growth. The Draft Fourth Outline does not allow us to be sure, but this seems unlikely. Planned public investment on rural electrification was 1·4 per cent of planned public outlay in the Third Plan and 1·6 per cent in the Draft Fourth Outline.[8] Primary health centres, the main means of bringing medicine to rural areas, increased from 2,800 to 4,800 during the Third Plan, and only 400 more are needed

---

[6] In money terms, private agricultural investment during the Third Plan was to be Rs 8,000 mn at 1960–1 prices; during the Fourth Plan, Rs 9,000 mn at June 1966 prices. Total planned agricultural investment was Rs 21,100 mn and Rs 34,390 mn respectively, and in organized industry and minerals the figures were 25,700 mn and 62,860 mn in Third and Fourth Plans (*4DO*, pp. 42, xii). Wholesale prices rose by 50·0 per cent, and farm product prices by 59·8 per cent, in this period (UN, *Monthly Digest of Statistics* (Jan. 1967), pp. 138–9, 164–5).

[7] Import content of planned public outlays for agriculture, Rs 259 mn; of all planned outlays, Rs 2,450 mn, both to be divided by 1·576 to get the post-devaluation value. *MFB*, p. 132. Total planned outlays from *4DO*, p. 42.

[8] Ibid. pp. 42, 229. The actual proportions attained in Second and Third Plan periods were 1·6 per cent and 1·4 per cent respectively. Ibid. pp. 43, 229; Hanson, p. 134.

by 1970–1 (pp. 352–3). New fertilizer plant receives 2·0 per cent of planned public investment in the Draft Fourth Outline, as against 1·9 per cent in the Third.[9] However, over half Fourth Plan fertilizer investment projects are 'not yet decided . . . foreign credits not yet arranged'. All the big increase in planned investment in tractor production is in the same category (pp. 284–8). Village housing, covering some 80 per cent of India's population, gets only 9·9 per cent of planned public housing outlay, an improvement on 4·6 per cent in the Third Plan.[10] Apart from the smallness of these changes, it is misleading to class (e.g.) fertilizer plant, which yields primary incomes entirely in the industrial sector, as quasi-agricultural investment. Agriculture benefits from fertilizers; cotton mills also benefit from raw cotton, but extra irrigation of cotton soils is not industrial investment.

9. Thirdly, the allocation of resources *within* agriculture may have been redesigned by the planners so as to yield more output and welfare per unit of input. This is the heart of the strategy for 1966–71: the attempt to rationalize Indian agricultural spending by irrigation schemes with shorter gestation periods, intensive concentration on selected areas, and redirection of expenditure from co-operation and community development towards schemes affecting farm output directly. But this cannot justify reducing the share of total outlay allocated to agriculture. If the marginal yield of agricultural outlay is much higher than before, and this is not true in other sectors, then agricultural outlay should form a bigger share of the total, not a smaller share as in the Draft Fourth Outline. It is surprising (though not necessarily mistaken) for the planners to seek maximum growth by reducing the share of outlay in agriculture. Can it be shown that India *ought* to put more than the present 20–25 per cent of investible resources into agriculture?

3. THE CASE FOR TRANSFERRING INDIAN INVESTIBLE RESOURCES TO AGRICULTURE

10. There cannot be anything in a *general* argument for raising

---

[9] *4DO*, pp. 42, 285; Planning Commission, *Programmes of Industrial Development 1961–66* (1962), pp. xv, xvii, xix. Since 45–50 per cent of the cost of fertilizer plant is in foreign exchange (*4DO*, p. 346), devaluation plus a 50 per cent rise in wholesale prices (1960/1–June 1966) probably means that the absolute value of proposed outlay on fertilizer factories is smaller in the 4th Plan than it was in the 3rd.

[10] Ibid. p. 359; Planning Commission, *Third Five-Year Plan* (1961), p. 679.

(or lowering) agriculture's share of investible resources.[11] If such an argument were sound, it would justify pushing agriculture's share up to 100 per cent (or down to zero), which is absurd. A *specific* but crude criterion for allocating investible resources is to get as much extra yearly output from them as possible: in the jargon, to minimize k, the 'marginal capital/output ratio', in the whole economy. This criterion implies that resources should go to sectors where k is low. On this very crude 'k-criterion', India's farms use extra capital more efficiently than its factories (see para. 11), and hence should get more of it than at present. Three familiar objections to the crude k-criterion are dealt with in paras 12–14, and actually seem to strengthen the conclusion that agriculture should get a higher proportion of investment. Nor does the conclusion seem to be weakened by two objections based on the 'long haul' argument for Indian industrial development: that farmers do not save and that industry ultimately yields more. These objections are discussed in paras 15–16 below. The final objection to the k-criterion, that Indian agriculture has reached the administrative or human limits of its capacity to absorb new investment, is discussed in para. 17, and turns out to beg the question of whether new investment can be so designed as to increase the 'absorptive capacity' of the farms.

11. It is almost certain that k is lower[12] (i.e. that average yearly output from new investment is higher) in Indian agriculture than in Indian industry. Reddaway[13] estimated k in 1960–5 at 0·9 for

[11] In India, at the present level of agricultural and other investment, some of the arguments are good (income equalization, nutrition, food surplus to obtain wage-goods without foreign exchange problems), some bad ('savings surplus for urban growth later'—why later? Why not from the urban sector itself, with its higher profit share and savings propensity?) Also there are some good ('you can't eat steel') and bad ('modernization') arguments for lowering India's present argicultural share. Plainly, for any economy, there exists a share of planned investment in any sector so high that none of the arguments for raising it holds good.

[12] Two problems of such comparisons can be simply dealt with. First, yearly farm output fluctuates because of monsoons, not because of 'capital'—k in agriculture shows great annual variation; therefore a yearly average or expected output must be used in estimating the yield of capital. Second, if output of a sector is projected in unusually high prices, its k will seem unusually favourable (i.e. low); either 'typical' prices or 'shadow' prices (reflecting planners' own valuation of outputs) should be used. Our prices (1960–1 and June 1966) may not be too untypical; anyhow they incorporate the relative valuations of the Third and Draft Fourth Plan documents respectively.

[13] W. B. Reddaway, *The Development of the Indian Economy* (London, 1962), p. 211. A. S. Manne and A. Rudra, 'A Consistency Model of India's Fourth Plan', *Sankhya* (1965), pp. 133–5, estimate 1·5 for agriculture and 2·3 for *heavy* industry in 1970–1.

7

agriculture, 2·6 for mining and manufacturing. For 1966–70 the planners[14] implicitly estimate k at 1·22 in agriculture, but 2·00 in industry. These are the ratios of direct investment in the sector itself, to extra yearly output in that sector; a refined k would measure 'indirect investments' in power and transport and perhaps in health and education, in so far as they raise factory or farm output, as parts of industrial or agricultural investment. This would raise k (lower the yield of investment) more in industry than in agriculture, since most investments in power and transport benefit the factory rather than the farm. Such a 'refined k' would probably be about twice as high for industry as for agriculture in the period 1966–70. In other words, the annual yield expected from investment, direct and indirect, is about twice as high in the farm as in the factory. This refers to *total* planned investment in each sector: does it suggest that *extra* investment would yield more in farm than in factory? As investment plans are expanded to cover the less profitable projects, yields may fall (k's rise) faster in agriculture than in industry, because of the severe limits on cultivable land. But this effect is unlikely to swallow up a difference in average yields of the order of 2 to 1; certainly there are no big agricultural projects with the enormous k's of the new steel and engineering works discussed by Dr Mirrlees (pp. 69–70).

12. One objection to the k-criterion is that it amalgamates different sorts of capital equipment into a single capital/output ratio, instead of maximizing the yield on scarcer varieties of capital. In so far as farm investment uses these scarcer varieties of capital especially sparingly, the above argument, that by the k-criterion Indian agriculture gets too small a share of investible resources, is strengthened. In three important cases the ratio of scarce to plentiful capital *is* lower in farms than in factories. First, the foreign-exchange content for Indian investment in 1966–70 is lower in agriculture than in industry (n. 7). Since the free market value of

---

[14] *MFB*, p. 9; with a 1964–5 base for agriculture, and a 1965–6 base for industry (i.e. mining, factory establishments with power, small enterprises), value added, in 1960–1 prices, is to rise by Rs 17,800 mn in agriculture, and by Rs 22,800 mn in industry to the adjusted 1970–1 figure. Converting to June 1966 prices by the farm product and wholesale price indices respectively (see n. 6), the figures become: agriculture Rs 28,302 mn, industry 34,200 mn. Fourth Plan investment (in June 1966 prices) is Rs 34,390 mn in agriculture, Rs 68,360 mn in industry (*4DO*, p. 42). This implies sectoral k's as estimated in the text. Since wholesale prices rose faster in 1960–6 than the appropriate industrial price index, our estimate for industry's k is on the low side.

the rupee is below the official value, India cannot buy foreign machines as cheaply as their price (relative to home-produced machines) suggests. Therefore, if the relative price of home-produced and foreign machines reflected their real scarcity value to India, the investment cost of extra factory output would be even higher, relative to that of extra farm output. Second, relative to industrial investment, a higher proportion of the value of farm investment consists of payments to unskilled labourers. Such workers would often be unable to get other jobs, especially in the agricultural slack season, when the expanded plans for minor irrigation works (p. 185) can be carried out. Again, a larger part of farm investment turns out to use plentiful or surplus resources; that is, factory investment contains a larger proportion of *scarce* resources. Third, most farm investment has fewer moving parts, slower obsolescence, and hence less depreciation. The only big exception is irrigation canals, but these are usually maintained by unskilled workers in the slack season. Therefore, agricultural investment makes fewer claims on future scarce resources than an equal amount of industrial investment.

13. A second objection to the k-criterion is that farm investment and factory investment are complementary; the yield of each depends on the level of the other, so that a high k in industry may be justified. For instance, if we take skilled engineers away from building (high-k) steel mills and employ them on (low-k) dam-building, we may starve tractor factories of essential steel, thus reducing output and hence the yield from the new dams. However, such *specific* complementarities work both ways; agricultural investment can lower k for industry. Thus extra irrigation works for cotton soils will increase the yield from new cotton mills. Moreover, there is a *general* complementarity favouring farm investment as a whole. Several times, most drastically in 1966–7, inadequate farm output has forced the Government of India to cut back industrial investment and output, firstly to divert foreign exchange from industrial raw materials to food imports, and secondly to curtail the inflation of food prices by reducing the wage demand for food. Extra farm output thus permits general industrial expansion, both by freeing foreign exchange for raw materials and by reducing inflationary pressures on food prices.[15] So extra farm output, by

[15] In 1964–5 about two-thirds of India's farm output, in 1960–1 prices, consisted of food. *MFB*, pp. 10–11.

allowing more freedom to Government reflationary action, stimulates extra industrial output. The converse does not apply; especially in the short run, extra industrial output does not stimulate food supply in India today. The fact that it increases the *demand* for food, therefore, does more harm than good. The above objection to the k-criterion, then, also reinforces the conclusion that Indian agriculture should get a bigger share of investible resources.

14. Another objection to the k-criterion is that capital is not the only scarce resource; one should also be concerned to lower India's engineer/output ratio, for instance. Again, the objection strengthens the claims of farm investment. Data are available only for doctors (para. 36), but these typify the general situation: agriculture's share of skilled personnel has been low and stagnant. So far, farm investment has been more economical than industrial investment in its use of technicians.

15. An upholder of India's present industrial priority might retort: 'It is myopic to use the k-criterion to advocate extra farm investment. For rapid growth, India must raise the proportion of income saved; this is as important as a low k. Most of the cost of farm projects comprises wage payments, and savings out of wages are low, but savings out of industrial incomes are much higher. Thus emphasis on farm projects means low savings and therefore slow growth. If India is to become self-sufficient, she must raise the proportion of income saved to prepare for the day when her savings are no longer supplemented by foreign aid. Moreover, industry's k is so high because factories take longer to build, and to overcome teething troubles, than farm projects—the gestation period is longer. If you look at the yield of 1966–71 investments in 1975, industrial projects will produce much more than in the short term'.

16. This 'long haul' case for industrial priority, associated with Nehru and Mahalanobis, contains two arguments.

(*a*) First, the value of k (extra capital/extra yearly output) is said to depend on the year in which extra output is measured. The later the year, the better the relative performance of industrial investment. But there is not much evidence of this from the Indian data because, however many years after investment we choose to measure output, k in industry is at least $1\frac{1}{2}$ times k in agriculture. So the gestation-period explanation for the relative performance of Indian agricultural and industrial investment gets less plausible as time goes by. Anyway, in the context of the present emphasis on quick-yielding projects, it is rather a self-defeating sort of argument for a high industrial share of investment!

(*b*) Second, it is true that a higher proportion of profits is saved than of wages, and that the profit-to-wage ratio is higher in industry than in agriculture. But to use this as an argument against agricultural investment is to assume that the financing of investment depends on private saving alone. For 1966–70, however, 25 per cent of investment finance is to be public;[16] admittedly it is easier to tax the *average* urban worker than the *average* farmer; but it is also easier for governments to raise their ability to finance investment, by taxation of *extra* income in excess of *extra* spending on current account, if high food output raises the taxable capacity of farmers and reduces outlays on famine relief. Eleven per cent of investment is to be financed by companies; they make higher profits (and thus save more) when there is enough food at reasonable prices, so that employers can satisfy their workers with low money wages because these workers can still buy plenty to eat. Twenty-five per cent of investment is to be foreign; aid-givers, where commercial pressures permit, are increasingly eager to direct aid to agriculture; further, since food shortages are more pressing than steel shortages, more foreign exchange may be saved[17] for investment by preventing the former. Only household saving, to finance 39 per cent of planned investment (1966–70), clearly benefits from the industrial emphasis of Indian output and investment; but it is misleading to link India's growth to personal saving but not personal consumption. Extra food consumption in India raises input and productivity of both labour and enterprise, much more for ill-fed farmworkers and smallholders than for well-fed urban workers and employers. If industrial investment yields more personal saving out of income (and hence more investment), agricultural investment yields incomes likelier to be used to feed the hungry (enabling them to work better).

17. While k is lower (i.e. the yield of investment is more) in agriculture than in industry, it is not so low that 1970–1 food targets can be achieved from present farm investment plans. This is shown in paras 23–27 below. But could the targets be achieved by raising

[16] *MFB*, p. 113, as for similar figures in this paragraph.
[17] During the Third Plan, 17·8 per cent of Indian cereal imports were not PL 480 (*4DO*, p. 102). PL 480 grain has saved many Indian lives, but is rather slow and inflexible during real hardship, and *marginal* imports are never PL 480; moreover the size of future PL 480 is uncertain.

the investment plans? It is sometimes argued that agriculture has low 'absorptive capacity' for new capital; that it is getting as much investment as it can use.[18] This argument has been repeated since 1950, although the real value of annual farm investment has been steadily rising despite the lack of that rural 'change of heart' allegedly required to raise absorptive capacity. The yield on new farm investment has *not* been diminishing—though it appears to have been, if we concentrate on the exceptionally good monsoons of the First Plan, and the disastrous monsoons of 1965 and 1966. The yields of farm capital are indeed kept needlessly low (only 150–200 per cent of the yields of industrial capital) by rural attitudes, institutions, and shortage of administrators. The remedy, however, is not to restrict farm investment because of low absorptive capacity, but to use farm investment to raise absorptive capacity. To some extent this happens automatically. Dams, improved seeds, and fertilizers raise the yield from good farming, and hence the incentive to abandon rural attitudes and institutions that keep absorptive capacity down. More specifically, some sorts of rural investment directly raise the farmer's capacity to absorb other forms of investment. This is especially true of investment in training extra extension workers and administrators, and in providing sources of credit and insurance outside the traditional structure. Finally, the argument from 'low absorptive capacity' suggests that extra farm investment will soon yield smaller returns than extra factory investment, which contradicts the expectations of the planners themselves (para. 11). These imply that the output targets for 1970–1 *could* be achieved by enough well-directed extra farm investment. So the planners, at least, cannot believe that it is low absorptive capacity that justifies the smallness of agriculture's share of investible resources.

18. Let us rehearse the surface evidence that agriculture is getting too few resources, remembering that this allegation really depends on the inevitably crude, superficial, and approximate cost-benefit analysis of paras 11–17 above. Total public provision for agriculture in 1966–70, including indirect help through transport, education, etc., is generously estimated at 31·2 per cent (p. 43) of planned public outlay—for the 70 per cent of the work-force making 45 per

---

[18] The image of 'absorptive capacity' begs the question. Agriculture is not a sponge, able to contain a fixed amount of productive investment. Yields on investment in agriculture (as in industry) fall as investment rises, but do not suddenly fall to zero when the sponge is saturated.

cent of national product, and the poorest and most undercapitalized 70 per cent at that. Four out of five Indians live in rural areas, but only 11 per cent of doctors practise there, and for most other technicians the ratios are even lower. Of the unemployed, however, *over* 80 per cent are rural.[19] All this has to be reconciled with the top priority accorded to agriculture and the known skill and integrity of India's planners. Can the explanation lie in the agricultural targets themselves?

4. THE TARGETS OF INDIAN AGRICULTURAL PLANNING

19. The specific targets of the Draft Fourth Outline look optimistic now (October 1967). This is largely due to India's second successive monsoon disaster in 1966. In discussing whether the aggregate output targets are (*a*) commensurate with Indian needs and (*b*) realistic in view of the input targets, we use the Draft Plan data for illustrative purposes only. Plainly, if industrial incomes grow less, so will the demand for food—and if farm outputs can grow less, so can farm inputs. But if the planners' own (June 1966) estimate of 1970's output is roughly commensurate with their estimate of 1970's need; if the latter estimate is roughly correct; and if the former estimate cannot reasonably be anticipated from the planners' own estimates of farm inputs—then there is nothing about the agricultural targets of the planners that can explain the low allocation of investible resources to agriculture. And that conclusion will still stand, if target estimates of needs, outputs, inputs, and resources are 'realistically' scaled down in about the same proportions.

20. It was frequently suggested in 1967 that a yearly growth rate of foodgrain output of 4 per cent, instead of 5 per cent as in the Draft Plan, would be compatible with the other Draft Plan targets. If this was so, the investment proposed in the Draft might suffice. However, a rough check of other targets does not support this view. India's ability to sustain the planned level of industrial imports requires that foodgrain imports end by 1970–1. By then, therefore,

---

[19] *Fact Book on Manpower* (Institute of Applied Manpower Research, Delhi, 1963), pp. 6, 200. The section in *4DO* on health, otherwise excellent, contains no discussion of how doctors are to be got into rural areas where the need is greatest, and no emphasis on debilitating rural disease—dysentery and worms. For 1967–8, however, about 1,000 medical students were to be bonded into the family planning programme.

domestic food supply must equal demand. How fast will demand grow? The planners expect population to grow at 2·5 per cent per year, and income per head at 3 per cent (pp. 61, 346). Therefore, if each 3 per cent rise in an average Indian's income means a 1·8 per cent rise in his spending on foodgrains, the demand for foodgrains will grow by 4·3 per cent yearly.[20] Now in 1964–5 demand was 94·7 mn tons. If this is to grow by 4·3 per cent each year from 1966–7 to 1970–1, and imports are to be eliminated, home foodgrain supply in 1970–1 must be 119·8 mn tons[21]—almost exactly the planners' target.

21. Our estimate of demand was on the low side. Since malaria kills at ages 4–5, but otherwise is usually not fatal,[22] the effect of malaria control in 1950–60 is to raise the adolescent and adult proportion of the population in 1965–80, and thus to raise the food consumption per head of population, at any given level of income. Moreover, India's population is slowly moving towards the towns, where food consumption is higher. Probably, therefore, a 3 per cent rise in income per head will raise the demand for foodgrains by *more* than 1·8 per cent.

22. The planners' food targets are also modest compared to the nutritional need. Between 1964–5 and 1970–1, food production is to rise 30 per cent; since it is intended that food imports shall end, this means a rise in the value of food consumption of about 25 per cent. Since people switch from cheaper to dearer foods as incomes rise—from cereals to dairy products, from coarse grains to wheat and rice—a 25 per cent rise in the value of food eaten implies a

[20] If D is the growth rate of demand for a product, P of population, and g of income per head, and p is income-elasticity of demand for the product, then $D = P + pg$. (J. W. Mellor, *The Economics of Agricultural Development* (Cornell, 1966), p. 75.) The estimates of Indian income–elasticity of demand for foodgrains are controversial, since they vary according to the *form* of the relation assumed between income and spending on foodgrains. Our estimate of 0·6 is deliberately on the low side; U.S. Dept. of Agriculture, *Elasticities of Food Consumption Associated with Changes in Income in Developing Countries*, 1965, pp. 16, 25, suggests an elasticity nearer 0·9 than 0·7, for income per head as low as India's, but for *total* food. The figure for foodgrains would be lower, but not very much, because extra foodgrains are often all the food there is to buy from extra income in India.

[21] *MFB*, p. 40, for the 1964–5 demand. On 1964–5 income levels, demand on the 1965–6 population was 94·7 × 1·025 = 97·1 mn tons. Growing at 4·3 per cent yearly, this becomes 119·8 mn tons in 1970–1.

[22] M. Lipton, 'Population, Land and Diminishing Returns to Agricultural Labour', *B. of the Oxford Univ. Instit. of Economics & Statistics*, vol. 26, June 1964, pp. 123–57.

considerably smaller rise in calorie and protein consumption: perhaps about 20 per cent for proteins, 18 per cent for calories. With a 17 per cent population rise, the nutritional improvement is very small.

23. So the low share of agricultural investment cannot be explained by saying that the targets for agricultural output are maximal, in the sense that investment *need* not be high enough to achieve them. But can these targets be approached by the proposed levels of investment? If they can, our argument that this proposed investment is insufficient is greatly weakened. A crucial piece of evidence is the Planning Commission's reading of past agricultural performance.

TABLE 2

Growth Rates, Past and Projected

| Crop | Past compound percentage growth over five years implied by: | | Planned five-year growth 1965/6 (base)–1970/1 | Weight of crop in index of agricultural production (1950) |
	Planners' trend, based on period 1950/1–1964/5	Comparable growth, good year to good year, 1951/5–1962/5		
Rice	19·6	13·0	31·8	35·3
Wheat	21·5	15·8	57·0	8·5
Other cereals	13·9	3·5	23·0	14·5
Total cereals	17·9	11·9	32·9	58·3
Pulses	8·3	3·3	47·3	8·6
Total foodgrains	16·5	11·1	34·9	66·9
Oilseeds	18·3	16·0	28·9	9·9
Sugarcane	25·8	20·7	9·8	8·7
Cotton	22·1	14·8	59·0	2·8
Jute	17·9	9·3	49·3	1·4
Tobacco	16·2	12·9	27·8	1·9
Tea	10·5	7·2	31·1	3·3

Method: Cols 1 and 3 are planners' estimates of trends over the periods shown. Col. 2 shows the quinquennial growth implicit in the rise of output from the *best* year of 1951–2, 1952–3, 1953–4, and 1954–5, to the *best* year of 1962–3, 1963–4, and 1964–5, for each crop or group of crops. Col. 4 is the percentage (by value) of 1950 agricultural output made up by each crop.
Sources: Cols 1 and 3 from *MFB*, pp. 10, 35; cols 2 and 4 from *Reserve Bank of India Bulletin* (Mar. 1967), p. 346.

24. The Planning Commission has projected rates of output in agriculture by estimating past trends and then allowing for new inputs. The planned growth rates for various crops are shown in the last column of Table 2. The planners' reading of past trends,

unfortunately, is somewhat rosy. Table 2, col. 1, which the planners
relied upon, shows the trend of official production statistics from
1950–1 to 1964–5. But 1950–1 was a bad year (food output was 9·5
per cent down on 1949–50).[23] It was followed by a dramatic upswing
in 1952–3 and 1953–4. This upswing partly reflected improving
monsoons, and it was held after 1953–4 partly because it had included
recovery from partition, unrest, and refugee resettlement. It is
mistaken to include such an upswing in a trend, and then to project
future growth from such a trend. Moreover, 1964–5 was an exceptionally good year followed by two disasters. Both at the start and
at the finish of the period used by the planners to estimate past
trends, therefore, abnormally rapid farm growth took place. In col.
2 of Table 2, we show the past growth rates for a more normal
period, comparing good years in the early 1950s and 1960s. These
rates are much lower than those on which the planners based their
future projections.

25. But even these data (Table 2, col. 2) are too optimistic,
because they are still based on the official output figures. The trend
rate of growth of officially estimated foodgrain output from 1949–
50 to 1960–1 was 3·4 per cent per year. Two careful cross-checks,
one from consumption (minus imports) and the other from estimates
of extra farm inputs and their yields, suggest an *actual* growth in this
period of 2·5 per cent per year at most.[24] If this overestimation
continued until 1964–5, the growth rate for foodgrains, over a
typical five-year period from 1954–5, comes down from 11·1 per cent
(Table 2, col. 2) to 6·3 per cent. The planners base their projections
on an assumed trend rate of 16·5 per cent.

26. Even the pessimistic estimate of 6·3 per cent cannot be simply
projected to 1970–1 unless inputs grow faster than before. And this
is not only because of the normal operation of diminishing returns
as more land is brought under the plough. The planners rightly take
1964–5 as the base-year in view of the 1965–6 drought, but do not
seem to have measured the full length of the shadow cast by the two
successive monsoon disasters of 1965 and 1966. Farmers eat or
market the seedcorn, postpone new investments, sell or starve their
cattle, and sometimes lose their land. In Bihar in 1967, many were

[23] *Reserve Bank of India B.*, March 1967, p. 346.
[24] V. J. Lele & J. W. Mellor, 'Estimates of Change & Causes of Change in Foodgrain Production in India', *Cornell Internat. Agric. Development B.*, ii (1964),
esp. p. 36.

too weak to dig wells, and some to sow seed. From a given yearly investment, such disruption pushes down the trend growth of output for several years. Two successive bad years have probably turned some farmers against risky new investments like IAAP. Certainly they have diverted administrators from development to relief work. With foodgrain output 89 mn tons in 1964–5, down to about 76 mn tons in 1965–6 and 1966–7, it is obvious that the Draft Outline *targets* for 1970–1 will not even be approached. The planners, of course, realize this; when they prepared the Draft Outline they could not allow for the 1966 drought. What the planners may not realize is that not merely the targets, but the *trend growth rates*, and with them the Intensive Programme itself, may be unapproachable by 1970–1.

27. Are the ambitious targets explained by extra farm investment? In real terms, little more is to be spent on farm investment than in the Third Plan (see para. 6 above). Moreover, most past growth has come chiefly from extra traditional inputs, not from increased investment. From 1949–50 to 1960–1, some 35 per cent of extra foodgrain output came from cultivating new dry land, and 26 per cent from extra labour per acre.[25] No estimate of the area to be cultivated in 1970–1 is available, but from 1964–5 the rate of growth of dry cultivated area is unlikely to exceed 0·5 per cent yearly, perhaps half the rate of 1949–50 to 1960–1. Labour *per acre*, which increased by over 1·2 per cent yearly in that period, is not expected to rise at all from 1964–5 to 1970–1 (labour input into agriculture and animal husbandry is to grow by some 3½ per cent in the whole period).[26]

28. We shall later consider the planners' belief that new inputs, especially new seeds within IAAP, can take over from increases in land and labour as the mainsprings of agricultural growth. First we must briefly look at the *size* of the increases in inputs, other than land and labour, envisaged for 1966–70. Certainly, if land and (according to the planners) labour per acre are to stagnate, the

[25] See Lele & Mellor.
[26] Calculated from *4DO*, pp. 107, 108, assuming that 70 per cent of the 1966 work-force were in agriculture. With land input rising at about 3 per cent from 1964 to 1970, a rise of only 3½ per cent in total farm labour means an almost stationary input of labour per acre. In my view this is somewhat pessimistic; but our object is to assess the output targets on the assumptions about inputs made by the planners themselves.

planned rises in output require enormous expansions or improvements in other inputs. The proposed expansions are: seed 30·1 per cent (as against 11·9 per cent achieved during the Third Plan); area under utilized irrigation, 17·9 per cent (13·9 per cent); organic manure, 30 per cent (14·9 per cent); fertilizer, 250 per cent (184 per cent); pesticides, 250 per cent (150 per cent).[27] *If* enough foreign exchange is obtained for fertilizer production, the extra farm inputs from the industrial sector should be attainable. How the relatively modest rise in the growth rate of intra-agricultural inputs is to be attained is another question.

29. For example, the target for organic manure seems remote. The planners urge that 'suitable cropping patterns should be propagated so that the loss on account of growing the green manure crops is compensated by growing other crops on the same land' and they hope for 'increased emphasis on utilization of . . . night soil'. This sounds rather unrealistic. New cropping patterns take several years to adopt, and most Indians just will not use night soil. 'Cow dung gas plants on a large scale' turn out to mean '5,000 family-size plants'.[28]

30. Final judgement on these input targets must await the revised Fourth Plan. Even if all the targets are attained, we shall have rises of 250 per cent in fertilizer, 30 per cent in agricultural throughputs, and 17 per cent in irrigation inputs, allied to rises of only $3\frac{1}{2}$ and 3 per cent respectively, in labour and land (at least half total inputs by value).[29] This is supposed to raise agricultural output by 25·4 per cent and foodgrain output by 33 per cent above 1964–5 levels (p. 39).

31. Before asking whether IAAP, including improved seeds, can reconcile the projected input growth with the expected output growth, we should point out four facts about Table 2. The forecast does not sufficiently disaggregate types of grain; we cannot see how the extra output of coarse grains is to be divided among such crops as ragi, maize, jowar, and bajra. Secondly, the pattern of planned

---

[27] *MFB*, p. 13. We compare growth rates of inputs from 1960–1 to 1965–6 for the Third Plan, with rates projected for 1965/6–1970/1. Irrigation data are calculated from *4DO*, pp. 185–6, 215–6, 219. Inputs other than labour and unirrigated land rose between 1964–5 and 1965–6, so that the latter year is a proper basis for calculation in this case.

[28] *4DO*, p. 190. As for urban compost, the negligible rise achieved in the early years of the Third Plan (Planning Commission, *The Third Plan Mid-Term Appraisal* (1963), p. 71) gives little promise for Fourth Plan targets.

[29] See, for example, Min. of Food & Agric., *Studies of Farm Management in Bombay* (Delhi, 1962), p. 86.

growth by crops bears little relation to past experience; the intention to hold back sugar production, thus freeing water and fertilizer for foodgrains, echoes a similar hope in the Third Plan, which did not materialize owing to lack of suitable price policy; the enormous planned acceleration in the growth rate for wheat, and to a lesser extent for tea and cotton, may be too hopeful to be explained by improvements within plan allocations. Thirdly, as we shall see, past experience with the Intensive Programme, and even at research stations, does not support the optimism of the output targets. Finally, the relatively slow growth, past and planned, of coarse grains—of crops high in protein, low in prestige, and consumed largely for subsistence in rural areas—suggests several things about what we shall call urban bias in agricultural planning: its primary concern with extracting a food surplus for the towns, its exaggeration of changes in the structure of food supply initiated by the more rapid growth of urban incomes and demand, and its failure to maximize the impact of a given agricultural outlay upon nutritional standards.

5. INCENTIVES AND RESOURCE USE IN AGRICULTURE

32. At first glance it is paradoxical to argue that the flow of resources into Indian farming has been inadequate. Surely, if demand for food rises faster than supply, the price of food will rise, and with it incentives to private farm investment? After all, in the Third Plan period, about 38 per cent of farm investment was private (p. 42). The private sector, if it responds normally to incentives, is still large enough to switch plenty of resources back to agriculture. And, although we shall argue in paras 56–61 that response to agricultural incentives is both restricted and perverted by attitudes (especially aversion to risk) and institutions, there is no doubt that peasants *do* respond to price incentives.[30] So, presumably, do the engineers, doctors, and teachers whose presence in rural areas may be relevant to increased agricultural output.

33. Unfortunately incentives have not been allowed to work in this way. The stimulus to suppliers of education, fertilizers, etc. to do more in the villages depends on rising farm prices, which enable

[30] R. Krishna, 'Farm supply response in India-Pakistan: a case-study of the Punjab region', *Econ. J.*, Sep. 1963; D. Narain, *Impact of Price Movements on Areas under Selected Crops in India*, Cambridge, 1965, esp. pp. 158–62; E. Dean, *The Supply Response of African Farmers: Theory and Measurement in Malawi*, Amsterdam, 1966, esp. pp. 74–79.

and encourage farmers to buy such services. But farm prices have
been systematically kept down; since 1960, by the release of 'not
less than $3\frac{1}{2}$ mn tons of imported food grains . . . each year by the
government for consumption—even in 1960–61 and 1961–62 when
bumper harvests resulted in peak levels of production'.[31]

34. The very sharp rise in the price of farm products in 1965–7
does not constitute a permanent correction of the pattern of incentives. Farmers appreciate that this rise is due to the two bad
monsoons of 1965 and 1966, and does not justify them in a lasting
increase in cost and effort to grow more food. More hopeful,
perhaps, are changes in Government policy. 'In 1966, minimum
support prices on a more realistic basis were fixed for rice and wheat
in certain States. Since January, 1965, an Agricultural Prices
Commission has been set up to keep the price situation under
constant review . . . Price and marketing policies will assume added
significance in (1966–70) in the context of a massive effort for
securing rapid increases in production' (p. 174). Similar assurances
on price incentives, however, were given in the Second and Third
Plans as well,[32] but very little was done to make them good.

35. It is arguable that food prices at retail level must be kept
below market level so as to enable poor people to buy food, that high
prices to farmers would therefore involve Government subsidies,
and that these are unacceptable, given the need to increase the
current budgetary surplus so as to finance public investment. This
argument loses much of its force in the context of PL 480 management. Moreover, there are ways round the argument. Incentives
to farmers might be restored despite low absolute procurement
prices for food, if the prices of farm inputs (such as fertilizer), or of
manufactured goods especially popular in rural areas, were kept
relatively low. But this has not been done. Fertilizer prices, relative
to farm prices, have been much higher in India than in Pakistan,[33]
and are among the highest in the world. Tea, soap, &c. are, in my
experience, considerably dearer in the shop of the village merchant
(thanks to his local monopoly) than in the town.

36. If the Central and State Governments are unwilling or unable
to raise the prices paid to the farmer (or let them rise by the pressure
of market forces), and also to lower the prices of farm inputs or

[31] K. N. Raj, cited in Mason, *Economic Development in India and Pakistan*
p. 58. See also Streeten and Hill's chapter in this book.
[32] *Second Five-Year Plan*, p. 40; *Third Five-Year Plan*, p. 323.
[33] Mason, p. 58. In 1967–8 the position has somewhat improved.

rurally-marketed manufactures, a third method is open to them. Through wage incentives, they can stimulate the supply of productive personnel to rural areas. But they seem to follow the reverse policy. Teachers and civil servants receive City Compensatory Allowance if they live in cities, but no allowance for living in rural areas. Rapidly rising urban incomes, together with the high income-elasticity of demand for private services, draw lawyers and doctors to the cities; only 11 per cent of Indian doctors practise in the villages, where over 80 per cent of Indians live.[34] On 31 March 1961, of the 26,802 Government of India employees under the Ministry of Food and Agriculture, 45 per cent received less than Rs 100 per month; the proportion in the Ministry of External Affairs was 30 per cent, and in the Ministry of Commerce and Industry 27 per cent.[35]

37. Nor is it a matter of purely monetary incentives. The educational system acts as a funnel for rural talent into urban employment. Agricultural education is seldom available at primary level, i.e. before the age of 12—and children at school after 12 seldom return to the farm. The Education Commission, by advocating Agricultural Universities outside the university system proper,[36] underlined the low prestige of agriculture as a discipline. At the level of research, few of India's leading social scientists would prefer the testing of hypotheses at village level to the construction of aggregative models in Delhi (or the USA); the allocation of finance for research projects, as suggested by Dr Pocock on p. 289, supports this preference. As for administration, the prestige, prospects, and pay of the Indian Administrative Service are at their height in the Foreign Ministry; agricultural administration, especially at the crucial level of the Block, is almost always in the hands of people with no chance of entering the IAS.

38. The structure of incentives reinforces, and is reinforced by, inequality between village and town. Output per person in 1960–61 was more than twice as high in urban areas as in rural areas, and the gap had increased since 1950–1;[37] the demand for the services of

[34] See n. 19 above.   [35] *Fact Book on Manpower*, pp. 70–71.
[36] Min. of Ed., *Report of the Education Commission* (Delhi, 1966) p. 656.
[37] G. Rosen, *Democracy and Economic Change in India* (California, 1966) pp. 159–65. His assumptions about the incidence of Government taxes and outlays and about relative prices, however, vitiate Rosen's conclusion that these 'possibly . . . eliminate the apparent income shift . . . in favour of the rural sector' (p. 163).

doctors, engineers, &c. rises faster than income per head; thus the shift of skilled persons to the towns, encouraged by the educational system, is the effect as well as the cause of growing inequality. Migration from country to town, being concentrated on young and literate men, robs the villages of their natural leaders. Moreover, such migration does not reduce the effects of urban-rural inequality by significantly raising the share of India's people who live in the towns. That is because migration creates a big surplus of men in the towns (substantially slowing down the urban rate of natural increase), but only a small surplus of women in the villages (affecting the rural rate hardly at all).[38]

39. It might be argued that all this is merely the natural play of market forces. We shall suggest in paras 96–121 that there is much more to it. But even if the pattern of incentives were wholly caused by spontaneous shifts of supply and demand, this would not justify it. Supply depends partly on monopoly power, and demand depends partly on the distribution of income. If growing urban–rural inequality and industrial concentration are socially disapproved, then the allocation of productive resources, induced by such trends, can be 'efficient' only in a special and specious sense of the word.

40. It is obvious that the trends described in paras 32–38 have lowered aggregate resource use in farming. Less obvious is their effect on the allocation of resources *within* agriculture: the possible link between 'urban bias' and 'big farmer bias'. As we shall see, co-operative production and credit, political representation, and even the Intensive Programme have benefited chiefly the big farmers. These farmers have the time to be active in district and State politics; they influence rural voters, and (because they supply most of the marketed surplus) their interests are much closer to those of urban industry than are the interests of smallholders. These pressures are felt only at State level and below; but it is at State level that official responsibility for agriculture lies. The Centre's share of agricultural outlays is to rise from 10·6 per cent achieved in the Third Plan to 17·2 per cent in 1966–70;[39] but the problem of implementing the

---

[38] See n. 22.

[39] *4DO*, p. 71. For planned public outlay in all sectors the rise in the Centre's share is smaller (49·6 per cent actual 3rd Plan, 53·3 percent planned 4th; ibid. p. 74).

correct allocation of resources, as between rich and poor farmers, remains with the States.

41. The fact that only the rich farmers are well represented in the urban decision centres is linked to an argument often advanced for public agricultural outlay: that it will 'release' surplus savings and food to the towns. The endowment per worker of capital, calories, and proteins is lower in the villages; improvements in any of these yield more extra output if initial endowments are low; equality apart, therefore, one would expect the seeker after growth to try to keep the food and savings surpluses, yielded by early farm invest-ment, in rural areas. But the *big* farmers have enough food and machinery for their requirements; they are therefore concerned with urban outlets, both for saving and for marketed surplus. Their wishes mesh perfectly with the townsman's desire for a bigger inflow from the country, both of food and of investible resources. Since big farmers are much better represented in the towns than small farmers (who 'urbanize' a smaller proportion of both savings and food output),[40] they are well able to combine with the urban interests to make policy in their favour. How does this affect allocation of resources?

42. Between a quarter and a third of India's farm operators are in overall deficit; i.e. to make ends meet, they must work for others, in addition to cultivating their operational holding.[41] Both per acre and per man, they have fewer assets, less irrigation (and hence more risk), a bigger proportion of output devoted to food crops, and much less saving with which to buy new inputs of seed and fertilizer. So far, the rich and influential farmers have got hold of much more inputs per acre. IAAP proposes not to discriminate between rich and poor farmers (p. 175) and in the Tanjore district the small farmers actually bought *more* of the 'package' of improved inputs,

[40] *Indian J. Agric. Economics*, Jan.–Mar. 1961, symposium on 'Problems of Marketable Surplus in Indian Agriculture', pp. 28 (P. C. Bansil), 53 (G. C. Mandal), 105 (V. S. Rao), 108–9 (M. Srinivasan); C. C. Malone, 'Some Responses of Rice Farmers to the Package Programme in Tanjore', *J. of Farm Economics*, May 1965; M. Raquibuzzaman, 'Marketable Surplus Function of Major Agricultural Commodities in Pakistan', *Pakistan Development R.*, Autumn 1966, pp. 380.

[41] A variety of non-random samples of villages suggests that 'the proportion of farmers producing less than the minimum subsistence output varies widely from 5 to 46 per cent'. Raj Krishna, 'The Marketable Surplus Function for a subsistence crop', *Economic Weekly*, Feb. 1965, p. 120 (n. 4).

per acre farmed, than did big farmers.[42] Bought, but not necessarily used; a later study[43] suggests that much was re-sold to bigger operators, and that tenants paying 60 per cent share-rent used about half as much 'package' as owner-operators. As for credit, verbal reports from Madras are confirmed by a study from Madhya Pradesh, where 'the Central Co-operative Bank in the district will not lend to farmers who owned less than three acres, [to whom] the village level workers paid relatively little attention'.[44] Since land is the security for most co-operative loans, tenants can seldom use them; since tenants have more obligations (frequently to pay a share of the crop) than owners, they market a smaller surplus from a similar output level; here again, cheap credit discriminates in favour of farmers marketing a surplus for the towns.

43. This drift of inputs to big farmers is inegalitarian, but what is its effect on growth? There are two considerations pointing in opposite directions. Extra food and income are less important for big farmers, so their labour input per acre is smaller; but they are better able to afford private investment. The small farmer usually has a higher output per acre, and works his new resources harder in the short run. The greater ability of big farmers to invest may make them better at exploiting new resources in the long run. The planners' current concern for quick-yielding projects should emphasize the first of these considerations. More and more studies are revealing far higher output per *acre* on small operational holdings.[45] This suggests that small farmers also work *new* inputs more labour-intensively and productively, though suggestion is not proof. The allocation of resources to big farms may accelerate the growth of marketable surplus only at the cost of the growth of total food output.

44. Another consequence of higher and more rapidly rising urban incomes is a shift in relative demand for foodgrains, and in particular the probable fall in the prices of coarse grains relative to rice and

---

[42] Malone, p. 259.
[43] Forthcoming in *Indian J. Agric. Economics*, verbal report by K. N. Raj.
[44] L. L. Hodgdon & H. Singh, *Adoption of Agricultural Practices in Madhya Pradesh*, Nat. Institute of Community Development (Hyderabad, 1966), p. 11. See also Rosen, pp. 167–8; his pp. 165–76 provide further abundant evidence for the drift of resources to big farmers.
[45] An excellent summary of the evidence is B. Mukhoti, 'Agrarian Structure in Relation to Farm Investment. Decisions and Agricultural Productivity in a Low-Income Country—The Indian Case', *J. Farm Econ.*, vol. 48, no. 5, Dec. 1966, pp. 1210–5. Cf. D. Kanel, 'Size of Farm and Economic Development', *Indian J. Agric. Econ.*, Apr.–Jun. 1967, p. 35.

wheat. As Table 2 suggests, the shift in relative prices has led farmers to aim at much higher growth rates in wheat and rice than in coarse grains. This trend will be accentuated by the emphasis on rice and wheat in IAAP seed programmes. Calorie and protein yields per acre will almost certainly rise less than if the incentives and improvements had been concentrated on coarse grains—especially if rice is husked, polished, and deprived of much of its protein. Moreover, the policy will retard the growth in availability of the cheapest forms of food, and hence reduce the usefulness of nutritional improvements to the poor and ill-fed,[46] whose productivity responds most when their diet is improved by a given amount. True, the emphasis on fine grain may mean a rapid growth of value added per acre, but the relative prices in which this growth is measured are themselves dependent on the distribution of income—and on relatively rapid urban growth. Income-elasticity of demand is a good servant of nutritional planning, but a bad master.

6. THE RESTRUCTURING OF AGRICULTURAL INPUTS

45. So far we have suggested (*a*) that agricultural outlay is a low and falling share of India's development effort, (*b*) that its yield is higher than the yield of some popular alternative uses of resources, (*c*) that the paradox cannot be explained by low requirements or targets for agricultural output, and (*d*) that the structure of incentives discourages human and other private resources from making good the possible deficiences of the public agricultural effort. It remains possible that (*e*) the agricultural programme has been so restructured as to produce a much higher yield per rupee than in previous plans. Table 3 shows the composition of agricultural outlay in the Third Plan (intended and realized) and in the Fourth Plan. Table 3 shows a rise in the proportion of the programme geared to food production, at the cost of major irrigation (with its long gestation period, severe maintenance problems and concentration on cash crops) and of social outlays like community development and *panchayats*. This change in the input pattern should raise the yield of agricultural spending in the current plan period, perhaps by enough to offset the effects of diminishing returns. However, with outlays more

---

[46] In 1955–8, consumption per person on dairy products was almost twice as high in urban as in rural areas; as for foodgrains, the villager ate about one-sixth more, despite his greater poverty. *Tables with Notes on Consumer Expenditure, National Sample Survey*, 13th Round, no. 80 (Delhi, 1963), pp. 267–8.

heavily concentrated on food production (where water is usually less
assured) the variance of annual output may also rise, unless IAAP
is really to concentrate on areas of assured water supply.

46. Not all the changes recorded in Table 3 will raise yields. What
of the big rise in spending on animal husbandry? Meat and diary

TABLE 3

Sector	3rd Plan (1960–1 prices)	3rd Plan Achievement (current prices 1961–6)	Draft 4th Plan (June 1966 prices)
Percentage share of total agricultural outlay in:—			
Crop production (a)	12·9	11·5	21·3
Major irrigation	37·4	37·3	28·6
Minor irrigation	10·2	15·3	15·4
Soil conservation	4·2	4·4	6·5
Animal husbandry	3·1	2·5	4·2
Dairying, milk supply	2·1	2·0	1·7
Forestry	3·0	2·7	3·6
Fisheries	1·6	1·4	3·3
Warehousing, marketing, storage	2·4	1·9	1·5
Co-operation	4·6	4·3	6·1
Community development, panchayats	18·5	16·5	7·7
Total = 100 (Rs at stated prices)	1,740·2	1,760	3,374

(a) Includes *ayacut* (multi-purpose river basin) development.
Source: 4DO, pp. 41, 43, 185.

products are likelier to be consumed by townspeople than by
villagers, and by rich people rather than poor. Thus the nutritional
yield of these outlays is less than might be suggested by the high
protein content of milk. Moreover, a serious problem is created for
the farmer by the combination of improved seeds with emphasis on
cattle. Farmers throughout India complain that the new varieties of
seed (especially millets) do not provide palatable fodder from crop
stalks. Yet 'the physical output of straw has been assumed to
increase in the same proportion as the output of foodgrains' by the
planners,[47] who concentrate discussion of feed and fodder development on the relatively small problem of fodder crops and grasses
(p. 200).

47. More fundamentally, the planners seem to have neglected the
central problem of animal husbandry in India. For the Indian

[47] *MFB*, p. 29.

farmer, the cow is part god, part mother, so he could not kill an old, dry, and useless beast. Of 54·3 mn adult cows in 1961, at least 55 per cent were dry, and the ratio of dry cows to milch cows was double the recommended ratio in Orissa, West Bengal, Madras, Andhra, Mysore, and Kerala, owing to 'religious sentiment against the slaughter of decrepit cattle'; the situation is worsening, since the population of milch cows grew by only 8·9 per cent from 1951 to 1961 as against a rise of 18·5 per cent in the total adult cow population.[48]

48. By providing more resources for cattle husbandry, the planners will increase the incentive to keep and breed cattle, and therefore the number of decrepit beasts five or ten years hence. Unless an area is suitable only for grazing, it seldom pays *nutritionally* to allocate Indian land to cattle, even if there is no taboo against killing cows or eating beef; for most purposes, pulse protein is as good as animal protein in an Indian dietary context, so that the scarce thiamin-building resources of tropical soils need not be filtered through animals hungry for B vitamins. Since Indian cattle are a burden for much of their lives, should huge funds be allocated to their support? The planners might claim that the extra milk yield is worth it, especially if breeds can be improved by somehow overcoming the farmer's rooted objection to castrating stud bulls; but the planners do not discuss the relative rates of return on spending for animal husbandry and alternative uses of resources. Of course the planners cannot convert Indian villagers to cow-slaughter overnight. However, even at this sensitive political juncture, they might publish estimates of the cost of refusal to slaughter cows. Should one not concentrate cattle improvement schemes in Moslem areas, and try to reduce Hindu cow-worship by larger allocations to possible substitutes for bovine services—village buses, calor gas, urban compost? Above all, what is the benefit/cost ratio of these huge allocations to cattle in India, given the unnecessary costs inflicted by each extra cow? It is hard to maintain that the structure of outlays in Indian agriculture has been ruthlessly revised with a view to raising yields.

7. RELOCATING AGRICULTURAL INPUTS: IAAP AND PEASANT BEHAVIOUR

49. Much the most important development of Indian agricultural planning is the Intensive Agricultural Area Programme (IAAP).

[48] M. B. Nanavati & J. J. Anjaria, *The Indian Rural Problem*, 6th ed. (Indian Soc. Agric. Economics, 1965), pp. 40–41, 142.

Unlike the measures discussed in paras 46–48, this is not principally designed to change the ratios between total farm outlays, but to concentrate the outlays in 'packages', and to allocate these packages to specific areas.

50. IAAP seeks to 'organize the use of high-yielding seeds together with high application of fertilizers over extensive areas where irrigation is assured'. The pilot Intensive Agricultural District Programme (IADP) covered 308 Blocks, or 5 per cent of India's cultivated area, by mid-1966. By 1970–1, these figures are to be quintupled. 'The programme is to cover [this] entire area with improved package of practices and tackle their whole crop economy instead of only their predominant crops' (pp. 176–7).

51. IAAP has several intellectual ancestors. Firstly, complementarities among technical inputs, and between them and structural reforms, are probably larger in underdeveloped than in advanced agriculture. Extra fertilizers with traditional seeds and water supply, or improved techniques and inputs with traditional share-rents and credit systems have disappointing results; reform of the total environment, socio-political and educational as well as technical, may pay off. The debate between this structuralist view of agricultural development and the gradualist approach should perhaps be the central controversy in development theory. The influence of structuralism explains the special efforts to introduce crop loans with supply of credit to meet the production requirements in the area covered by IAAP (pp. 176–7), the special emphasis on plant protection measures for IAAP (p. 190), and why in the context of IAAP, agricultural research work is being reoriented radically (p. 196). The programmes for agricultural education, better agricultural implements, crop insurance, soil conservation, and land reform, however, do not concentrate on IAAP areas. Above all, though most observers agree on the benefits from the approximate doubling of extension and administrative personnel in IADP areas, it does not seem practicable to extend this to IAAP, which is eight times as large, without severely depleting the non-intensive areas—a policy specifically rejected by the planners (p. 175). This adds up to a curious sort of half-structuralism. It is not clear why complementarity is sufficient to justify the concentration of all the 'package' inputs (plus plant protection, crop loans, and research) on 20–25 per cent of Indian farmland, but insufficient in the case of crop insurance, land reform, and administration.

52. Secondly, IAAP is based on the justified belief that any reasonable strategy is better than none. But were alternative strategies tested before they were rejected? In particular, the bundle 'improved implements, land consolidation, improved traditional practices of composting and storage, crop insurance' might have produced greater additions to output than IAAP, for less resource outlay. I believe this is so, but nobody, in the present state of research, can really *know*.

53. Thirdly, IAAP derives from the planners' determination not to waste yet more resources on areas with unreliable water. If the rains fail, the farmer's purchases of fertilizer may have cost him more than the value of the extra crop produced; in severe drought, fertilizer may even reduce the crop by burning. Planners are aware that, when they persuaded farmers to raise output at the expense of security, poor rainfall destroyed not only crop but also confidence in future extension. IAAP is supposed to concentrate on areas of assured water supply, thus reducing the variability of total food output, since growth will be fastest in IAAP areas, which have lower variability. However, *actual* area selection has not followed this principle in the past (para. 71). Even if it does in future, it is ignoring the farmer in low-rainfall areas. He is faced by the greatest risk, and is thus especially likely to keep investment down so as to avoid yet more risk. He is also poorer than most farmers with adequate rainfall, and thus even more likely to insist on security even at the expense of output. Since the dry farmer's policies are more distorted by risk than are those of farmers with assured water, he will probably increase investment more, in response to the same outlay on reducing risk. To give him such incentives within IAAP, a way must be found to redistribute output (or income) from Intensive Areas to other areas in bad harvests, and thus to pay out claims by dry farmers for crop insurance on risky investments. No such scheme seems to have been devised.

54. There are three ways to achieve any desired reduction of the effects of the variability of crop output around the trend growth path: (i) to concentrate investment in regions with low variability of water supply, as in IAAP; (ii) to reduce variability of *each* region's output, by increasing secure but lower-yield investment (irrigation, pesticides, *robust* new seeds) relatively to risky but higher-yield investment (fertilizers, more *profitable* new seeds); or (iii) to protect farmers against the risks of investment by crop

insurance, backed by some combination of larger grain stocks and compulsory procurement from surplus zones (food aid is too unreliable). All three methods have costs; short-run growth is maximized by putting each year's investment where it is expected to earn the highest yearly return, and the encouragement of private investment by risk reduction is a long-run affair. The planners have concentrated on the first method, but the cheapest way of achieving a given risk reduction (or the least risky way of achieving a given growth rate) generally involves some outlay on each of the three methods.

55. Above all, IAAP derives from the conversion of the planners, through brilliant intermediaries like Raj Krishna and David Hopper, to the agro-economic ideas of T. W. Schultz.[49] Both the argument and the terminology make this obvious: 'It is inherent in the process of transformation of traditional agriculture that the primary producer—the farmer—should be enabled by adult education to understand and adjust himself to new technology' (p. 196). IADP was first proposed by the Ford Foundation team in 1959,[50] and aid was tied to this initial pilot programme; but the Indian Government's enthusiasm for IAAP is based on genuine intellectual conversion rather than on aid pressures. When the Minister of Food and Agriculture, Mr Subramaniam, explained on BBC television how the dry farmer had faced an almost unchanging environment for many years, and had learned to make the best use of traditional resources, he argued that a big rise in output was therefore possible only from a whole sheaf of new factors and techniques, concentrated on the 10–15 per cent of land area that enjoyed assured water supply. This is pure Schultz. His arguments must, therefore, be examined if the logic of IAAP is to be assessed. The following discussion is bound to be rather technical; non-economists might skip to para. 64.[51]

56. Schultz argues that underdeveloped peasant communities as a whole (not merely the individual farmers) are 'efficient but poor'. Each farmer, by maximizing profits, prevents 'any major inefficiency in the allocation of factors'. So 'no appreciable increase in agricultural production is to be had by reallocating the factors at the

[49] T. W. Schultz, *Transforming Traditional Agriculture* (Yale Univ. Press, 1964).
[50] Agric. Production Team (sponsored by Ford Foundation), *Report on India's Food Crisis and Steps to Meet It* (1959), p. 5.
[51] A fuller exposition of the following arguments appears in M. Lipton, 'The Theory of the Optimizing Peasant', *J. Development Studies*, Apr. 1968.

disposal of farmers who are bound by traditional agriculture'.[52] The appeal of this theory lies in its common-sense picture of a peasant learning from long experience in an unchanging environment how to make the most profit with his traditional resources. If Schultz is right, then a massive infusion of new factors and techniques is needed to 'transform traditional agriculture'; tampering with the use of existing resources cannot do so. Such massive change, with India's enormous agricultural sector and limited savings and skills, implies selection of areas. Well-watered areas, especially if irrigated and hence already exposed to some use of non-traditional factors, are the obvious choice. Hence IADP and now IAAP.

57. Schultz's account of optimizing peasant communities implies that traditional agriculture is close to neo-classical perfect competition: neo-classical because fixed factor proportions are implausible (Schultz rightly rejects them when he dismisses the possibility of zero marginal product of labour); perfect competition because otherwise individual profit-maximizing actions do not add up to a social optimum, so that Schultz's conclusion—that interference with the allocation of traditional resources is almost useless—would not follow. The Schultzian base for IAAP thus rests on the claim that each peasant acts like a profit maximizer in perfect competition: that he equates the marginal value-product of money in each use. Schultz does not explicitly consider risk, but his policy conclusions are seriously affected by it.

58. Rainfall (and thus output) varies from year to year. So the peasant does not know how much extra output will be produced from an extra rupee's worth of land or fertilizer. He still has a profit-maximizing policy, however: to make sure that the last rupee of his outlay, in each and every use, is adding the same sum to the average, typical, 'expected' value of his yearly farm product. In other words, to maximize profit taking the good years with the bad, the peasant must ignore risk, and sow his seeds as if this year's rainfall was sure to be the same as the average of all previous years (in general this average is the best estimate of this year's rainfall). Unfortunately, the average of previous years' rainfall is a less reliable

[52] Schultz, p. 39. The theory is more interesting than its statistical underpinning. Schultz complains (p. 40) of 'the propensity to take (weak) estimates . . . and force them into a Cobb-Douglas . . . production function', yet his main statistical source material does exactly this; the inputs are so closely related (collinear) that one cannot separate their influence and thus see how well the function explains the observations of output.

predictor of the current year's rainfall in monsoon areas than in temperate zones of similar total rainfall. Moreover, the lower the average rainfall of a village, (*a*) the more likely is a big difference between this year's rainfall and the average of previous years,[53] and (*b*) the bigger is the loss of crop if the rainfall is less satisfactory than was predicted when the farmer's early decisions (and risks) were taken. Profit maximization involves the farmer in deciding how to farm his land on the basis of *some* predictor of rain; but the best predictor is least accurate in the very places where it is most important. True, *any* rule of good farming has to rely on this predictor, but to maximize profit is to ignore risk, and to hope to come out on top in the long run. Among rational policies—rational in the sense that the farmer cannot, with the same resources, *both* raise his expectation of profit *and* risk—this policy is the riskiest, the most dependent on this paradoxical predictor. By failing to insure against risk, the policy has the effect of concentrating the farmer's losses in the years of poor harvest, when the value of extra output to him is greatest.

59. The logical oddity of profit maximization for the Indian peasant is underlined by another argument. The policy is bound to succeed only if continued for enough years to cancel out any runs of bad luck. But the peasant's low income and assets imply that two or three successive years of bad rainfall with a risky cropping pattern may mean ruin, forced sale of land, and thus inability to carry out the policy for long enough to succeed.

60. Apart from the logical oddity of profit maximization with fluctuating rainfall, it is an observed fact that people take out insurance policies. That is, they give up some expectation of profit, so as to reduce risk. Indian peasants, being poor and without social security, are especially likely to act like this. Gould[54] and Das Gupta[55] have shown that, among cropping patterns 'rational' in the

[53] S. Naqvi, 'Coefficient of Variability of Monsoon Rainfall in India & Pakistan', *Pak. Geog. R.*, pt iv, no. 2 (1949).

[54] P. R. Gould, 'Man Against his Environment: A Game-Theoretic Formulation', *Ann. Assoc. Amer. Geog.* (1963), pp. 290–7. A mixed-strategy maximin (maximizing the minimum income if Nature is malicious) is an excellent approximation to the behaviour of Jamaican fishermen in W. Davenport, 'Jamaican Fishing: A Game Theory Analysis', *Publications in Anthropology*, no. 59, ed. C. W. Mintz (Yale University, 1960).

[55] S. Das Gupta, 'Producers' Rationality and Technical Charge in Agriculture, with special reference to India'. Ph.D. thesis (available at Library of London School of Economics).

above sense (that re-allocation of land or effort cannot *both* raise expected profit *and* cut risk), most peasants choose the pattern with least risk, although this sacrifices a good deal of profit. There are numerous divergences from individual profit maximization, in the interests of insurance—intertillage of major crops with robust but low-value legumes; crop-sharing rents that mean low rent if the harvest is poor; fragmentation of land so that no son shall suffer the ultimate insecurity of landlessness. All these things suggest that State action can provide less inefficient insurance, and that it *can* thus persuade the peasant to improve the way in which he allocates existing resources.

61. Even if the peasant knows exactly what rainfall to expect, traditional restrictions on the sale of land and the use of labour prevent him from approaching as close to profit maximization as he might wish (given his desire for leisure, security, and status). Caste decides who does which jobs; family decides who farms what land; and exchanges of land or job are rare, even when both parties could benefit from exchange. For example, a leisure-loving and an output-orientated peasant may, respectively, be stuck with high-yielding but difficult land and low-yielding but easy land. If each peasant greatly prefers the taste of his own crop, or if the cost of marketing is considerable—or if the crops are the same—even a perfect product market cannot make up for imperfect markets in labour and land.

62. The learning process, claimed by Schultz to make the peasant into a profit-maximizer, depends on a secularly constant environment. This has been shattered by population growth, and by the near-exhaustion of opportunities for bringing new land under the plough. Agricultural practices born of long Indian experience are likely to use more land and less labour than is desirable per ton of output produced now. Many of the aspects of Indian farm behaviour that surprise Western observers, yet are not traceable to insurance, are of this type: failure to make compost heaps, insufficient weeding, reluctance to sow seed rows at a distance that would make weeding possible.

63. Even if *each* peasant maximized profit, this would not be optimal for *all*. Individual maximization under irrational constraints, e.g. against the slaughter of dry cows, helps the constraints to survive. Apart from this, a planner would reject even 'social profit maximization' in favour of a definition of optimal resource allocation

that gave some cost to risk (though less than the peasant does), to inegalitarian income distribution, to techniques that reduced employment, and to production that yielded incomes of which very little was reinvested or taxed.

64. It has been argued in paras 58–63 that the peasant is logically unable to get the information needed to maximize profit; that even if he could, he would sooner protect himself against risk; that even if there were no risk, the traditional restraints on the use of land and labour would prevent profit maximizing; that even if they did not, population growth has made many of the lessons of the past inappropriate, and vitiated the maximizing farm practices derived from them; and that, in any case, private profit maximization will not produce an optimum for the community. I shall now examine Schultz's hypothesis in the light of my research in a single (but fairly typical) dry millet village in Maharashtra in 1965.

65. Three types of village observation cast doubt on the notion of the peasant as profit-maximizer, and instead suggest that he seeks a survival algorithm—a set of rules of farming that ensure a tolerable minimum output. First, he accepts constraints that would be irrational for the profit-maximizer, ranging from hereditary allocation of jobs and land to the sacrifice of seed corn to appease a village deity. This acceptance makes sense 'just in case' misconduct is punished. Second, disagreement on practices persists; for instance, half the farmers adopt the same millet seed rate on good soil as on average soil, one-third a higher rate and the rest (correctly) a lower rate. Different farmers can learn different survival algorithms, but only one can maximize profit. Third, agreement on discredited practices also persists; 9″ instead of 12″ gaps between millet seed rows, open-heap manure storage, etc. These practices are traditional and therefore relatively safe. The peasant justifies all three types of behaviour 'from long experience', and he recognizes that his neighbours' experience with identical soil and crops often differs.

66. All this does not support the notion of peasant as maximizer, or the associated strategy of break-through by farmer, village, or Intensive Area to a progressive world of new factors and techniques. One finds, within a village, people whose inherited survival algorithm includes this or that good farm practice: a progressive ploughman, a progressive sower, a progressive manurer—and often they are different people. Similarly, the village that sows improved seed is

not necessarily the village using the best fertilizer mix. A person, or perhaps a community, inherits a group of practices, some progressive, others not. Farming depends on many practices, any one of which can be varied; and the small farmer is near to the breadline. How can he adopt an individual, uninsured, *ad hoc* adjustment to a single part of a farm procedure? Yes, his neighbour uses improved seed and gets more output; but his neighbour's inherited wisdom contains a whole group of different, yet complementary, practices. To learn just one of them, and attach it to one's own quite different group, may be disastrous.

67. This suggests that education and demonstration, directed at the improvement of traditional practices, may be a better strategy (either *instead of* or *as well as* some of IAAP) than the planners indicate. Hopper finds huge variations in efficiency *within* a village, with the top 20 per cent of farmers obtaining yields well above those at the research station.[56] Cannot radios, agricultural extension workers, and colleges do more to get farmers to learn from one another? The experience of the agricultural economists at the Gokhale Institute (Poona) is instructive here.

68. Two considerations deepen my worry about the logic of IAAP. First, the older work with improved seeds, even at research stations, does not suggest the break-through implicit in the 1970–1 targets. Paddy yields rose by under 1 per cent yearly from 1948 to 1963 even on experimental plots; in villages with comparable soils, one in five farms were getting higher yields than the research stations in 1963–4. The experience with wheat is disappointingly similar.[57] Secondly, the ambidextrousness syndrome ('on the one hand, on the other hand') damages IAAP. 'Though priority in the allocation of essential inputs will be given to (IAAP) areas, there is no question of ignoring the non-intensive areas in provision of inputs and administrative and technical personnel' (p. 175). The plan espouses an inegalitarian strategy to meet a foodgrain crisis. This may be right, but equalization in the face of such a strategy requires specific measures of redistribution.

69. Is all this too pessimistic, in view of the new seed varieties developed since 1963? Some experts estimate that high-yielding foodgrain varieties added 2–2½ mn tons already in 1966–7; all agree

[56] D. Hopper, *Allocation Efficiency in Indian Agriculture*, IADP Staff Working Paper no. 6203.
[57] Ibid.

on the huge excess demand from farmers for the new seeds. On the other hand, this demand may fall off because farmers anticipate that the price of new varieties will fall, relative to the price of traditional strains; this anticipatory decline in demand, according to a verbal report, has already happened in parts of Kerala. Secondly, it is not clear whether seed farms can approach the targets for output of the improved seeds. Thirdly, scarcity of complementary fertilizers is substantially reducing the outturn from the improved seeds, though this should be a short-term problem only. Fourthly, many new seeds produce stalks which are unsatisfactory for fodder. For all that, the overall picture is promising, but it is one of slow, steady improvement, not dramatic break-through.[58] An expert writes of his visit in early 1967:

The new high-yielding varieties of wheat and rice are as yet unproven for disease resistance in really extensive cultivation; moreover, the main wheat (Mexipak) and rice (IRR8-288-3) are soft and unpalatable. Further, they *only* yield sufficiently highly to justify the higher cost of fertilizer if water is constantly and accurately available. They prove uneconomic when grown under less controlled conditions which arise both from power failures for the pumping system (which are frequent) and from delays and shortages in fertilizer or credit. They may well need a massive pest-control organisation which is not yet built up.[59]

Laymen cannot judge between agronomists; but even laymen know that risky improvements, exciting as research engineering, often prove economically disappointing in the field. This time it may be different; but different enough, after two disastrous monsoons, to transform the situation by 1970–1?

8. THE SELECTION OF AREAS WITHIN
THE INTENSIVE PROGRAMME

70. IAAP is a clear, considered strategy, whether or not it is the best available. In formulating it, intensive areas must be selected. This seems to be done from the top. 'In the Fourth Plan, an attempt was made in May, 1965, to indicate production targets to each State, [which was to] break them up into . . . programmes and targets [for districts, which would] further break them up into block programmes

---

[58] Malone.
[59] G. Hunter, *A Note on a Visit to Pakistan and India*, Jan. 1967, Joint Inst. of Race Relations–Overseas Development Institute Project (London, 1967) (unpubl.), p. 5.

and targets' (pp. 181–2). The criterion for area selection is availability of irrigation and personnel, and, as an assumed consequence, maximum rate of return: 'IADP and IAAP areas ... offer the maximum potential for production' (p. 175). However, area selection is bound to involve political pressure, especially if the general guidance is as general as all that.

71. Robertson and Sharma have analysed the seven pilot IADP districts selected in 1960–1. They compare the improvement achieved by 1963/4–1964/5 over 1957/8–1959/60 levels with the improvement in the adjoining district. Four of the IADP districts achieved considerably more agricultural growth than their neighbours; three considerably less.

Despite the definition of maximum irrigation facilities and minimum of natural hazards as two of the basic criteria for choice of the package districts, some ... were poorly off for irrigation at the outset ... Little progress has been made in [extending the irrigable area], except in [one] district.[60]

The real value of irrigation investment planned for 1966–70 is *less* than in the Third Plan, and even allowing for schemes 'in the pipeline' it is hard to see how this is supposed to correspond to much *more* extra irrigation. Political pressures on area allocation will be magnified by IAAP's huge share in the plan, and possibly by the post-electoral spectre of separatism. It is a bad omen that the carefully selected pilot districts, where experience is longest, have performed badly—and that the irrigation criterion, with its implicit recognition of the peasant's unwillingness to innovate under conditions of great risk, should have been disregarded.

72. Area selection requires more disaggregation than the Planning Commission has so far undertaken. In 1965 B. S. Minhas was undertaking research into variations among districts in their agricultural growth rates, but he found big gaps in the data. Are these gaps being filled? Do we know whether small villages grow faster than big villages, one-crop villages than multi-crop villages, etc.? Do the boundaries between IAAP areas define genuine economic units? Is the escalation of Intensive Programme units from districts to areas sensible, or should one go the opposite way and identify *blocks* where the rate of return on the 'package' is especially favourable? Until we have answers, however tentative, to such

[60] C. A. Robertson & R. K. Sharma, 'Lessons from the Package Programme', *Ind. J. Agric. Econ.*, Oct.–Dec. 1966, pp. 124–5, 127.

questions, can we really present the location of agricultural outlays as a scientific exercise, and thereby try to defend it against local political pressures?

73. Village studies, some of them rigorous, comparable, and regular, exist. They are not, to my knowledge, used at any stage of the process of planning in India. To derive and test hypotheses from these studies, regarding the rate of return on various types and packages of agricultural outlay by crop, size of village, literacy rate, &c., should be the first priority for the research programmes division of the Planning Commission. If new sorts of questions or of village study are needed, they should be promptly designed and implemented. Where agricultural outlays earn the biggest return is the biggest single issue facing Indian planning. It is a pity that this issue must be dealt with mainly by a plea for information that, but for the direction of Indian statistical resources towards the measurement of big aggregates, would have been available long ago.

74. So the paradox of Indian agriculture—high priorities, yields, and targets, yet low allocations—is not really cleared up either by the improved structure of agricultural outlays or by their improved location within the Intensive Programme. The latter seems to depend on an untenable analysis of the peasant's behaviour (especially under conditions of risk), and neither past performance nor area selection suggest that the expected outturn of IAAP can be attained. Does the explanation of the planners' optimism lie in improved prospects of implementation?

9. IMPLEMENTING THE AGRICULTURAL PLAN

75. 'In each of the Five Year Plans, there has been a significant gap between planning and implementation' (p. 154). The Fourth Draft Outline, in a careful and interesting chapter on implementation, does not mention that the gap is biggest in agriculture (Table 1), where the public sector is smallest in relation to total output, investment, and employment. As far as Block-level decisions go, there is little indication of how fulfilment of output targets shall be rewarded; and the Draft Plan's suggestions for other improvements in administration do not sound very promising.

76. 'Lack of co-ordination between different departments and institutions dealing with complementary aspects of the same programme' (p. 180) was indeed a problem in implementing the first

two plans. Now, however, it is hard to understand the call for 'a single organisational unit having responsibility and authority over the basic factors of production, extension and co-operative services in rural areas' (p. 180); what is a Block, if not just that? Similarly, the call for a 'wholetime Agricultural Production Officer at the district level' has long been satisfied in many districts. Apart from the problem of whether these proposals are relevant to the real problems of block administration—paperwork before fieldwork, shifting and ill-qualified personnel—the whole section on co-ordination (pp. 180–1) is puzzlingly couched in the language of 'ought', not of 'shall'. It is thus hard to assess its practical effects on plan implementation. These will be bad if Block Development Officers (BDOs), still reeling from the early snowstorms of *panchayati raj*, are buried in a further avalanche of paper. The proposal that 'the BDO should function primarily as an Agricultural Production Officer' (pp. 180–1) will improve direct supervision of agricultural investment programmes, but to do this properly he needs freedom from routine forms and reports, and time to get into the villages. Also it is unclear how this proposal affects the specialist agricultural officers subordinate to many BDOs.

77. BDOs are well equipped to supervise specific programmes. What they are expected to do through 'Block plans' (p. 181) is surely more than this: to oversee the balance of effort, and in particular to tilt it towards foodgrains. This requires BDOs to combine adherence to a central plan with flexibility towards local conditions and profitabilities. Once more, a plan better informed about specific local conditions would help. In any event, implementation of the agricultural programmes stands or falls by the BDOs and their assistants, especially in Intensive Programme Areas.

78. It is therefore disquieting to note the treatment of training for Block assistants and village-level workers (VLWs) in the planners' brief discussion of 'agricultural and allied personnel' (pp. 120–1). Rumour has it that the number of villages per village-level worker is to fall from eight to five by 1971. This sounds splendid, but many existing VLWs are renamed *patwaris* (village revenue collectors), with little agricultural training, and far less experienced than the farmers they are supposed to instruct. Pay, conditions, and prospects are poor, and the incentive to accept illegal payments (especially for access to the record of land rights) is great. Farmers' confidence in

agricultural extension will not be increased by extending and diluting this inadequate service. There are already 100 'training centres where selected *gram sevaks* (field assistants) are given higher training to improve their professional competence and effectiveness'; 20 were upgraded in the Third Plan, and the other 80 are to be upgraded by 1971 (p. 121). But to upgrade is not necessarily to enlarge or to improve; and there are far more than 100 agronomically or socially distinct sets of conditions in which *gram sevaks* serve. My experience suggests that such training is centralized, general, and remote from the specific problems a VLW faces in the field. Until the VLW is known to succeed *as a farmer*, and to have roots in local conditions and problems as well as scientific training directly relevant to them, he is unlikely to win the respect of the farmers.

79. Guy Hunter's account of VLWs may be juxtaposed with the huge demands made of them under IAAP.

[The] extension service is too thin on the ground (about one VLW as field assistant to 2,000 farmers), without adequate transport (one jeep to a block of 100,000 inhabitants [was] usual), low in prestige and . . . wrongly structured. The field assistant (High School plus two years' training) is paid about 100 Rupees per month . . . . In order to live he often has to attach himself to a large farmer for food and even housing and becomes dependent on him. [Usually] he has little to give the farmer—neither credit nor fertilizer because it is [scarce or] handled through other channels. Above [him] there is no middle grade (as in Africa) of practical diploma level officers. The next step is straight to a young graduate [BDO], often with a Master's degree [and] 10,000–20,000 farmers in his parish. [In IADP districts] the extension service is more than doubled . . . but I suspect, without knowing, that it is still not spreading very far down the social scale . . . . [The attempt] to distribute fertilizers and [insecticides] through the extension service both immobilized the officers in looking after sales and storage, and was beset by . . . bribery and undue influence.[61]

80. Of all the components of IAAP, spill-off to areas outside the programme will be hardest to implement, because neither the officers responsible nor the methods of transferring resources are well-defined. A research officer at the Ministry of Agriculture has tried to express the rationale of spill-off: 'Secondary and tertiary effects [of IAAP in a region] spread out beyond the confines of that region, viz., increased availability of food [would release] foreign exchange for other sectors; increased production of commercial crops would lead to an expansion of the industrial sector which uses

[61] Hunter, pp. 3–4. In my experience, many field assistants are less trained than is suggested here.

them as raw material'.[62] None of this helps villages outside IAAP. If IAAP succeeds, food prices should fall relative to prices of urban products, and non-IAAP areas will suffer absolutely as well as relatively. Spill-off could remedy this, by taxing a proportion of the value which IAAP added to land, and redistributing this proportion (as higher procurement prices, crop insurance schemes, or fertilizer subsidies) to non-IAAP areas. Without some such scheme, there will not be much spill-off. Long-distance diffusion of innovations is unlikely; they would have to pass from IAAP areas where they are subsidized and supported by large-scale extension, to poor and less well-watered areas without such benefits. As for risk in non-IAAP villages, a success by IAAP in reducing the variabilty of total food output would deprive non-IAAP surplus farmers of one of their most valuable forms of insurance: the likelihood that poor rainfall will be compensated by high farm prices. Crop insurance for some non-IAAP regions, financed out of spill-off, could remedy this. However, spill-off requires much more precise plans for implementation if IAAP is to have the desired results.

10. LAND TENURE AND LAND REFORM

81. There remains one possible explanation of the paradox of low agricultural outlay, combined with high agricultural priority, targets, and yields of outlay. The ancillary services to agriculture may have been expanded (or changed in structure) so as to raise the yield of directly agricultural outlays. In this context, we shall examine land reform, co-operative credit, and social services. Land reform in India means 'land to the tiller' (p. 125).

82. Land to the tiller implies (*a*) smaller holdings, raising labour-input (and hence output) per acre in the short run, but reducing investible resources per acre and hence possibly lowering output per acre in the long run; (*b*) probably a shift from cash crops to foodgrains, but an increased reluctance to market surpluses; (*c*) removal of the disincentives to investment created by crop-sharing and insecurity of tenure. Research is needed into the short-run and long-run effects of distributist land reforms on the inputs and productivity of land, labour, and investment, for various crops in India. Only such research can provide priorities, by telling planners

---

[62] M. L. Manrai, 'Intensive Approach to Agricultural Development', *Ind. J. Agric. Econ.*, Oct.–Dec. 1966, p. 113.

the regions and crops where land reform will have better, faster effects on output. Although the planners tell us that the main objective of land reform is to raise agricultural output (p. 123), the chapter on land reform nowhere analyses its effects on production. It therefore seems unlikely that types and areas of land reform have been selected so as to maximize the rate of return to plan projects.

83. The scope for distributist land reform is anyway not as large as is sometimes claimed. In 1960–1, 78 per cent of India's farmland was wholly cultivated by its owners, and 4 per cent partly. Already one in five operational holdings was smaller than 1 acre, 63 per cent were smaller than 5 acres, and only 1·1 per cent (occupying 12·2 per cent of India's cultivated area) were over 50 acres.[63] The scope for distributist reform is also limited by its uneconomic effect on plot size. The big holdings are fragmented into larger plots than small holdings,[64] so that redistribution tends to reduce the size of plot, unless combined with consolidation (and effective action against future fragmentation) to retain economies of scale to the plot.

84. Apart from the apparent failure to link land reform to productivity, and the small scope for land distribution, the record of evasion makes it doubtful that land reform can do much to raise productivity of outlays in agriculture. Ceilings on landholdings and rents, usufructuary rights for tenants, &c. are welcome on social grounds—if they are enforcible, and if resource use is not worsened by such measures or the attempts to evade them. Despite the morass of evasion, Indian land reform has peacefully, gradually reduced concentrations of under-farmed land. Even *mala fide* transfers to brothers and cousins mean the dispersion of ownership and income (albeit confined to the caste). The Draft Outline (p. 127) is realistic about evasion, though the concealment and shortening of tenancies (to prevent the authorities from identifying the tenant, and thus allowing him to buy the land) should be added to the list of evasive practices; since it reduces output and investment, its eradication should receive high priority. But the omission confirms that India's programme of land distribution is social rather than economic.

85. The chapter on land reform is further removed from direct relevance to the productivity of plan outlays by the undue tendency of urban reformers to rely on contract law. 'The rents as fixed by law are still high in several States and should be brought down to . . . one-fourth . . . of the gross produce' (p. 130)—if land scarcity pushes

[63] Nanavati & Anjaria, pp. 222–6.   [64] Ibid. p. 227

up rents to half the gross produce, and this is thought excessive, then detailed and enforced intervention is required, not more laws. Sometimes this contractualism is underlined by ignorance of rural life, as in the suggestion that 'produce rents . . . should be abolished and replaced by fixed cash rents so that uncertainties arising out of annual fluctuations in rents may be eliminated' (p. 130). Both landlord and tenant usually prefer share-rents; tenants to reduce rent payments when the harvest is poor and thus *reduce* uncertainty, landlords because they are rich enough to prefer the higher average yearly value of the share-rent to the greater security of a fixed payment; so how is abolition to be enforced? Similarly 'immediate legislation to break the landlord-tenant relationship, the State interposing . . . to collect fair rents from tenants and pay them to landlords after deducting land revenue and a collection charge' (pp. 128–32) is as unrealistic as the abolition of dowries by law. Again, the status of the dicta on land reform is obscure—'ought', 'should', 'States might consider' (p. 105).

86. Is the discussion of land reform quite unrelated to the problem of increasing output? The fear mounts when we discover that tenurial conditions were ignored in selecting IADP areas. 'In four out of the five (package) districts visited by us the tenurial situation is not satisfactory . . . if land tenure conditions were a part of the criteria for selecting a package district, [two of the five], West Godavary and Tanjore, would not qualify at all'.[65]

87. We have mentioned that undoubted economies of scale exist, not to the holding but to the *plot*. Achievement of the ambitious consolidation target (p. 133) was thus perhaps the best agricultural news of the Third Plan period. By 1964–5, 54·8 mn acres were consolidated, about one-sixth of India's net sown area. Consolidation is unlike most land reform in clearly and quickly raising productivity of land *and* labour. Unfortunately, progress has been slowest where need is greatest. The smaller a holding, the smaller the *plot* resulting from a given degree of fragmentation—and, in practice, average plot size; the bigger, therefore, the economic gain from consolidation. Average household operational holdings in 1960–1 were smallest in Kerala (1·8 acres), Jammu and Kashmir (3·8 acres), West Bengal (4·1), Madras (4·6), and Assam (4·7).[66]

[65] W. Ladejinsky, *A Study on Tenurial Conditions in Package Districts* (Planning Commission, 1965), p. 9.
[66] Nanavati & Anjaria, p. 221.

Therefore the need for consolidation was greatest in these five States. Yet by the end of the Third Plan Madras and Kerala had enacted no legislation for consolidation, and in the other three States progress has been negligible.[67] The planners' discussion of allocation of funds among States (p. 136) suggests that States with experience of consolidation will get priority, and the rest encouragement ('Other States should initiate preliminary steps and take up pilot projects . . .'). This rewarding of success appears sensible, but the least consolidated States need consolidation most—if the aim is to raise output. The real problems—the $2\frac{1}{2}$-3 years that a village needs from application to completion of consolidation, the shortage of competent and incorruptible administrators—are not discussed by the planners. Nor do they say which villages should receive priority for consolidation—IAAP villages, big villages, one-caste villages, highly fragmented villages. With consolidation of plots, as with distribution of holdings, land reform does not seem to be geared to increasing agricultural output. This is not to deny its substantial, and often grossly underrated, social achievements.

11. CO-OPERATIVE CREDIT

88. The provision of credit can substantially raise the ability of the small farmer to benefit from, and complement, public farm outlays. By 1961–2 about a quarter of new rural borrowing was from co-operatives, as against 3 per cent in 1951–2 (p. 136). The share of *outstanding* debt is admittedly far smaller, and the reported share of new yearly borrowing is inflated, both by the inclusion of large sums that are merely automatic annual renewals of old co-operative loans, and by the concealment of private loans at illegal interest rates. Some co-operative loans go to big moneylenders, who re-lend at much higher rates; some credit societies pass into the hands of big merchants and landlords, who use them to reinforce the traditional power structure;[68] some secretaries abscond with funds. For all that, co-operative credit has made a remarkable breakthrough. At worst, it has kept rural interest rates below the levels that would otherwise have prevailed. At best, in villages with owner-occupied farms of similar size, it has transformed the credit

[67] Ibid. pp. 133, 236–7, 400.
[68] D. Thorner, *Agricultural Co-operatives in India* (Asia Pub., Bombay, 1965).

situation, and has forced the moneylenders to use their spare cash for productive investment instead of extortionate loans.

89. The success of co-operative credit depends on the extent of owner-occupancy, and on the size of the typical holding. Maharashtra and Gujerat were the two States most successful in raising the co-operative share of total yearly borrowing by 1961–2 (p. 136); these States feature operational holdings well above, and an incidence of tenancy well below, the Indian average. The reverse is true for Assam and Bihar, two of the three States least successful in expanding the share of co-operative borrowing.[69]

90. The obvious importance of credit in allowing the efficient small farmer to take full advantage of IAAP, plus the failure of co-operative credit to get to such people (see para. 42), fully justifies the planned shift from mortgage loans (secured by owned land) to loans secured by the coming harvest (p. 136). This shift ought to allow tenants and smallholders to benefit from co-operative credit, and also to provide a more credible means of enforcing repayment. Properly used, the scheme can become a valuable channel both for crop insurance and for compulsory procurement at prices creating appropriate incentives; it might be desirable, for both reasons, to give several years' notice of the prices at which the co-operative would buy each main crop. These purchase prices would, of course, fall as the length of the loan (the time until the harvest) increased.

91. Past and planned expansions of co-operative credit, then, have done something to raise the yield to be expected of Government outlays, by enabling farmers to afford ancillary expenditures. However, progress has been limited (and co-operative credit has not replaced the moneylender) chiefly because of two accounting fictions, disguised as economic principles, and not yet rejected by the planners. Co-operative loans are supposed to be short-term (normally for one year or less), and not for consumption. If such laws are enforced, they drive the borrower to the moneylender. Generally they are unenforcible. In my experience, almost every villager 'repays' yearly and borrows again a day later. No doubt the provision of cash for Repayment Day, when most villagers want it, is profitable for somebody. As for the division between investment and consumption loans, it is quite mythical. Even with no loan, a farmer would need to buy most of the seed, manure, cattle-cake, &c. for which co-operative credit is advanced. The addition to his total

[69] Nanavati & Anjaria, pp. 221, 224.

cash reserves, made by such credit, allows him to spend more on food or weddings. It would greatly enhance the ability of co-operative societies to oversee farm investment and budgeting if they faced these facts, and went all out to replace the moneylender by providing general-purpose, secured long-term loans. This policy, given the shortage of personnel, would imply some concentration of effort as regards co-operative credit, perhaps in IAAP areas; but this may be desirable in any case. Only those societies with facilities to store improved seeds and fertilizers, and to advise on their use, are likely to succeed in tying credit to *extra* investment in a credible and enforcible manner. This criticism does not apply to the bigger, longer-term *tagai* (Government) loans for well-building, &c., where both the genuine 'extra-ness' and the execution of the project can be overseen. It does, however, limit the scope of co-operative credit for raising the yields on public agricultural outlay, and thus for resolving the paradox of low planned outlay and high production targets.

12. EDUCATION, HEALTH, AND AGRICULTURAL PRODUCTIVITY

92. Can the social services in rural areas be used to raise yields on outlay, hence resolving this paradox? Some observers are pessimistic. 'Attempts to train for vocational competence in farming through formal schooling in agriculture at primary and lower secondary levels have failed and further efforts should be held in abeyance'.[70] The Draft Outline expresses general agreement (p. 327) with the Education Commission's massive report; one must hope this does not extend to this proposal, which was supported by *a priori* judgements—but no evidence—about 'the rural boy' and what 'appears rather unlikely',[71] and by speculation about the causes of migration and of vocational competence. What is the comparative performance of farmers with different types and levels of agricultural training? How does it compare with agriculturally untrained, but otherwise similarly educated, farmers with similar physical resources? Schooling in agriculture is often oddly designed; usually it is not available until the child is twelve. If he is still at school then, he is headed for urban work. Root-and-branch attacks on agricultural schooling should not be based on such programmes. Accurate

[70] Education Commission, *Report 1964–6*, p. 657.   [71] Ibid. p. 360.

judgements require careful assessments of the real social rate of return over cost, for a variety of schemes. Until such assessments are attempted (however crudely) by the planners, education will remain largely an unknown quantity in its effect on the proper size and use of other forms of rural development spending.

93. The planners' discussions of health also omit to estimate the effects of various forms of outlay on rural productivity. It is possible that such effects have been neglected, since nothing specific is said about worm infestation, though there is a welcome rise in the share of plan outlays devoted to rural water supply.[72] If a 1,000 rupee outlay on improved water supply will reduce worm infestation by the same amount in two villages, should not priority be given to the village where the effect on output is larger? At present, there are no inquires afoot in India that might allow us to discover which village this is.

94. In nutrition too, there are no quantitative studies of the effects of specific improvements on output, though economists have written for years of the vicious circle relating hunger to low food production. Healey has estimated that a 40 per cent rise in builders' wages would have improved nutrition enough to raise productivity by 50 per cent in the construction of Bhakra Nangal dam.[73] The existence of a potential labour surplus in agriculture does not mean that the effect of nutrition on farm labour can be ignored. First, ill-fed workers will provide much less than the potential labour input; they will go to a festival (or to bed) instead of composting. Second, the average labour surplus is not evenly distributed through the year; it becomes a labour shortage at harvest time, and underfed labourers will not do much productive 'overtime' then. Third, nutrition affects the quality as well as the quantity of labour input; hungry workers do not concentrate on picking all, and only, good bolls of cotton.

95. Where will improved nutrition most influence farm output? It depends on initial nutritional levels, intensity and timing of effort, climate, and much else. Again, local study is essential. Least-cost diets might be prepared for a variety of types of Indian village, and the effects on labour-input and labour-efficiency of extra nutrients, over and above these dietary minima, might then be estimated. As with health and education, so with nutrition: 'top priority for

[72] *Third Five-Year Plan*, p. 654; *4DO*, p. 349.
[73] J. M. Healey, *The Development of Social Overhead Capital in India 1950–60* (Blackwell, 1965), pp. 120–3.

agriculture' implies the concentration of rural spending on projects and areas where the effect on output is greatest. Both the 'priority' and the implied policy can reasonably be subjected to social and humanitarian constraints; but these should be clearly defined.

13. URBAN BIAS: NATURE, ACHIEVEMENTS, AND LIMITATIONS

96. We have not yet resolved the paradox of Indian agriculture: necessarily ambitious production targets, low and sometimes unproductive public outlays, low incentives to private outlays, yet a high rate of return to *potential* extra spending. The explanation lies neither in the composition and location of plan outlays within agriculture, nor in a direct linkage of ancillary spending to investment in production. Nor is there any conscious failure by the planners to appreciate the abstract need for 'top priority in agriculture'. Two successive plans have aimed at self-sufficiency in foodgrains. To ram home the lesson, the adverse conjunction of population growth, poor harvests, and scarce foreign exchange in 1965–7 showed how an underdeveloped agriculture can stultify industrial development by diverting foreign exchange from industrial raw materials to food imports. Economics is reinforced by psychology. Only 3 per cent of Indian workers are employed in modern industry.[74] India's planners have lived through the colonial atmosphere of enclave development; they understand the futility of trying to promote attitudes favourable to economic growth (or political stability) by development allocations that widen the huge gulf between this 3 per cent and the rest. Yet this understanding remains somehow abstract, and so does 'top priority for agriculture'.

97. We have seen that neither allocations of public money, nor incentives to the movement of persons and other resources, have favoured agricultural development; that 70 per cent of the workers get less than 35 per cent of investment finance and a far smaller share of human skills. Several types of pressures on opinion and policy have combined to bias the allocation of cash, effort, personnel, and research away from rural needs. First, skilled, literate, and articulate persons congregate in cities. There, they have access to senior

---

[74] P. N. Dhar and H. F. Lydall, *The Role of Small Enterprises in Indian Economic Development* (Inst. of Economic Growth, Delhi, 1961). 'Modern' means 'using electric power *or* in plants with more than 50 persons'.

political and administrative officers. However conscientious these officers may be, the balance of pressures on them is overwhelmingly urban. A BDO spends most of his life in the biggest town in his Block; so does his agricultural assistant. A CEO spends most of his life in the district capital. Tours of duty take them to villages, and by and large they welcome such visits; but 'visits' they remain. A BDO covers 30–50 villages, and does well to visit each village twice a year. The influences, pressures, and conversation of the market town outweigh the contradictory, unorganized complaints of numerous villages, each fleetingly experienced. For the CEO the balance is even more urban. And in centres of State Government, where business, trade union, and mass pressures are constantly heard and felt, the pressure of the remote village is very faint. Riots for lower foodgrain prices (and strikes and *gheraos* for higher wages, i.e. for dearer manufactured goods for farmers) are an immediate threat; famine, caused by failure to use price incentives to persuade farmers to grow enough food, seems a distant cloud. The high and rising representation of villagers in State Parliaments[75] is hardly relevant as a counterpoise; these MLAs are usually big landlords and their interests are those of the urban élite, not of the often more efficient mass of small farmers.

98. The second aspect of urban bias concerns the relative pay and status of urban and rural personnel. We saw something of this in paras 36–37. It means that the best doctors, lawyers, businessmen, and administrators gravitate to cities and influence policy there. This impedes the development of worm-free farmers, litigation-proof consolidation schemes, private agricultural investment, and the efficient organization of rural life.

99. Townsmen naturally prefer those villagers who speak and write their language, sell them food, and invest in urban industry. In so far as a direct rural presence is felt in the towns, it is unrepresentative. It is the big landlords and moneylenders that can afford city houses, and sometimes control rural votes. Laws to reform tenure and credit therefore have built-in loopholes. As for the permanent migrants from villages to towns—if employed, they identify themselves with the urban élite they have joined; if unemployed, they have little influence on policy. Full-time small farmers have practically no direct impact in State capitals. Hence, as we have seen, agricultural development is geared to bigger farmers, with

[75] See Rosen, pp. 72–73.

irrigated land and a marketable surplus, in ways that often increase risk and reduce incentives for other farmers.

100. Another aspect of urban bias is an intellectual successor to Brahmanism. Gandhi was Banya by caste; but growing population gives urgency to his advocacy of manual work, and outside South India it is hard to find a Brahman who religiously refuses to touch the plough. It is, however, very common to find smooth-handed Agricultural Development Committees at all levels from Zilla Parishad (district) upwards. I asked the headmaster of a boys' high school in Maharashtra how many of his candidates for the Senior School Certificate (taken at age 18) returned to agriculture. Ah, he sympathized, a tragic problem; some of these intelligent young men actually did have to go back to the villages. In Delhi, research village studies are sometimes dismissed as 'cow-dung economics'.

101. The planners' emphasis on industry is not due only to the fact that industrialists are more powerful, articulate, and accessible than farmers. Output is more easily measured, and relevant inputs more easily specified, in industry than in agriculture. This has long been a partial explanation of their respective plan allocations; tangible yields, traceable to specific inputs, are attractive because they can be put into a growth model (or a Plan Frame) and checked afterwards. However, since 1958, the Agro-Economic Research Centres have been producing quantitative studies of villages at five-yearly intervals, designed to illuminate the processes of agricultural change; studies which, for all their deficiencies, are the raw material for similarly precise planning in agriculture. Yet they are not used for policy-making at any level. The IAAP has been submitted to closer analysis than the earlier arrays of agricultural schemes, and the projections for 1970–1 divide farm output into more components than was the case in previous plan periods. But research into the relations between inputs and outputs still concentrates on industrial sectors. We do not know, even roughly, whether IAAP yields more than an equal outlay on (say) improving traditional implements and practices; or whether an extra hundred rupees yields more rice in Kerala or West Bengal, in dysentery relief or in fertilizer subsidy.

102. It is quite mistaken to suggest that Indian agricultural planning has achieved nothing. 'The growth rate [since Independence is] a marked improvement over ... preceding decades, when

agricultural output grew by less than 1 per cent per annum' (p. 172). Indeed, urban bias in agricultural planning has great rural achievements to its credit, especially in schemes that can be organized centrally without treading on powerful urban toes. 'The village, unchanged for 2,000 years' is romantic (or Cassandra-like) rubbish. The village, since Independence, has seen a social revolution, raising the level of living in ways that seldom express themselves as rises in estimated income per head. Malaria affected 108 per 1,000 in 1953–4, and 5 per 1,000 in 1965 (p. 340). Since Independence, primary-school enrolment has almost trebled (p. 328). Most villagers can get some sort of medical help, and can educate their children. A much higher proportion than ever before can get conveniently to the nearest town by road, at least in the dry season; possess a hurricane lamp, and see to it that the village street is lit at night; have access to a communal radio—and so on, over a wide range of social and private durable consumer goods. What, then, is wrong with urban bias in agricultural planning?

103. Anyone who has observed a particular village must admire the achievements of planning in village India, but he will be saddened by the small extent to which social advance has led to increased agricultural efficiency. Social change *has* been induced. Caste restrictions on well-use, commensality and joint farmwork are weakening, both because population growth has loosened job rigidity and because of direct Government pressure. Economic change, however, has been small. The proportion of Indians dependent on agriculture was much the same at the 1951 and 1961 censuses; yet food production per head of population in 1964–5 was barely 1 per cent higher than in 1953–4, and agricultural output per person 2 per cent higher.[76] In view of the increases and improvements in non-human inputs over the period this is disappointing progress. Most Indian farmers plough too seldom, sow their seed rows too close, make inefficient manure heaps instead of compost pits, and waste their crops through poor protective measures, both in the field and in storage. In every case the expected value of extra output exceeds the extra labour cost.

104. The small farmer's reluctant economic response to social improvement and technical change is not born of stupidity. Farmers first seek to insure themselves against disaster, not to incur *certain* efforts and costs with new techniques for a merely *probable* return;

[76] FAO, *State of Food and Agriculture 1966* (Rome, 1966), p. 198.

second, they seek to maintain their family's status by means including expensive weddings in the ploughing season, division of holdings among the sons to avoid landlessness, and cow-worship—all this, if necessary, at the expense of investment and output. Such behaviour is fully compatible with the farmer's known readiness to change his cropping pattern if the price incentives are right. The farmer's behaviour is not irrational, but its rationale is not simply the maximization of expected profit. Effective agricultural planning must recognize and bridge the gap between the peasant's varying mixture of goals (status, income, security) and the planning maximand (value added in agriculture).[77]

105. The most serious aspect of urban bias is the city dweller's inability to appreciate the peasant's thought processes. This is less marked in the Draft Fourth Outline than in earlier planning documents, as is clear from its more realistic discussion of land reform. A sense of unreality nevertheless permeates the agricultural sections of the Draft Outline (see para. 114). The effect of this remoteness from rural realities on agricultural planning has been discussed at several points. The suggestion that crop-share rents *increase* the tenant's insecurity (para. 85) is an extreme example. The origin of the remoteness lies in the almost exclusive exposure of planners and politicians to the thought, pressure, and company of the tiny sections of India's population involved in modern urban politics, trade unionism, industry, universities, and administration. Planners and Ministers show a deep, sincere concern for the welfare of farmers, and (foreigners often assume) understand rural India because they are Indians. However, concern and goodwill are not substitutes for direct, prolonged contact with particular villages, and study of micro-level data collected from many more.

106. Planning under urban bias is well able to treat rural backwardness, provided the treatment satisfies three conditions: amenability to large-scale central organization, absence of affront to powerful interests in the villages, and lack of conflict with rural values and attitudes. Thus Indian planning can eradicate malaria, build big dams, provide big areas with electricity. But if there is an intra-rural power struggle, as with land reform; or a complex situation requiring detailed case studies, as with diffusion of innovation; or a need to transform attitudes, as with castration of stud

[77] F. G. Bailey, 'The Peasant View of the Bad Life', *The Advancement of Science*, Dec. 1966.

bulls—then planning under urban bias is unlikely to succeed. The townsman is a contractualist (para. 85) and thus disguises his failure from himself by paper legislation[78]—ceilings on holdings evaded by *mala fide* transfers to relatives, laws against dowries and untouchability, limitation of rents and interest rates to unenforceably low levels. The townsman's life is compartmentalized, and he can learn to improve some aspects of it without much effect on others; so he also honestly believes in 'showpiece planning' through model farms and isolated research stations.

14. VILLAGE POWER, ATTITUDES, AND INSTITUTIONS

107. India has about 646,000 villages. One of the themes of this chapter is that the type of village—its size, caste structure, cropping pattern, nutrition, tenure, and urban contact—affects the rates of return to various types of farm outlay, and that the urban bias of Indian agricultural planning has stopped planners from discovering these rates and adjusting planning accordingly. Nevertheless, some generalizations can be made.

108. The Draft Fourth Outline, like its predecessors, contains no discussion of the rural balance of power; we have seen how resources drift to big, powerful farmers irrespective of efficiency (paras 40–44), and urban bias is relevant both to the drift itself (paras 119–21) and to the neglect of the research required to evaluate its effect on agricultural growth. Three aspects of the rural balance of power are obviously relevant to agricultural planning. Do the new institutions of co-operation and *panchayati raj* change the power structure? How far does power lie with groups or individuals hostile to economic advance, either because they fear a threat to their dominance or because they are old, set in their ways, or detached from fleshly interest by spiritual involvement? Who are the 'progressive farmers', and what political structures will increase their influence on their neighbours?

109. Potter has shown[79] that *panchayati raj* in Rajasthan leads to disproportionate representation of the high castes, the richest, and the landlords; and that the degree to which town dwellers are

[78] Attitudes *can* be changed by legislation, if those affected (*a*) respect or fear contract law, (*b*) believe the legislation will be enforced. That is the difference between the effective legislation against racial discrimination in the US and the ineffective legislation against dowries in India.

[79] D. C. Potter, *Government in Rural India* (Bell, 1964), pp. 53–54.

over-represented increases with the power of the democratic body. Thorner reaches similar conclusions[80] about co-operative farming. Mrs Epstein shows[81] how modern economic opportunities within the village also tighten the grip of traditional ruling groups. If these groups were also agriculturally progressive, or were made so by the new institutions, democratic regret would be tempered by economic delight; but is this so? Does not entrepreneurship come from the group trying to improve its status through economic activity, rather than from the protectors of entrenched power? Bailey's account[82] of the Boad and Ganjam Distillers in Orissa and Basu's discussion[83] of the Subarabaniks in West Bengal suggest that this is certainly true of backward, rigid, multi-caste villages.

110. In many parts of West and North India, a single cultivator caste (e.g. the Marathas in Maharashtra) has a majority in most villages. This caste takes more than a proportionate share of economic decisions in the new institutions of *panchayati raj*, co-operative credit societies, &c., which, together with land reform, have improved its position *vis-à-vis* Brahmans. Research is needed to decide if this trend is economically desirable. In my experience, Marathas have more and better (though more fragmented) land than ex-untouchables; they tend to be more traditional, less experimental farmers, though perhaps superior in their use of traditional methods. Under the new institutions craftsman castes—forced into farming by population growth, and with quite good, unfragmented land recently acquired—lose power, as do the ex-untouchables. In West Bengal, Bose shows[84] that a village with an overall majority of traditional cultivator-castemen showed faster agricultural progress than similar villages nearby, with no clear majority caste. The point is not to praise or condemn 'majority-casteocracy', but that it has little-analysed economic implications, e.g. for optimal area selection under IAAP.

111. While there is little knowledge of the effects of the new power structures upon economic efficiency (and less attempt to bring such knowledge into the planners' allocative decisions), more is known, from long experience, of the economic impact of traditional power

[80] D. Thorner.   [81] S. Epstein, *Social Change in South India* (Manchester, 1964).

[82] F. G. Bailey, 'An Oriya Village: II', in M. N. Srinivas, ed., *India's Villages* (Asia Pub., Bombay, 1960).

[83] T. K. Basu, *The Bengal Peasant from Time to Time* (Asia Pub., Bombay, 1964).

[84] Bengal, Dept of Agric., *Eadpur: a West Bengal Village*, by S. P. Bose (1963), pp. 36–40, 55.

structures. Within a village, many of the old economic links are still strong. In my experience, a Brahman landlord (owning about 100 acres) was faced by State legislation entitling tenants who paid more than one-fifth of their crop as rent to buy the land. He responded by shifting tenants round his land every year or two, while continuing to charge the market rent—half the crop. That way, nobody is seen to farm a piece of land long enough to establish a plausible claim to settlement. The fact that this is tolerated, e.g. that tenants do not insist on written rent receipts, suggests that most villagers accept traditional property rights. The consequent insecurity of tenure greatly strengthens the usual objection to share-rent: that tenants do less labour and much less investment than owner-occupiers.

112. If the Brahman's reaction and the tenants' tolerance are typical, it is damaging (not merely futile) to change the legal super-structure of property relations without doing anything to alter the 'who-whom' of power, custom, and respect. The tenant and the landless labourer will continue to defer to the landlord, the merchant, and the moneylender, until the Government provides *substitutes* for the trade credit, employment, and contacts with officials that (as well as exorbitant rents and interest rates) come from the old rural establishment of India. It may be costly to provide such substitutes—crop insurance, loans secured against the harvest, rural labour exchanges. But it is self-defeating to act as if such substitutes existed already and to ignore the effects on agricultural legislation of the real, feudal power relations in the villages.

113. Traditional 'who-whom' relations survive purely legislative reform, partly because the powerful have resources (land, credit) to bind the weak, but partly because Hinduism comforts the weak with promises that adherence to their justly allotted status ensures rebirth in a higher caste, and reassures the powerful that their status is the consequence of good acts in previous incarnations. Attitudes of rural people to economic change affect the optimal allocation of resources. In particular, the Draft Outline's discussion of improved attitudes helps us to see the characteristics that planners associate with 'progressive farmers', who are claimed to be an important source of growth.

114.

Attitudes and behaviour patterns ... have to undergo as much of a fundamental change as ... when a country gets engaged in war. These changes have to be such as to maximize work, efficiency, savings, and resource mobilization. They must motivate and move the people in the direction of economic development . . . . There has to be a change in the attitude of the well-to-do . . . towards consumption. Austerity should be encouraged not only in daily life but also extended to . . . conspicuous expenditure . . . on ceremonial occasions . . . . Taxation should be recognized as an instrument of resource mobilization. . . . Social displeasure should . . . be brought to bear on tax evaders . . . it is also necessary to stimulate in the people . . . willingness to put up with reduced availability caused by . . . exports . . . . There has to be a deliberate building up of an attitude of preference for *swadeshi* . . . . It is also necessary to bring about a preference for small families (pp. 36–37).

(*a*) Work, efficiency, savings, and resource mobilization are 'maximized' by distinct sets of policies. Clearly the planners wish to improve attitudes to all four aims. Peasant attitudes to *work* are determined by diet, especially protein; climate, especially humid heat at peak seasons; health, especially worms and dysentery; and by the yield of, and need for, effort. We have seen that the impact of diet and health on agricultural efficiency is not analysed (para. 94–95). As for the effects of climate, the planners' view of short crops (pp. 175–6) is enthusiastic, but too general to consider the regional impact on work loads—or whether these will fall when humid heat is at its worst. Yield of, and need for, efforts must vary with mechanization and size of holding; yet the benefits of IAAP are to be applied with 'no discrimination between cultivators on the basis of resources or the size of holding' (p. 175). In each case, appropriate policies to change attitudes require local fact-grubbing rather than exhortation.

(*b*) Economic *efficiency*, within a given structure of ownership, means that (i) each productive unit (given its location) uses its resources as efficiently as possible; (ii) units are arranged in a spacial optimum—best size, location, and degree of fragmentation into plants (or plots). For the peasant to play his part in (i) by maximizing profits (paras 58–63), he needs some assurance that the reward for ambition will not be bankruptcy in bad years. For (ii) the planners rightly emphasize consolidation (pp. 133–4), but overlook certain locational aspects. Farmers put more effort (weeding especially) into big plots, and into plots near home.[85] This suggests the reallocation of land among villages which goes beyond the present framework of consolidation schemes. Also, consolidation of *plots* need not lead to a more efficient size of *holding*. Again,

[85] M. Chisholm, *Rural Settlement and Land Use* (London, 1962).

exhortation seems to be advanced as a substitute for highly localized enquiry and action.

(*c*) *Savings* are reduced by taxing rich people, unless the Government can replace their lost saving. The planners eschew deficit finance, yet propose 'narrowing the disparities in incomes and property ownership' (p. 22).

(*d*) This would be no paradox if *resource mobilization* could be achieved by exhorting people to pay taxes. Pressures against this, however, are such that other States may follow Madras and abolish land revenue.[86] The planners obviously want to reverse this trend (pp. 87–88) but it is not clear how they propose to do it.[87] This enormous topic cannot be discussed here, except as another example of the use of 'rural attitudes' as a catch-all for a number of policy problems, calling for local inquiry into peasant response.

(*e*) The well-to-do might be discouraged from consumption by making it more expensive, and savings more profitable. The Indian Post Office Savings Bank offers unattractively low interest, around 4 per cent. Profit need not accrue in ways amenable to the economic calculus; the most profitable ways for a rich farmer to use his spare cash may be to lend it at illegally high rates, to educate his sons for urban jobs, and to buy status through expensive weddings. It would help if co-operatives were actively encouraged to make consumer loans (para. 91) and if village funds were set up for communal finance of ceremonials. Berating individuals for extravagance in supporting rural people's few enjoyments is less useful than trying to arrange alternative support (or alternative enjoyments) which are less damaging to investment finance.

(*f*) Social displeasure might be brought to bear on tax evaders if police displeasure were to help it along. The village police headman is often a big farmer, or dependent upon one, and hence may not always enforce the tax legislation to the full. Kaldor estimates[88] that less than half Indian income taxes are actually collected.

(*g*) Preference for *swadeshi* (Indian-made goods) is not helped by stores that openly stack row upon row of illegally-imported luxury foods. The British and the Indians are both gifted at self-denigration; villagers' attitudes (for example) to Indian and German Petromaxes

[86] Economist Intelligence Unit, *Qtly. Econ. Rev. of India and Nepal*, Dec. 1966.
[87] If drinking were penalized by high taxes instead of by evaded laws, more resources would be mobilized. The abolition of prohibition by two big States (July 1967) may open the way.
[88] Min. of Finance, *Indian Tax Reform*, by N. Kaldor (Delhi, 1956), p. 76.

are based on pure prejudice. The tax system might again prove helpful.

(*h*) 'Preference' for big families illuminates two peasant attitudes: the adaptive lag and the insurance principle. Twenty years ago, a rural couple was well advised to have five children to ensure one surviving son; today, three will do. This is a great achievement of free India, yet it has not been communicated to the peasants. But the trouble lies deeper. Peasants maximize subject only to guarantees of survival, and many children mean many friends in need. This is part of the case for social security and crop insurance; in their absence, big families are one of the wasteful forms of insurance that planners must expect from villagers, as Cassen shows, pp. 252–4.

115. In part, all these demands for changes of attitudes are ways to pass the buck; but they also demonstrate the townsman's vision of the village divided into 'progressive farmers' (with approved attitudes) and stupid, innately conservative peasants. The latter are urban myths; their distant cousins, farmers confirmed in a set of practices that guarantee a livelihood, and reluctant to learn risky new methods from neighbors or village-level workers, are a hard reality. Conversely the search for 'progressive farmers', to serve as foci for development, may be misconceived. There *are* big, rich farmers; their lessons are for others in that tiny minority. Among small farmers, there are progressive composters, weeders, storers—and they are not the same people. Each family finds, inherits, and defends 'from long experience', farming procedures that ensure survival as a landowning unit. This *survival algorithm*[89] suits the family's risk aversion, preference between income and leisure, liking for various seldom-traded vegetables intertilled with the main crop, auspicious days, and *dharma* (spiritual and caste duty). In a complex affair like farming, it may be fatal to detach and learn a practice that is 'improved' only in the context of someone else's algorithm.

116. Townsmen tend to berate or to legislate when confronted with rural institutions hostile to growth. Institutions have functions, and will not be readily abandoned until they are replaced by other institutions fulfilling similar functions, unless the rural environment or value-structure changes so that the peasant no longer seeks the fulfilment of these functions. Caste, for instance, has economic

---

[89] In the American sense of an intellectual short cut, a calculating device, guiding the family to a set of farming tactics that ensures survival.

drawbacks; it impedes specialization of labour according to comparative advantage, it compels the duplication of wells, it slows the response to economic incentive where such response conflicts with *dharma*, and it perpetuates inequalities that reduce the enjoyment yielded by the few commodities available. Yet all this will leave the villager unmoved, as long as caste, and caste alone, provides social order, cohesion in the sense that such order is generally accepted, and (especially through single-caste factions) some social security.

117. Similarly, there is little point in attacks and laws against moneylenders while co-operative credit societies may not replace them as sources of consumer loans; or against the use of land to sustain cattle of little economic value, while most peasants are encouraged to worship them by the absence of alternative sources of draught power, transport, fuel, soil enrichment, protein, or reserve capital.[90]

118. Many practices inimical to modernization are disguised insurance policies. Among them are: tenants' preference for share-rents over fixed rents; borrowers' preference for grain repayment over cash repayment;[91] willingness of both to pay for their preference; hoarding of marketable surpluses; reluctance to use fertilizer where water is unsure; intertillage of cereals with robust but low-value legumes; and persistence in 'improvident maternity'. Alternative sources of security, especially crop insurance schemes, might alleviate these evils. The plans for crop insurance come very late, and States are free to finance them or not, as they choose (p. 182). The Central Parliament enacted a crop insurance scheme in July 1967, but we must see how and by whom it is to be administered and financed, how the States will respond, and whether the limited resources are to be concentrated on IAAP farmers (with new inputs but assured water in most cases) or on high-risk dry farmers.

15. URBAN POWER AND AGRICULTURAL DEVELOPMENT

119. We have seen that farm policy is made by the towns, and to some extent for the towns. Business and trade union leaders both

---

[90] A forthcoming paper by K. N. Raj will show a high rank correlation coefficient, for States, between the proportion of 'useless' cows and of pasture land.

[91] This preference is nothing new, nor is the higher grain-rate of interest; cf. R. Kumar, 'The Deccan Riots of 1875', *J. Asian Studies*, Aug. 1965, p. 615.

want low food prices. They can 'buy' them from the big landlords in return for loopholes in land reforms and in laws limiting interest rates; for low agricultural taxes; and for subsidized inputs (especially irrigation and fertilizer) for the big farmers. Such a deal is politically stable, because urban business and labour can be easily organized into monopolies and cartels; because the *powerful* rural groups are included, and the smallholders and landless labourers are deprived of their natural leaders by emigration; and because millions of small illiterate farmers are almost impossible to organize into unions.

120. The deal between urban élites and big farmers has been compatible with considerable rural progress; but it has meant too small a proportion of total outlays for agriculture, and it has distorted the structure of agricultural spending. Inequality within the village, and between village and town, has been worsened, and growth has suffered. Production of dairy products (and perhaps rice and wheat) gets too big a share of farm investment; coarse grains (and probably pulses) get too small a share. Urban power grows as skilled graduates concentrate in the cities. Meanwhile the planned share of public investment in organized industry goes on rising.

121. One group within the urban élite may try to resist these trends: the planners themselves. There is reason to believe that they have been shocked into a new realization of the role and needs of agriculture. But the planners are in Delhi, and seem to have been getting weaker in 1967; and the main agricultural decisions are in the State capitals. Moreover, planners are human; like most of the urban élite, they are not long 'emancipated from the rural morass'. They are not eager to plunge back in, despite their great and genuine sympathy for the peasant. Yet we have been driven to the conclusion, in almost every field of rural policy, that disaggregated, local-level research and action are needed. If the planners and their research staffs go back to the grass roots, they may still command the prestige to take the necessary steps. But they will be opposed by a formidable urban coalition, and by their own background and inclinations as well.

16. THE URBAN ALLIANCE: THE CASE OF EMPLOYMENT

122. The use made of labour is perhaps the clearest illustration: the provision of work opportunities in successive plans has shown

systematic urban bias. Between the 1951 and 1961 censuses, the proportion of workers outside agriculture (30 per cent) hardly changed, yet 6·5 mn of the 8 mn extra jobs created during the Second Plan were outside agriculture. 'During the Third Plan the addition to the labour force may be ... 17 mn, about a third of the increase being in the urban areas' yet the Third Plan proposed to provide 10·5 mn non-agricultural jobs and only 3·5 mn agricultural jobs,[92] though 4 mn seem to have been achieved. It is not easy to make sense of the concept of unemployment in India, but on any definition it is hard to believe that in 1966 only 'about three-fourths [of the unemployed] are in the rural areas' (p. 106).

123. The same imbalance appears in the employment plans for 1966–71. The workforce is expected to rise by 23 mn between mid-1966 and mid-1971 (p. 108). It would be surprising if townward migration outweighed the effect of urban sex ratios (see para. 38) sufficiently to put as much as one-third of the extra workers into the towns. Thus at least 15 mn will be in rural areas. Yet the 18·5 to 19 mn extra jobs to be created in 1966–71 (p. 108) are to include only 4·5 to 5 mn in agriculture. So at least 15 mn extra rural workers may expect—if we make a generous allowance for extra non-agricultural work in the villages—at most 6·5 mn extra jobs in 1966–71, while urban unemployment is intended to fall sharply.

124. The failure of various schemes of local works, rural works, &c. to employ the rural labour surplus is attributed to fortuitous factors by the planners, who hope to achieve an improvement if such works are 'incorporated as an integral part of the plan' (p. 111). Yet the employment target for local works is only 1·5 mn 100-day man-years, as against 2·5 mn in the Third Plan (achievement 400,000) (pp. 111–2). Nothing is said about voluntary and semi-voluntary unemployment due to village festivals, dysentery, worms, and job restrictions based on considerations of caste impurity. Yet the jobs are waiting to be done in every village—roof repair, well desilting, composting, weeding, even washing children. Misery is caused impartially by voluntary, semi-voluntary, and involuntary joblessness. Has a mistaken transference of Western concepts of unemployment led Indian planners to concentrate exclusively on the third type?

125. Further, Healey has shown how employment opportunities

---

[92] *Third Five-Year Plan*, pp. 156–9. Some of the non-agricultural jobs are in the villages, but not enough to distort the comparison very much: many of these jobs are temporary dam-building &c.

in dam-building are restricted, and costs raised, by failure to schedule work into the agricultural slack season.[93] The Draft Outline does not discuss this, but the proposed reduction of real outlay on major irrigation means less scope for counter-seasonal rural employment. The imbalance of new job opportunities, the decline of local works, and the lack of seasonal jobs renders the planners' claim of priority for employment (pp. 106–9) hard to follow, at least in the rural areas. 'Maximise growth, never mind employment, and tax the employed to compensate the jobless' could be a humane and sensible development strategy, but it is not articulated by the planners. Once more, the practical consequences of policies for the villagers do not seem to be analysed.

17. CONCLUSIONS

126. The share of agriculture in the Draft Outline of the Fourth Plan is smaller than has ever been planned before. However the data may be adjusted for devaluation or indirect contributions from other sectors, agriculture still does not seem to be getting the priority claimed by the planners.

127. The overall food targets are not too high, given that the vagaries of climate (and aid) render foodgrain self-sufficiency a prudent aim. But investment is insufficient to achieve these targets, especially in view of the structure of incentives, which tends to discourage farmers from growing foodgrains.

128. Capital/output ratios are substantially lower in agriculture than elsewhere. Agriculture uses relatively little foreign exchange and few scarce skills. It seems impossible to account for its low share of planned resources in economic terms. There is a real paradox here: high targets, high yields for extra outlay, yet low planned outlay. Moreover, incentives are so structured as to discourage the private sector from making good the deficiencies of public agricultural outlay.

129. The paradox is not fully resolved by the expectation of higher yields in IAAP. IAAP is advocated in the belief that peasants themselves exhaust all opportunities to improve traditional factors and techniques. This belief rests on a questionable interpretation of peasant motive. Poor farmers are too concerned with risk to behave as simple profit maximizers; rather they inherit a bundle of

[93] Healey, chs 9–10.

farm practices, some good, some bad, together constituting a survival algorithm.

130. To reduce agricultural risk, planners can (*a*) concentrate output in low-risk areas, as in IAAP; (*b*) select low-risk investments—irrigation rather than fertilizers; (*c*) insure against things going wrong—foodgrain stocks. Current planning concentrates almost exclusively on (*a*), but there is no evidence that this is the cheapest policy.

131. IAAP is inegalitarian, and in a way that may harm growth, since it reduces risk only for peasants already enjoying assured water supply. These are already the richest and most risk-free of farmers. Since risk is a bigger deterrent to the poor, and to those who suffer a lot of it, IAAP farmers are likely to raise private investment less than dry farmers, in response to a given public outlay to cut risk. The 80–85 per cent of farmers outside IAAP, already poorer than the rest, will receive lower prices if IAAP succeeds. Neither the experience of IADP districts, nor comparisons of performance by research stations and good farmers, suggests a dramatic breakthrough.

132. New seeds may make the decisive difference, but probably not as quickly as the planners suggest. The new varieties have drawbacks (palatability, fodder value, risk) for which special arrangements are needed.

133. Selection of IADP areas was unsatisfactory; in IAAP, area selection requires more attention and analysis. Owing to the aggregative and industrial nature of economic research in India, we do not know where the expected rate of return on the package is highest. Similar criticism applies to most agricultural outlays—land reform, farm education, health and nutritional improvements, irrigation, &c.; hardly ever do we know the rates of return on scarce resources by area and crop.

134. The administrators and VLWs to carry out IAAP seem to be lacking. Their training is too centralized, their stay in one place too short, and their work too clerical. A big increase in the number of such personnel will reduce their quality, and hence farmers' confidence in extension—especially when risky new inputs are being offered. For successful implementation in agriculture, the pay and status of rural civil servants, especially VLWs, must rise.

135. Agriculture's persistently low share of development resources must be traced to urban bias in the Indian policy. Rewards and status

are higher in urban areas, even for jobs where the social rate of return is obviously much higher in villages (e.g. doctors). Policies are made under urban pressures. Research concentrates on more easily measured industrial processes.

136. Agricultural planning under urban bias has registered considerable achievements, but fails to grasp the villager's decision processes. It neither exploits nor changes his motivations, especially concerning status and risk; it relies too heavily on paper legislation based on contract law; and, by failing to grasp the facts of rural power, it allocates resources to the powerful, whether or not they use those resources best.

137. Such allocations, often through democratic institutions, also reflect the unity of motive between the townsman (who wants a marketed food surplus) and the big farmer (who sells it). This is damaging for two reasons. First, the small farmer, often with higher output per acre, is deprived of resources of credit, fertilizer, &c. Second, the nutritional pattern of output is distorted. The faster growth of urban incomes, and the higher income-elasticity of demand for milk and polished rice, anyway cause the prices of such products to rise relative to coarse grains; and the *big* farmer, as he sells to the towns, switches production accordingly. If he outbids also small farmers for scarce resources, the prospects in cheap coarse grains are even more likely to be neglected. Yet it is the consumers of such grains who need extra food most. Moreover, 'big farmer bias' and present price policy may (as in the past) divert the new inputs from the cereal fields to cotton and sugar.

138. Both past output trends (which the planners interpret too optimistically) and present input plans suggest that planned growth rates of agricultural production may not be approached by 1970–1. Extra land and labour, which accounted for over half the farm growth of the 1950s, will increase much more slowly in future. Industrial inputs to farming depend on hopeful projections for foreign exchange. Agricultural inputs depend on unrealistic assessments of the possibilities (green manure, urban compost, changing cropping pattern). The effects of the droughts of 1965–6 and 1966–7, both on inputs and on incentives, may severely damage future growth in agriculture.

139. There has been much more real land reform than the usual catalogue of evasion suggests, but there is still too much reliance on paper laws, and too little fieldwork to estimate the effects on output.

More should be done about consolidation, especially in States where holdings (and therefore plots) are small.

140. The history of rural credit, too, does not support the extreme pessimism now current, but more can be done to get credit to small farmers, especially tenants. The crop loan scheme should improve this. Abandonment of accounting fictions concerning annual repayment and consumer loans would be helpful.

141. The allocation of agricultural outlay among *types* has been improved, but some aspects still need explaining. In view of the high and rising share of useless cattle, and of the low calorie/land ratio, the renewed emphasis on animal husbandry is hard to understand, and may be a reflection of middle-class urban diets.

142. There is not enough integration of social programmes into plans to raise farm output. The Education Commission's casual treatment of agricultural education is unempirical; the rate of return on different types of education, in different forms of agriculture, should be estimated. Such evidence as exists on the returns to nutritional improvement suggests that they are appreciable, especially among the ill-fed. The pattern of investment by crops (and the distribution of farm outputs, whether through compulsory procurement or through market incentives) should take more account of this, and less of the vagaries of income-elasticities of demand, overweighted as they are by growth in the better-fed urban sector.

143. Employment opportunities continue to favour the towns. No strategy is proposed in the published documents to correct the distributional effects of this, either by an attack on 'voluntary' rural unemployment or by counter-seasonal timing of rural investment projects; but some such strategy may nevertheless exist.

144. Planning under urban bias, with its excessive reliance on town demands and big farmers' supplies, has nevertheless achieved a great deal in rural India. Whatever their drawbacks, the Intensive Programme and the new seeds may seem to consolidate this achievement. In the long run, such an impression would be unfortunate. It would obscure the real needs: for intensive research, at local level, to discover the returns on alternative schemes; for rural development directed at maximum returns rather than at surpluses for low-yield urban reinvestment; and for a break with the whole ideology of premature industrialization. India's experience since Independence proves that neglect of agriculture is a recipe for slow industrialization, not for rapid economic growth.

5

Economic Overheads: Co-ordination and Pricing

J. M. HEALEY

In the introductory section of this chapter there will first be a brief discussion of the nature of economic overheads, the balance between public and private participation in overhead development, and the principles for allocation of public overhead investment. This will be followed by an examination of the pattern of overhead investment in the current plan. The third section will consider the need for co-ordination between different overhead services and the need to relate plans for certain overheads to the agricultural objectives of the Planning Commission. Fourthly, there will be a discussion of the need for a more commercial approach to the operation of public overhead services and of the importance of productivity considerations in investment decisions about overheads.

1. INTRODUCTION

'Economic overheads' is a term of art. There is a widely recognized group of sectors which are understood to fall in this category, but it is not entirely clear what unifies them in the sense of justifying their separate treatment as a group.[1]

Overhead facilities often, but not always, provide services necessary for a whole range of other activities. They usually provide

---

[1] Perhaps it is useful to regard 'overheads' in philosophical terms as a 'cluster concept' or 'family resemblance word', like 'game'. The characteristics of such a concept are like a group of interlocking circles; each example lies in some, but not all. No single characteristic is necessary or sufficient. Thus some games are competitive; some are entertaining; some involve teams; some have firm rules; but a dishonestly played patience has nothing in common with a dour international professional football match, save through intermediates (e.g. a bridge game) with resemblances to both. Cf. L. Wittgenstein, *Philosophical Investigations* (London, 1958), pp. 31–32.

inputs which are not specific to one particular use. Power and transport satisfy this criterion but irrigation does not. Other facilities, such as steel mills, satisfy this criterion but are normally excluded.

Overhead facilities are usually 'lumpy' and hence yield economies of scale, though many industrial investments also have this characteristic. The yields from overhead facilities tend to be spread over a long period of time, and it is usually difficult to trace and charge all the beneficiaries from the services provided. Thus overheads are usually state-financed and managed: to avoid private monopoly, to overcome individual myopia, and to exploit external benefits.

For the planner, the significant common feature of most overheads is that their services are not importable. Therefore, overhead capacity has to be more carefully planned and ensured than in other sectors, as shortfalls cannot be filled by imports directly. Since most overhead services are essential for production in many other sectors and since a shortfall cannot be made up from imports, widespread damage to the growth of an economy may be done by inaccurate prediction of the demand for overhead services and inadequacy of supply. It is argued by some that it is better to err on the safe side and plan an excess of overhead capacity, since the risks are asymmetric. The cost of too little electricity is likely to be greater than the cost of too much electricity, because a shortage which cannot be made up by imports will reduce potential production in a whole range of manufacturing, agricultural, and service industries.

In theory, imports can make up for any shortfall in final goods arising from inadequate overhead services. This, however, is extremely difficult in a country with an acute foreign exchange shortage (like India). Moreover, the foreign exchange foregone in the short period by establishing excess overhead capacity may be small (e.g. railways in India). And even if the foreign exchange component of investment is substantial (e.g. electric power in India), it is usually easier to obtain foreign aid tied to power investment than for the imports of a wide range of goods in short supply as a result of inadequate power supplies. Of course, the alternative uses of domestic resources locked up in excess overhead capacity need to be taken into account also.

If this view is accepted, there does seem to be a justification for grouping certain types of facility together under the overhead category, possibly for special priority in national investment plans.

Should such investment be entirely or largely the responsibility of the public sector (as in post-war India), or is there a case for greater private participation? If, as argued above, the non-importability of these services makes adequate provision crucial, there appears to be a strong case for the government to estimate these requirements and guarantee their provision. Moreover, there may be lack of incentive and foresight among private investors in this field. Limits on financial charges and restricted private access to foreign exchange for import requirements are centrally-imposed obstacles, but in many cases the scale of resources required, and the long period necessary for the recovery of capital cost, inhibit private investment—especially as interest rates (and profit opportunities elsewhere) are higher in less developed countries.

However, there are some types of overheads (e.g. road transport, minor irrigation, some electricity projects) where the necessary scale of investment is relatively small. In these fields there may be positive advantages from encouraging greater private participation. First, there would be economy in the public sector's scarce and overstrained managerial capacity for development and operation of these services. Second, these investment opportunities should stimulate greater private saving. This is a particular advantage in view of the poor savings record of public undertakings in under-developed countries. Third, there may be speedier private response to existing or anticipated overhead bottlenecks, if only because the government usually lacks the local knowledge of the private entrepreneur and because of the slow working of political and administrative processes leading up to public investment decisions. In addition, private provision of overhead services would be concentrated at growth points in the economy rather than spread widely and thinly, as it has tended to be in publicly constructed and controlled irrigation systems in Asia.[2]

No generalizations can be made, except on the need for a flexible approach to the balance between public and private participation in overhead development. Where there is evidence of a willingness of private investors to establish these facilities, governmentally imposed obstacles should be removed and assistance provided (e.g. credit facilities). If the government believes that private provision will not be adequate, it can step in to supplement private facilities. West

---

[2] See pp. 160–3 below.

Pakistan has shown such flexibility recently in transferring responsibility for tubewell development from the public to the private sector. India is also proposing to give greater scope for private motor transport operators after a long period of official discouragement. These are welcome signs of a less doctrinaire, more pragmatic policy.

Finally, what criteria should guide the allocation of funds to overheads in total, and among types of overheads? One simple rule is that the physical requirements of different services (power, water, transport) should be estimated for the various areas and provided at minimum cost. This means choosing the techniques of power generation or transport media which will provide the services at minimum cost.[3] There are at least two ways in which such a procedure may differ from that involved in allocation of resources between directly productive activities.

First, there may be social grounds for estimating demand on the basis of charges which do not cover the marginal cost of overhead services. Requirements of power or transport in backward areas may be estimated on the basis of subsidized charges to provide an inducement to infant industries and to aid the geographical dispersal of development, especially in countries where labour mobility is low and there are regional political tensions. In the case of roads, for example, charges can seldom enter into estimation of requirements.

Second, investment in overheads may be planned somewhat in excess of anticipated demand for risk-avoiding reasons, given earlier. This is a difference of degree rather than kind compared to decisions on directly productive investment.

In general, the provision of funds for different overhead services will have to be determined by the need to provide complementary services for the anticipated development of productive activities in each area.

2. THE PATTERN AND ADEQUACY OF OVERHEAD INVESTMENT IN THE DRAFT FOURTH PLAN

The distribution of public sector outlays on overheads is set out in Table 1. The table permits a comparison between the actual pattern of expenditure in the Third Plan and the proposed expenditure for 1966–70.

---

[3] Clearly, there are further complexities here. With an estimated growth of demand through time, the choice arises between a larger investment now with economies of scale, or a smaller investment with additions to capacity as demand increases later.

TABLE 1

Overhead Investment

	Expenditure in 3rd Plan* Rs mn	Per cent of total overhead expenditure	Proposed expenditure in 4th Plan Rs mn	Per cent of total overhead expenditure
	(Current Prices)		(Prices of June 1966)	
Soil Conservation	780	1·8	2,180	3·3
Minor Irrigation	2,690	6·2	5,200	8·0
Irrigation and Flood Control	6,570	15·1	9,640	14·8
Power	12,620	29·0	20,300	31·1
Railways	13,230	30·4	14,100	21·6
Roads†	4,450	10·2	7,600	11·6
Ports	910	2·1	1,700	2·6
Civil Air Transport	500	1·2	1,250	1·9
Posts and Telecommunications	1,180	2·7	2,350	3·6
Inland Water Transport	30	0·1	130	0·2
Total overhead outlay	42,960		64,450	
Percentage of total plan outlay	50·3		40·8	

* Based on actuals for 1961–5, and likely actuals for 1965–6.
† Private investment in road transport for the 4th Plan is estimated at Rs 6,300 mn compared with Rs 2,500 mn in the 3rd Plan.
Source: 4DO, pp. 72–73.

In the whole public sector programme (1965–70) the balance has shifted substantially away from overheads towards 'directly productive' expenditure (mainly agricultural production, organized industry, and mining), compared to the last plan. This change in balance can be largely explained by the reduced shares of railways and power in *total* plan expenditure. Railway investment, in fact, is likely to be lower in real terms in 1966–70 than in 1961–65.

(a) Railways

The two largest elements in the overhead programme are still railways and power. It is important to ask whether the allocations for these sectors will be adequate to meet demands in the years up to 1970–1. In the case of railways, investment in real terms appears to be smaller than in the Third Plan, and doubts may be raised about whether such an allocation will be adequate, given that the expected increase in freight traffic in 1966–70 is double that which actually occurred in 1961–5.

11

One reason for optimism is that traffic demand may be over-estimated. In the Third Plan traffic demand was substantially over-estimated, because aggregate output did not rise as fast as anticipated. National income rose 12·7 per cent compared to a target of 32 per cent, and industrial production 40 per cent against a planned 70 per cent. This may well happen again, but planning cannot proceed on such an assumption. Moreover, it was the demand for specific categories of freight—especially coal, materials for steel plants, and finished steel products—which failed to rise as expected, rather than general freight, as Table 2 indicates.

TABLE 2

Increase in Railway Freight in Third and Fourth Plans (mn/tons)

	1960–5		1965–70
	Estimated increase	*Actual increase*	*Estimated increase*
Steel products and raw material for steel plants	+21·3	+9·1	+22·1
Coal	+41·2	+13·7	+36·9
Cement	+5·6	+2·5	+7·0
General goods	+24·4	+24·5	+36·0
Total	+92·5	+49·8	+102·0

Source: 3rd Plan, p. 542, 4DO, p. 296.

Experience in the last two plans shows up the failure to predict the demand for *specific categories* of freight. Such errors may cause excessive investment in specialized types of rolling stock or specific route capacity, e.g. over-capacity on the Bihar-Bengal routes, which is often difficult to adapt to meet other kinds of freight demand. However, the Planning Commission has made detailed commodity projections and point-to-point studies of freight movement, so that more accurate projections should result for the next five years.

Passenger traffic is expected to rise from 1966–7 to 1970–1 at approximately the same rate (24 per cent) as in the Third Plan. If passenger traffic depends on population, urbanization, and income per person, this is a conservative estimate, since income per person is predicted to rise 3 per cent per annum in 1966–70, in contrast to 1961–5 when it changed very little.

However, road transport is assumed to take an increasing share. Moreover, substantial excess capacity exists at the beginning of the Fourth Plan, because rolling-stock ran ahead of requirements in the Third Plan. On the published estimates of surplus rolling-stock and planned additions, the achievement of *freight* targets will demand about 15 per cent better operating efficiency.[4] Improvements are expected from the expanded dieselization and electrification programme as well as from better organization.

There seems little warrant in recent experience for believing that this will be attained. Average wagon turn-round time, planned to fall by 17 per cent between 1960 and 1965, actually increased. Gross ton-miles per engine hour, which measures the combined average speed and loads of trains, increased by only 4–5 per cent during the same period.[5] (However, greater improvements were achieved in the Second Plan.)

This past failure to raise operating efficiency occurred despite a substantial rise in the proportion of diesel and electric traction during the period and despite a high level of investment in track renewal. The most important factor is likely to be organizational; and experiments began in 1963 to develop programming methods to control freight movements and to utilize rolling-stock more effectively. These methods should yield results in the next few years.

(b) Power

The Energy Survey Committee, on the basis of data for the economy as a whole and for individual industries, has made demand estimates which are very close to those made by the Planning Commission. There are reasons to believe that current plan investment will be adequate to meet this demand. The balance of investment is to be changed in favour of transmission and distribution. In the Third Plan, inadequate provision was made for transmission, but correction of this imbalance will permit fuller utilization of existing and of new generating capacity. In addition, the operation of power systems in neighbouring States is to be integrated, and regional grids are to be set up. Provided the investment cost of transmission does not exceed the extra cost of generation capacity required for a given electricity supply, this policy should permit economy in power investment in the current plan period. Some economy will also be

---

[4] Railway Board, *Report, 1965–6*, ch. 3, & *4DO*, p. 295.
[5] Railway Board, *Report*, Statistical App., sect. 13 (annual).

possible by spreading the load more evenly over a period of time through industrial two-part tariffs.[6]

(c) *Agricultural overheads*

The emphasis on agricultural production claimed in the Fourth Plan would be expected to influence the pattern of the overhead programme. The share of major and medium irrigation in total plan expenditure has fallen, and a rise of under 50 per cent in money investment between the Third and Fourth Plans—a fall in real terms—is expected to more than double the quinquennial addition to gross irrigated acreage. This assumption is not as optimistic as it seems. Expenditure is to concentrate on 'continuing' rather than 'new' major projects, so that ongoing Plan investment should have a shorter average gestation period. Moreover, several major schemes from earlier plans are only now starting to yield their full benefits.

Minor irrigation receives a larger share of resources. Since it is quicker-yielding, and has more than fulfilled its past acreage targets, it seems sensible to give it greater priority.

The adequacy of the overall irrigation programme will depend heavily on the extent to which India is successful in raising the proportion of capacity utilized, the intensity of cropping on utilized supplies, and hence on yields per unit of water.

Proportionately more resources are devoted to soil conservation than in the past. There is to be more expenditure on rural electrification, to be concentrated on areas with development potential and near to transmission lines. Although roads increase their share of overhead investment, there is no clear indication that sufficient attention or resources have been provided for village-access roads, vital in a policy to increase the flow of fertilizers to cultivators and produce to markets.

3. THE NEED FOR CO-ORDINATION

One important theme in the Draft Fourth Plan is the resolve to achieve greater co-ordination in the management and development of certain public services. The main emphasis is on co-ordination within the transport sector—especially between road and rail

---

[6] The subject of power is treated only cursorily here. It is considered at length by Prof. Robinson, pp. 173–83 below.

development, but also between other forms of transport.[7] Co-ordination is also called for within the irrigation sector. One aspect of co-ordination that receives little prominence in the Draft Outline is the need to relate policy on overheads, such as roads and broadcasting, to the newly emphasized agricultural development programme.

(a) Co-ordination on Transport Policy: road and rail

The planners now recognize the need to view the transport sector as a whole, rather than allowing each agency (Ministry of Railways, Ministry of Transport, State Governments) to work and plan independently.[8] This new emphasis on co-ordinating the different forms of transport means the beginning of a more rational approach to estimating demands, making investment decisions, and drawing up rate structures and transport regulations.

The planners have also indicated that the first steps are being taken to create a framework of economic policy and institutions which will permit greater integration and co-ordination of the various transport services than has occurred in the past. 'Road communications and rail and road transport services have to be thought of together as complementary services and incorporated into a single integrated plan of development' (p. 299). Although coastal and inland waterways, pipelines, and airways are also transport media in need of co-ordination, road and rail are the most important and require immediate attention.

Already the broad lines of a common rail/road policy seem to be emerging, based on the estimated comparative advantages of these two forms of transport. First, new investment in railways is to be devoted largely to building up the efficiency of the existing network rather than seeking to expand it.[9] The comparative advantage of

---

[7] Co-ordination is defined by the Committee on Transport Policy and Co-ordination as the 'Development of the various modes of transport as complementary services in such proportions and combinations as will meet the total need of the community at each stage at minimum cost to the economy'.

[8] *4DO*, pp. 52, 299, 304–5.

[9] *4DO*, pp. 296, 298–9. The railway programme in the current plan shows evidence of this approach. New line outlay is down from Rs 2,130 mn in the 3rd Plan to Rs 1,610 mn in the 4th. Track doubling, on the other hand, has risen from 1,860 mn to 2,320 mn and the *increase* in the stock of diesel locomotives is to be raised from 545 (Third Plan) to 882 (Fourth). Additional electric locomotives are to rise from 183 (Third Plan) to 605 (Fourth), while extra steam locomotives are to be halved.

railways over roads lies in moving assured and steady flows of bulky traffic, particularly mineral products and manufactures of heavy industries, over long distances.[10] The main emphasis is on increasing line capacity on already congested or high-density routes, while improving the speed and power of trains on these routes by dieselization and electrification. Certain new rail lines constructed or relaid in the past ten years have proved unprofitable, as the traffic flows were not dense enough to ensure full utilization of the very expensive capacity created.[11] There is evidence of a more careful and critical approach to the development of new lines, despite the strength of political pressure for them in India.

Conversely, it is now recognized that extra road transport often has a comparative advantage over new railway lines, particularly in opening up new and less developed areas and regions. This view is presumably based on the greater flexibility of road transport capacity, viz. that it can be marginally adjusted to small and slowly-changing demands. However, the Committee on Transport Policy recognizes that fiscal incentives may sometimes be necessary to persuade private transport operators to serve the hill and backward areas, bring their agricultural produce to the market, and open them to market influences.

The Central Government has committed itself to improving the existing network of national (trunk) roads by filling in large gaps left by past neglect (missing links, weak bridges, inadequate surfaces, &c.) Central Government expenditure on roads is to rise from Rs 800 mn in the Third Plan to Rs 4,000 mn in the current plan period—nearly half of it for the existing national road system.[12] Many of these roads run parallel with major railway routes, so road transport is presumably seen as taking an increasing share of those services in which the railways have a disadvantage: movement of small consignments, quick delivery, high-value freight over short and medium distances, and freight which involves considerable trans-shipment by rail.[13]

---

[10] Ibid. p. 298.

[11] See Planning Commission, *Preliminary Report on Transport Policy & Co-ordination* (1961), p. 122.

[12] *4DO*, p. 301.

[13] Railways have been steadily losing this type of freight. Between 1954–5 and 1963–4 the proportion of wagons loaded with small consignments declined steadily from 13·7 to 7·2 on the metre gauge and 9·0 to 4·4 on the broad gauge. The tonnage of high-rated freight has fallen from 36·8 per cent of total freight in 1956–7 to 28·4 per cent in 1964–5, though there has been some recovery in the last 2 years. (See Railway Board, *Report*, ch. 3, sect. A.)

With this more integrated and clearly-defined policy there is evidence of measures to make the planning and the operation of transport services more rational. The Ministries of Railways and Transport and the Planning Commission have set up a joint group for transport planning, to determine more accurately the present and future demand for certain types of freight between important centres, before deciding which transport media will most economically meet these needs. This marks an improvement on the past, when each agency made its own independent estimate of demand, and of capacity needed to meet it. Before new road or rail projects are to be implemented, careful cost/benefit studies are to be undertaken, according to the Draft Fourth Plan, and measures have already been taken to improve the statistical information on the costs of moving specific flows of traffic by different methods.[14]

Unlike railways, road transport services are operated largely by private enterprise in India. Efficiency and co-ordination in this field have been handicapped in the past, not only by a poor and incomplete road network, but also by weak internal organization and inefficient and piecemeal public regulation of private operators. The planners list measures to encourage the many small private-road operators to merge into more viable units; to form regional and State associations of operators to provide common booking, maintenance, and other facilities; and to promote co-operative undertakings.[15]

Road transport operation is to be left largely to private initiative, but limited Government participation is anticipated for three major purposes: to ensure co-ordination of road and rail goods services over long-distance inter-State routes (an Inter-State Transport Corporation is envisaged which will be jointly owned by the Central and State Government and Railways); to meet the transport needs of backward regions where private operators fail to respond to fiscal and other incentives; and to set standards of performance for private industry.[16] The planners, however, say nothing about the 'imperative need to simplify and introduce greater uniformity in the existing approach to procedures for regulation of road transport', (issue of permits, distance limits, etc.) which is stressed by the Committee on Transport Policy.[17]

---

[14] *4DO*, pp. 299, 301. Planning Commission, *Final Report on Transport Policy & Co-ordination* (1966), pp. 176–81.
[15] *4DO*, pp. 301–2. [16] *Final Report on Transport Policy*, ch. 6.
[17] Ibid. pp. 87–94.

The ability of the road transport industry to meet increased passenger and goods demand during the next five years will be largely determined by the country's ability to produce motor vehicles. Road freight (in ton-miles) is expected to rise by 82 per cent, while trucks on the road increase by 70 per cent. Passenger traffic is expected to rise by 50 per cent, with a 43 per cent increase in buses on the road. This is estimated to require a net increase of 205,000 commercial vehicles between 1966 and 1971.[18] On the assumption that about 25 per cent of the existing fleet will be replaced in the next five years, the gross requirements will be about 300,000 vehicles (1966–71). Given the high proportion of aged vehicles in India, replacement requirements for efficient operation are probably higher than this estimate suggests. An expansion of production capacity to 90,000 is anticipated by 1970–1, but this is unlikely to meet requirements if utilization of vehicle-manufacturing capacity does not improve considerably and rise from 55 per cent in 1966–7 to near 90 per cent for the next five years.[19]

(b) Co-ordination on Ports

Little can be said on the basis of plan information. Some questions may be asked relating to co-ordination. Is there a national plan for operating existing port capacity? Could congestion in some ports be relieved by fuller utilization of capacity in others by re-routing shipping? Are demands on inland transport capacity being minimized by ensuring that cargoes go to the ports nearest to the ultimate inland destination of the goods, or to those which involve the least congested routes? These two objectives may not always conflict.

(c) Co-ordination on Irrigation

One of the main weaknesses of the irrigation programme has been the poor utilization of capacity from major and medium irrigation schemes. This appears to be largely a result of inadequate co-ordination between different administrative departments and authorities, and of inadequate complementary policies.

Between 1960–1 and 1965–6, the proportion of potential irrigation utilized has risen from 77 per cent to 88 per cent. Despite the improvement, there still seems to be a large margin of under-utilized capacity.[20] The main reasons given for this under-utilization are poor

---

[18] *4DO*, p. 310.   [19] Ibid. p. 289 (Table).
[20] Ibid. p. 216. This is a paradoxical example of capital-intensive resources being wasted because of a failure to organize a classically labour-intensive activity.

phasing of major projects (so that benefits were not reaped at the intermediate stages of projects construction) and the time lag between the provision of water in the main canals and its use in the fields. This has been due to a failure of co-ordination between project authorities, district and local authorities, and agricultural departments. Agricultural departments often failed to determine the appropriate crops, cropping patterns, and irrigation practices, and to advise and convince the cultivators on these. The appropriate seeds, fertilizers, credit, and marketing facilities were not always made available. The result was that field channels, needed to utilize the waters provided by the projects, were not constructed by cultivators or the responsible local authorities.

The degree of under-utilization of irrigation capacity varies with the experience of the irrigation administration in different States. There are few recent data by States, but an earlier study showed that under-utilization of irrigation varied widely from State to State. In 1960–1 utilization was greatest in Madras, Punjab, Kerala, Andhra, and Rajasthan, and least in Bombay and Mysore.[21] The good record of Madras at that time was attributed to proper phasing to avoid time-lags between completion of headworks, canals, and minor distributories. This was made possible by extending the responsibility of the public works department to cover the excavation of field channels where necessary. If Madras can do this, why cannot other States?

In addition to under-utilization of *capacity* from major schemes, there has been a shortfall between *constructional* targets and achievements during the Third Plan, which contrasts with the slight over-fulfilment for minor schemes. Thus:

Extra Irrigated Acreage Potential
(mn gross acres)

| | 1961–5 | | 1966–70 |
	Target	*Actual*	*Target*
Major Irrigation	12·8	5·5	9·0
Minor Irrigation	12·8	13·1	12·0

Source: 4DO, p. 185 (Table).

[21] *3rd Plan,* p. 410.

The main reasons for the shortfall in major irrigation potential appear to be: (*a*) unrealistic target setting, (*b*) escalation in costs of projects and shortages of construction materials, (*c*) diversion of funds by States from continuing schemes to new schemes.[22] There may be some justification for (*a*) and (*b*), but (*c*) is indefensible policy when quick returns on investment are so urgently required. In the light of this experience, what new approach to irrigation policy is evident in the planners' current thinking?

In the first place, few *new* major projects are to be financed in the plan period 1965–6 to 1970–1. Major irrigation expenditure of Rs 8,700 mn (Rs 5,720 mn in the Third Plan) is to be largely concentrated on schemes already initiated in earlier plans. New schemes are to be chosen which yield phased and early benefits.[23]

Secondly, proper phasing of projects is recommended, so that benefits are secured as each stage of the projects is completed. Concerted action is to be taken by the Irrigation and Agricultural Department of State Governments to synchronize the programmes for construction of head works, canals, and field channels. Measures are also required to ensure that cultivators are prepared in advance for the use of water made available, and for the supply of complementary inputs.[24] All this was said in the Third Plan and, indeed, in the Second Plan before it.[25] It is not clear, however, what new measures or new administrative vigour are to be applied to the task.

Will the project authorities or the local authorities be made responsible for constructing field channels and charging the cultivators? Or are the cultivators expected to carry out the work and be provided with loans? If the field channels are constructed, what further incentives or penalties will there be for use or non-use of irrigation water made available? Financial incentives or penalties seem the most obvious policy. A Committee of State Ministers has recommended that water rates should be raised to something between 25 per cent to 40 per cent of the additional net benefit to a farmer from irrigation facilities. The planners say only that this recommendation is to be acted on by State Governments.[26]

[22] Ibid. (Apr. 1965).   [23] *4DO* pp. 48, 218.   [24] *4DO*, pp. 216–8, 274.

[25] *2nd Plan*, p. 350; *3rd Plan*, pp. 383, 386, 389–91; *4DO*, pp. 174, 216–8.

[26] *4DO*, p. 220. Water rates have been too low and inflexible for years, despite repeated resolutions of past plans. Most irrigation projects run at a loss. There is some evidence, however, in the States' budgets for 1966–7 that water rates are being raised in some States (e.g. Bihar, Rajasthan) and the estimated contribution of irrigation projects to State budget revenues appears significantly higher for 1966–7 than in any previous year. (See *Reserve Bank of India B.*, May 1966.)

Fuller use of irrigation potential requires not only compulsory construction of field channels and charges, but also a compulsory water cess on the irrigated areas (whether or not the water is currently used), to induce the cultivator to use the water and raise his yields. A policy of this kind, however, requires an adequate complementary programme to provide the cultivator with the necessary advice, supplies, credit, and marketing facilities. It may also require land reform measures, such as consolidation of small-holdings and action against sharecropping, to make water-use economically worthwhile.

The third and perhaps most significant feature of the planners' approach to irrigation is the shift in the balance of public expenditure from major to minor irrigation.[27] This is a complex issue and no generalizations can be made. Some evidence suggests that very big and very small schemes yield higher value added per rupee of investment than most minor irrigation schemes in between.[28] In any case the balance of major and minor schemes in any area will be mainly determined by constraints such as the terrain, extent of surface water, depth of water table, &c.

However, two general factors suggest that the change in favour of minor schemes is a sensible one. First, given the urgency of the agricultural problem, the emphasis should be placed on quick-yielding types of investment. Second, there should not be the co-ordination problems for minor irrigation that have hampered the major irrigation programme. If the new programme is to assist the development of private tubewells and wells, there is also more likelihood that the water will be used intensively instead of being spread evenly over the maximum acreage as in the case of the major public irrigation schemes in India (see pp. 170–2 below).

(d) The Link between Overheads and the Agricultural Programme

1. *Rural Roads.* Good road links between villages and urban markets and industrial centres are essential to ensure a supply of fertilizers, tools, and incentive goods to agriculturalists, and the movement of food and other agricultural produce to markets. The

[27] The distinction between major and minor schemes is based on the size of the financial costs of schemes. Minor schemes must cover a wide range of techniques (wells, tubewells, tanks, streams, &c.). This distinction between major and minor does draw attention to certain important differences in gestation periods, administrative problems of construction, and operation. But for allocation of expenditure more details are surely required.

[28] See NCAER, *Techno-Economic Survey of Maharashtra* (New Delhi, 1963).

development of village approach roads will speed up the movement of goods, reduce the possibility of damage to goods carried, and improve the dependability of transport, as well as reducing its costs.

India has the lowest mileage of road per cultivated acre in the world. Large areas have no access to roads at all. Only 11 per cent of the 646,000 villages are connected with the rest of the country by all-weather roads. One out of three villages is more than five miles from a dependable road connexion. The isolation of many villages impedes the spread of new attitudes and techniques as well as movements of physical goods.

Rural market roads are the responsibility of the State Government and, in the past, considerations of administration rather than of economic growth seem to have been pre-eminent in decisions about the construction or improvement of these roads.[29] Village approach roads (linking the market road network with villages) have in the past been left to the limited resources and efforts of local rural communities. Roads constructed have been largely unmetalled and inadequately maintained, and are usually impassable except in the dry season.

It is not clear from the planners' statements what emphasis is to be placed on rural road development. The Draft Outline says, 'Rural roads need to be given distinctly higher priority than in the past' (p. 301). But nothing is said about the allocation of funds for this purpose, strengthening of local bodies, where the effort is to be concentrated geographically, or what quality of roads are to be constructed.

States' expenditure on *all* roads is to rise from Rs 2,800 mn in the Third Plan to Rs 3,600 mn in the current plan period.[30] The allocation to rural roads appears to be Rs 650 mn, but no physical targets for rural roads are laid down. This appears an inadequate allocation, given the vital role of roads in stimulating a greater marketed supply of food.

The provision of an adequate all-India rural road network requires enormous resources and cannot be achieved in the next five years. Given the limited funds, it would be sensible for the State Governments to concentrate their efforts on areas where intensive

[29] *Final Report on Transport Policy*, p. 65.
[30] *4DO*, p. 73. In view of the rise of about 50 per cent in wholesale prices, this represents a reduction in real terms, unless considerable economies in road-building are possible.

agricultural development programmes are being undertaken or where new reserves of water and power have been made available. This approach is not indicated in the Draft Plan. Moreover it is not clear whether the Central Government will provide assistance (e.g. matching grants) to the States for rural road development.

A further issue not mentioned involves the choice between metalled and unmetalled roads. A given expenditure on the former will build fewer miles of road, but if unsurfaced roads are not passable in the monsoon, how effective can they be in opening up rural areas?[31]

2. *Rural Broadcasting.* Broadcasting is a service which should be effectively co-ordinated with the new agricultural programme. Does India make the fullest use of this powerful medium for instruction in better agriculture practices? The average all-India radio time devoted to rural audiences appears to be about 10 per cent, and many community radio receivers are out of order.

There is a case for stepping up the rural broadcasting effort and improving maintenance of village receivers. Lipton points out, however, that many States have only one transmitter covering wide variations of weather, soils, crops, and topography. Farm information is thus over-centralized, often useless, and possibly sometimes harmful. Maharashtra's twice-weekly 'Rural Farm Forum', a model in some respects, is relevant to any particular village perhaps one-tenth of the time. Nevertheless, more resources and personnel could be devoted to rural broadcasting. Should this not receive priority over the programme for strengthening the television centre at Delhi?

4. NEED FOR HIGHER RATES OF RETURN ON OVERHEAD CAPITAL

There is a new emphasis in the Draft Fourth Plan on the urgent need to run public overhead services on a commercial basis and raise rates of return. Management improvement, cost reductions, revised charges, and greater self-finance of investment are urged on railway, airline, and shipping corporations, state transport undertakings, port authorities, and electricity undertakings. For the first time, the principle is established that public utilities should earn a minimum

---

[31] Moreover, the savings in vehicle operation costs and speed of movement on adequately surfaced roads probably outweigh the extra road investment. J. M. Healey, *The Development of Social Overhead Capital in India* (London, 1965), pp. 73–78.

rate of return on capital employed. The rate suggested is 11–12 per cent, and reduction in costs rather than revision of charges is advocated to achieve this.[32]

The case for setting target rates of return has clearly been based on the view that the return on public services should approximate to that earned on capital in other sectors of the economy, especially those which supply similar services (e.g. railways and private road transport).

Up to 1964 most of the major public utilities (power, railways, ports, &c.) were operating at the limit of their capacity and therefore presumably in the zone of rising short-run marginal costs. Since most electricity undertakings have been running at a loss and railways have been earning only low rates of profit, it seems likely that charges have not covered marginal costs. In these conditions it can be argued that charges which reflect costs more closely will improve the use of aggregate resources following the profit-maximizing decisions of users of these services. Investors will take these 'real-cost' charges into account when deciding the appropriate technology for their plants (whether to use coal, or oil, or electricity), and also will take cost-determined transport charges into account when deciding the best location for their plants. With shortages of power and transport facilities, prices are a method of rationing these scarce services. Higher charges will help to limit the growth of demand for them, and hence the heavy drain on scarce capital and foreign exchange resources which are required to meet this demand in India. Further, higher profits on public undertakings will increase the resources for financing their heavy investment programmes. There is no obvious reason why the burden of finding these savings should be thrown on to the rest of the economy.

However, some implications of this policy must be noted. Public undertakings are urged to reduce their operating costs to achieve higher rates of return. But their new licence to raise charges may weaken the pressure on them to increase efficiency. Further, a

---

[32] *4DO*, pp. 1, 82–83, 86, 219, 230, 304. Railways are expected to finance 18 per cent of their current plan investment from their profits compared with about 6 per cent achieved in the 3rd Plan. Port authorities are also expected to finance nearly 30 per cent of their investment from their own earnings.

The Central Government has of course the power to implement this policy in undertakings under its control (e.g. railways), but the problem remains that it can only urge the State Governments to follow a commercial policy on their undertakings.

policy of higher rates of return on public projects could mean substantial increases in prices of public enterprises, since a large proportion of public sector output is consumed by the public sector itself. Thus thermal power stations will find their costs raised by higher costs of coal transport, while having to make a higher rate of return themselves. The same will be true for steel plants. Furthermore, some export costs could be substantially affected by higher charges for transport and power, and these exports might require extra subsidies.

Finally, the Indian economy since 1965 has entered a period of recession owing to two successive droughts and the low level of activity. This has given rise to excess capacity on railways and possibly in the power sector also. In this situation, which may well continue into 1968, not only will it prove very difficult to earn greater returns by increased charges but a pricing policy designed to do so will lead to less than optimum use of under-utilized capacity. The timing of the new policy, therefore, appears to be particularly unfortunate.

Railways

The higher rate of return for railways presumably reflects the rate of return capital would earn, or expect to earn, in the private sector, more particularly the rate of return in the private road transport industry which provides comparable services to railways. According to Lefeber and Chaudhuri, a 10 per cent yield, net of depreciation but before taxes, represents the *average* return on Indian enterprises in general, and road transport in particular. However, they estimate that the minimum *marginal* net rate of return expected by private investors approximates to 20 per cent, and this covers the road transport industry too.[33]

What has been the rate of return on railway capital in the past? In 1960–1 the average net rate of return was approximately 3·6 per cent.[34] Between 1960 and 1964 estimated net fixed investment was

[33] 'Transportation Policy in India', in P. N. Rosenstein-Rodan, ed., *Pricing and Fiscal Policies* (London, 1965), pp. 99–100. In all the above calculations depreciation is assumed at 4 per cent. This is probably a conservative estimate, given the rate of technological obsolescence of rolling stock for example. However, it seems to be the marginal depreciation rate allowed by Indian railways in 1960–4.

[34] Gross profits in 1960–1 were Rs 1,440 mn, the capital stock was valued at approximately Rs 19,000 mn and depreciation was assumed to be 4 per cent. (See Railway Board, *Report, 1961–2*, ch. 2, sect. A.)

Rs 9,750 mn while the addition to gross profits was Rs 720 mn. With depreciation assumed to be 4 per cent, this implies a marginal net rate of return of 3·8 per cent.[35] These figures for average and marginal yields on railway capital are well below those expected and earned in the private sector of the economy. Moreover, the above marginal yield for 1960–4 takes into account the substantial increases in rates for coal and other freight, especially over long distances, between 1961 and 1964.

Thus, if railways are to achieve even the stipulated minimum average rate of return, they must either reduce operating costs substantially, or raise charges more drastically for types of freight and passenger services in inelastic demand. They will certainly have to assess much more carefully the yields on new investment.[36]

The low rate of return on railway capital has been largely due to the railways' faulty rate structure in the past. This had discriminated in favour of low-value bulk freight, especially over long distances.[37] Charges for certain categories of low-value freight did not even cover operating costs. In general, the overhead costs of low-value freight were subsidized from charges on high-value freight.

This has obscured the real cost of transporting various types of freight. In the case of coal, for example, there has been no effective encouragement to the use of coal substitutes (e.g. fuel oils) in *existing* industrial plants and no incentive for *new* industrial capacity to be located nearer to coal fields or other sources of power. This may have assisted regional dispersal, but not economic allocation of resources.

Some steps have recently been taken to bring charges on low-value

[35] This is a crude estimate of the marginal rate of return and does not take into account lags in the yield on investment. Net fixed investment was derived from figures for gross investment by assuming that 25 per cent of rolling stock expenditure, 20 per cent of plant and machinery, 50 per cent of bridge expenditure, and the whole of track renewal, was for replacement. All other fixed investment was assumed to be net. (Railway Board; *Report*, ch. 1, sect. B; ch. 2, sect. A; ch. 5, sect. A.)

[36] There was quite a substantial amount of investment during the 1960–4 period in facilities which did not provide immediately, or even ultimately, for significant extra traffic movement. New lines cost Rs 1,710 mn; staff quarters and welfare and users' amenities cost Rs 560 mn. If these items are omitted, the marginal net yield becomes 7 per cent (1960–4).

[37] Freight with low value in relation to bulk includes coal, ores, sugar-cane, &c. High-value freight includes manufactures such as cotton, iron and steel, cement, &c. and also some industrial materials such as raw cotton, jute, and fuel oil. Rates were adjusted 'telescopically' (so that cost of transport of freight did not rise proportionally with the distance carried).

freight more into line with costs generally.[38] The demand for bulk movement of low-value freight is likely to be price-inelastic; road transport cannot offer as cheap or as convenient a service as railways, especially over long distances, and 70 per cent of total rail freight traffic is of this kind. It should therefore be possible for the railways to achieve a higher rate of return on capital by exploiting their advantage on bulk low-value freight.

There are probably greater difficulties in raising passenger fares. Although first-class fares appear to be subsidized from third-class revenues, there will be difficulty in raising first-class fares without inducing a substantial fall in demand, because they are very nearly as high as air fares. The demand for third-class travel is probably very price-elastic on most routes, but some increase in revenues should be possible by raising suburban fares.

The plan clearly expects a substantial increase in the railway surplus from cost reductions. It does not make clear where these are to come from. Some reduction in fuel costs and greater efficiency should result from greater dieselization and also from closed-sector train working.

Power

State electricity undertakings are also required to earn the stipulated return within the next three to five years.[39] The price of electricity is too low for a capital-intensive product with a high foreign exchange content, and there is evidence that the fertilizer industry, for example, would have been willing to pay much higher charges if it had been assured of adequate power supplies. It has blamed its low utilization of capacity on the frequent breakdown of power supplies.

[38] Rates were raised from 4–6 per cent on certain low-value freight in 1965, and in 1966 tapered rates for coal and coke were introduced. 1966 also saw a 3 per cent surcharge on all goods, and 10 per cent on passenger fares. Little information has been published on the costs of transporting specific types of freight. The railways have recently made efforts to estimate costs of this kind, although there are obvious difficulties in the imputation of common costs. In 1959–60 the average cost of hauling coal (including interest at 3½ per cent) was estimated at 3·85 n.p. per ton-mile on broad gauge railways in India. The average revenue per ton-mile of coal fell below this in 1959–60, but by 1964–5 was 5·13 n.p. Unless costs have risen very steeply it seems likely that in 1964–5 coal revenue covered its costs. However, coal transport on the metre gauge system, where costs are substantially higher, is still probably run at a loss. (See Healey, p. 41; Railway Board, *Reports*, Statistical App., Sect. 9.)

[39] *4DO*, p. 230.

There are also wide regional differences in electricity charges which do not appear to reflect similar differences in costs. However, a committee is currently investigating the possibility of standardizing power charges.

Two-part tariffs have been introduced for industry recently, to try to spread the power load more evenly over the day, and to encourage the use of electricity at night. Since shift working should not add substantially to labour costs in the Indian economy (as it might in a labour-scarce economy) there should be considerable scope for improved utilization of capacity and hence higher returns from this policy in the long run.

Higher returns on investment should also be possible from the Fourth Plan policy of greater interconnexion and integration of power systems. This raises utilization of generating capacity by saving standby capacity, matching diverse load patterns, and permitting larger generating units. Although progress in laying interconnecting lines appears to have been slow in the Third Plan, the Draft Fourth Plan states that work on interconnexion will proceed with greater vigour in the next five years. The ratio of planned expenditure on transmission to expenditure on generation is to be 4:5 in the Draft Fourth Plan, compared to 1:2 in the Third Plan.[40]

Irrigation

The Draft Plan does not require any minimum rate of return from irrigation projects, but it stresses that projects are not giving adequate financial returns and recommends an upward revision in water rates. It is suggested that water rates be fixed at 25 per cent to 40 per cent of the additional net benefit from an irrigated crop.[41]

Most irrigation projects run at a loss, and in some cases operating costs are not covered. One reason for this is presumably the under-utilization of capacity. This is greatest on the newer projects, which also keep down water charges so as to promote the use of water newly made available. There is little justification, however, for long-established projects, where irrigation capacity is fully used, basing their depreciation and interest charges on historic cost, instead of covering their current costs.[42]

---

[40] *3rd Plan*, p. 401. *4DO*, p. 227.   [41] Ibid, p. 220.
[42] See *Combined Revenue & Finance Accounts of Central & State Governments* (annual), passim; Healey, pp. 31–37.

Further, water rates in most States have not kept pace with the increase in the value of crops grown. Since the majority of State politicians represent rural areas and many are landowners, there is not likely to be general support for higher water charges in State legislatures. Moreover, resistance to raising water rates is also likely to result from the cultivators' feeling that the money collected would be spent on urban projects that would not benefit the local community. Objections to higher charges are likely to be weaker if the revenues are spent locally. In Madras, water charges are now included as part of the local rather than the State taxation system. These revenues are used for the development of local amenities such as schools and roads, and thus seem to cause little resentment: indeed, in some areas, water rates have been raised by 150 to 200 per cent. This policy might be extended.

A third aspect of policy, which has a bearing on both the real and the financial returns from irrigation, is the intensity with which available water is used (see also pp. 160–2). The planners point out that 'the existing irrigation practice in many parts of the country is to apply water thinly in order to extend the benefits of irrigation and afford protection against drought to as large an area as feasible. This does not serve the needs of intensive agriculture for securing high yields per acre'. It adds 'there is a need for re-orientation of this policy', but does not state categorically that there *will* be such a re-orientation.[43]

A change from a 'drought protection' policy to one which concentrates water supplied on high-yielding areas would clearly raise the real return on irrigation investment and reduce salination at the same time. Higher financial revenues should also result, and it would be possible to subsidize or rehabilitate any families who were badly affected by reduced water supplies in the low-yield areas.

On the approach to *new* investment little is said in the Draft Fourth Plan. Cost-benefit studies are recommended before choosing between new roads and rail in a particular area. There is no reference to such an approach to irrigation projects, ports, broadcasting, or telecommunications. Yet there is a strong case for assessing the marginal social productivity of investment more carefully, especially in irrigation where past project reports have been inadequately prepared, and where financial criteria have been adopted for deciding irrigation priorities.[44]

[43] *4DO*, p. 173.
[44] See NCAER, *Criteria for Fixation of Water Rates and Selection of Irrigation Projects* (1959); Healey, pp. 99–101.

One of the main drawbacks of this technique is the difficulty of anticipating all the future benefits likely to arise from such a scheme. This, however, is not an argument against undertaking such studies. Given the substantial autonomy of the States in irrigation, it is unlikely that a cost-benefit approach to irrigation investment could equalize returns on marginal irrigation expenditure among States. Within each State, however, a more rational choice of projects would be possible; cost-benefit is particularly effective for choosing among techniques for achieving a given objective, e.g. among types of minor irrigation to achieve a given water supply.

5. CONCLUSION

The main themes of the foregoing discussion may be summed up as follows:

1. The need to ensure adequate overhead capacity is particularly crucial because shortfalls in these facilities will cause widespread disruption of production in the whole economy. This arises from the difficulty of importing most overhead services.

2. Co-ordinated development, in particular of transport facilities, is required so that needs are met at minimum cost. The programme of agricultural development should be complemented by adequate provision of rural roads and rural broadcasting.

3. Higher rates of return are required on overhead capital, so as to ensure that charges approximate more closely to costs, and hence to permit more socially rational investment decisions in other sectors of the economy.

6

The Case of Energy Investment

E. A. G. ROBINSON

1. THE GROWTH OF DEMAND

ANY justification for devoting a large proportion of India's available investment resources to infrastructure, and particularly to energy, must rest primarily on the necessity for such investment, if Indian economic and industrial development is to reach the designed levels. The justification of the energy investment has recently been examined by the Indian Energy Survey Committee[1] of which I have been a member.

What quickly emerged from the initial examination of the problem was that Indian development had, until recently, been very seriously held up by shortages of energy. In the case of coal, the principal problem was, until lately, inadequate transport facilities, due to shortages of locomotives and rolling stock. These difficulties have now been largely removed. The difficulties of oil supplies have derived from India's limited foreign resources and the limitations of indigenous oil hitherto available.

In the case of electricity supplies the problems are much more complex. The consumption of electricity, as in most countries, has been growing rapidly. From 1958/9 to 1962/3 it increased on average by 14·1 per cent per annum. But the growth of actual consumption has been considerably less than the growth of demand. Not only have there been very numerous occasions of break-down of supplies and load-shedding, but it has been impossible to connect numerous applicants to the system at all. For others, connexion has been conditional on very tight restrictions on amounts and time of load. Businessmen in Calcutta, Bombay, and other large cities reported that much-needed small-scale developments were being frustrated for lack of possible electricity connexions.

[1] See Energy Survey Committee, *Report* (Govt. of India Press, 1965).

173

Until lately India's electricity system has also been very inadequate to the needs of an industrializing country in other respects. It would, indeed, have been misleading to describe it as a system at all. It began, as in all countries, with small isolated stations in the bigger towns, mostly owned by private companies at first. Despite rapid progress after independence, electricity has continued to be provided by numerous small stations, many very small and very old, obsolete by modern standards, operating at low fuel efficiency and inadequately interconnected. Of just under 800 stations at the end of 1961/2, only 29 were of more than 50 MW installed capacity; of 2,741 generating sets in service, only 16 were at or above 50 MW capacity, the minimum size that one would ordinarily think of installing to-day.

It is less easy to indicate statistically the inadequacies of the distribution system. Inadequate interconnexion among local systems meant that a shortage in one area could not be made good by spare power from another. Without interconnexion, there was a need to hold excessive total reserves of capacity. In the major cities, particularly Calcutta, Bombay, and Delhi, rapid population growth had meant that increasing loads had been met by an endless series of improvisations which left the distribution systems very seriously overloaded and in constant danger of breakdown.

2. THE INDIAN ENERGY SURVEY COMMITTEE

These deficiencies had, of course, been recognized by the responsible officials, both at the Centre in the Ministry of Irrigation and Power, and the Central Water and Power Commission, and in the various State Electricity Boards; and investment plans had been drawn up to meet the deficiencies. The size of these plans, and of the consequent demands for aid to meet them, led to the setting up in 1962 of the Indian Energy Survey Committee to examine them critically. The Committee, composed of eighteen Indian members and associates and four foreign members, made a very full examination of all the problems involved and signed its final report in 1965.

It was the primary task of the Committee to see how far the estimates of future demands for energy in all various forms, including electricity, were realistic. First it needed statistical evidence of past performance sufficiently accurate to provide a bench-mark for the future. Having done this, the Committee made its own estimates of future energy requirements on three alternative assumptions of possible rates of Indian economic growth over the plan periods 1965/6 to 1970/1, 1970/1 to 1975/6, and 1975/6 to 1980/1. The Draft Fourth Plan corresponds most nearly with the second assumption, a 6 per cent growth rate of gross national product. Since the projections made for the Committee were based on specific assumed outputs in each major sector of the economy and each main industry, it is not difficult to adjust (as I have done) the energy estimates made by the Committee to the Draft Plan estimates in specific sectors.

In 1960/61 the Committee estimated the total primary energy consumption of India to have been 242 mn tons of coal equivalent, 96 mn tons from commercial fuels (coal, oil, and hydro power), and 146 mn tons from non-commercial fuels (principally firewood, but including also cow-dung and vegetable wastes). To reach the Draft Fourth Plan's targets for 1970/71, on the basis of the specific consumptions per unit of output assumed in the studies made by the Committee, the total primary consumption would grow to 403 mn tons of coal equivalent, including 220 mn tons in commercial fuels. The growth of the gross generation of electricity required would be from the 20.15 TWh of 1960/1 to about 82 TWh in 1970/1, involving an installed capacity of a little under 20 GW.[2]

If one looks a further plan period ahead to 1975/6, for which much of the investment will need to be planned and started in the present plan period, the estimated primary consumption is expected to grow to 550–600 mn tons of coal equivalent, of which about 350–400 mn tons would be in commercial fuels. The gross generation of electricity required is estimated to reach 125–150 TWh, involving an installed capacity in 1975/6 of about 29–34 GW.

These estimates are very close to those now incorporated in the Draft Outline and in the Fourth Plan Material and Financial Balances.[3]

3. REGIONAL PROBLEMS

These overall national estimates must of course be reconciled with the estimates by States of the growth of demands for energy in general and electricity in particular. In the field of electricity this is

---

[2] TWh (TeraWatthours) = 1,000 GW.; GW (GigaWatt) = 1,000 MW; MW (MegaWatt) = 1,000 KW.
[3] See *4DO*, p. 226, and *MFB*, p. 49.

now the responsibility of the Electric Power Survey, set up in 1962 as one of the earliest outcomes of the work of the Committee. Its task is to consider the annual development proposals of the State Boards, to examine critically the demand assumptions, and to see how far the proposals are on the one hand justified and on the other hand adequate in the light of what is known about the actual growth of demand and the construction of new undertakings requiring electricity. While some States have tended in the early stages to overestimate demand, experience has been accumulating of a careful and strictly realistic watch over the timing as well as the planning of all developments.

In the earlier stages of electricity development there was inadequate investment in interconnexion, particularly between separated systems in different States. And because electricity development was primarily a State responsibility, there was initially undue reluctance to depend on uncertain supplies from a neighbouring State, and an excessive desire to possess within the control of each State Board adequate reserve of capacity for all emergencies. In the past few years much better interconnexion has been provided, and it is now generally possible for one State Board to help another in such emergencies as result from shortage of rainfall and interruption of hydro supplies. But on a wider scale such joint planning between States has been encouraged by the establishment of regions for the combined planning of all electricity development. This is particularly important, both where it is being attempted to incorporate large nuclear stations into the system and to give them adequate night load to keep them on a high plant factor, and also where it is being attempted to make use of waste- and by-product coals near the mines and the coke-oven washeries for the low cost generation of electricity and its transmission over long distances to areas of consumption in other States.

4. RURAL ELECTRIFICATION

Rural electrification, in India as in most countries, is not a strictly economic activity and, as the Survey commented, 'has indeed many of the characteristics of a social service'. Only some 4,500 'places' in India—well under 1 per cent—have populations of over 5,000. They house under 18 per cent of the population. It was hoped that, by the end of the Third Plan, all of these, and some 41,000 smaller 'places' would have electricity. About 68 per cent of the population live in 'places' with a population of less than 2,000. To most such 'places' the supply of electricity is in the strict sense uneconomic. The main elements of the load in these rural areas are irrigation pumping; small industrial purposes such as processing industries associated with agriculture; the provision of drinking water supply; and street lighting. The domestic lighting load is in most cases negligible. The revenue seldom covers a minimum return on the cost of the lines and transformers required, apart from the cost of generation.

Even if one is prepared to assume a high shadow price for marginal food production, it is very doubtful whether, on a purely economic basis, it is in the national interest to devote considerably increased resources to rural electrification rather than to the installation of diesel-engined pumps. Such resources as are available for the development of electricity can more economically and more profitably be used to expand the still inadequate supplies for industrial development in the urban areas, and to improve the dangerously overloaded distribution systems of many of the cities.

The contribution of rural electrification to national development is much more intangible and non-economic: a matter of welfare and of a psychological feeling that the rural areas as well as the great cities are benefiting from the modernization of the economy. But if one assumes that it is right to make such limited contribution as India can afford to welfare, it is obviously best to make it where it will bear most fruit. In the past year the criterion that has been adopted for the electrification of a village or a group of villages has been that a sufficient number of tube-wells or other wells for irrigation purposes are available to be provided with electricity. This is clearly a move in the right direction. But it is an over-simplification to suggest that, wherever electricity might be used for irrigation purposes, it is only maladministration that fails to supply it.

5. PRICING OF ELECTRICITY

John Healey's chapter stresses the importance of ensuring that the prices charged for energy cover the full costs of generation and distribution. With that I entirely agree. In fact, however, partly as the result of the work of the Energy Committee, State Electricity Boards were instructed in 1963 that prices should be based on the assumption that a return of 11 per cent should be earned on invested capital, and have been in process of revising their prices on that basis.[4] The justification of this was two-fold. In the first place, it represented approximately the opportunity-cost of the capital that would be employed. Industrial capital, at somewhat greater risk, earns around 15 per cent. In the second place, it is calculated that in this way the State Boards will be able to finance from their internal savings about half the capital costs of future developments, and will have to depend only for the other half on the limited resources of the Indian capital market. Those are to my mind more convincing arguments for higher prices than had ruled previously.

If Dr Healey has in mind that the higher prices will significantly reduce consumption, I am more doubtful whether he is right. For the majority of consumption of electricity (about 70 per cent) is industrial, and in most cases energy costs represent only about 2–3 per cent of total industrial costs, so that the demand does not in consequence have a high price-elasticity.

Nor am I convinced that a major contribution to economy of capacity can be secured by higher peak-load charges and more encouragement to shift working. With the objective, of course, I agree, and the Committee urged a reconsideration of charges along these lines. But shortage of capacity has meant that more direct pressure has already been put on all large consumers to spread their load over the twenty-four hours, and limitations of acceptable load by day have already meant that most of these large consumers are working a night shift of their more energy-intensive operations.

6. CHOICE OF TECHNIQUES IN ELECTRICITY GENERATION

The choice of techniques for generating electricity is a subject about which economists, in my view, very frequently fall into error. There is in practice much less freedom of choice than is often supposed. There are few countries in a position to choose between a system based wholly on hydro-electricity and a system based wholly on thermal or nuclear generation: India is not one of them. Apart from a small area of North India, hydro potential is nowhere adequate to carry the full load twelve months in the year. There are limited river flows and amounts of water that can be impounded. Moreover, the hydro developments are almost always dual-purpose; the release of water has to be related to the needs of agriculture at

[4] See also pp. 165–6.

least as much as to those of electricity consumers. In practice, except in the small area in the north, hydro must everywhere be combined with, and backed up by, thermal or nuclear generation. It then becomes a problem of how hydro and thermal or nuclear generation can best be integrated into a system. This is a subject to which the Committee gave close and detailed attention.[5]

At all load factors hydro is cheaper than thermal or nuclear generation, unless there are waste coals available (as there may be in limited amounts in particular areas) at zero cost or somewhere near to it. But at the low load factors (30 per cent or thereabouts) at which peak load has to be met, hydro generation is incomparably cheaper than any alternative. The cheapest provision for peak load is to build into a dam system the additional penstocks, turbines, and generators to use the available water intermittently in large volume on peak load. This is the most efficient way of using hydro, provided that all annually available water is utilized for generation, including of course, the water which must be released for irrigation purposes at certain fixed times of year. The most efficient use of the thermal or nuclear plant is to use it on 75 per cent plant factor, or better, on the base load. In almost all parts of India, therefore, that is the now accepted strategy.

How, then, should one plan thermal and nuclear power? The problem is complicated by the fact that coal is found only in certain limited areas (there is scarcely any coal west of a line from Delhi to Cape Cormorin). There are, moreover, large prospective tonnages of by-product coals from the coke-oven washeries; but all coking coal is in the Bengal-Bihar coalfields, and the washeries are there, or near the steelworks. The by-product coals have a high ash content and are correspondingly expensive to transport. The Committee made a very thorough analysis of the relative costs of long-distance transmission of electricity and coal haulage. At distances up to about 800–1000 km, transmission at very high voltages and of large amounts of power is more economical than present methods of rail transport, but closed-circuit train operation is fractionally cheaper, unless the amounts to be transmitted are very large.[6]

Nuclear energy provides a more difficult problem. On the one hand the conditions of India are very different from those of most European countries. The distances from Calcutta (in the neighbourhood

---

[5] See Energy Survey, *Report*, paras 340–59 and Tables 138–9.
[6] Ibid. paras 352–67.

of the main coalfield) to Bombay and Madras are 1,450 and 1,500 km respectively. Coal costs about Rs 25 at pithead, but about Rs 55 at the most distant coal-using stations. On the other hand the use of heavy oil, though possible in small amounts near coastal refineries, cannot be extended greatly because of foreign exchange limitations. At 75 per cent plant factor, nuclear power is expected to be appreciably more economic than thermal power in the areas of high-cost coal:[7] it is not a mere prestige extravagance, and nuclear developments in the areas chosen so far are not foolish. But longer term expansions of nuclear power will necessarily depend on the solution of the technical problems of using thorium, since India is not well-endowed with uranium but plentifully supplied with the former.

7. THE IMPORTANCE OF ACCURATE PLANNING

Any attempt to plan energy in India quickly reveals two things. First, one cannot have industrial development without an adequate infrastructure. What was said in this note about energy supplies could be said with equal force about the necessity for an adequate transport system to move food, materials, and finished goods.

But second, and equally important, the cost of infrastructure investment is high. Excess may swallow up the resources needed for the very industrial investment that it is primarily designed to assist and encourage. In the case of energy investment, the Committee's estimates were that it would involve an annual expenditure rising from about Rs 6,500 mn in 1966/7 to about Rs 7,500 mn in 1970/1, and representing about 13 per cent of all investment of the period. It was expected that by 1980/1 yearly energy investment would have risen to some Rs 14,500 mn, representing, however, about 11 per cent of all investment. These are formidable figures.

Evidently no country in India's position can afford to invest excessively in infrastructure. On the other hand the risks of under-investment and over-investment are asymmetric. Even slight under-investment saves infrastructure at the cost of frustrating other development through inability to organize production, or at the cost of such interruptions of production as are not unknown in the United Kingdom, and have been one of the normal features of life in India, as in many developing countries. The losses resulting from such shortages are considerably larger than the marginal losses from

[7] Ibid. Table 139a.

slightly excessive infrastructure. But considerably excessive infrastructure investment, based on guesses of future demand that will never be realized, can force a nation in India's position into policies of import restriction, penal interest rates, and other deflationary measures which will equally reduce the industrial output.

It is tempting to argue that, in practice, the industrial development will be less than the planners suppose, and to reduce the planned growth of electricity demand (and the proposed construction of capacity) to allow for this. This argument, however, assumes that the shortfalls of all the electricity-using industries will be as calculated, while those in electricity supply will be wholly absent. Experience does not justify such an assumption. Delays in completion of electric plant and equipment have been as great or greater than those in most industrial enterprises, and have in most cases derived from the same causes. Thus, while there is an unanswerably strong case for brutally realistic planning over the whole field, there is real danger in a mixture of unrealistic and realistic planning—realistic about other people, unrealistic about yourself.

For all these reasons it is most important to guess the future demands and the dates of completion of new capacity as nearly right as is possible. In the case of energy investment, this is the more difficult because the period of gestation of much energy investment is of the order of seven to ten years, from the first stages of planning the project to the first actual delivery of energy. The task of the planner is, I would suggest, not unlike that of William Tell. It is of the essence of his task that he shall hit the apple. But, if error is to be made, it is better that he should be a fraction high than a fraction low.

TABLE 1

Estimates of Demands for Energy 1970–1
(million tonnes of coal replacement)

	1960–1 actual	*1970–1 5% growth*	*1970–1 6% growth*	*1970–1 7% growth*	*1970–1 adjusted to Draft Fourth Plan*
Transport	30·7	55·3	61·8	71·7	56·9
Industry	39·6	84·7	97·5	119·8	101·4
Domestic	163·3	225·0	225·0	225·0	225·0
Agriculture	3·4	9·7	9·7	9·7	9·7
Others	2·4	4·2	4·2	4·2	4·2
Energy Sector	3·1	5·1	6·1	8·2	5·5
Total all Fuels	242·5	384·0	404·3	438·6	402·7
Total Commercial Fuels	96·4	201·3	221·6	255·9	220·0
Total Non-Commercial Fuels	146·1	182·7	182·7	182·7	182·7

Notes: (*a*) The year 1960–1 and the estimates based on 5 per cent, 6 per cent, and 7 per cent growth of national incomes are taken from the Energy Survey of India Committee, *Report*, Table 85.

(*b*) The adjustments to the basis of the Draft Fourth Plan have been made by the present author, using the data available to the Energy Survey Committee.

(*c*) The units of coal replacement used in the Survey express the amounts of coal needed to substitute other forms of fuel, taking account of the efficiencies involved in typical cases of substitution.

TABLE 2

Estimates of Demand for Electricity 1970–1

	1960–1 actual	*1970–1 5% growth*	*1970–1 6% growth*	*1970–1 7% growth*	*1970–1 adjusted to Draft Fourth Plan*
Final consumption (TWh)	16·9	59·0	64·7	74·0	69·0
Gross generation (TWh)	20·2	69·7	76·6	88·3	81·8
Gross generating capacity (GW.)	5·6	18·4	19·2	21·4	19·9
Coal used for generation of electricity (m. tonnes)	9·1	16·5	19·0	24·4	22·7

Notes: (*a*) Figures for 1960–1 and estimates for 1970–1 from the Energy Survey of India Committee, *Report* Tables 148, 150, and 153.

(*b*) Adjustments to Draft Fourth Plan made by the author, using the methods employed by the Survey.

TABLE 3

Relations of Estimated Gross Investment in Energy to Estimates of National Income and Total Gross Investment
(Rs mn are 1963–4 prices)

	1960–1	*1970–1*	*1975–6*	*1980–1*
Estimated National Income	147,000	276,000	386,000	540,000
Estimated Total of Gross Investment	17,500	59,000	86,000	127,000
Estimated Gross Investment in Energy	—	7,550	10,500	14,400
Ratio of Investment in Energy to All Investment (%)	—	12·8	12·2	11·3

Note: These calculations, taken from Table 165 of the Energy Survey *Report*, are based on the 7% rate of growth assumed in the plan then under consideration. Adjustments to the scale of the Draft Fourth Plan would probably reduce the 1970–1 estimates by between 10% and 15%, but would not greatly change the final ratio.

The Human Factor

7

Investment in Human Capital*

DAVID OVENS

1. THE ROLE OF EDUCATION AND HEALTH IN ECONOMIC GROWTH

To describe people as 'human capital' is to adopt a restrictive economic concept, which emphasises the material aspects of life, to the exclusion of the cultural and spiritual. But in a country which has a material standard of living as low as India's, the emphasis on strictly economic objectives is justified. When many are hungry, the cost of any economic sacrifice made in pursuit of other aims is very high.

As a strictly economic concept, 'human capital' defines people as capital assets which yield a stream of economic benefits over their working lives. Expenditure on education and health can be regarded as an investment made to improve the quality and adaptability of these capital assets, to make them more productive and, in some cases, to lengthen their working lives. This is the 'investment in human capital', which is justified, from a strictly economic point of view, if it earns an economic return comparable to the return earned on physical investment in other sectors of the economy.

It is notoriously difficult to estimate even the direct economic benefits of investment in education and health, and more difficult still to measure its indirect effects. For the yield on educational and health expenditure is dependent on complementary investments made in other sectors of the economy; and improved performance in these other sectors may equally be regarded as an 'external benefit' derived from investment in education and health. Further

* I gratefully acknowledge the help given me by Paul Streeten and Michael Lipton, who commented extensively on an earlier draft of this chapter; and I am especially indebted to Richard Layard and Andrew Shonfield for their help in preparing it for publication.

187

complications arise when part of the expenditure on social services is made with political and social objectives in mind: securing greater equality of educational opportunity; achieving a broadly literate and numerate electorate; forging a national culture and encouraging the political and social integration of the country; raising health standards for all—for the elderly as well as for the working population. The achievement of these political and social aims will yield incidental economic benefits, of course. But when resources are severely limited, as are the resources available to implement the Fourth Plan, any expenditure on non-economic objectives reduces the resources available for the direct promotion of economic growth. How big an economic sacrifice is being made?

No country can claim to have made an accurate or comprehensive assessment of the relative costs and benefits of all its education and health programmes. It would therefore be unfair to criticize Indian planners for their failure to employ techniques of economic analysis which have yet to prove their worth in this field elsewhere. But in the absence of any attempt to calculate these costs and benefits it is very hard to assess the realism of the Draft Fourth Plan. The argument of this chapter is that, despite all the known difficulties, an attempt should be made to apply cost-benefit analysis to investment in education and health in India, for three reasons: first, even the *attempt* to measure the social return on particular investments in the social services would help to clarify the planners' objectives, and reveal more of the implications of alternative policies; second, while the margin of error will remain uncomfortably wide, it should be possible to indicate areas where a change of emphasis—more expenditure here and less there—would have a beneficial effect; and, third, the broad order of magnitude of the economic sacrifices made in the pursuit of non-economic aims may be more widely appreciated. The kind of framework needed for a rigorous assessment of costs and benefits is discussed, in relation to education, in an Appendix to this chapter. It is too complex, however, to apply to the Draft Fourth Plan. Instead, we can ask a series of questions, which will form the theme of this chapter:

(1) What relative priorities, between education, health, and other sectors, and within the education and health sectors, are implied by the financial provisions of the Plan?

(2) How has the emphasis given to each head of expenditure on education and health been justified in the Plan—by qualitative

arguments about the aims to be achieved, if not in quantitative economic terms?

(3) How far are these aims, which are held to justify the expenditure, likely to be achieved *in practice*, through the expenditure of the money provided in the Plan budget?

(4) In the light of this probable performance, can we do anything to rectify the omission from the Plan of any calculation of relative costs and benefits? Or are the conceptual and practical difficulties of calculating the rate of return on investment in education and health so great as to invalidate any findings we might reach?

(5) Within the margins of error to which rate of return calculations in the social services are subject, what can we conclude about the relative priorities that have actually been accorded in the Plan to the education and health sectors, and to the various types of expenditure within those sectors? Is India devoting too small (or too great) a share of its limited resources to education and health? And within the social services, is the money being spent on the right objectives?

2. PRIORITIES IMPLIED BY THE FINANCIAL PROVISIONS OF THE PLAN

Some indication of the relative priorities accorded by the Planning Commission to education and health, in relation to the rest of the public sector outlay on the Plan, can be obtained from the record of actual expenditure during the first three five-year plans, and from the several proposals which culminated in the Draft Fourth Plan.

The figures in Table 1 can be used as an illustration (albeit an imperfect one) of the *relative* priorities accorded to education and health in the plans, but not of the absolute changes in the real resources devoted to education and health from one plan to the next. Wholesale prices rose by 36 per cent[1] during the Third Plan period alone, so the Draft Fourth Plan outlay, expressed in June 1966 prices, cannot be directly compared with the expenditure made during the Third Plan between 1961 and 1966 at current prices. Even the relative priorities would be changed, to some extent, if prices in the health and education sectors rose less sharply than prices in the rest of the economy.

[1] *4DO*, p. 4.

TABLE 1

Draft Fourth Plan Outlay on Education and Health
(*Rs mn*)

	Actual Expenditure in Earlier Plan Periods			Proposed Outlay in Fourth Plan		
	1st Plan at Current 1951–6 Prices	*2nd Plan at Current 1956–61 Prices*	*3rd Plan at Current 1961–6 Prices*	*Oct. 1964 Memorandum in 1963/4 Prices*	*Sept. 1965 Memorandum in 1963/4 Prices*	*Aug. 1966 Draft Outline in June 1966 Prices*
Education & Training						
General education	1,330	208	5,960	14,000	10,080	9,570
Technical education	200	350			2,520	2,530
Craftsman training		130	570	1,300	1,300	1,300
Total Education & Training (Excluding medical education)	1,530	2,560	6,530	15,300	13,900	13,400
Health						
Family planning	7	30	270	950	950	950*
Drinking water supply & sanitation	490	760	3,300	3,400	3,710	3,730
Other health (including medical education)	903	1,460		6,550	4,830	4,920
Total Health (Including medical education)	1,400	2,250	3,570	10,900	9,490	9,600
Total Plan Outlay (Public sector)	19,600	46,000	86,300	156,200	145,000	160,000
Percentage of total outlay devoted to education	7·8	5·6	7·6	9·8	9·6	8·4
Percentage of total outlay devoted to health	7·1	4·8	4·1	7·0	6·5	6·0

* The proposed outlay on the family planning programme was subsequently increased to Rs 2,290 mn. If this increase is achieved within the same total plan outlay, but without cutting back other health programmes, the total provision for health rises to Rs 10,940 mn, or 6·8% of total plan outlay of Rs 160,000 mn.

Source: Cols. 1 & 2, 3rd Five Year Plan, pp. 32, 576–7, 651; *Col. 3, 4DO*, p. 43; Memo. on the 4th Five Year Plan, Oct. 1964, p. 67; *Col. 4*, Memo. on the 4th Five Year Plan pp. 11, 67, 73; *Col. 5:* Sept. 1965 Memo.; *Col. 6: 4DO*, pp. xii, 325, 338, 347.

The boundary between investment in human capital and other forms of investment is arbitrary. In this chapter the boundary has been drawn fairly restrictively, by defining investment in human capital as comprising the expenditure sanctioned in the Plan under five budget headings: family planning; education; the training of craftsmen; health; drinking water supply and sanitation. The training of craftsmen in government institutions can be regarded as an extension of their formal education; and the provisions for pure drinking water and sanitation can be included as an integral part of the public health programme. Family planning has been included as a special case: expenditure made to restrict the growth in the stock of human capital, in order that more resources may be devoted to raising its quality and improving its performance.

The total provision in the period 1966–70 for education and health is significantly greater than that shown in Table 1, because additional provision for education and health is made in other plan programmes. Out of Rs 1,800 mn provided for the promotion of the welfare of scheduled castes, scheduled tribes, and other backward classes, no less than Rs 600 mn is provided for their education—and this is not included in the education budget. Additional provision for education, training, and health is made in the programmes for agriculture, community development, and co-operation; for the development of hill areas and special areas; for the rehabilitation of refugees; and in several other plan programmes. A more elastic definition of expenditure on health would include Rs 500 mn spent on social welfare; and provisions made for housing and other programmes which have a direct bearing on health.

3. TYPES OF COST

The concept of 'investment', when applied to human capital, is a very broad one. For the expenditure made on education, health, and family planning is a combination of capital investment (in buildings, equipment) and running expenses which recur year after year (on the salaries of teachers, doctors, and nurses, for example, and on materials consumed). The return on this investment in human capital, thus broadly defined, can in principle be compared with the return on investment in other sectors of the economy—using either internal rates of return or the net present value of the cost and benefit streams at given interest rates. It would be quite logical to compare the internal rate of return on investment in a college producing engineers, or in a training institute producing skilled craftsmen, with the internal rate of return on investment in a factory making machine tools—all three, in a sense, capital goods industries. In each case the cost stream would include both the initial capital investment in buildings, plant, and machinery, and the operating costs of materials and labour over the life of factory (or teachers' and instructors' salaries over the life of the institution). The costs of education would also include, however, the value of the product of an untrained or less educated worker, which the economy loses during the period of his education or training.

The calculation of the benefits stream is more complex. For the machine tools factory, one might assume a set of ex-factory prices, which would represent the capitalized value of the future stream of services rendered by each machine tool produced. For the engineering college or training institute, the corresponding benefits stream would be the capitalized value of the future services rendered by each annual batch of trained engineers or craftsmen—to the extent that the value of these services could be attributed to their education or training alone. As a first approximation of this incremental value of an engineering training one could estimate the future lifetime earnings of each annual batch of trained engineers and deduct from it an estimate of the future lifetime earnings of an equivalent batch of workers who had been educated only up to the entry standard of the engineering colleges. The difference between the two earnings streams, adjusted for any differences in earnings attributable to factors other than education, would represent the benefits attributable to investment in education.

The distinction between capital investment and current outlay is very important, because the element of capital investment in the total plan expenditure on education, health, and family planning is very low, and the element of labour costs (particularly the cost of qualified people) relatively high, compared with most other programmes in the Plan. In some health programmes, such as the provision of water supply, the capital element is itself largely composed of labour costs incurred in construction—in this case consisting mainly of unskilled labour. Therefore if we attempt to compare the return on the current Plan expenditure on education or health with the return on Plan expenditure on other sectors, such as heavy industry, we shall not be comparing alternative uses of similar

resources. We may be comparing the returns on alternative employment of scarce *financial* resources (if we assume that government
revenue from taxation or borrowing is available for either capital
investment or current outlay). But we shall not be comparing the
returns on alternative employment of the same scarce *physical*
resources. Our comparison will not be valid unless *all* factors of
production, including capital equipment, foreign exchange, and
labour are priced at their social opportunity cost.

The significance of this proviso can be seen clearly from the outlays
proposed in the Draft Fourth Plan. Of the total expenditure under
the education budget, less than 40 per cent is capital investment in
buildings and equipment, and over 60 per cent is current outlay.[2]
The provision for water supply and sanitation is entirely on capital
account, although the resource composition of that investment is
very different from that of capital investment in manufacturing
industry or other sectors which require expensive imported equipment. In the other health programmes, less than 42 per cent is
capital investment on buildings and equipment. Education and
health expenditure together accounts for nearly Rs 40,000 mn out
of the total plan outlay of Rs 160,000 mn in the public sector.[2]
And of the remaining Rs 120,000 mn less than 10 per cent is current
expenditure (mostly in agriculture and community development).

Education and health outlays also have a relatively low foreign
exchange content—5 per cent for education, and less than 7 per cent
for health and water supply, compared to over 36 per cent in the
rest of the Plan (when calculated at post-devaluation exchange rates).[3]
Only if the prices of capital, labour, and foreign exchange correctly
reflected the social opportunity cost of the resources used could these
wide disparities in import content, capital intensity, composition of
capital, and requirements for trained manpower and unskilled labour
be taken adequately into account in comparing the true cost of the
expenditure made in education and health, with that incurred in
other sectors. With costs adjusted to reflect the true scarcity of the
resources used, the return on investment in education and health
would be seen to be much higher in relation to the return on investment in other sectors.

When the Indian rupee was devalued in June 1966, thus bringing
the rupee equivalent of the foreign exchange cost closer to the social
opportunity cost of foreign exchange, the rupee cost of the same

[2] *4DO*, p. 41.   [3] Ibid.   [4] *MFB*, p. 132.

physical expenditure on education rose by only Rs 220 mn, or less than 2 per cent; and the rupee cost of the health and water supply programmes rose by only Rs 240 mn, or just over 2 per cent. But the rupee cost of the same physical expenditure in the rest of the Plan rose by Rs 13,910 mn, or over 11 per cent, thus reducing the relative share of education and health in the total financial outlay. The apparent reduction in the relative priority assigned to health and education as between the September 1965 proposals and the Draft Outline, is therefore merely a reflection of the change in the exchange rate. Similarly, if the cost of capital were increased to reflect its social opportunity cost, then as education and health expenditure has a relatively low capital content compared with the rest of the plan outlay, the real share of education and health in the total Plan outlay would be seen to be even lower. To put it another way, in order to maintain the *apparent* priority accorded to education and health in 1965 (before devaluation), while counting both foreign exchange and capital at social opportunity cost, the physical expenditure on education and health would have had to be sharply increased, relatively to expenditure in other sectors.

The share of total plan outlay allotted to education and health is not, in any case, a true indication of the relative priority accorded to education and health, either by the Indian Government, or by Indian society as a whole. The Plan provides for the establishment of new institutions, and for the expansion or improvement of existing facilities. But it excludes the much larger sums required to maintain and operate all the institutions which had already been established by the end of the Third Plan. For a typical development project, such as a hospital or an engineering college, the Plan budget will include all building, equipment, and other capital costs, but the salaries of additional teaching and medical staff will be included as plan current outlay only during the 'development phase' of the institution concerned. When this 'development phase' is completed— usually in less than five years—these recurring costs become 'committed', and have to be met thereafter out of the ordinary revenue budgets of the Centre and State Governments. In 1965-6, for example, plan expenditure accounted for only Rs 1,800 mn[5] out of the total estimated expenditure on Indian education of Rs 6,000 mn.[6] Of the balance, Rs 2,470 mn was provided out of the

[5] *Annual Plan 1966-7* (Mar. 1966), p. 70.
[6] Education Commission, *Report 1964-6* (1967), p. 471.

revenue budgets of the Centre and the States, and Rs 1,730 mn by the private sector and local authorities. Similarly, the plan outlay on the training of craftsmen covers only the expenditure on government industrial training institutes, and on the government apprenticeship scheme, but does not include the expenditure made by both public and private sector firms on their own training schools and in-plant training programmes.

The true priorities accorded to education and health, by the Government as a whole, will depend on the extent of the expenditure made on the State education and medical services out of the ordinary revenue budgets of the States, and on the willingness of village authorities to raise funds for elementary education. For the country as a whole, it will also depend on the extent to which this public expenditure is supplemented by private expenditure on education, training, and health. These non-plan expenditures are so large, in relation to the development expenditure in the Plan, that any changes in the relative priority accorded to education and health in the development budget from one plan to the next may be illusory unless it is matched by an equivalent change in priorities in non-plan public and private expenditure. What may appear to be a decreased emphasis on education or health in the Plan may merely reflect a policy decision to shift responsibility for a given part of the educational or health programmes from the development to the non-development budgets of the States. Support given previously from plan funds to enable teachers' salaries to be increased has been withheld in the Draft Fourth Plan, with the exception of relatively small incentive payments, and the responsibility for any further increase, which the Plan recommends, has been put on the ordinary revenue budgets of the States. Conversely, an apparent increase in priority may merely reflect a broadening of the scope of the development budget, as happened in the case of water supply, when responsibility for expenditure formerly provided out of State revenue budgets was included as part of the Plan programme.

A more reliable indication of the relative priority accorded for example to education as a whole, allowing for both public and private expenditure outside the Plan, as well as for Plan outlay, is obtained by relating total expenditure on education to the net national income. Expenditure on education has risen twice as fast as the national income, the share of education in the national income rising from 1·2 per cent in 1951 to 2·4 per cent in 1961 and about

3 per cent in 1965–6.[7] But in absolute terms the expenditure on education per head of the population is still very low, amounting to only 12 Rs out of a per capita income of 409 Rs in 1965–6 at current prices. Young persons are a high and rising share of India's population.

In the rest of the paper we shall concentrate first on investment in education and training, leaving the discussion of health and family planning (apart from its manpower aspects) to the latter half.

4. PLANNED EXPENDITURE ON EDUCATION

Table 2 shows how the expenditure made within the development budget for education has been distributed in the first three five-year plans, and how it is proposed to be distributed in 1966–70, by level of education.

As most other vocational education and training—the education and training of engineers, for example—is included in the development budget for education, we have included medical education and training in Table 2, although provision for this is actually made under the health budget. Although this figure also includes provision for medical research, the actual expenditure on medical education and training may well be larger, as a substantial part of the increased provision for family planning is to be spent on training personnel for the programme, and this provision is presumably additional to the provision for medical education and training made in the rest of the health budget.

In one respect, Table 2 substantially understates the relative priority accorded to elementary and secondary education, because it excludes expenditure under other programmes. The special provision for the educational development of the scheduled castes, scheduled tribes, and other backward classes has been put at Rs 600 mn, which adds 5 per cent to the total education development budget of Rs 12,100 mn. This expenditure is excluded from Table 2, because we do not know what form this *extra* expenditure outside the normal education budget will take. But as most of it is likely to be spent on elementary and secondary education, this will increase the relative financial priority accorded to school education in the Plan—although it appears to have been already allowed for in the estimates of school enrolments.

[7] Ibid. p. 465.

TABLE 2

Draft Fourth Plan Outlay on Education

	1st Plan	2nd Plan	3rd Plan	4th Plan Outlay	
	Percentage of Total Expenditure on Education (planned)			*Rs mn in June 1966 Prices*
Elementary education	56	35	34	32	3,860 (*a*)
Secondary education	13	19	21	22	2,710 (*b*)
University education (general)	9	18	16	15	1,750
Technical education (*c*)	13	18	22	21	2,530 (*c*)
Social education	3	1	1	5	640
Cultural activities	} 6	{ 1	1	1	150'
Other programmes		{ 8	5	4	460
Total education (*d*)	100	100	100	100	
Rs mn in current prices	1,530	2,560	5,600	12,100	12,100 (*d*) (June 1966) prices)

Notes: (*a*) Provision for elementary education in Draft Fourth Plan includes Rs 640 mn for teachers' training.

(*b*) Provision for secondary education in Draft Fourth Plan includes Rs 280 mn for teachers' training.

(*c*) Provision for technical education excludes craftsman training (allotted Rs 1,300 mn in Draft Fourth Plan).

(*d*) Total excludes provision for medical education which is included in the health budget (Rs 1,780 mn allotted to medical education, training, and research in Draft Fourth Plan); also excludes Rs 600 mn provided in Draft Fourth Plan for special programme of educational development of scheduled castes, scheduled tribes, and other backward classes.

Source: 3rd Five Year Plan, *Cols 1, 2, & 3*, pp. 576–7; *4DO, Cols 4 & 5*, p. 325.

Within a limited development budget there has to be a compromise between satisfying the social, economic, and political demands for more school and university places, and meeting the urgent need to improve the quality of the education provided. The more provision that has to be made on social and political grounds, for the elementary education of the rapidly-growing child population, the less the resources that can be devoted to the improvement of the quality of the educational system. Table 3 shows, very roughly, where this basic compromise between quantity and quality has been struck, within the development budget for education for the period from 1966–7 to 1970–1.

The provisions for additional enrolments reflect, in part, the pursuit of the political and social objective of free and universal

TABLE 3

Fourth Draft Outline Outlay on Education (a)
Rs mn in June 1966 prices

	Elementary Education	Secondary Education	University Education	Technical Education
Provision for additional enrolments	2,440	1,300	500	430
Provision for improvement in quality:				
Teacher training (b)	680	330	} 230	110
Postgraduate studies & Research	—			} 50 (d)
Scholarships	—	90	350	100
Vocational Courses	100	240	—	
Other improvements in courses and facilities (c)	640	750	670	} 1,840
Total Expenditure (a)	3,860	2,710	1,750	2,530

Notes: (a) Excludes medical education, craftsman training, social education, cultural activities, 'other programmes', and special educational programmes for backward classes.

(b) Includes incentive payments and awards to teachers (Rs 40 mn for elementary teachers, Rs 50 mn for secondary teachers, Rs 20 mn for university teachers, and Rs 10 mn for technical teachers).

(c) Includes special programmes for girls' education (Rs 200 mn in elementary schools and Rs 70 mn in secondary schools); also includes some miscellaneous expenditure not directly related to improvement of quality.

(d) Excludes postgraduate studies and research in Central Government institutions, Regional Engineering colleges, and in the Indian Institute of Technologies.

Source: 4DO, ch. xvi, pp. 311–30.

education. In part, they are a response to the private demand for education, and to the strong political pressures which are exerted to reinforce that demand, and to put more of the financial responsibility for meeting it on to the public budget. And in part—but only in part—they represent the deliberately planned expansion of enrolments for the specific purpose of satisfying requirements for educated manpower in later plan periods. Expenditure made in response to social and political pressures will, of course, yield incidental economic benefits; and the private demand for education presupposes individual assumptions (which may well be false) about the future private rate of return to education. But only that part of the expenditure on additional enrolments which has been deliberately made to provide for future manpower requirements could be said to be made in pursuit of strictly economic objectives.

By contrast, a much greater part of the expenditure made in an attempt to improve the quality and change the character of Indian education can be regarded as being made in pursuit of economic objectives: to produce the right kind of workers, suitably educated and trained, to meet the needs of economic development. There is, of course, some social pressure in India for higher educational standards as well as for more school and university places. But the main weight of the political and social pressure, with its emphasis on unrestricted admissions, easier examinations, and more lenient marking to minimize the risk of failure to secure that vital paper qualification, militates strongly against any attempt to improve the quality of the education provided.

The professional bodies, like the lawyers, appear to be powerless, in the face of political pressure from students and their parents, to insist on higher standards. And although private employers can put some premium on quality by showing preference for candidates from particular institutions of above-average quality, the public sector employers find it very difficult, politically, to discriminate between applicants with theoretically similar paper qualifications.

The expenditure on teachers' training, shown separately in Table 3, is obviously affected by enrolment policy: the greater the increase in enrolments, the more teachers required, and the more that need to be trained. But to the extent that expenditure on teachers' training is intended to increase the *proportion* of trained teachers in the system as a whole, and to raise the average standard of teaching in the country, we can regard this expenditure as being devoted to the pursuit of quality, rather than quantity.

We now have a rough conceptual framework within which to examine the effective priorities which emerge from the financial provisions of the Plan.

5. OBJECTIVES OF THE EDUCATIONAL PLAN

Three overriding (but conflicting) aims are stated in the educational chapter of the Draft Fourth Plan: (1) the political and social aim of free and universal elementary education; (2) the economic aim of meeting manpower requirements, not so much in the Fourth Plan period itself, when the supply of educated and trained people is already largely predetermined by the expenditure made in previous plans, but in the Fifth, Sixth, and subsequent plan periods; and (3) the economic aim of improving the quality of the education provided at all levels, and altering the character of education and training in order to integrate it more closely with manpower requirements. In this context only does the Plan state as a specific objective an improvement in return on investment in education, to be achieved by reducing the extent of wastage from the system—a proposition which implicitly assumes that the resultant increase in the supply of educated people will be matched by increased opportunities for employment.

The political and social aim of free and universal elementary education is enshrined in a Constitutional Directive that 'free and compulsory' education for all children up to the age of 14 is to be provided by the State—and this objective was to have been achieved by 1960. Although the Constitutional Directive is stated in absolute terms, with no attempt to calculate the costs and benefits of fulfilling it, in practice the limitation of resources, coupled with the rapid increase in the school population, has forced the Government to compromise. An apparent indication of the progress made towards the goal of free elementary education for all is given by the figures of enrolments in Table 4.

The Draft Fourth Plan now states that this goal 'is not expected to be achieved before 1981' (p. 313), and a realistic estimate would put the date much later. For the figures of enrolments are a poor guide to the education actually received. The Draft Fourth Plan points out that 'drop outs' from primary classes are as high as 60 per cent. What is more, as the Education Commission confirms, over two-thirds of all the children who 'drop out' from the primary schools do so in their first year, so they hardly receive any education at all, and remain illiterate. Out of every 100 children who start school at the age of 6, only about 25 are still in school at the age of 12 or 13. The emphasis given in the Plan to the reduction of wastage in elementary schools is therefore made in pursuit of the political and social aim of free and universal education, as well as in pursuit of the economic aim of improving the return on expenditure on elementary education. Whether this reduction in wastage, if it is achieved, will have much economic return will depend mainly on the ability of the economy to provide sufficient jobs to enable the

TABLE 4

Enrolment in Education 1950–1971

	1950–1 Actual	1960–1 Actual	1965–6 Provisional	1970–1 Target
Elementary Education				
(a) *Primary stage (age 6–10)*				
Total enrolment (mns)	19·15	34·99	51·50	69·50
% of age group enrolled (%)	42·6	62·2	78·5	92·2
Girls as % of total enrolment (%)	28·1	31·3	35·3	42·9
(b) *Middle stage (age 11–13)*				
Total enrolment (mns)	3·12	6·70	11·00	19·00
% of age group enrolled (%)	12·7	22·5	32·2	47·4
Girls as % of total enrolment (%)	17·0	21·9	25·4	30·5
Secondary Education (age 14–16)				
Total enrolment (mns)	1·22	2·96	5·24	9·00
% of age group enrolled (%)	5·8	11·7	17·8	22·1
University Education (age 17–23)				
Total enrolment (mns)	0·30	0·73	1·10	1·60
% of age group enrolled (%)	0·7	1·5	1·9	2·4

Source: 4DO, p. 326.

elementary school leavers to make full use of the education they have acquired.

The complicated interaction between social and economic objectives, and the difficulty of measuring the indirect economic benefits derived from the pursuit of social aims, is well illustrated by the education of girls in India. Although the Constitutional Directive of free and compulsory education up to the age of 14 applied equally to girls and to boys, in fact far fewer girls than boys go to school. In 1965–6, of all girls aged between 11 and 13, less than 17 per cent were at school; and of all girls aged between 14 and 16, less than 8 per cent were at school. The Draft Fourth Plan accordingly includes special programmes, costing Rs 270 mn, to accelerate the enrolment of girls in the elementary and secondary schools. What economic benefits will this expenditure yield?

More girls will complete secondary education, and become eligible for training in medicine, teaching, and other social services. If they qualify and subsequently work in these professions, they will fill urgent needs, and are likely to be highly productive, especially if they can be persuaded to work in the rural areas. But the great majority of Indian girls who do acquire an education do not intend to enter the workforce at all. The main economic benefit their education gives them, perhaps, is the prospect of a more suitable marriage—an important private return to education, no doubt, but not necessarily much of a social return. According to the 1961 Census, of all women with matriculation and above, only 23 per cent were in the labour force. If these workforce participation rates remain typical, then to enrol one woman matriculate for further training in medicine or teaching, or in any other further training or employment, it will be necessary to educate four—one to work and three to stay at home.

6. FORECASTS OF MANPOWER REQUIREMENTS

The major economic aim, of meeting manpower requirements in the Fifth and subsequent plan periods, is supported by long term forecasts of manpower requirements only in the case of specialists, who might be expected to be in short supply. Requirements are estimated for agricultural and veterinary graduates; for doctors, nurses, and other medical personnel; for engineers, at both graduate and technician level; for skilled craftsmen; and for teachers at various levels.

Two methods are used by the Planning Commission to forecast the requirements of these specialists. The first of these is to establish detailed manning patterns for the various development programmes included in the Fourth and longer term Perspective Plans. This method has been used to forecast the requirements for agricultural graduates and other trained personnel needed to implement specific agricultural development programmes. The second method, used to forecast requirements for engineers, relies on the basic assumption that requirements for educated people will rise in direct proportion to net output in each of the sectors where they are employed.

The advantage of the first method of forecasting—provided that the long-term programme is defined in sufficient detail and is likely to be carried out without major revisions—is that the manpower forecast can be made by occupation, specifying the education and training required for efficient performance in each occupation, and regionally, by States, Districts, and even Development Blocks, with a distinction made between requirements in urban and in rural areas. The main disadvantage, which applies in practice to the agricultural, family planning, and other health programmes, and to all other development programmes for which the programme method of forecasting might conceivably be attempted, is that none of these programmes is yet defined in sufficient detail, over a sufficiently long period (of ten to fifteen years)—and with sufficient certainty that it will not be drastically modified in response to major changes in government policy during the period of the forecast. In most cases the programmes that have been drawn up are not sufficiently comprehensive to show the staffing patterns required.

7. MANPOWER PLANNING IN AGRICULTURE

The agricultural programmes illustrate both the advantages and the shortcomings in the programme method of forecasting manpower requirements. Detailed plans for the employment of people trained in various aspects of agriculture have been drawn up at District, Block, and even village level, for the more fortunate parts of the country (about 5 per cent of the total cultivated area) which are included in the 'Intensive Agricultural District Programme' (IADP). Rather sparser manning patterns for qualified people have been established for the less intensive 'Intensive Agricultural Areas Programme' (IAAP), but to the extent that part of the area included under this programme, together with the IADP districts, will be brought under the more recent 'High Yielding Varieties Programme' (HYVP), the strength of the technical and administrative personnel will be augmented. In the less fortunate areas of the country that are too poor in resources to be included in any special agricultural programme, a more skeletal manning pattern has been adopted so far.

The Draft Fourth Plan, however, estimates future requirements for agricultural graduates on the assumption that, by the Fifth Plan, ten agricultural extension officers will be in position in each Block (roughly one officer to every ten villages). Does this imply that all Blocks, even the poorest of those outside the special agricultural programme areas, are to have the same staffing pattern by 1971? And will the educational and training requirements for agricultural personnel be the same for all parts of the country? It seems unlikely that such a policy would be implemented—and if it were, it would almost certainly be uneconomic.[8] The manning patterns which are

---

[8] For equal staffing in all Blocks to be economic, the marginal product of the tenth extension officer in promoting the output from each Block would have to be equal for all Blocks despite the wide variation in natural resources of soil and water from Block to Block.

eventually adopted will also depend on the role given to the agricultural universities in the promotion and supervision of agricultural extension work, and upon the relationship—which is at present far from clear—between the agricultural extension service and the State agricultural services, which will still be responsible for all supply matters at least.

While these policy issues remain unresolved, a nationally coordinated programme showing the type and location of all posts to be filled cannot be drawn up. Also missing is a clear idea of the education and training required for efficient performance in each post.

With the exception of those who have attended one of the few outstanding agricultural institutions in India, the graduates of Indian agricultural colleges are seriously lacking in practical farming experience, and seldom well qualified for work in the agricultural extension service. The agricultural polytechnics, on the other hand, do not yet exist; no financial provision for them has been made in the Fourth Plan; and no studies have yet been made to demonstrate where the future agricultural diploma holders who would emerge from these new polytechnics would find appropriate employment— either within or outside the context of official agricultural development programmes.

A similar uncertainty prevails at lower levels. The Education Commission rejects agricultural schools out of hand, on the rather slim evidence of the poor performance of the existing ones. The Planning Commission disagrees, and provides Rs 80 mn for the establishment of 300 new agricultural schools (with another Rs 80 mn for vocational training in agriculture in secondary schools, and a further Rs 80 mn for other post-elementary school vocational training in agriculture). But indecision about agricultural education policy, doubt about the quality and practical value of the training given in these schools, and uncertainty whether the boys who take these vocational courses will subsequently be prepared to work in agriculture in the rural areas—all these still persist.

The separate training programmes for the *gramsevaks*, the Village Level Workers, who are relied upon to promote and maintain the closest links between the government agricultural development programmes, the village *panchayats*, and the individual farmers, are equally open to criticism. The *gramsevaks* are trained in 100 special training centres, of which 20 were upgraded and orientated more directly towards agriculture in the Third Plan period, with the remaining 80 due to be up-graded in similar fashion during the Fourth Plan period.[9] The intention is that, in future, the *gramsevaks* should spend almost all of their time on agriculture—which means that other workers have first to be hired and paid by the village *panchayats* to do the rest of their work. But despite these attempts to strengthen the *gramsevaks'* education and practical training in agriculture, many of them are still ill-equipped, both in formal education and in vocational training in agriculture, to carry out the demanding tasks allotted to them under the government agricultural development programmes.

If firm, realistic, and nationally co-ordinated targets were agreed on for the employment of trained people in agriculture, specified down to Block and village level, over a ten or fifteen year period, and if agreement could be reached on the combination of formal education and specialized training required for efficient performance in each job, then the manpower planners would at least have a clear objective. But a clear picture has first to be obtained of the way in which the existing stock of suitably qualified personnel is at present employed.

This illustrates some of the problems encountered in developing the programme method of manpower planning. And the programme personnel are, of course, only part of the total requirement for trained people in agriculture. Other agricultural graduates and post-graduates will be required for teaching and research, for industry (especially in fertilizers and pesticides), in the agriculatural co-operatives, and—not least—as farmers.

Manpower planning in this detail presents formidable difficulties, and there is a great risk (discussed later in this chapter) of inflexibility through over-specialization. But the number of major policy issues affecting agricultural manpower which still remain unsettled, the lack of a co-ordinated national programme, and the lack of detailed and comprehensive knowledge about the existing manpower distribution in agriculture, alone suffice to throw considerable doubt on the statement in the Draft Outline that there will be 'an overall numerical balance between the Fourth Plan additional demand [for agricultural and allied personnel] and [the additional] supply'.

[9] As there is a shortage of suitably qualified instructors for these training centres, the practical effect of 'up-grading' them may be less than the Draft Fourth Plan implies.

(pp. 120–1). Even if there were an 'overall numerical balance', numbers mean little without regard to quality, or if, as we discuss later in this chapter, they are wholly unrelated to the working of the labour market.

8. MANPOWER PLANNING IN THE MEDICAL SERVICES

Where comprehensive long term development programmes are not available, or where they are too general or too uncertain to provide a useful basis for a manpower forecast, a global forecast is sometimes made on the basis of desirable or feasible norms, or target ratios. Thus the Draft Fourth Plan aims at the achievement of a doctor:population ratio of 1:3,500 by 1976—compared to the existing ratio of 1:5,800 in 1966. Target norms are also set for the nurse:population ratio, or doctor:nurse ratio; and for the ratio of doctors and nurses to auxiliary medical personnel of various kinds. These target norms are usually fixed in the light of experience in other countries, but adjusted for the feasibility of achieving them in India over a ten or fifteen year perspective planning period.

The main disadvantage of these global forecasts is that they are related neither to the location of the posts to be filled, nor to the character of the work to be done. In a country the size of India, a ratio of one doctor to every 5,800 people, obtained by relating the total number of doctors in the country to the total population, means very little. It conceals the fact that, while 80 per cent of the people live in the rural areas, less than 20 per cent of the doctors practise there—so that the doctor:population ratio in the countryside is more like 1:23,000, against about 1:1,400 or 1,500 in the towns. In 1961 there were only 8,560 women doctors in the whole of India, and of these only 1,082 were practising in the rural areas—one woman doctor to every 200,000 village women and girls. And as the growth in the number of women doctors practising in the rural areas has probably barely kept pace with the increase in the rural population during the last five years, the situation today is roughly the same.

The Draft Fourth Plan does not even suggest target ratios of men to women doctors, or indicate the proportion of both men and women doctors who need to be persuaded to work in the rural areas. It is not clear, therefore, from the Draft Fourth Plan, by how much the Government aims to reduce the disparity between the medical services available in rural areas, and the services available in the towns. Certainly, a target doctor:population ratio of 1:3,500 would be much more ambitious, and call for an entirely different order of supporting investment and current outlay, if it meant that *every* group of 3,500 people in India, however remote, should have at least one doctor to serve them.

Not only do the global forecasts fail to indicate *where* the additional doctors should be employed; they also fail to indicate *what kind* of doctors are needed. Even if the target norms were fully achieved, therefore, the medical education and training given might be quite unsuitable, if it is not related to the jobs to be done, in the health programmes which need to be staffed, and in the places where the posts are created. Training should be aimed at detailed, mutually consistent, and interrelated long-term plans for each health programme.

9. EMPHASIS ON FAMILY PLANNING

The family planning programme is discussed on pp. 251–68. Only the personnel requirements of that programme need be commented upon here. They cannot be estimated until the full details of the expanded family planning programme are available, and have been related to the provisions for medical education and training included in the rest of the health budget. It is clear that substantial provision for specialized training in family planning will be included in the expanded Rs 2,290 mn programme, as the earlier Rs 950 mn programme itself included Rs 170 mn for a training programme for 160,000 auxiliary nurse-midwives, 250,000 *dais* (village midwives), and 60,000 basic health workers. But it is not clear whether any additional provision will be made for the formal medical education of doctors and nurses, beyond that included under the health budget in the Draft Fourth Plan. It is generally accepted that the expanded family planning programme will require many more doctors and nurses; that these doctors and nurses will need specialized training, although they might be given a shorter course, spending less time on the more traditional aspects of medical education; that a high proportion of the family planning doctors will have to be women; and that most of these women doctors and nurses should practise in the rural areas. Unless provision for the entire medical education and training of these additional doctors and nurses is included in the expanded family planning programme, or unless the Rs 1,780 mn provided for medical education, training, and research in the health budget is suitably increased, the implication is that the expansion of the family planning programme will be achieved by diverting more of the newly-trained doctors—and as many as possible of the women doctors—away from other health programmes and into family planning. In other words, even if the financial provision for the remaining health programmes (including the provision for medical education) is preserved intact, while increasing the financial provision for family planning from Rs 950 to Rs 2,290 mn, there will be a substantial diversion of scarce trained medical personnel from the other health programmes into family planning

The family planning programme provides a good example of the influence of the technical characteristics of a health programme on the kind of medical personnel needed to operate it—and especially on the required ratio of men to women doctors. If the responsibility for contraception is to be borne mainly by women (as in the case of the IUCD), more women doctors are needed; if the responsibility is to be borne mainly by men (as with sterilisation), then more men doctors are needed.

As many more women doctors and nurses are needed in any case, especially in the villages, it might matter little if fewer women were required for family planning. But a more satisfactory solution would be to devote more resources to male sterilization without reducing the impetus given to the promotion of the use of the IUCD by women. In the absence of a well-defined programme, the training of medical personnel may be inefficient; and if the emphasis of the programme is likely to be changed in mid-stream, a training which enabled doctors, nurses, and auxiliary medical personnel to be more flexible, more prepared to switch their services from one technique or health programme to another, would have obvious advantages— if the cost of acquiring such flexibility were not too high.

Assuming that the expanded family planning programme does keep the emphasis on the IUCD, it is still far from clear whether the manpower implications have been fully taken into account.

10. MANPOWER PLANNING IN INDUSTRY

In other sectors of the economy, such as manufacturing industry, where comprehensive long-term development programmes are not available in sufficient detail to use the programme method of fore-casting, the basic assumption made by the Planning Commission is that requirements for educated and trained people will rise more or less in direct proportion to net output. This assumption is made in the Draft Fourth Plan, as a basis for the forecast of requirements of engineers. The Planning Commission estimates that the net output of the 'engineering intensive' sectors of the economy will grow by 10.3 per cent a year (not 10 per cent) during the next fifteen years (p. 117). In order to achieve this growth rate, and provide for non-plan requirements and replacements, it is assumed that the total stock of graduate engineers and diploma holders, taken together, should increase by 11 per cent a year over the next fifteen years. An employment norm of one graduate engineer to three technicians (engineering diploma holders), based on experience in more advanced industrial counties, is then adopted as a target ratio for 1986 (against the existing ratio of 1 graduate engineer to 1.4 diploma holders in 1966), so that within the 11 per cent annual growth, the stock of diploma holders has to grow much faster than the stock of graduate engineers. In order to step up the annual supply of trained people to match these forecasts of requirements, and to raise the ratio of technicians to engineers progressively towards the 1986 target ratio of 3:1, the Draft Fourth Plan makes provision for a substantial increase in the capacity of the engineering polytechnics.

Requirements for skilled and semi-skilled craftsmen are also esti-mated globally, by assuming an employment norm of 15 craftsmen to every graduate engineer. So that these estimated requirements can be met, the Plan provides for the training capacity of the Govern-ment Industrial Training Institutes (ITIs) to be nearly doubled, and for the Government Apprenticeship Schemes to be expanded, at a combined cost of some Rs 1,300 mn.

The main weakness of this method of forecasting is that, even if the planned targets of net output were achieved, sector by sector, and even industry by industry, manpower requirements may still not increase at the anticipated rate. The Planning Commission's assumption that the stock of educated and trained people should increase in direct proportion to the increase in net output is partic-ularly suspect. There is no empirical evidence to support this assumption; and what evidence there is suggests that, in manu-facturing industry at least, requirements for high level manpower will rise more slowly than output.

In the first place, no allowance is made for the fact that the base year of the manpower forecast, 1966, was one in which the Indian economy was in fundamental disequilibrium. The employed labour force was seriously under-utilized, in some industries by 50 per cent or more, and net output per worker was well below the level that can reasonably be expected to be achieved, in future, with the same capital equipment and labour force. In continuous process industries, such as chemicals, most existing plants are already fully manned for three-shift operations, but many of these plants are operating at only 50 or 60 per cent of capacity. A sharp increase in output could therefore be achieved, by pushing up operating rates closer to design capacity, without requiring any significant addition to the labour force. In mechanical and electrical engineering, present output rates are often based on two-shift or even one-shift operation, so additional shift workers would obviously be required to operate the capital equipment at capacity, on a three-shift basis. More supervisory and production-planning staff might also be required to ensure continuous operation at near-capacity rates. But even in that case, there need not be a corresponding increase in the staff of the overhead departments, such as research and development, where a large proportion of the employees are likely to be highly qualified.

There was also a serious disequilibrium, in the base year of the manpower forecast, in the educational characteristics of the labour force, in relation to the education and training required for efficient performance in each occupation. The existing relationship between education, training, and occupation is, to a significant extent, a historical accident—a product of the supply of educated people and the demand for them at the time they were hired. When insufficient suitably qualified people were available, unsuitably-qualified candidates had to be accepted, and these older men still hold responsible positions for which, by education and formal training, they are underqualified. In-plant training facilities were often inadequate in the past, so many of the older employees received none of the formal training which might now be regarded as essential. More recently, when the output from the educational system caught up with and surpassed demand, employers found themselves flooded with applications from candidates who—on paper at least—were often over-qualified for the job to be done. In engineering in particular, many engineering graduates have been forced to accept technicians' jobs which could have been more efficiently filled by people with a less advanced theoretical education and more practical experience.

Forecasts based on existing labour/output ratios, and on the existing average relationship between occupation and education, will merely compound the extent of the imbalances which already exist. They would be valid only if it were reasonable to take the pessimistic position that the labour force will be just as under-utilized, in proportion to its capacity, and just as ill-educated, in relation to the requirements of the job, in fifteen years' time as it is today. There are many reasons why at least the first of these assumptions is likely to be false. Labour utilization is invariably inefficient during the first two or three years after a new plant has been com-missioned, while teething troubles with the new equipment are being overcome and the labour force gains experience with an unfamiliar technology. The higher the proportion of new to old plant, there-fore, the greater the difference between the actual and the potential output of the existing labour force and capital equipment. But as the industry expands, the proportion of recently commissioned plant to total installed capacity is likely to fall, with a corresponding rise in the rate of labour utilization. Output was held back in many factories in 1966 by acute shortages of foreign exchange for essential maintenance imports—but when the flow of non-project foreign aid was resumed, output per man rose. Labour productivity is low in many industries in India today—machine tools, for example—because production is held back whenever expansion in one industrial sector is out of phase with the expansion in the other sectors which supply its raw materials and components, or consume its prod-ucts. But as the phasing between sectors improves with the completion of many projects now under construction or planned, and as the economy becomes less dependent on imports, labour productivity should rise.

Another major objection to the projection of manpower require-ments on the assumption of a fixed one-to-one ratio between the percentage increase in net output and the percentage increase in the demand for high-level manpower, is that no account is taken of the impact of technological change on manpower requirements—except for the implied but unsubstantiated assumption that any rise in crude labour productivity will take the form of a reduction in the ratio of unskilled and uneducated workers to output, while the ratio between high-level manpower and output remains constant because more qualified people are needed to operate and maintain the more sophisticated equipment. When technological change and the widening of the market is accompanied, as it often is, by economies of scale, the resultant improvement in crude labour productivity, *and* the impact on the relationship between high-level manpower and output may be quite dramatic.

In general, requirements for high-level manpower per unit of output are higher in the capital goods sector than in the consumer goods sector of the engineering industries—mainly because capital equipment must be capable of maintaining consistently high standards of performance over a long period, and because it is more likely to be 'tailor made' to customers' requirements, which precludes production in large batches of standard design. Under these circumstances, changes in the nature of demand may have a significant impact on manpower requirements. In the machine tools industry, for example, a recession in the demand for the more simple, standard machines has been accompanied by a growing demand for more sophisticated automatic and special purpose machines, which may have to be produced on a 'one-off' basis, with correspondingly high labour requirements per unit of output. The production of complex machines of this type requires not only more skilled craftsmen, but also more engineers, who are needed to supervise the design and assembly stages of manufacture.

In all industries, manpower requirements will be directly affected by the changes in the structure of the industry which accompany its expansion. An expansion of output may be achieved, especially in the earlier stages of industrialization, by the creation of new industries to manufacture products which were formerly imported. Because they are new, and because both the management and the labour force is inexperienced, such new industries are often overmanned with qualified people as well as with unskilled labour, so the employment of high-level manpower per unit of output is likely to be high—even after efficient utilization of the capital equipment has been achieved. At one remove from the creation of a new industry is the erection of new plant to be run by new public or privately-owned organizations. Again, as these new units have to be organized from scratch, their manning patterns are likely to be less streamlined than those of established plants, and manpower requirements per unit of output will still be relatively high. But when a new plant is put up by an established firm, experience will suggest economies in the staffing pattern, and the new plant will have the benefit of technical services provided by the central departments of the holding company, so the additional manpower requirements per unit of additional output are likely to be lower. Lowest of all will be the additional manpower required per unit of additional output where the increase in output is achieved by expanding existing plants, in a way which enables economies to be made in the service and other overhead departments. As India's industrial development has already reached the stage where an increasing proportion of total new investment is made in the form of the expansion of existing plants, or the erection of new plants by established firms, the requirements for high-level manpower per unit of additional output are likely to be markedly lower than those derived from a straight projection of the existing relationship between output and employment. Partially offsetting this trend, however, is the concentration of a higher proportion of new investment in public sector projects, which, with their more rigid manning patterns and hiring practices, tend to employ more people at every level than private sector firms, to obtain a given increase in output.

Requirements for highly-qualified people in research and development depend on factors which are related only tenuously to current output, or to the expected increase in output. India's current imports, sustained by foreign aid, have a substantial content of highly-qualified manpower—comprising not only direct expenditure on foreign consultancy, design, and engineering services, and direct payments for foreign technical know-how and patent rights, but also the import of capital equipment, components, and materials which already embody the results of foreign research and development, design, and engineering services. If these import costs are to be reduced, in order to achieve the planners' current aim of self-reliance, without any more foreign aid, by the end of the Fifth Plan period in 1976, then the equivalent high calibre research, development and design personnel will have to be recruited from the Indian universities, and will have to be given adequate opportunity to acquire training and experience through appropriate employment. The Draft Fourth Plan (pp. 118–19) stresses the need to provide the the necessary scientists and other highly-qualified research and development staff, and to expand and diversify the indigenous engineering consultancy and design services which have been already established. This raises a host of wider issues—of public sector versus private sector investment; of attitudes to foreign aid; and of the preference of foreign investors (and of the countries providing most of the aid) for turnkey projects which rely heavily on foreign research, development, design, and engineering services—as well as on foreign capital equipment—and make a minimum call on indigenous research, design, and engineering talent. The fertilizer industry provides a most striking example of this dilemma. There are many others. An analysis of this problem would take us far beyond the scope of this chapter—but its relevance to Indian investment in human capital is undeniable.

11. A SURPLUS OF UNSUITABLY EDUCATED PEOPLE

All these qualifications apply to the Draft Fourth Plan forecasts of the requirements for specialists. They suggest that, on balance, requirements have been substantially overestimated in engineering—but probably not in agriculture and certainly not in medicine. For the general matriculate, or intermediate, or arts graduate, the targets in the plan relate only to enrolments, not to requirements—it being assumed with good reason, that the educational system is already set on a course which will produce more than enough people with a general non-technical and non-professional education. As in the case of elementary education, the enrolment targets for secondary, university, and vocational education are a very poor guide to the likely output of students who have completed the course. At the secondary stage, according to the Draft Fourth Plan, about 50 per cent of the students appearing for the final examination fail to pass—and there is certainly no suggestion that the qualifying examination has been made too stiff. Of those who do matriculate, a high proportion—nearly two-thirds—stay on for some form of higher education, but there is a 'high proportion of failures and third classes, especially in pass courses' (p. 311), and only about a third of those who enter the intermediate colleges obtain a first degree. Therefore the future output from general education at secondary school and university level, which is already largely pre-determined by past and present enrolments, will be even higher if the Plan aim of reducing wastage from the system at all levels is achieved. As in elementary education, the return on investment in secondary and university education, and the return on the particular expenditure made with the specific objective of reducing wastage, will depend on availability of productive employment for the increased output of educated people.

Where long-term manpower requirements are specifically estimated, the Planning Commission appears to regard the meeting of these requirements as an absolute priority—in terms of quantity, if not of quality—without regard to the costs of education and training. The implicit assumption is that the benefit of avoiding the risk of manpower shortages in key sectors is so great that the cost of meeting estimated requirements needs no further justification. The output from the system is assessed on the basis of existing and anticipated enrolment policy (or the assumed response to continuing pressures for more higher education) and expected wastage rates, and any deficiency between the anticipated output of educated people and the forecast of requirements is then made good by expanding educational facilities. But with the major exception of doctors and other medical personnel and qualified teachers of all kinds, and the probable exception of agricultural graduates, the likelihood is that the educational system will produce more than enough people with the required paper qualifications, especially those of a general, nontechnical nature. Indeed, again with the exception of health and agriculture, and of good quality teaching staff, the tendency in the Planning Commission has been to overestimate the long-term requirements of high-level manpower, and in general to overestimate the amount of additional employment generated by the planned investment during each plan period. Consequently, if additional investment in education is made on the basis of over-generous forecasts of requirements, there is a strong probability of a continuing surplus of educated people which will depress the economic return on the additional investment in education.

This surplus has already emerged in the figures of educated unemployed recorded by the employment exchanges. By June 1966 the total number of educated unemployed (matriculates and above), recorded by these exchanges, had risen to 889,000. These registrations are incomplete in some respects, and inflated in others, so they are not a very good guide, either to the absolute extent of the unemployment of educated people today, or to the trend over time. Although only a very small proportion of the graduates registered as unemployed at the beginning of the Fourth Plan period had engineering or any other technical or professional qualification, there is evidence of an increasing number of engineering graduates unable to find jobs,[10] and the unemployment figures take no account of the increasing underemployment of educated people who are forced to take jobs where they are unable to make good use of their education.[11]

In general terms, the Draft Fourth Plan takes account of this growing surplus of unsuitably-educated people. 'Efforts will be made to prevent the current rush to the universities ... The limitation on numbers will be effected by raising the qualifications for admission ... by multiplying terminal courses at the secondary stage, and by discouraging the opening of sub-standard affiliated colleges' (p. 315). But except where an *increase* in enrolments is planned—as in medicine, agriculture, engineering, and teaching—these general aims are not defined in terms of numbers. The absence of any attempt to convert them into specific programmes casts doubt on the priority that the government will give in practice to measures designed to limit the outflow of unsuitably-educated people. And if the estimates of manpower requirements are likely to prove excessive in many cases, while the educational system is already set on a course which will supply substantially more educated people than would be needed to match even these inflated requirements, one is left with the strong impression that the Planning Commission is much more concerned to eliminate any risk of manpower shortages than to avoid wasting resources by educating more skilled people than the economy needs.

The argument usually made in support of this policy of erring on the side of over-supply is that manpower shortages have a cumulative effect in retarding economic growth—retarding it directly in the sector where the manpower shortages first appear, and indirectly in other sectors of the economy which are dependent on the first sector for their essential supplies. The total cost to the economy—in terms of a general reduction in the return on capital investment—of allowing shortages of engineers and other qualified people to

[10] At the end of 1967, 7,000 graduate engineers (against the present annual output of 13,000), and 28,300 engineering diploma holders (against the present annual output of 21,620) were reported as unemployed. See the *Hindu Weekly Review*, 11 March 1968, p. 9. Other unofficial estimates broadly corroborate these figures.

[11] H. N. Pandit, 'The Nature and Dimensions of Unemployed Educated Manpower in India, 1953 to 1964', *Manpower J.*, Oct. 1965–Mar. 1966. See also Working Paper no. 14, 1965, with the same title, publ. by the Institute of Applied Manpower Research, New Delhi.

occur, is therefore so great that the risk of shortage must be minimized, and, if possible, eliminated. Even if there were an overall
statistical balance between the total supply of educated people and
the total demand for them, there might well be damaging regional
shortages, particularly in the less attractive rural areas where the
need for trained people is acute. On the other hand, if the supply
of educated people is likely to exceed the demand, the risk of damaging regional shortages is lessened, and there will be more chance
of persuading educated people to fill vacancies in unattractive rural
areas, if their only alternative is to remain unemployed. Some
unemployment of educated people can therefore be tolerated, even
at the expense of reducing the marginal return to investment in
education, because the cost of allowing manpower shortages to
impede economic growth would be greater.

The relative costs and benefits on which this argument rests have
never been calculated. Much would depend, of course, on the
extent of the unemployment and underemployment of educated
people that occurred. If it became very large, the argument in
favour of erring on the side of over-supply would be hard to justify—
especially as there is no risk of a shortage of people with a general
education who are likely to form the bulk of the unemployed.

As the Draft Fourth Plan admits, the main damage done as a consequence of the rapid rise in enrolments at all levels during the last
fifteen years, and of the 'open door' policy of unrestricted admission
to higher education, has been a deterioration in the quality of the
education provided. Such a large part of the limited resources
available has been consumed in expanding the system, that very
little has been left to maintain and improve its quality. Uncertainty
about the prospects of employment when the flow of graduates
exceeds demand, has been one of the causes of the student riots
which are now such a common feature of the Indian university
scene—with predictably damaging effects on the quality of university
education.

12. IMPROVING THE QUALITY OF EDUCATION

The Draft Fourth Plan's aim of improving the quality of Indian
education, while integrating it more closely with manpower requirements and at the same time making the educational system more
efficient, is based on an assessment of the defects of the existing
system. Quality is poor in two respects: the economically-useful

15

content of any given paper qualification is low; and the educational system has failed to provide a form of education which is closely linked to the requirements of the economy—and to do so at least cost. Efficiency is low because the cost of producing a given output of educated and trained people is inflated by high wastage rates and by the poor utilization of existing facilities.

Three-quarters of all Indian graduates are B.As or B.Scs without any technical or professional qualification. These are 'half-way' degrees, taken usually at the age of nineteen or twenty, four years after matriculation. As the Education Commission points out, holders of Indian first degrees in arts and science are generally equated with matriculates in major universities in Europe, where they are considered eligible for admission only to the first year of the first degree course. A similar disparity is to be found both at lower levels and in higher technical education.

13. SELECTION ON MERIT FOR HIGHER EDUCATION

What indication is there that the planners' stated aims of improving the quality of education are likely to be achieved in practice? The first requirement, as the Draft Outline points out (pp. 311, 316), is to restrict the entry of unsuitable students into higher education, by introducing and enforcing a policy of selection on merit. This implies not only that entry into higher education should be denied to those who are unlikely to be able to make good economic use of it, but also that gifted students should not be enrolled in courses for which they are temperamentally unsuited. A policy of selective admissions would weed at least some of them out.

But the restriction of admission to higher education, and the enforcement of a policy of selection on merit, will not be achieved merely by the expenditure of Plan funds. What is needed is essentially a political decision to enforce a policy which is bound to be unpopular. The Plan may aim at a reduction in the relative number of arts students, for example, but the applicants for arts courses are often those who have failed to gain entry into the more coveted technical faculties, yet continue to demand a university education. It is this pressure which has led in the past to the haphazard proliferation of affiliated degree colleges. Every town, however small, wants its own degree college—and every politician wants the political kudos of inaugurating it. These colleges, poorly staffed and equipped, and loosely administered, consume a large proportion of the limited resources available for higher education—and consume them least efficiently. But education in India is primarily the responsibility of the individual States, and the State Governments are most vulnerable to this kind of political pressure.

Some discipline might be exerted by emphasizing the need for realistic manpower planning at State level, so that the disparity between manpower requirements and the outflow from the colleges could not be so readily ignored by local administrators and electorates, and the absurdity of uncontrolled expansion would become more apparent. And the power of the Centre to influence the States, and to stiffen their resistance to political pressure for more higher education irrespective of the need for it, could be augmented if a higher proportion of total expenditure on education in the States were made out of funds supplied in the first instance by the Centre. With more 'power of the purse', the Centre could insist that these funds be spent only on approved projects designed to raise the quality of existing institutions, rather than to multiply the inefficient. If the Centre is short of funds, can foreign aid, for expenditure in rupees (because the foreign exchange content of educational investment is negligible), but specifically tied to educational policies, be a useful tool? One might look to PL 480 counterpart funds, but these could be used only if the educational investment were made, by prior agreement, at the time the food imports are sold—thus avoiding inflation. Aid for education out of PL 480 rupee *balances* is just as inflationary as financing the educational investment by creating Central Bank credit. Direct foreign aid, specifically tied to education but spendable in rupees, would provide the necessary capital resources and strengthen the Centre's ability to enforce unpopular policies—while inflation would be avoided by the increased flow of imports paid out of a foreign exchange counterpart fund which would be totally unrelated to the expenditure on education. Such a policy would help, of course, only if the Central funds, which would have been devoted to education in any case, are not diverted to other purposes, thus offsetting the increased flow of foreign aid.

14. VOCATIONAL EDUCATION AND TRAINING

The Draft Outline aims to give education a higher economic value by integrating it more closely with manpower requirements—'to give secondary school leavers a training which has an employment value' (p. 315), by increasing the emphasis given in the school curricula to science and mathematics, and by increasing the number of vocational courses of a terminal nature in industry and agriculture. In the universities, 'it is proposed to slow down the number of persons enlisting for arts and commerce courses' (p. 316), and to expand facilities for science and agriculture and for technical and medical education. But will the cost of providing more vocational courses be justified by the resultant benefits? Will the vocational courses be good enough, and be related closely enough to employment opportunities? And will secondary school boys and girls be willing to enrol in these terminal vocational courses, and forego the prestige of a university education, however unsuitable? They will do so only if the jobs offered to those who have taken the vocational courses are sufficiently attractive—in terms of money, prestige, opportunities for promotion, and security of employment—when compared to the employment opportunities open to university graduates.

15. THE NEED FOR FLEXIBILITY AND ADAPTABILITY

There is also a risk that the emphasis on a relatively narrow vocational training and on a greater degree of technical specialization at university level may conflict with the need for flexibility and adaptability. In a rapidly changing industrial environment, where manpower requirements cannot possibly be predicted far ahead with any precision, there are obvious advantages in educating people to be adaptable to changing conditions in the labour market.

Certain subjects of universal applicability, such as mathematics and science, including agricultural science, should be emphasized more at the school stage, and should probably be taken to a much higher level much earlier in degree courses, as they are the basis for—and greatly shorten the study of—any of a wide range of specializations. There would still be specialization within the formal educational system, although perhaps more of it might be deferred to the postgraduate stage. The specialist knowledge acquired within the universities should have a reasonably wide field of application over a broad range of employment.

Formal education of this more general character can then be supplemented by specialized in-plant or field training, which can be more directly related to the skills known to be required, and need be given only if the future employment of people with those skills is assured. The return on both the formal education and the specialized training will be much higher than at present, because the formal education will have an economic value in any of a wide range of jobs, while the costs of the specialized training will not be incurred unless the future employment of the trainees is assured, and the content of the specialized training will be more closely related to the skills known to be required.

All this implies a fundamental change in the content of existing courses and examinations at all educational levels. Any suggestion that rote learning for examinations—the rule rather than the exception in most Indian schools and colleges—has any practical value, must be strongly resisted. For standards can be raised only if students are taught to apply the principles they have learned to the solution of unseen problems—and if examinations are designed to test this ability.

16. IMPROVING TEACHING STANDARDS

There were about two million schoolteachers in India in 1966, but some 600,000 of them were untrained, and there was still an acute shortage of qualified teachers, especially in science and mathematics, and for technical and vocational courses, including agriculture. Including provision for replacements, nearly a million more teachers will be required for the schools alone during the Fourth Plan period—800,000 in the elementary schools and 200,000 in the secondary schools—and a further 30,000 teachers will be needed in the general education faculties of the universities. Acute shortages of qualified teachers have also to be remedied in the engineering polytechnics and other technical faculties of the colleges and universities, especially in medicine and agriculture, where the number of student places is being sharply increased.

There may be little difficulty in finding sufficient *unqualified* general teachers—even at existing pay scales—to fill the gaps in the elementary schools, at the cost of a further deterioration in standards. The acute shortage is of qualified teachers. This lack will be remedied to some extent through the provisions made in the Draft Fourth Plan for teachers' training—as shown in Table 3 (on p.198). Additional provision for the training of teachers is made, to some extent, under specific programme budgets—for example in the provision for medical education and training in the health budget. But despite these provisions, and especially when account is taken of the Plan's aim of improving the quality of education at all levels, the shortage of suitably qualified and trained teachers will remain acute—and this will prejudice the achievement of virtually all the objectives of the education programme.

17. TEACHERS' PAY

This is the context within which the case for increasing teachers' pay must be examined. The Education Commission has made higher salaries for teachers one of its principal recommendations. But, as Professor V. K. R. V. Rao, then Member for Education on the Planning Commission, pointed out, 'the amounts involved are so substantial that there was no chance of including them in the Plan outlay . . . .' and the Draft Fourth Plan, therefore, states that 'the general rise in the salaries of the teachers should be in the normal budget (of the States) as in the case of other government servants' (p. 324). This leaves it to the States to find the extra revenue to pay higher salaries to teachers—but at the same time the Planning Commission exhorts the State Governments to restrict the increase in their non-plan expenditures to a maximum of $3\frac{1}{2}$ per cent a year.

The validity and relevance of these statements is open to question. Given the resources available, would any conceivable general increase in the pay scales of *all* Indian teachers make good the existing deficiency in the quality of teaching, and increase the supply of *good* teachers into the profession? The ratio of teachers' pay to income per head is already far higher in India than in more industrially developed countries, such as the UK, and the pay and status of university teachers, in particular, puts them among the more privileged members of Indian society. According to the Education Commission,[12] the average salary of all Indian teachers, including both school and university teachers, is about three and a half times the Indian national income per head—whereas in the UK average teachers' salaries are just over twice as high as the national income per head. What justification is there, therefore, for the payment of higher salaries, especially to the large proportion of teachers who are still unqualified and untrained? If many untrained teachers are themselves rejects from the educational system, and if the supply

[12] Education Commission, *Report 1964–6*, p. 47.

of these unqualified teachers exceeds the demand for them, why should their pay be increased?

The answer to this is that pay increases must be selective. The private return on an education and training for teaching must be as high as the private return on an equivalent education employed in other government service or industry. As the Education Commission points out,[13] while the salaries of qualified teachers in India are high in relation to the national income per head, they compare unfavourably with the salaries of other public servants in the government administrative service—and even less favourably with earnings from technical, administrative, and managerial positions in industry.

Pay increases for qualified teachers should be selective regionally, favouring posts in the rural areas, where the shortage of qualified teachers is most acute. And by making pay increases selective, budgetary demands become more manageable, and the unbalancing social and economic effects of raising the salaries of teachers as a class, relative to salaries in other occupations, would be avoided.

18. THE LANGUAGE OF INSTRUCTION

What is perhaps the most important of all the factors responsible for the progressive deterioration in the quality of much Indian education receives no mention in the Draft Outline. This is the politically sensitive issue of the language of instruction.

From a strictly economic point of view, the language of instruction should be that which produces the highest return on educational expenditure, by enabling a subject to be studied most effectively in a form which will be most useful in subsequent employment. This will depend on the language in which good textbooks are available; in which other necessary literature on current developments in the subject is readily accessible; in which good teachers can instruct most effectively; in which the education acquired will subsequently be put to practical use in employment; and—especially in the case of science, engineering, and other technical subjects— the language in which the most important technological developments in the subject are most frequently made. The economic return on teaching in this language will be high, provided that the cost of ensuring that students are proficient in the language of instruction

---

[13] Ibid, p. 58.

is not itself too great in relation to the benefits of more effective instruction.

Despite the political and social pressures to promote the commercial use of indigenous national or regional languages, English is likely to continue to perform an essential economic role in industry and commerce and as a language of instruction in technical subjects well beyond the end of the Fourth Plan period. While English continues to perform this role, the quality of educational attainment is bound to be affected by the proficiency in the English language of both students and instructors in technical subjects. The consensus of opinion in India today is, however, that the ability of students, especially in the engineering colleges, to understand and express themselves clearly in English, and particularly in writing, is deteriorating noticeably.

One of the main impediments to the improvement of Indian education at present is uncertainty about language policy. Decisions are postponed, because any decision is so controversial that it is bound to have far-reaching political repercussions. The consequence is either continued drift, with English retained as a medium of instruction in technical courses in the polytechnics, colleges, and universities, while less and less attention is paid to the proficiency in English of the students who enter those institutions; or—an equally disastrous possibility—the precipitate enforcement of a shift towards technical instruction in indigenous languages, without first ensuring that sufficient good teachers are available, or that good textbooks and other literature are available, or that industry can develop efficiently with technical personnel trained only in indigenous languages. A further deterioration in educational standards, and a sharp reduction in the return on expenditure on education, seems the only possible result from either policy.

19. REDUCTION IN WASTAGE AND OTHER ECONOMIES

The plan also aims to improve the efficiency of the educational system by improving the utilization of existing physical facilities and by reducing wastage rates—one of the few instances where an improvement in the return on investment in education is mentioned as a specific economic objective. Success in achieving these aims will be mainly dependent on the factors already discussed in relation to quality—better teaching, selection for higher education on merit, and more vocational education with a direct employment value.

To reduce the very high rate of wastage in the elementary schools, the plan relies on better teaching, better school organization, the free supply of text books, and the provision of free mid-day meals. It also expresses the hope—without adducing any very convincing evidence to support it—that the adult literacy programmes will encourage parents to keep their children at school. School hours and vacations are also to be better adjusted to free children to take part in agricultural operations such as sowing and harvesting.

In the engineering colleges and polytechnics, the high rate of wastage (through 'drop outs' and examination failures) is attributed to 'an overall shortage of 35 per cent in teachers, of 53 per cent in equipment, of 51 per cent in instructional buildings, and of 55 per cent in hostels' (p. 319). Wastage is accordingly to be reduced by making good these deficiencies. Economies of scale are to be achieved by consolidating existing institutions, which are often too small and isolated to be adequately staffed and equipped—except at prohibitive cost per student—and by improving instructional buildings, equipment, and student hostels.

The Plan contains no convincing demonstration that these measures are likely to achieve the intended results—especially in the face of local political pressure for unrestricted admissions to all forms of higher education, with scant regard for quality. No attempt is made in the Draft Outline to define these general aims by setting quality norms or by setting physical targets for the reduction in wastage rates. How much reduction in wastage is envisaged at each level, and how is this reflected in the enrolment estimates? What is the probability that the expenditure of the funds provided for reducing wastage will bring about the intended reduction? And how do the benefits of reducing wastage compare with the costs incurred in reducing it? How important, in financial terms, are the economies of scale and other economies that the Plan seeks to achieve by consolidating and improving existing institutions and by securing fuller utilization of existing buildings, equipment, library facilities, and staff? The defects of the education system are to be remedied to an indeterminate extent, but the relative costs and benefits of doing so are not assessed.

20. ADULT LITERACY PROGRAMMES

The Draft Fourth Plan outlay on adult literacy programmes is shown under the heading of 'Social Education' in Table 2 (on p. 197).

Of all workers in 1961, 73 per cent were recorded by the Census as illiterate; in the rural areas 78 per cent were illiterate. Against this background, which has improved only slightly during the last five years, the Draft Fourth Plan provides Rs 640 mn with the objective of taking nearly 100 mn people up to the 'first stage of literacy', and making 12.5 mn of these 'functionally literate'.

If this objective could be achieved, and if all the 100 mn could eventually become functionally literate, the return on expenditure under the literacy programme would be very high. If instruction is not maintained for a sufficiently long period, if reading materials are not readily available, and if the initial instruction is not followed up persistently until functional literacy is assured, a speedy relapse into illiteracy becomes a virtual certainty, and most of the resources spent on the programme would be wasted.

Given limited resources, higher returns could be achieved by limiting the size of the programme to ensure that expenditure per head is sufficient to ensure functional literacy. There is also a case for discriminating, where possible, in favour of those whose productivity is likely to be most increased by becoming functionally literate—such as the farmers who are fortunate enough to be included in the IADP.

This means, inevitably, compromising the social aim of equal opportunity—of achieving literaly, as of receiving a free school education. The indirect economic returns from a more literate and numerate population, reflected in attitudes to innovation and birth control for example, or the freeing of illiterate villagers from exploitation by unscrupulous politicians, moneylenders, and scribes, could be very large. But there is neither social nor economic benefit to be gained from spreading a limited budget indiscriminately over so many people, on grounds of equity, that each one receives less than the necessary minimum of assistance. All the funds are spent, but very few of the beneficiaries become functionally literate, and most of the resources are therefore wasted.

21. THE INFLUENCE OF THE LABOUR MARKET

One of the most glaring defects of the manpower and educational planning policies outlined in the Draft Fourth Plan is that they completely ignore the influence of the labour market on employers' demands for people with various skills, and on the supply of skilled people willing to satisfy those demands.

An 'overall numerical balance' between demand and supply becomes meaningless, if no account is taken of the economic mechanism by which vacant jobs are actually filled. That mechanism is the labour market—and however imperfectly it may operate in India, its influence cannot be ignored.

The problem of matching manpower requirements with a supply of trained people who are willing to accept employment in the places where they are most needed is well illustrated by the following factors affecting the supply of doctors:

First, will there be a sufficient number of good school leavers, both boys and girls, able to satisfy the entry requirements for a medical education?

Second, will enough of these suitable boys and girls think that a medical career is attractive enough, in terms of potential earnings and working conditions, to be worth pursuing?

Third, will the facilities for medical education and training be adequate, so that, after allowing for wastage, sufficient men and women doctors will qualify to meet the needs of all the health and family planning programmes, as well as the needs of private practice?

Fourth, will enough of these qualified doctors be willing to make their career in the State medical services in India, instead of entering more lucrative or less demanding private practice in the towns, or emigrating for further study and probable future employment overseas where working and living conditions may appear more attractive?

And fifth, if enough doctors can be persuaded to choose the State medical services as a career, will enough of them—and particularly of the women doctors—be prepared to practise in the particular health programmes and in the rural areas where they are most needed?

Belatedly, and in a rather half-hearted way, the Government is now considering the introduction of various incentive schemes, and in a few cases has begun to offer incentive payments—for example, to teachers who improve their qualifications or teaching ability. Scholarships are to be offered to medical students, on condition that the students undertake to work, for a specified time after qualifying, in particular government programmes such as family planning. In the State medical service there is talk of discriminating in favour of employment in the rural areas, where working and living conditions are less attractive and there is less opportunity to earn a supplementary income from private practice. And there are suggestions that promotion within any government service should be made dependent on willingness to serve a term in the villages.

But the steps actually taken so far do not go nearly far enough. There is no doubt that the pay offered for work in the rural areas—to doctors, qualified teachers, and agricultural graduates alike—is not nearly high enough to compensate them for the many hardships of working and living there.

Much could be done, if the resources were available, to lessen the physical hardships of working and living in the countryside. Primary health centres and district hospitals could be better equipped; better housing could be provided for doctors and teachers and other government servants; more public funds could be spent on improving water supplies, on providing free transport to the nearest town, and on the promotion of other development programmes which would reduce the feeling of isolation experienced by educated people working in the villages. More generous arrangements for home leave, with free travel for wives and families would also help. In programmes as large as the family planning and other health programmes, it cannot be assumed that more than a very small fraction of the necessary staff will be dedicated people to whom the amenities of life are unimportant.

But there is a limit to the physical improvements that can reasonably be expected. And, at any feasible level, monetary incentives alone are unlikely to offset the remaining hardships of rural life. The question therefore arises whether monetary incentives can be supplemented by some form of direction of labour. A step in this direction is the proposal that scholarships—or the waiving of repayment of student loans—should be made conditional on the students' undertaking to work, for a specified time after qualifying, in a particular government programme, or in one of the less attractive posts in the rural areas. But there is a risk that the imposition of conditions, even when associated with financial assistance while studying, might deter good students—and especially women students—from choosing a socially useful career. The obligations would appear less onerous if they were imposed universally—if *all* candidates for higher education of any kind, including all those seeking technical or professional qualifications, were compelled to accept equally stiff national service obligations. A few years of work in the villages, or in particular government programmes, could then be chosen as one means of satisfying a universal and compulsory national service requirement. Such a policy could succeed only if the political will to impose it—and enforce it—is strong enough. As a first step, the formal award and recognition of academic, technical, and professional qualifications might perhaps be made dependent on the demonstrated fulfilment of specified 'public interest' work obligations. And public sector employers, at least, might be enjoined to refuse employment, in any capacity, to anyone whose public interest work obligations had not been fulfilled.

22. PLANNING FOR FULL EMPLOYMENT

Before we can discuss the many issues raised by any attempt to determine the rate of return on various forms of expenditure on education or health, we must first examine another aspect of manpower planning which has a direct impact on *all* returns to investment in human capital: planning for the full employment of the existing labour force. Planning supply to match forecasts of manpower requirements is one objective; planning economic development with the aim of ensuring the full employment of the existing labour force, quite another. These two aspects of manpower planning do not necessarily coincide, for manpower requirements may be met while leaving an excess supply of educated people unemployed. As the potential productivity of educated and trained people will not be realized if they are unemployed or underemployed, the employment policy followed in the Fourth Plan period will have a critical bearing on the return to all forms of investment in human capital. Investment which yields an increased flow of educated people who cannot find employment is a waste of scarce resources.

The employment opportunities expected to be generated by the Fourth Plan are, to a large extent, a by-product of investment and other planning decisions made on grounds other than the provision of employment. The Draft Fourth Plan makes the point explicitly: 'To achieve a balance between development and investment on the one hand, and growth in employment on the other, is an essential objective of planning. However, such a balance has to be sought as an indirect rather than as a direct consequence of planning; . . . the scope for large changes in the plan from the angle of employment is somewhat limited' (p. 106).

The consequences of this approach can be seen in the extent and nature of the additional employment which was actually generated

by the investment made in the Third Plan period. Over the entire
five year period, the recorded increase in employment in the 'organized' sector, outside agriculture, was only 3.3 mn.[14] About a
third of these new jobs were in the Central and State government
administrative services, and only 860,000 of them were in 'organized'
manufacturing industry.[15] If total employment outside agriculture
rose by 10.5 million, as the Draft Fourth Plan claims, then about
70 per cent of these new jobs must have been found in the 'non-
organized' sector—in construction, in establishments employing less
than twenty-five people, in household enterprises, and in self-
employment. Much of this additional employment—perhaps half—
is likely to be created in the rural areas, where the non-agricultural
labour force is as large as the entire urban labour force. But in this
'non-organized' sector much of the additional employment is more
in the nature of work sharing—with underemployment rising as the
same output is produced by more people. Where such a large
proportion of the additional employment takes this form, productivity will be low, and the earnings of educated people who cannot
find employment in the 'organized' sector will be correspondingly
reduced.

At the start of the Fourth Plan period there were an estimated
9 to 10 mn unemployed[16]—an estimate which almost certainly
seriously understates the true extent of unemployment, and takes
no account of the much larger numbers of underemployed. Against
a predicted increase of 23 mn in the labour force during the Fourth
Plan period, it is expected (in the Draft Fourth Plan) that the plan
investment will generate 18·5 to 19 mn new jobs (4·5 to 5 mn in
agriculture and 14 mn outside agriculture), leaving a gap which, if
not filled by special measures such as relief construction works,
would see unemployment increasing by a further 4 to 4·5 mn.

The estimates of employment generated are based largely on
investment/employment norms, which have been revised to some
extent to take account of changes in technology and scale, using
project reports when these are available, plus an arbitrary allowance
for the additional employment generated indirectly in the 'non-
organized' sectors of the economy. No attempt has been made,
however, to reconcile the forecasts of employment generated, with the

[14] *4DO*, p. 3.
[15] Directorate General of Employment and Training, *Employment Review*, *1961–6* (Min. of Labour, Employment and Rehabilitation, 1967), p. 9.
[16] *4DO*, p. 106.

forecasts of additional manpower required, and quite different estimating methods are used for each of the two forecasts. Nor has any attempt been made to relate the anticipated increases in employment in 'organized' industry to the relatively low rate of increase in employment in this sector recorded during the Third Plan period. Whether the additional employment actually generated during the Fourth Plan period will correspond to the estimates—in terms either of the total number of new jobs or of the nature of the additional employment—will depend primarily on the following factors:

(a) The degree to which the Draft Fourth Plan physical targets of investment and output are achieved;

(b) The degree to which increases in output are achieved by the improved utilization of existing plant and equipment and the existing labour force—i.e. the adequacy of the allowance made for improved capital and labour productivity with existing facilities; and

(c) The accuracy with which the assumed investment/employment norms reflect the influence of technological change and scale of plant on manpower requirements.

Because of the rapid pace of technological change with its accompanying economies of scale, and because of the emphasis given in the Draft Fourth Plan to improving the utilization of past investments—especially in plants which are in many cases already fully manned for capacity operation—the degree of *additional* employment generated per unit of additional investment or output is likely to be even less than in earlier plans.

Increased labour productivity which results from the more efficient use of existing facilities in which scarce capital resources have already been invested, is a clear gain to the Indian economy. But the benefits are less obvious when we consider new investments of a capital-intensive nature, which create relatively little additional employment in a labour-surplus economy. The choice of techniques will, of course, affect not only the total amount of new employment generated, but also the numbers and kinds of educated and trained people required to produce a given output. It is an issue which has been much discussed by the Planning Commission: what are appropriate technologies for a developing country, and what preference should be given in the Plan to labour-intensive techniques? This question is of such fundamental importance to any policy of investment in human capital that it is worthwhile attempting to summarize the main considerations which appear to underlie the cautious attitude to 'employment orientated' investment adopted in the Draft Fourth Plan:

(1) Labour-intensive techniques should be encouraged if they are as efficient as capital-intensive techniques. They should not waste scarce raw materials (a common disadvantage of most labour-intensive methods of food processing, for example) and their total costs of production should be no higher. Costs might be interpreted in a wider sense, however, if the adoption of more labour-intensive techniques stimulated the development of industry in the rural areas, and limited the flow of population to the cities, thus avoiding some of the increased costs of housing and other services which are associated with this internal migration.

(2) It is recognized that the market prices of capital, foreign exchange, highly qualified and skilled manpower, and unskilled labour, do not reflect their relative scarcities in India, and that a system of shadow prices which did reflect social opportunity costs would show some labour-intensive techniques to be more economic.

(3) Shadow prices can be used by the planners to allocate scarce resources between sectors, and to evaluate the potential return on investment in specific projects. But at the level of the individual firm—especially in the private sector, but also in day-to-day operations in the public sector—shadow prices are unlikely to be workable if they diverge from market prices. Market prices can be aligned with the appropriate shadow prices if the political will to do so is strong enough; the devaluation of the rupee in June 1966 brought the internal market cost of foreign exchange much nearer to its true cost.

(4) Once prices did reflect the true relative costs of capital, qualified manpower, and unskilled labour, appropriate technologies could be designed and engineered to make the most efficient use of the resources available in India—and some, at least, of these new designs would be relatively labour-intensive. In the long run, therefore, given a successful design effort and the widespread adoption of the new indigenous technologies, fuller employment of the labour force might be achieved. This fuller employment would be a function mainly of the higher long run rate of economic growth which would result from more balanced development reflecting Indian factor endowments.

(5) But this would inevitably be a very slow process, with employment effects governed by the speed at which more appropriate—and therefore more economic—new indigenous technologies could be first successfully designed and engineered, and then adopted commercially on a wide scale.

(6) Within the time context of the Fourth and Fifth Plan periods, the scope for increased employment promoted by the adoption of more labour-intensive techniques is severely circumscribed. Many of the labour-intensive techniques proposed for adoption are inefficient—even given appropriate shadow prices—in terms of total costs of production, especially when full account is taken of the economic losses incurred in the cruder forms of processing which waste scarce food and raw materials, or fail to recover valuable by-products.

The main objective of most of these labour-intensive schemes is to utilize more *unskilled* labour, and the technical possibilities of doing this economically are limited, in the absence of radical changes in design. In agriculture and services the degree of labour intensity is very high already—too high, in view of the failure of these sectors to employ their workers *fully*. In the more capital-intensive sector of 'organized' industry, most of the existing projects are already heavily overmanned with both clerical and unskilled labour—they are often both capital intensive *and* labour intensive in practice. The benefits to be derived from the adoption of more appropriate technologies lie therefore more in the saving of scarce capital resources—thus improving the return on the capital invested by achieving higher productivity per unit of capital—than in increasing the absolute number of unskilled, semi-skilled, and clerical workers employed.

For all of these reasons it is likely that an employment-orientated Fourth Plan which deliberately sponsored *known*, and relatively inefficient, labour-intensive techniques in the manufacturing sector, would merely increase total production costs without making much impact on total employment. But an important exception must be made for inter-sectoral shifts in investment, in favour of sectors where the return on capital invested in labour-intensive projects may be exceptionally high. Such an exception is investment in the basic necessities of the rural economy—especially in minor irrigation works. The return on investment in these rural construction projects—such as the construction of waterproof irrigation channels, the improvement of field drainage, the digging of tanks (small reservoirs), and the drilling of tube wells—is very high under present conditions of acute water scarcity. And labour-intensive methods, using largely unskilled labour, are both technically possible and economically efficient. If shadow prices were consistently applied to allow for the negligible foreign exchange requirement of these investments, and if capital costs were adjusted to allow for the resource composition of the capital invested, the true return on investment would be seen to be even higher.

These possibilities are recognized, to a limited extent, in the Draft Fourth Plan, but there is a tendency to regard many of these rural construction schemes as merely relief works, intended to provide temporary or seasonal work for the rural unemployed. They could with advantage be given much higher priority, not as relief works, but as high-yielding projects in which a much larger proportion of the Plan's financial resources could be invested on a continuing basis—as a major component of the planned investment programme, and not merely as temporary measures in times of drought to alleviate hardship in the rural areas.

Even if rural construction works were given higher priority, however, the planners still seem to be relying heavily on technological advance, especially in manufacturing industry, to achieve a rapid increase in output by methods which are essentially capital-intensive. Because of the increasingly sophisticated nature of the technology employed, the demand for high calibre technical and managerial personnel will continue to rise, and the return on the resources devoted to their education and training will be correspondingly high—provided that they are productively employed. But the numbers of educated and trained people required will still be small in relation to the increase in the total labour force. The bulk of the unemployed will still be unskilled, but as progress is made (on social grounds) towards universal education, even the unskilled will have at least an elementary education. Thus, as unemployment and underemployment rise, the economic return on the resources devoted to elementary education will diminish. A more deliberate attempt to plan for full employment with the aid of labour-intensive techniques in those sectors where the return on investment using these techniques is high (given the use of shadow prices), might not raise the return on elementary education much, until techniques which made use of that education had been developed. But even if most of the additional jobs were unskilled, the return on health expenditure would be substantially improved. If more resources were devoted to, say, rural construction projects, this would leave less resources available for investment in the more advanced sectors, and the requirements for high-level manpower would rise less rapidly. And if less high-level manpower were needed, because technology had been adapted to make the most efficient use of the physical resources available in India, then some of the resources now used to educate and train people to apply the more sophisticated imported technology could be saved for investment in other aspects of education, or in health, or in any other part of the economy where the return on investment would be higher.

23. HEALTH AND FAMILY PLANNING

An indication of the relative priorities accorded, in the development budget, to the various health and family planning programmes, is given by the financial provisions of the Fourth Plan, as recorded in the Draft Outline. These are shown in Table 5.

TABLE 5

Draft Fourth Plan Outlay on Health and Family Planning
(Rs mn)

Medical education, training, and research	1,783
Control of communicable diseases	866·8
Medical care, including hospitals, dispensaries, and primary health centres	1,810
Other public health systems	360·2
Indigenous systems of medicine	100
Water supply and sanitation:	
Rural water supply schemes	1,500
Areas endemic with cholera and filariasis	330
Urban water supply and sanitation schemes, including metropolitan schemes	1,900
Family planning (expanded programme)	2,293·1
Total health and family planning	10,943·1

Notes: (*a*) It is assumed that the increased provision for family planning (which was allotted only Rs 950 mn in the Draft Fourth Plan) will not be made at the expense of any other health programme.

(*b*) In addition to the provision of Rs 1,783 mn for medical education, training, and research, a substantial portion of the expanded family planning budget will be devoted to the training of medical and public health personnel in family planning techniques.

Source: 4DO, pp. 338, 349.

A substantial part of the health budget is devoted to medical education and training of a general character, which is not directly related to any one health programme, but is necessary, in some degree, to the implementation of all health programmes. This expenditure is related to forecasts of manpower requirements in health and family planning, which have been discussed in the context of education. The return on this expenditure on medical education and training will depend, however, on where the doctors and other medical personnel actually practise—in the State medical services or in private practice (or not in India at all), and, in the case of State employees, in which particular health or family planning programme they are employed.

The cost of medical education and training should therefore be allocated between the various programmes, in proportion to the manpower requirements of each programme. This would establish the total cost of each programme—to the extent that it is financed out of the development budget—and it is to this cost that the benefits derived from that programme should be related. As in the case of education, however, the total cost of each health programme is higher than that shown in Table 5—notably to the extent that maintenance of existing facilities and the salaries of State medical personnel are financed out of the ordinary revenue budgets of the States. The exception is the family planning programme which, although implemented by the State Governments, is financed to the extent of 90 per cent to 100 per cent (according to the category of expenditure) by the Centre out of the expanded Draft Fourth Plan allocation. In terms of total expenditure, therefore, the relative priority accorded to family planning, as compared with the other health programmes, is not as high as it appears to be from Table 5.

24. ANNOUNCED AIMS OF THE HEALTH PLAN

With the exception of family planning, where the announced objective is to reduce the birth rate from the present level of 40 per thousand to 25 per thousand 'as expeditiously as possible', the aims of the health programmes outlined in the Draft Fourth Plan are stated in general, social, and humanitarian terms. The return on health expenditure made under earlier plans is normally measured by the sharp fall in the death rate—from 40 per thousand in the 1920s to about 12 per thousand today, with a corresponding increase in the expectation of life at birth from about twenty-seven years to about fifty years—the sharp fall in infant mortality rates, and the success achieved in controlling the incidence of major diseases such as malaria, smallpox, and cholera. Expenditure on health in the Draft Fourth Plan is justified in similar fashion—as contributing to the continued fall in the death rate, improving the health standards of the population in general, and 'intensifying the campaigns against communicable diseases which sap the health and efficiency of our people' (p. 339).

These are social aims, rather than economic objectives. And although it is implicitly assumed that all health expenditure will yield economic benefits, no attempt is made to estimate the economic return on different types of health outlay—or to emphasize those which are likely to yield the highest economic returns. It is therefore useful, for economic purposes, to distinguish between:

(a) expenditure which is primarily intended to prevent death— e.g. expenditure on casualty wards in hospitals, or the treatment of 'killer' diseases which would prove fatal if left untreated; and

(b) expenditure which is primarily intended to prevent or to cure debilitating diseases, such as dysentery and worms, which are not usually killers—except to the extent that, if left untreated, they would shorten life expectancy.

Expenditure to prevent death has a positive economic return if the patient subsequently produces more than he consumes. But expenditure made to prevent or to cure debilitating diseases may well yield a larger return, because the increase in productivity made possible by the prevention or cure of the disease would be very likely to exceed only to the *increase* in consumption made possible by the achievement of better health and a higher income.

The cost per person *prevented* from contracting any disease is likely to be much less than the cost per person *cured* of that disease after he has caught it. The rate of return on expenditure made to provide pure drinking water, for example, would normally be much higher than the return on expenditure on medical care for people who had caught dysentery or cholera through drinking impure water. Although the benefit is the same in each case (or greater if illness is prevented), the cost per head of providing pure drinking water is likely to be much less than the cost per head of providing effective medical care. The difference between the two rates of return would probably be even greater if the cost in each case were calculated with the use of shadow prices for all the resources used. In the case of malaria, the economic maxim that prevention is better than cure has clearly been followed with great success. But it is very surprising to find the Draft Fourth Plan defending the admittedly inadequate provision made for drinking water supply in these terms: 'With the limited resources available, it is not possible to wipe out all the backlog in rural and urban water supply and sanitation facilities during the Fourth Plan. Priorities have to be assigned to tackle more pressing problems' (p. 349).

Health expenditure is usually defended more on social or humanitarian grounds than on economic grounds. *Any* reduction in the death rate, or in infant mortality rates, is a good thing *per se* and *any* cure of disease is to be welcomed as full justification of the expenditure incurred. All sick people should have the same opportunity to obtain treatment, irrespective of their incomes and irrespective of their age and ability to work. It is also usually held, again on humanitarian or ethical grounds, that prevention of death should take priority over the prevention or cure of illness, if the illness is unlikely to prove fatal. But expenditure made to produce a decline in the death rate may yield different returns according to whose death is prevented. Prolonging the life of the urban elderly may yield little direct economic benefit—for it will add nothing to production, while adding significantly to consumption. But the prevention of death, and the lengthening of the *working* life, of skilled workers in industry or agriculture may yield substantial economic benefits. The ethical argument, even if applied to the reduction of infant mortality, is certainly in conflict with the economic argument for birth control—which assumes that an uncontrolled increase in the population would not produce a large enough excess (if any) of additional production over additional consumption.

With most types of health expenditure, therefore, a fundamental conflict arises between the social, humanitarian, or ethical considerations, and the economic objective of securing the greatest economic return from the employment of scarce resources. Most societies prefer to pursue the social aim of equality of medical treatment, reducing the death-rate and preventing or curing illness indiscriminately wherever it occurs. But can a country as poor as India afford to have the same non-economic objectives? If total resources are inadequate, but the entire population is provided with a modicum of medical care on a proportionate per capita basis, costs per head are likely to rise and efficiency in preventing and curing disease to fall—so that neither social nor economic aims may be achieved. Several small, isolated, and inadequately staffed and equipped primary health centres—some of which are little more than bare shells—are likely to be less effective in curing disease than one larger one which can be fully staffed and equipped, so that all its facilities can be fully utilized. And the economic return on health expenditure could be raised by relating it more directly to productivity, giving priority in the provision of medical services to classes of people whose productivity is most likely to be increased by the prevention or cure of illness. If the prevention or cure of a debilitating disease earns relatively high economic returns, should it not be given higher priority in the allocation of scarce resources? And if social aims are pursued at the expense of economic benefits, then at least society should know the extent of the economic sacrifice implied by the choice of ends it has made.

Certainly, both in preventing death and in reducing the incidence of disease, there is no conflict if the same objective can be achieved at lower cost. The case for prevention of disease at source—as in the provision of pure drinking water supply—is greatly strengthened by the fact that no compromise need be made between the achievement of social and economic objectives.

If the humanitarian aim of equal treatment for all, without discrimination on grounds of age or potential productivity is abandoned in favour of the pursuit of strictly economic objectives, economic arguments can readily be made for many forms of discrimination. Money spent on improving the health of the employed labour force, especially of the younger and more productive members of it, or money for improving the health of children and students so that they can more readily absorb education and put it to good use in subsequent employment, or money for improving the health and capacity for decision of high level administrators and managers—all are likely to yield a greater return than the same sum spent on improving the health of the urban elderly. Spending money on eliminating dysentery and worms may so increase agricultural production that it will save more lives than would have been saved by the elimination of, say, tuberculosis amongst unskilled workers in urban areas. Again, a conflict arises between social aims and economic priorities. But society is in a better position to decide whether it can or cannot *afford* to pursue social aims, such as equality of opportunity for medical treatment, if it can first calculate the cost in terms of economic benefits foregone.

Whether or not a *potential* rise in productivity, due to better health, will be translated into an *actual* rise in productivity, will depend, of course, on the prospects for employment. A healthier man who remains unemployed will still produce nothing—though he may consume more if he is given financial assistance. The benefit from health expenditure will also be reduced if the improved health of the work force results in a reduction in its size—for example if a firm finds that it has to carry a smaller reserve to allow for absenteeism, which was formerly largely due to the sickness now eliminated. But the return on health expenditure may be very high if better health improves the *quality* of a given work force, without reducing its size. There is convincing evidence that, in many factories, output could be substantially increased with the same labour force if the workers were healthier and more able to concentrate on the job for longer periods of time.

The poorest unskilled workers, both in the towns and in the rural areas, may be the most susceptible to illness. Therefore a given expenditure on health may yield a greater return—in terms of the number of sick people made well—if spent on those lowest paid workers. Under conditions of full employment, the improved health of these unskilled workers may also raise production more than it would be raised if equivalent resources were spent on improving the health of other, better off, people. But if there is a substantial level of unemployment in the economy, and if this unemployment is expected to prevail in future, an addition to the unskilled labour force brought about by preventing early death from disease or by preventing chronic sickness, may merely add to the number of unemployed—and produce no economic return at all. This argument may not be conclusive, however, even under condition of persistent unemployment, because the main effect of improving the health of unskilled workers may be to improve the *quality* of their work—and this improvement in quality may not be offset by the employment of less workers. The unskilled labour force may remain the same size as before, but it will be more productive, and the productivity of scarce capital resources will be raised to a corresponding extent.

Both ill-health and unskilled labour requirements may be seasonal, especially in the rural areas, and the season of ill health may coincide with the season of unemployment. Under those conditions the economic loss attributable to ill health is reduced, because no employment would have been available at the time anyway. Conversely, the economic return on improved health will be low because that improved health will coincide with the onset of seasonal unemployment. Where there is chronic underemployment in agriculture, improved health may still be accompanied by the same amount of involuntary underemployment. On the other hand, if ill health is the traditional *cause* of less intensive employment, an improvement in health may result in more regular employment—unless involuntary underemployment is converted into voluntary underemployment because traditional attitudes cannot easily be changed.

CONCLUSION

A general theme running through this chapter has been the need to look at social outlays in terms of costs and returns. While some of the investments planned, for example, in agricultural and medical education and in family planning, seem fully justified, others, for example in undergraduate arts courses, seem uneconomic. Indeed economic considerations argue strongly for more expenditure on the first group of activities and for less on the second. However, neither health nor education programmes can be viewed in isolation, and plans to produce more doctors or agricultural graduates will fail unless the incomes policy is also altered to encourage such people to work where they can, in large numbers, be more productive—in the countryside. It is vital that education and health should not be looked at only as ends in themselves, but as part of a set of complementary inputs necessary for economic growth.

APPENDIX: MANPOWER PLANNING AND THE RATE OF RETURN ON INVESTMENT IN EDUCATION—A COMPLEMENTARY APPROACH

Of all the inadequacies for which manpower and educational planning in India may be criticized, perhaps none is more wasteful than the neglect of economics—not only in ignoring the influence of the labour market, but also in making no attempt to calculate the relative rates of return on each form of investment in human capital. The absence of any calculation of relative costs and benefits makes it hard to assess the implications of the relative priorities actually accorded in the Draft Fourth Plan, in its proposed financial outlays on the various education, training, health, and family planning programmes, and the priority accorded to the social services as a whole in relation to investment in the rest of the economy. Nor is there any calculation of the extent of the economic sacrifices made in the pursuit of social and political objectives, which yield smaller economic benefits than investment made in pursuit of strictly economic objectives.

Theoretically, an optimum allocation of resources would be achieved if the marginal return on plan expenditure were the same in the social services as in any other sector, and, within the social services, if it were the same on each kind of investment in education, training, and health. The last rupee provided in the plan for a particular level and type of education, or for in-plant training in industry, would earn the same return as the last rupee spent on medical care in the hospitals, or on family planning, or on the supply of pure drinking water. And this would be the same as the return on the last rupee provided for agriculture, or for physical investment in plant and machinery in manufacturing industry.

In the ideal approach to this problem of resource allocation, manpower planning and rate-of-return calculations would be interdependent, the one complementing the other. Starting with a forecast of manpower demand and supply, we could attempt to determine the rate of return on additional expenditure on education and training. Then, by adjusting educational investment programmes so that the returns on marginal expenditure in each programme are equated (both within the educational system itself, and between it and other sectors of the economy), we would influence manpower supply, the labour market, and manpower demand—and change the marginal return on investment in education. Could we then repeat the process, *ad infinitum*, moving closer and closer to an optimum allocation of scarce resources? The conceptual and practical difficulties encountered in making an analysis of this order of complexity are very great. How near can we come in practice to this planners' ideal?

A rigorous attempt to combine manpower planning with the calculation of economic costs and benefits would comprise the following initial steps:

(1) Given the investment priorities already established in other sectors, forecast the numbers and kinds of people required in each occupation, and at each level of skill and supervisory or managerial responsibility.

(2) Determine the education and training required for efficient performance in each occupation and at each level of skill and responsibility.

(3) Consolidate these findings into a forecast of the numbers and kinds of trained people required as an output from the educational system and training centres.

(4) Determine the additional expenditure to be made on facilities for formal education, in school and university, and on facilities for in-plant training in industry, in order to provide the required output of educated and trained people.

(5) After allowing for private expenditure on education and training, and for non-plan expenditure by the Central, State, and local governments, determine the outlay to be provided in the development plan in order to meet the supply objective.

(6) Cost each type and level of education and training separately, using shadow prices for the resources used in each case, to arrive at the true marginal costs of providing the additional supply of each kind of educated and trained manpower.

(7) Pay people in accordance with their marginal social productivity in each occupation and in each location (e.g. in rural as opposed to urban areas). If the social productivity of agricultural graduates who actually work on farms, or of doctors who actually practise in the villages, is very high, then they should receive comparably high rewards. This should help to ensure:

   (a) that sufficient students of adequate calibre are persuaded to enrol in the additional educational and training facilities provided; and

   (b) that sufficient graduates from the educational system and training centres are persuaded to work in the occupations and in the places where they are most needed, and where their marginal social productivity will be highest—because this is also where they will earn the highest private return.

(8) In the light of these anticipated earnings, calculate the marginal social rate of return on the additional expenditure made on each level and type of education and training. If the allocation of resources is optimal, the marginal social return on each category of expenditure should be equal—and equal to the marginal social rate of return on plan expenditure on health, and on all other sectors of the economy.

The main practical difficulties besetting each step in this initial approach are:

(1) Forecasts of manpower requirements are, as has already been demonstrated, subject to wide margins of error—especially if they are made ten or fifteen years ahead to allow for the time lag between educational investment and the output of educated and trained people.

(2) The expenditure made, at each level, to supply the additional requirements for educated and trained people may not have the intended results, for a variety of reasons. The assumptions made about the future efficiency of the educational system may prove to be too optimistic; wastage rates may be higher than anticipated; and all the measures relied upon to improve the quality and the employment value of the education provided may be less effective than expected—as they would be if political pressures for more university places, at the expense of quality, proved irresistible.

(3) The allowance made for private and government non-plan expenditures on education and training may be inaccurate—for example, if Plan priorities were based on a false assumption about the extent of the complementary expenditure sanctioned by the States out of their revenue budgets to permit selective pay increases to be given to qualified teachers, or to subsidize private industrial training schemes.

(4) The costs of the additional facilities provided for each level and type of education and training may be very difficult to establish in practice—especially as the relevant costs are the *marginal* costs of the additional facilities provided, and not the average costs recorded for each level and type of education and training. If the capacity of existing educational and training facilities is under-utilized, marginal costs may be low; if it is already fully utilized the costs of marginal increases in capacity may be high. And when prices are rising very sharply, as they have been in India during the last five years, marginal costs, at *current prices*, may be much higher than average costs at historical prices. Unless all investment is made at precisely the same time (or unless suitable adjustments are made to allow for price inflation), any comparison made between the returns on various forms of educational or training investment, or between the returns on educational and other investment, will become hopelessly distorted.

(5) The labour market may not operate in such a way as to attract a sufficient number of suitable students into the additional educational and training facilities provided, or may fail to persuade them to enter the occupations where they are most needed, or to work in the places where they will be most productive. This would be the case whenever the inter-occupational or inter-regional wage and salary differentials in the labour market did not reflect marginal social productivity— including the indirect social benefits derived from the removal of impediments to the balanced growth of the economy as a whole. Failing government action to influence wage and salary differentials in the public sector, a wide disparity between actual earnings and marginal social productivity must be expected to persist. Allowance must therefore be made for this disparity in calculating the true rates of return on educational investment.

(6) The impact of an international market in the skills produced by higher education may be incorrectly foreseen, and the emigration of trained doctors, engineers, and scientists to Europe and the United States may reduce the supply to the Indian economy below expectations.

(7) The return on investment in education and training will be strongly affected by the complementary investments made in other social services and in other sectors of the economy. Expenditure on health, for example, will improve both the performance of students within the educational system and their potential productivity in subsequent employment. And the potential marginal social productivity of educated and trained people will actually be realized only to the extent that sufficient opportunities for productive employment are created by complementary investment in agriculture, manu-facturing industry, and other sectors of the economy. Appro-priate allowance must therefore be made for the impact on employment, and on the earnings of educated people, of the planned level of complementary investment in all other sectors—and if relative priorities are changed, allowance must be made for the effect of changes in this level of complementary investment.

(8) The benefits resulting from expenditure on education and training will be realized over the entire future working lives of today's schoolchildren and students. The return on

investment in education and training will therefore depend on marginal social productivity of employment in particular occupations over a long period of time, and will be responsive to shifts in manpower demand caused by technological change, and by changes in the pace and pattern of economic growth. In order to take these factors into account it would be necessary to forecast the demand and supply schedules for each category of educated and trained worker over his entire working life— which has yet to begin. To construct these demand and supply schedules we should need

(*a*) a detailed forecast of manpower requirements;

(*b*) a forecast of the supply of trained people from each part of the educational system; and

(*c*) a forecast of the imperfect workings of the labour market, and of the extent and nature of educated unemployment— all on a year-by-year basis over a period of some forty years. The margin or error in such a forecast would be very wide. But when all future earnings are discounted to present value, the significance of the larger errors made in the latter part of the forecast would be much reduced. And the margin of error in a static calculation which took no account of future developments would almost certainly be even greater.

It is essential to adopt a dynamic approach, using improved techniques of manpower planning to draw up future demand and supply schedules on a logical basis, as a foundation for the calculation of more realistic rates of return on investment in education and training. The complementary nature of manpower planning and the rate of return approach now becomes clear, because the return will depend on the future demand and supply schedules, and the future supply will itself depend on the educational investment made in the light of anticipated rates of return on that investment.

(9) The stream of benefits flowing from investment in education and training is unlikely to follow the same pattern, over time, as the stream of benefits flowing from other kinds of investment, such as physical investment in plant and machinery. There is typically a much longer gestation period, or time lag, after the investment in education and training is made, and before the benefits attributable to it begin to be earned. When they do begin, they are likely to be relatively low for the first

few years, but may then be expected to rise steadily year by year. In contrast, the yield on physical investment in plant and machinery may begin much earlier, reach a peak fairly quickly, and then remain relatively stable. These two dissimilar benefit streams can be compared only by discounting all future benefits to their present value, or by calculating an internal rate of return to each category of expenditure. The comparison between the net present values of educational and other kinds of investment will therefore be affected by the rate of interest used to discount future benefits. In most cases, a high discount rate—a preference for quick returns—would favour investment in other sectors of the economy and militate against investment in human capital. Such a preference for quick returns could explain attempts to cut the education and health budgets more sharply than the other Fourth Plan outlays—thus sacrificing the greater economic benefits which might have been earned in the Fifth and subsequent plans. But where the return on education and training is exceptionally high in the early years—as it would be if a crash training programme successfully overcame acute manpower shortages which had prevented the efficient utilization of capital investments already made—then a high discount rate might favour *certain kinds* of marginal expenditure on education and training relatively to marginal investment in new physical assets.

The few attempts that have been made so far to calculate the economic return on investment in education and training do not overcome any of these problems. The first difficulty usually encountered is the lack of the data needed for the construction of education/age/earnings profiles as a basis for the calculation of the discounted present value of the lifetime earnings attributable to education and training. All that can usually be done—and the information available to do even this is often far from adequate—is to take a snapshot of the existing labour force at a given point of time—usually, perforce, the present—relating the age and education of workers in given occupations to the earnings they receive. This cross-sectional approach, which provides a very rough proxy for lifetime earnings, is essentially a static concept. The earnings differentials attributable to education and training will vary over time, according to the demand and supply schedules which apply, over their working lives, to workers with different educational qualifications. The cross-sectional approach reflects only the situation as it is today, with existing levels of technology, existing levels of unemployment, and the existing imperfect state of the labour market. It may also reflect historical imbalances between supply and demand, which may have led to the employment of over-qualified or under-qualified people in positions which, once filled, become insulated from later changes in the labour market. Changes in technology, or changes in the future pace and pattern of economic growth, may produce quite different levels of demand and supply.

The same difficulty arises with the calculation of earnings foregone by students, which can be regarded either as part of the cost of their education and training, or as negative earnings which reduce the present value of the future stream of benefits attributable to education and training. Again, much depends on the opportunities for productive employment which would have been available to anyone who elected to enter the labour force, with lower qualifications, at an earlier age instead of continuing his education. At first sight, it might seem that the earnings foregone by students would be equal to the earnings received by boys and girls of the same age who entered the labour force earlier. But if manpower planning were perfect, so that supply and demand at the lower educational level were perfectly matched, then any marginal increase in the labour force at that educational level would result in unemployment. It might therefore be argued that, under conditions of excess supply at lower educational levels, the marginal social productivity of the student who gives up his higher education to enter the labour market before qualifying is nil—because manpower requirements at that lower level are already fully satisfied by the supply which was planned on the assumption that students would be excluded from the labour force.

Another difficulty is that we are interested in the *marginal* return on investment and training—the return on the additional expenditure made in the Plan on each level and type of education and training, not the *average* return on existing educational facilities, which is what we should obtain from the static cross-sectional approach to education/age/earnings profiles.

There are also, of course, many well-known conceptual difficulties[17]

[17] For a detailed discussion of all the technical objections see M. Blaug, 'The Rate of Return on Investment in Education in Great Britain', *The Manchester School*, Sept. 1965, pp. 205–61.

which have been exhaustively discussed in the literature on the application of rate of return calculations to investment in education. What part of the observed earnings differentials can properly be attributed to differences in education and training? In India, in particular, differences in earnings may be as much due to differences in caste, or in family status and income, or in innate ability and drive, as they are to education and training. And when formal education is supplemented by in-plant training, how much of the difference in earnings can be attributed to differences in formal education, and how much to differences in the amount of in-plant training received? Attempts can be made to control the influence of all these other factors, and by adopting simplifying assumptions it is possible to isolate the return on in-plant training from the return on formal education. But as more of these interdependent variables are taken into account, the calculation of meaningful rates of return becomes an increasingly complex operation.

Finally, even if the rate-of-return calculations could be made both accurately and dynamically, reflecting future demand and supply schedules, we are still left with a feedback problem. For it would be fallacious to suppose that the Indian economy is today set on a path anywhere near that of dynamic equilibrium, in which the marginal rate of return on all forms of investment, including investment in education and training, is already approaching equality. When the rate-of-return calculations, made on the basis of estimated future demand and supply schedules, demonstrate that priorities should be changed within the educational system or between education and other parts of the economy, then the level or character of investment in education will change, the supply schedule of educated and trained people will shift, and their marginal social productivity will change. Given the demand schedules for particular skills at various prices, the shift in the supply schedule will change relative earnings and affect the rate of return on educational investment—implying a further adjustment of investment priorities in education and training. All other factors remaining constant—which implies a perfect forecast of the impact of technological change on the manpower demand schedule—investment priorities could be progressively adjusted in this way until a state of dynamic equilibrium had been reached.

8

Population Control:
Aims and Policies*

ROBERT CASSEN

FEW people would deny that the rapid rate of population growth in India is one of the greatest threats—if not the greatest—to her hopes of prosperity. The total population almost certainly passed the 500 mn mark before the end of 1966, and, at the estimated rate of 2·4 per cent, is currently growing by 1 mn a month. There is not much evidence that would offer the expectation of any decline in fertility in the near future, while the death-rate is expected to continue to fall. In the absence of any decline in fertility, the rate of population growth may be expected to increase, reaching, according to one estimate,[1] 3·1 per cent in 1985. At that rate, the population would double in less than twenty-three years.

2. Given what seems almost to be a law of demography in developing countries—that all population estimates are under-estimates—one can hardly feel that this forecast is too gloomy. The emphasis given to population control in the Draft Plan, and the tremendous effort which is now being made in India, are therefore both very natural and very welcome.

3. This chapter has three main sections. In the first there is some discussion of factors other than birth-control measures and their

---

* This chapter was written while the author was employed by the UK Ministry of Overseas Development. No part of its contents should be taken necessarily to reflect official policy. The author is indebted to his colleagues there for comments on this and connected work, and particularly to Mr D. Seers and Mr W. A. B. Hopkin. I have benefited greatly from discussion at the Conference, and most especially from the comments of Prof. Paul Streeten and Michael Lipton. The customary absolution from responsibility applies.

[1] UN Dept. Economic and Social Affairs, *Report on the Family Planning Programme in India* (Feb. 1966), UN doc. (TAO/IND/48, Photo-offset) p. 95 (henceforth 'UN *Report*'.) For trends in total population, &c. see Appendix, Table 1, p. 269.

possible influences on the growth of Indian population. In the second the economics of reducing the birth-rate are examined in general terms. In the third the programme of the current plan period is considered.

1. THE INFLUENCE OF FACTORS OTHER THAN BIRTH CONTROL

4. The view has been expressed that the population problems of developing countries may 'solve themselves'. Although there is no satisfactory quantitative explanation of the decline in birth-rates experienced by the developed countries, the list of contributory factors believed to be the causes of the decline is fairly well defined. It has even been graced with the title of the 'theory of demographic transition',[2] though as more and better historical demographic data are compiled, this theory becomes more rather than less puzzling.

5. At any rate, there is agreement among demographers that fertility decline is associated with economic development, and in particular with 'modernization'. The growth of urban industrial society makes itself felt as an influence in the direction of changing social customs which affect fertility—most particularly in raising the marriage age—and of raising the economic cost of having children.

6. As far as India is concerned, there is little basis to hope that such factors will operate significantly in the near future. Urbanization, which figures importantly in the theory of demographic transition, does not yet appear to be having much effect on the overall birth-rate. The urbanization which has taken place in India has not been accompanied by the types of social change which favour lower birth-rates. Indeed, the social system and family structure of rural life seem to survive transplantation to the town or city quite remarkably, according to sociological studies. Marital fertility is somewhat lower in cities than in rural areas, and urban birth-rates are lower than rural rates, in part as a consequence of the high male-female ratio in cities.[3] But the differences are not very great, and the rural-urban distribution of population has changed little between the 1951 and 1961 censuses.

7. As far as marriage age is concerned, the UN Report on the

---

[2] For a discussion of this theory, see D. M. Heer, 'Economic Development and Fertility', *Demography*, iii, no. 2 (Chicago, 1966), and works there cited.
[3] See Appendix, Table 2, p. 270.

Family Planning Programme in India calculates[4] that if the average age at marriage rose from 16 to 20 over the period up to 1985, the birth-rate would fall by about 7 per 1,000—that is, from 41·4 in 1965 to 34·4 in 1985. This by itself would be only a slight contribution to the solution of the population problem. And, as the Report emphasizes, this is not an extrapolation of any trend, but an upper limit to the results both of changes which are occurring and of possible policies to be pursued by the Government of India to raise the marriage age.

8. One aspect of the 'transition', possibly more hopeful than those mentioned hitherto and largely neglected by the UN Report, is the relation between death-rates and birth-rates. A commonly quoted cause of high birth-rates in developing countries is the combination of high death-rates and no social security, or, to put it another way, the desire of parents to ensure that some at least of their children will survive as long as they themselves do. Demographers at the Harvard School of Public Health have produced studies showing that, in a cross section of forty-one countries, the strongest relation among numerous variables with fertility was that of infant mortality— where one was high, so was the other.[5] They could, of course, be positively correlated simply as a result of some other factor or factors acting on both. But simulation studies of mathematical population models have yielded results described as 'generally realistic', showing slower population growth rates, over a range of mortality rates, the lower the mortality.[6]

---

[4] UN *Report*, pp. 97–98. More precisely, the Report estimates such a reduction in the birth-rate on the basis of assumptions that by 1985 no girls will marry before 18, 15 per cent will be married at 18, 30 per cent at 19, 60 per cent at 20 'and so on', making an allowance for increased marital fertility as a consequence of the likely reduction in the period of delayed consummation of marriage.

[5] D. M. Heer.

[6] D. M. Heer & D. O. Smith, *Mortality Level and Desired Family Size*, Contrib. no. 26 (Harvard Center for Population Studies, 1966). Another simulation study has however found, on the basis of different assumptions, an increase in the population growth-rate, the decline in the death-rate outweighing the associated decline in the birth-rate. Cf. J. C. Ridley and others, 'Effects of Changing Mortality on Natality: Some Estimates from a Simulation Model', *Milbank Memorial Fund Q.*, Jan. 1967 (New York), pp. 77–97. This study, emphasizing the effects of increased marital duration and increased intervals between births resulting from lower death-rates and lower infant mortality (unlike Heer and Smith's study, which emphasizes desired family size) is based on parameters derived from Indian demographic data, and may well be the more realistic as regards the near future of the Indian population.

9. Of course, there are historical cases of simultaneously falling death-rates and rising birth-rates. To treat death-rate reductions as a hopeful source of fertility reductions in India, one would need to know something of the time lags involved, or threshold values of death-rates, or changes in death-rates that would support the case. Historically, the time lags appear to have been rather long.

10. This is not an adequate discussion of autonomous factors influencing the rate of growth of population in India. It has only attempted to draw out one or two important points. The UN Report concludes that some decline in fertility would undoubtedly take place in the future, even in the absence of a birth control programme, 'as a result of modernization and changes in customs and social factors, particularly a slow but steady rise in the average age at marriage'. However, it goes on to say, it is not excluded 'that this decline in fertility will, at least partly, be counter-balanced by an increase in fecundity,[7] and by an increase in the proportion of live births to total births, as a result of improved health conditions. Future decline in adult mortality may also reduce the frequency of widowhood and keep a larger proportion of women in marital status; and a weakening of taboos against re-marriage might tend to raise the present relatively low level of fertility in India'.

11. It is this analysis, together with the expectation of a continued decline in death rates, which led the Report to project an increase in the growth-rate of the population in the absence of any measures to control it. We have not found much, if any, cause to challenge this view. One last point, however, may be of some significance. Although such social and economic change as has been occurring in India may not have brought with it any fall in fertility, this may in part be due to a lack of knowledge of, and means for, birth control. It may well be that this change is nevertheless engendering a sharpening of the motivation to adopt measures of birth control when these are made available.

[7] 'Fecundity' in demographic parlance refers to the biological potential for reproduction, while 'fertility' is simply the number of births expressed (usually) as a rate per 1,000 women. The latter is distinguished from the (crude) birth-rate, which is the number of births per 1,000 people. A factor of some importance, which the UN *Report* has not taken into account, is the impact of the eradication of malaria in 1945–55. This considerably reduced child mortality, and results currently in a rising share of women of child-bearing age, making the task of achieving an actual fall in the birth-rate, even with a successful family planning programme, a very daunting one, at least before the mid-1970s.

2. THE ECONOMICS OF REDUCING THE BIRTH-RATE

(a) *The General Argument*

12. We consider the question first quite generally, with the proviso that we are referring to countries where the pressure of population on resources is already considerable. In crude aggregate terms one can set out the problem quite simply. A fall in the birth-rate reduces the number of children in the year in which it occurs relative to the number there would otherwise have been (and in subsequent years if the lower birth-rate continues—we will assume that it does). If we assume—which may not be entirely correct—that a child performs no productive service until the age of fifteen, then we can be confident that income per head during those fifteen years will be higher than it would otherwise have been, if only because there are less heads. (This will be true provided that, as seems plausible, the reduction of numbers of people of non-working age does not affect output. Though it is of course possible that, had there been more children, their parents would have made greater efforts.) But the effect on growth is more complicated than this. The increase in income per head through the reduction of numbers[8] in early years may itself lead to additional increases in incomes. What happens will depend on how the resources, released by the relative reduction in the number of children, are used.

13. These resources may be used in a number of ways. They may simply be consumed—if so, the consequences for economic growth are hard to calculate. There is some effect of consumption on productivity in developing countries, but it would be a major task requiring original research to quantify it. Nevertheless, even if all the released resources are consumed, there is likely to be some improvement of economic performances. The resources may also be saved and invested, though once again only a firm believer in aggregate capital-output ratios would put a definite quantity on the effect of this investment on growth, except to say that it would be positive.

14. Further to this, as well as the resources directly released through the reduction of the number of children to be clothed and fed, there are likely to be investment resources shifted from the social

---

[8] Here and at other points in the paper 'reduction in numbers' should be read as an elliptical expression for 'reduction in numbers relative to those which would have occurred otherwise'.

uses encouraged by a growing population to the provision of productive equipment. It is possible that the contribution of this effect to economic growth may be at least as significant as those mentioned in the previous paragraph.

15. It is, then, fairly clear that for the early years after the fall in the birth-rate there are unambiguous gains in income per head (*a*) simply as a result of the reduction of numbers, with no loss of output, and (*b*) as a result of the application of the resources made available by the reduction of numbers. But, after fifteen years or so, the reduction of numbers affects the size of the labour force, and calculation becomes difficult. One can put the question simply: will the relative loss of labour offset the gains during the early years?

16. We shall not attempt to pursue this question in full. We shall ignore the arguments which purport to show the economic advantages of rapid population growth, since they are hardly relevant to the Indian case. But reference should be made to two important features of the problem. The first is unemployment. Clearly, in a country which has difficulties in absorbing its existing labour force, additions to the labour force cannot be of immediate benefit. Thus, while it is fifteen years before the labour force is affected by a reduction in the birth rate, it may be twenty or thirty years before the numbers actually employed are significantly affected. The second is the so-called 'burden of dependency'. As can be seen from the Appendix (Table 1) fertility decline has the effect of raising quite sharply the proportion of people of working age in the population. These points imply that, whatever sacrifices of output are made by a reduction in labour-force size, they occur a long way in the future and are partially cancelled out by changes in the age distribution. The benefits of reduced numbers, however, occur immediately.

17. (Strictly speaking, the presence of unemployment means that one is concerned with the absolute number of dependents, adult or child, rather than the ratio of people of working and non-working age. A constant dependency ratio as indicated by the size of age groups may conceal a worsening or an improving situation, depending on what is happening to employment. One should add that, for precise calculation, two further aspects at least should be taken into account: (*a*) the fact that declining fertility increases the participation of women in the labour force; and (*b*) the relative consumption standards of children and adults. If welfare is a matter of consumption per head and not output per head, one should note that the dependency ratio need only be corrected for a participation rate to

estimate changes in output per head, but further correction is required for estimating the effect of a change in the dependency ratio on consumption per equivalent adult. See also the quotation from Coale and Hoover in n. 9.)

(b) *The Indian Case*

18. Let us now consider these arguments in the Indian case. The purpose of doing so is not to demonstrate that the gains from reducing the birth-rate in India outweigh the losses. It is rather to see what steps would be necessary to calculate the economic effects of reducing the birth-rate, and thereby to evaluate the return to expenditure on birth control.

19. Unfortunately, as we shall see, it is not possible to estimate at all accurately the 'returns' to birth control, if the above general argument is roughly correct, since on almost all points where quantitative estimates are necessary, they are lacking in the literature known to the author, and it is beyond the scope of this study to provide them.

20. In particular, an estimate of the effect on income per head of a reduced birth-rate would require at least: (*a*) an estimate of the marginal propensity to save, not out of aggregate income, but out of income per head. It may be that studies exist for areas of India showing savings at different levels of income and family size, which would go some way towards assisting a calculation of the additional savings that could be expected from growing incomes with lower, as compared with higher, population growth; but the author has been unable to locate any such studies; (*b*) in so far as additions to income per head are consumed, an estimate of the effect of increased consumption on productivity. Although this effect may be substantial, the author has not found any quantitative work on this subject in India adequate for the purpose; (*c*) an estimate of the extent to which the composition of investment as between social overhead capital and productive equipment might be affected by a reduction in the rate of growth of population. In this case it would be hard to provide a quantitative estimate, since public policy would weigh so heavily as a determinant. In the case of India it might be argued that, in the short run at least, a reduction of the rate of growth of population would not have much effect on the composition of investment, on the grounds that the need for social investment is already far from being met, and that a small reduction in this need is unlikely to reduce to any significant extent the pressure for social

investment, at least in the public sector. On private sector housing, there might be some effect.[9]

21. What we have in mind here is a model of economic-demographic growth, in which the marginal propensity to save is a function both of income and of population; output is a function of consumption per head, as well as the usual variables; and the capital-output ratio is a function of population (this would seem to be the simplest way of taking account of the effect of population change on the composition of investment). But since we cannot estimate, or even guess intelligently, many of the coefficients involved, further elaboration of such a model would not be useful for present purposes. Nevertheless, spelling this out does achieve one thing: it introduces a criticism of one aspect of those cost-benefit analyses of birth control which include in their estimate of benefits no recognition of the interactions of population change and economic growth. (This is one of many criticisms to which Enke's celebrated analysis[10] is subject, concentrating, as it does, simply on the discounted present value of an individual 'life'.)

22. Without some such model as above described, it is hard to make an accurate assessment of the effect of reducing the rate of growth of population on income per head. However, since these considerations all work in the direction of raising income per head (there are others, not yet considered in this section, which work in the opposite direction, which will be mentioned below), a cruder calculation may suggest a lower limit to this effect.

[9] One might compare A. J. Coale & E. M. Hoover, *Population Growth and Economic Development in Low-Income Countries* (Princeton Univ. Press, 1958)—still the most painstaking attempt at an estimate of the economic consequences of reduced fertility in India, even if its demographic basis has been overtaken by the 1961 Census. They allow for increased savings, but the main difference between the high-fertility and low-fertility income projections comes from the change in the composition of investment. Over numerous variations in the values of parameters, they estimate that the low-fertility case typically shows a 1 per cent gain in the annual growth of *total* output over a thirty-year period, so that gains in consumption per head are very considerable. (Another interesting feature of their analysis is an estimate of the very long run; using a Cobb-Douglas production function, which allows for substitution between labour and capital, they estimate income per consumer in the low-fertility case to be nearly double that in the high-fertility case after fifty-five years, claiming that 'the economic advantages of reduced fertility are distinctly *not* limited to a transition period before labour force growth is affected' (p. 327).) We cannot here attempt any critique of their approach.

[10] S. Enke, 'The Economic Aspects of Slowing Population Growth', *Economic J.*, Mar. 1966 (Cambridge).

23. For reasons which will be made clear in the last section, we will examine here the effects of a programme which would effectively reduce the 1975 population by 40 mn over the ten years from 1965, relative to what it would otherwise have been; that is, we will compare the alternatives of 630 mn people and 590 mn people in 1975.

24. The simplest calculation is the effect on income per head of the fact of there being less heads. If income growth were entirely independent of population growth, income per head in 1975 with a population of 590 mn would be approximately 6·8 per cent higher than with a population of 630 mn. As has been suggested, the effect of a reduced birth-rate on economic growth is likely to raise this figure within the ten year period, but we were, for reasons explained, unable to make this calculation.

25. However, there is some cost involved in achieving the lower population. An acceptable figure for the upper limit of the cost of a 'prevented birth' is $10.[11] With an average of 4 mn prevented births per year, this gives an annual expenditure of $40 mn per year, or Rs 300 mn (post-devaluation). Assuming an incremental capital-output ratio of 4, and a marginal savings rate of 0·16, and no depreciation of capital, the increment to total income in 1975 of an annual investment of Rs 300 mn for ten years is about Rs 800 mn, or less than Rs 1·5 per head.[12] Let us say Rs 2, to err on the side of caution.

[11] The figure is taken from G. Ohlin, *Population Control and Economic Development*, O.E.C.D., Development Centre Studies no. 8, p. 138. This implies another criticism of Enke, whose much lower figure comes from estimating only the medical charges involved, omitting organizational and educational costs.

[12] We have calculated this in the following way. If an amount C is invested each year, with capital-output ratio k, and marginal savings ratio m, the addition to the capital stock after T years is given by the formula

$$C \frac{(1 + m/k)^T - 1}{m/k}$$

assuming no depreciation, and assuming that all savings are invested. Since, however, we are interested in the income generated by this investment in year T, we should not include in the formula for the relevant capital stock the capital generated indirectly by year T's investment, so that the formula should become

$$C\left[1 + \frac{(1 + m/k)^{T-1} - 1}{m/k}\right]$$

Dividing the resulting capital stock estimate by k, estimated income in year T from the stream of investments is derived. (This is an improvement on the formulation in Ohlin, p. 149, where the increments to the capital stock due to the savings generated by each year's investment are neglected.)

26. At the time of writing, no estimate was available of Indian national income in 1975. The Draft Fourth Plan[13] indicated that work on such estimates was still in progress. But taking the target income for 1970–1 of Rs 231,000 mn, and assuming a growth rate of 5 per cent per year gives roughly Rs 300,000 mn for 1975, or about Rs 508 per head at 590 mn population, and about Rs 476 per head at 630 mn. (Our calculation is, in any case, insensitive to changes in the estimate of 1975 income.)

27. We have still to allow for the alternative use of resources. Correctly, we should not have calculated the growth of total incomes at the same rates, since the high-population total income should be greater to allow for the use of resources not devoted to family planning. But Rs 300 mn is a very small fraction of total investment (less than 1 per cent of total annual investment as projected in the Draft Plan). An acceptable, if rough and ready, way of making this allowance might therefore be to subtract the increment in income per head due to the alternative use of resources from the higher figure, giving Rs 506 and Rs 476 respectively, or a net increase in income per head due to birth control of over 6 per cent. Over ten years, this represents somewhat more than an additional $\frac{1}{2}$ per cent per year on the rate of growth of income per head.[14] The above calculation can be summarized as follows:

Alternative Situations in 1975

Population	Cost of FP Programme in foregone 1975 income	Total income	Income per head
630	Rs (nil)	Rs 300,000 mn	Rs 476
590	Rs 1,500 mn	Rs 298,500 mn	Rs 506

28. It must be emphasized that we have been trying to calculate the *lower limit* of the net increase. At every stage of the calculation we

[13] *4DO*, p. 28.

[14] This analysis is challengeable at many points. We have made a set of calculations with various levels of marginal savings rates and capital output ratios: see Appendix, Table 3. It is obvious that, at any reasonable values of these parameters, the superiority of investment in birth control is unchallenged. As one would expect, the calculation is more sensitive to changes in k than changes in m.

have adopted figures which favour the return to the 'alternative use of resources' and diminish the return to birth control. We have ignored the positive effect on growth of reducing the birth-rate; we have taken the highest suggested figure for the cost of preventing a birth; we have ignored depreciation and gestation lags in calculating the return to the alternative use of resources. This has been done partly because no figures are available, and partly because, where a range of figures is given, one has often no particular reason for choosing the higher or lower end of the range. But we have also been motivated by the existence of some suspiciously high estimates, and a desire to produce another estimate which commands some confidence.

29. It may be useful to compare our result with the kind of calculation made by Enke. As is well known, his conclusion was that the return to investment in birth control may be as much as 100 times as high as the return to other forms of investment. We have not in fact calculated a 'return to investment', but rather have attempted to assess the difference in per capita income after ten years with and without a programme comparable to that being undertaken by the Government of India. In our calculation, the net gain from birth control of per capita income in 1975 is Rs 30, representing fifteen times as large a return as that from other investment. A true cost-benefit analysis would of course take the annual stream of benefits and costs and compare their discounted values. The 'value' of a prevented birth diminishes over time with the increase in the probability of death, as well as from possible effects of changes in the size of the labour force in later years, so that a great deal depends on the discount rate employed. We have preferred to avoid introducing yet more untrustworthy numbers into the calculation.

30. An interesting point, raised by Michael Lipton in discussion, is the implication of the difference between the average and the marginal investment in birth control. Although the average return is very high, the costs of extending particular aspects of the programme in particular areas may be very considerable—sufficient possibly to compare unfavourably with alternative uses of resources. In fact, if one disaggregated the programme on a local basis, one would have a series of programmes, the cost curve of each of which would probably have the shape of an inverted, recumbent 'S', rising at first as the programme spreads to remote areas and people unfamiliar with birth control, then falling, as with 'contagion' models of disease or information, as widespread knowledge makes acceptance

simpler, and finally rising again as it attempts to reach the most scattered or most uninterested inhabitants of the area. This last phase of an area programme might well lack economic justification, but one would expect the bulk of the population to be reached on the declining-cost part of the curve in each area. It is nevertheless an important qualification to our argument that not all expenditures on birth control are justified. In defence of our analysis, however, it can be said that we were using the UN Report's maximum feasible programme, whose feasibility should in part have depended on considerations of the costs of further extension.

31. One could go deeper still, and examine the sensitivity of the results of given outlays on birth-control measures to variations in complementary educational and medical measures, in rural and urban demographic patterns, in income distribution, in administrative expenditure and techniques, and so on.[15] Information on some of these questions is available from studies of programmes in other countries; and it is to be hoped that the continuous evaluation proposed in the Indian programme will not lose sight of these points. Certainly an analysis of returns to expenditure, with medical, administrative, and educational charges lumped together in a figure for 'cost per prevented birth', gives little guidance for the detailed preparation of a programme. Our intention, though, has been mainly to give substantive justification to the over-all policy decision to spend very large sums of money on family planning, and give some indication of the likely return.

32. The effect on the labour force is worth a further mention. It has been assumed throughout that there are no adverse effects on economic growth of a reduced rate of growth of population. This is roughly correct for the early period, since the reduction in the birth-rate does not affect the size of the labour force for fifteen years or so after its onset. But here we see the importance of the age-distribution. Even with a rate of fertility decline slightly greater than the one we have postulated (44 mn prevented births by 1975), the difference between the 15–59 age groups in the populations with constant and with declining fertility is about 36 mn in 1990. (50·4 per cent of 983 mn, compared with 68·0 per cent of 668 mn.) Assuming 0·7 of this age group to be the labour force, one could expect a substantial proportion of these 25 mn extra workers to be unemployed. But even if they were all employed, the productivity

[15] The author is indebted to Prof. Paul Streeten for these points.

of the labour force as a whole in the higher population would have to be about 37 per cent greater than that in the lower population, just in order to provide the same income per head. If one were to talk of consumption standards rather than income per head, this figure would be substantially reduced, since the bulk of the difference between the two populations consists of children whose consumption is much lower than that of adults.

33. However, as has been suggested, the lower population is more likely to enjoy greater productivity of the employed than the higher one. It is as much due to this, as to the fact that even if there were gains from the higher population their present value at twenty-five years' distance would still be insignificant, that we feel justified in ignoring any possibility of an adverse effect of fertility decline on income per head.

3. FAMILY PLANNING IN THE FOURTH PLAN

34. The precise programme envisaged during the Fourth Plan period is still under review at the time of writing; the details of the programme as set out in the Draft Fourth Plan are no longer the basis of policy. A paper prepared by the State and Central health authorities, however, gives an indication of the scale of programme which is likely to emerge.[16] The details given there are of a plan for 1967–8, and some broad targets for the remainder of the period. The plan for 1967–8 comprises the following targets (as far as concerns numbers of people to be reached with birth control measures):

IUDs	2 mn people
Sterilizations	1·5 mn people
Conventional contraceptives	2 mn people

The goal for the plan period as a whole is 'to expose at least 50 per cent of the 90 mn couples in the age-group 15–45 to one or other method of contraception'.

35. Since a great deal of emphasis is placed on the IUD programme, it may be as well to discuss this first. On the basis of trials in

---

[16] 'Family Planning Programme' (1967, mimeo).

various countries, it is believed that two out of every five loops inserted in every year will be expelled or removed before having much effect, while each loop which remains in position might (in India) prevent an average of 1·3 births over a five-year period. This implies that 'for every five loops inserted, four births will be prevented over a five year period'.[17] The 1967–8 target for IUDs implies, on these assumptions, about 1·6 mn prevented births over the five years.

36. On the basis of assumptions of effectiveness as used by the UN Report, the whole 1967–8 programme would imply about 3 mn prevented births. If the programme were to expand with the same proportionate emphasis on the different techniques of contraception, and 45 mn couples were reached within the Plan period, this would imply more than 25 mn prevented births as a result of action taken within the period (though some of the 'prevented births' would occur outside the period). In Section II above, we discussed the possibility of 40 mn prevented births in ten years on the basis of equal annual numbers of prevented births. In fact, we may expect an accelerating programme. Even so, the tentative figures outlined here are ambitious; our target figure of 40 mn prevented births would be passed before 1975.

37. The UN Report concluded that a programme rising to 9 mn prevented births in 1975 would achieve the target, and estimated that this might be managed in the following way:

Method	Number in 1975	Prevented births
Rise in age at marriage	—	1·9 mn
Sterilization	3 mn	2·1 mn
IUD	5 mn (insertions)	4·0 mn
Condoms	300 mn (pieces)	1·0 mn[18]

38. The Report felt that this target might be reached as the

17 UN *Report*, p. 101. The expulsion/removal rate may be pessimistic, though recent research may bear it out.
18 Ibid. p. 103. Some of these 'prevented births' occur after 1975. The *Report* does not give figures for all intervening years, and is ambiguous as to whether 40 mn births *which would have occurred by 1975* are prevented by the programme, or 40 mn births some of which would have occurred after 1975. We have assumed the former, which is not impossible on the basis of the figures given, and compares with the low fertility case of Table A.

result of very vigorous Government action. Evidently the authorities have felt that the target was too low, since, although they do not mention any efforts to raise the age at marriage (the Report on *this* issue may well have been optimistic), they do indicate an intention to make substantially greater efforts with the main birth control methods.

39. The planners are undoubtedly right to raise their sights, though there may be some doubt as to whether performance better than that indicated in the UN Report will be attainable. The UN Report assesses the need for additional trained personnel of various kinds before the end of the current plan period to be over 70,000. The Indian document above has much higher targets: 40,000 additional auxiliary nurse midwives (A.N.Ms) alone, compared with the Report's 30,000. It is virtually impossible for an outsider to evaluate what the Draft Plan proposes about training, other than to say the obvious: the training requirements are immense on any assumptions, and may well prove a bottleneck.

40. Concerning training, one difficult question deserves attention: namely the distribution of operations between doctors and medical auxiliaries in the IUD programme. Extensive medical training is not required for insertion of the IUD; but it is far from being a trouble-free device, and failure in even a few cases can lead to adverse public opinion which might discredit the family planning effort over a wide area. Doctors are important both for the pre-insertion check-up, and in general as confidence creators. This is why, in some countries, family planning has progressed most satisfactorily in relation to a general public health programme, which has the additional advantage of relieving a 'family planning' doctor from the claims of other kinds of medical attention which arise where medical facilities are poor. As against this, the greater the share of highly-trained medical personnel in the programme, the slower is its possible rate of expansion.

41. Fundamentally the problem is one of weighing risks—the risks of medical complications or failure (leading to the possible disruption of a programme) which one would expect to increase with the less highly skilled people that are employed—against the possible gains to be derived from faster implementation of the programme. This is one of the more complex questions in the whole field of the training, pay, and employment of medical personnel, which will probably (and certainly should) be one of the first tasks of the

18

committee set up to evaluate the programme. As more reliable information comes to hand concerning the first years of activity, it should be possible to come to some conclusions on the subject.

42. A few words about sterilization and other birth control methods may be of use. To date (June 1967) there have been approximately 2·34 mn sterilizations (male and female).[19] The 1967–8 target looks feasible by past standards of performance. The demographic effect of sterilization is hard to assess; it depends on the age and fertility of couples, and the existing family size when the operation is performed. Condoms appear to be a cumbersome method for a large-scale programme, an estimated 300–475 being required per prevented birth. [20]

43. The relative costs of different methods are:

Method	Rs
IUDs	20–35 per insertion (mainly medical costs)
Condoms	20–30 (?) (year's supply)
Sterilization	40 (of which Rs 30 are for publicity, transport, and compensation)[21]

Given the rates of demographic effectiveness, the cost per prevented birth favours the IUD. There are, of course, 'programme costs' on top of the above figures. The usual estimate of a prevented birth is Rs 35–75 (post-devaluation).

44. Without any knowledge of the details beyond 1967–8, it is clear that either the cost of preventing a birth is higher than is customarily believed, or that a great deal of this expenditure is an investment for future acceleration of the programme (presumably much of it in training). Otherwise the implied scale of expenditure would be sufficient to prevent from 35 to 60 mn births in the period up to 1975 (independently of any expenditure after 1970), or between one-and two-thirds of the 100 mn births expected in the period, which even in the lower case is an extremely ambitious aim. The rate of expansion of the programme as a whole is colossal. Some 4–5 mn couples have been reached already; the 1967–8 programme should

---

[19] 'Family Planning Programme'.　　　[20] UN *Report*, p. 102.
[21] Ohlin p. 136–8. These figures are an international average, and should be treated as a rough guide only.

bring this to 10 mn. That leaves 35 mn to be reached in the ensuing three years if the target of 45 mn couples is to be attained.[22]

45. The Government of India has repeatedly said that finance will be made available up to any amount that can be usefully spent. As far as the physical aspects of the programme are concerned, this is undoubtedly a sensible policy. It is fairly obvious that the availability of physical resources will limit expenditure within what could or should be made available. The question of incentive expenditures, however, does remain open. But it can only be settled on an area basis. In many areas experience shows that all facilities offered are utilized, indeed demand is often greater than supply. Thus the amount of useful incentive payments may also be limited by physical availabilities, especially if the programme were concentrated in areas where problems of popular response are less of an obstacle to it.[23]

46. (There is also the question of removing fiscal and other assistance to childbearing. The Indian tax system gives concessions

[22] Since writing this paper, the author has had an opportunity to collect some more up-to-date information in India. As of October 1967 the figures for achievement of the programme are as follows:

Loops in place	1·5 mn
Effectively sterilized couples	2·6 mn
Couples employing conventional contraceptives	0·8 mn

The programme is stated not to be going well in Assam, Bihar, Rajasthan, and Uttar Pradesh. Plans have been issued for the year 1967–8 as follows:

IUD insertions	4·1 mn
Sterilization	2·0 mn
Conventional contraceptives	3·1 mn

There is said to be an acute shortage of contraceptive supplies, particularly those of a conventional nature. A total of Rs 310 mn has been voted by Parliament for family planning during 1967–8, Rs 256 mn of which is for expenditure by State Governments. One or two details may be of particular interest; for example the State Government of Maharashtra has passed legislation depriving families who do not restrict themselves to 3 children, or to their present size, of various fiscal and welfare benefits. In some States, incentive programmes have been adopted for the employment of part-time doctors. As regards the IUD—most controversial part of the programme—there is a vast variety of experience; it is by no means the case that the IUD is a failure, but future plans for this method of contraception remain open to change. The plans referred to above for 1967–8 may look ambitious, but they could be attainable. In 1966–7, for example, sterilizations numbered over 860,000, and may soon become the programme's leading sector.

[23] This is to speak only of incentives for the clients of the programme. There is also a complex question of incentive payments to employees of the programme, which we have not gone into here. At the time of writing, there is no published data on the success of the programme on an area basis.

for the first two children. But the vast majority of the Indian population, and particularly that part of the population which is prone to having large families, is outside the tax net. There are also maternity and child benefits for an estimated 3 mn workers under the Employee's State Insurance Scheme, and in some other conditions of employment. The abolition of all such allowances and benefits, although politically awkward and unlikely to have any large impact on the birth-rate, would accord with the spirit of the family planning programme and the climate of opinion related to childbearing which the Government of India is trying to create.)

4. CONCLUSIONS

47. A considerable effort will be required even to prevent an increase in the rate of growth of population. The challenge of bringing this rate within bounds that promise prosperity for India is indeed enormous. Our examination suggests that autonomous factors—other than Malthusian ones, which we have avoided examining—do not promise any reduction. Prospects for reducing the rate of growth rest with distributing and encouraging the use of birth control facilities, and perhaps with attempts to raise the marriage age.

48. There is some indication that the programme is not yet progressing very fast. Although the authorities give the highest priority to it, evidence suggests that the programme has not until very recently had the attention it deserves—particularly as regards its administration. Plans for production of materials, training of personnel, and the organization of distributional and educational facilities down to the village level appear to be adequate, as does the financial provision. It is therefore mainly on the administration of the programme that its success now depends.

49. One aspect we have not covered is the question of external assistance for the programme. Several Governments (the United Kingdom's now among them) are willing to provide personnel, contraceptive materials, and other forms of assistance for population control policies. The major role for aid donors is unlikely to be the actual provision of medical personnel, since these are scarce even in the developed countries, and in any case may be less suitable than indigenous doctors and auxiliaries. But they can do a great deal in the field of training. As far as contraceptive supplies are concerned, one would hope that India will soon become self-sufficient, though in

the meantime, donors should be willing to provide supplies and assistance for their production in India. It should not be forgotten that technical progress in family planning is very rapid, and improved methods are currently being tested; here again donors can assist in the rapid diffusion of new techniques. Finally, there is a range of ancillary equipment (mobile film units, clinics, and so forth) for which donors can provide assistance. In the current state of opinion among donors, no part of the Indian programme should be held back for want of foreign exchange. If, as now seems likely, the facilities of the World Health Organization can be made available for family planning, that would be a very suitable body through which assistance could be channelled.

STATISTICAL APPENDIX

TABLE 1

Prospective Trends in Total Pop., Birth-Rates, Rate of Pop. Growth, No. of Births & Age Distribution in India, 1965–90

Year	Mid-year total pop. (mn)	Crude birth-rate (mn)	Rate of pop. growth (per 1000)	No. of births (mn)	Pop. by broad age groups (per cent)		
					Under 15	15–59	60 & over
I. *Constant fertility*							
1965	484·3	41·4	24·1	20·0	40·7	53·8	5·5
1970	548·8	40·5	26·5	22·2	41·5	52·8	5·7
1975	629·0	40·1	28·2	25·2	41·9	52·1	6·0
1980	725·0	40·0	29·5	29·0	42·3	51·6	6·1
1985	841·4	39·9	30·9	33·6	42·8	51·0	6·2
1990	983·2	39·9	32·1	39·2	43·4	50·4	6·2
II. *Moderate fertility decline (birth-rate 25 in 1985)*							
1965	484·3	41·4	23·3	20·0	40·7	53·8	5.5
1970	544·1	36·5	22·9	19·9	41·0	53·2	5·8
1975	607·3	32·2	20·9	19·5	39·8	54·0	6·2
1980	669·1	28·4	18·4	19·0	37·5	55·8	6·7
1985	729·0	25·0	16·2	18·2	34·6	52·2	7·2
1990	785·8	22·0	15·1	17·3	31·8	60·4	7·8
III. *Rapid fertility decline (birth-rate 25 in 1975)*							
1965	484·3	41·3	24·1	20·0	40·7	53·8	5·5
1970	538·7	32·2	19·2	17·3	40·4	53·8	5·8
1975	585·7	25·0	14·4	14·6	37·6	56·0	6·4
1980	621·6	19·4	10·0	12·1	32·7	60·1	7·2
1985	647·0	15·1	7·3	9·8	27·1	64·8	8·1
1990	668·2	15·1	6·5	10·1	22·9	68·0	9·1

Source: UN *Report*, p. 123.

TABLE 2

| | Birth-rate (per 1,000 people) | | Marital fertility (per 1,000 once-married women) | |
	Rural	Urban	Rural	Urban
Assam	44·9	42·3	271	268
Jammu & Kashmir	33·5	25·5	165	146
Kerala	36·2	31·3	229	203
Madhya Pradesh	n.a.	n.a.	188	199
Mysore	34·2	31·3	182	178
Orissa	36·5	31·9	173	160
Punjab	39·2	34·5	232	207
Rajasthan	40·4	41·1	200	209
Uttar Pradesh	36·8	32·7	179	179
Delhi	41·9	36·7	225	216

Source: Min. of Home Affairs, *Vital Statistics of India for 1961* (1964), Table 29A, pp. L–LI. As the text makes clear, the figures are not very trustworthy. Some States were not included for lack of data. The figures for marital fertility are based on sample surveys and census data. In all cases the figures quoted above are less than 'computed' figures, i.e. those rates implied by the growth of numbers between the 1951 and 1961 Censuses.

TABLE 3

Calculated Additional Income per Head in 1975 from Non–Birth Control Investment (various values of marginal savings rate and capital output ratio)

| Extra savings per rupee of extra income m (Rs) | Extra capital requirements per rupee of extra annual output | | |
| | 2 Rs | 3 Rs | 4 Rs |
	Extra income per person (Rs)		
0·1	2·86	1·80	1·30
0·15	3·16	1·90	1·32
0·2	3·49	2·03	1·43
0·3	4·24	2·33	1·58

9

Social Anthropology
Its Contribution to Planning

DAVID POCOCK

1. HAVE THE PLANNERS A CONSISTENT STRATEGY?

THE starting point for the social anthropologist faced with the Draft Fourth Plan is not primarily the proposals, but the planners themselves. This is difficult for a planner to swallow, in so far as he thinks of himself as standing back from his material and discussing it in an objective manner. I hope, however, to show that by considering the position of the planners in modern Indian society, we can firstly understand the document itself better, and secondly put ourselves in a position to be constructively critical.

Michael Lipton's references to urban bias[1] touch on a cleavage in Indian society between what can be fairly characterized by two 'ideal types'. On the one hand we have a minority, based on the cities, valuing change, oriented towards the nation; on the other a majority, based on the villages, indifferent to change, oriented towards the neighbourhood. The fact of being involved in the planning process not merely places the planners in the first category, but approximates them to the purest expression of the type. They are committed to an ideology which is not only not shared by the majority of their compatriots, but is opposed to the ideology of the majority. The planner derives from western models an ideal of the unified secular state; he is planning for a people who, for the most part, think in terms of the localized unities of castes, hierarchically organized according to religious values. Thus the situation is one of conflict, and the ends of the planner are revolutionary.

In a country which has accepted democratic procedures one cannot, of course, expect a planning commission to declare war on

---

[1] See above, pp. 130–5.

271

the electorate in so many words. We may be sure that in defining the situation as one of conflict we are not saying something of which many planners are unaware. But the Draft Fourth Plan shows that the implications of the conflict have not been clearly thought out. We certainly would not expect to see a clear outline of the proposed strategy, but at the same time we should hope not to find evidence that none exists.

It is, however, difficult to derive from the outline any clear picture of the future life envisaged for the rural masses of India. One thinks first of all of the effect of the Plan's proposals upon the caste system, taking that as the embodiment of traditional values. The planners have little to say directly about this. They observe:

In spite of efforts to end the practice of untouchability the evil still persists to some extent, specially in the rural areas. Provisions in the Constitution banning the practice of untouchability and making its practice a cognizable offence have not been found adequate . . . . It is clear that in this sphere there is no room for complacency and there is need for a nation-wide effort to create a sense of worth and equal dignity for every citizen in the land (p. 380).

The first comment to be made on this is a correction of the phrase 'to some extent'. The practice of untouchability is pervasive in the rural areas.

The Commission suggests two sorts of remedies: those which would improve the general economic condition of the scheduled castes as a result of an overall improvement in the rural economy, and those which would lift members of the scheduled castes out of the rural milieu primarily by means of education and industrialization. Since it will obviously be many years before the latter outlets are accessible to most members of scheduled castes, clearly the former remedy is supposed to be the effective one. But the hierarchy of caste is not an economic hierarchy. The link between economic standing and caste status is far from perfect. In Gujarat I have observed long-established co-operatives (founded by missions) which have raised the standard of living of untouchables above that of some purer castes without affecting relative caste status. And in the same villages landless Brahmans remain at the head of the hierarchy, while entirely dependent economically upon the local landowners. A more general theoretical point follows: the practice of untouch-ability flows from the basic religious principles organizing the caste hierarchy and will not be abolished until those principles have been replaced by secular ones.

Is this sociological purism, in that greater economic independence will go far to make the scheduled castes indifferent to the judgement of their neighbours? I shall later give some evidence for this view. What I am at present concerned with, however, is the small extent to which the Planning Commission appears to have any such strategy based upon an understanding of the total social situation in which untouchability is practised.

For example, the Draft Plan seeks to answer the question of decentralizing industry *both* through 'small industries, especially for the production of a variety of ancillary parts and components required by large industries' *and* by the development 'of some of the traditional village industries which have been languishing' (p. 240). This demonstrates a failure to distinguish between the social functions of these two kinds of small-scale industry. The first, whether it is established in a village or a town, encourages workers to move away from the village ethos, which is the ethos of caste, and creates contractual relationships between employer and employee in a labour situation to which caste is much less relevant. To this extent it gives the labourer, of whatever caste, a moral and economic independence from traditional relationships and pressures. The 'traditional village industries' on the other hand are without exception linked to caste and thus to the caste hierarchy. To revive those that are languishing is, whatever the economic benefit to the individuals concerned, to reinforce caste values and thus to encourage the practice of untouchability. The apparent failure to see this distinction, strengthens my suspicion that the Planning Commission has not taken the measure of the rural society that it must restructure if the Plan is to succeed.

Alternative strategies to deal with caste will be considered later. All that need be said here is that the average educated townsman in India today has little experience of untouchability. The more he moves in educated circles, the less he has to do even with lesser caste distinctions. The only experience of caste that he may have is the fact that he is almost certainly married into his caste, and to the extent that this gives stability and community to his marriage, he cannot think of it as sociologically linked with discriminations contrary to his ideology.

2. IS ANTHROPOLOGY TOO SMALL-SCALE TO HELP?

Two arguments against this general line of criticism have been advanced by defenders of the Plan. It is said that the variety in social organization from one part of the country to the other, and the differences even within one small area, make it impossible for the Planning Commission to enter into regional details. Secondly, it is argued that the primary concern of the planners is with large-scale economic phenomena, the implication being that the benefits resulting from the manipulation of these phenomena will seep down to the masses. Thus we are told:

Since 90 per cent of the scheduled castes live in the villages and a considerable proportion among them engage in agricultural labour or in occupations of low skill and productivity, whatever measures can be taken to build up the agricultural economy and to diversify the rural occupational structure, will be of benefit to the scheduled castes (p. 380).

As regards the first argument, the notorious diversity of the Indian social scene is more apparent than real. The prevalence of the caste system from one end of the country to the other might make us suspect underlying similarities permitting a remarkable degree of generalization. In fact, the detailed study of a caste or a village in South India has immediate comparative relevance for the social anthropologist working in the North. The traditional value pattern is the same throughout. The concept of the 'dominant caste', first put forward by M. N. Srinivas, is universally applicable in India.[2] Connected with the dominant caste is the so-called 'jajmāni system', which, despite variations as to detail, expresses the political and economic dependence of the specialist castes (including Brahmans where these are not also dominant) and, more generally, of all inferior castes.[3] To be aware of this alone is to be chary of developing 'traditional village industries'.

In short, one does not ask that the planner immerse himself in all the social anthropological literature on India. There are not, nor are there ever likely to be, detailed studies of each of its 646,000 villages,

[2] M. N. Srinivas, 'The Social System of a Mysore Village', in McKim Marriott ed., *Village India* (1955), p. 18.
[3] I have discussed this with particular reference to change in D. Pocock, 'Notes on Jajmāni Relationships', *Contributions to Indian Sociology* (the Hague, 1962), vi.

but one is entitled to ask for some awareness of the degree of generalization which social anthropology has been able to achieve in India. Were this reflected in the Plan, it would be much easier for any development officer, concerned with any particular village, to appreciate in considerable detail in what particulars it was unique, and to modify his approach accordingly. If, for example, social anthropologists have advanced the generalization that power within *panchayati raj* tends to be preserved in the hands of the dominant caste, and have described the circumstances in which this tendency is strongest, the local worker is in a better position to observe the conditions in which this is not so, or is less so, and to ponder the advisability or feasibility of encouraging these circumstances elsewhere.

The second defence of the Plan, that it is properly concerned with the manipulation of large-scale economic phenomena, is more simply dismissed. If progress depended entirely on the correct incentives and depressants properly applied at the right time, a generation of economic planning would presumably have discovered the right brand of carrot and the suitable length of stick. But the planner must know also to whom the benefits are flowing, and whether it is in the long-term interests of planning that they should so flow. There is, for example, no evidence that a build-up of the agricultural economy would inevitably benefit the scheduled castes. On the contrary, wherever there has been an improvement in the peasant condition in India, this has been monopolized by higher land-owning castes, and the condition of the landless has remained unchanged (see p. 137). In Gujarat it was not the growing prosperity of the tobacco- and cotton-growing Patidar of the Kaira District that doubled the cost of seasonal labour after independence; it was the competition of small local industries.

Furthermore, the planners do not in fact limit themselves to large-scale economic operations. Against untouchability, for instance, they urge the provision of unsegregated housing sites in the village for scheduled caste families (p. 381). There is no indication how the ancient prejudice making for segregation is to be overcome. I shall later give an instance of just such a victory, admittedly in favourable circumstances; it is quite wrong to attribute some kind of perverse invulnerability to the 'eternal dharma'. It is true that every man has his price, but we have to find out in what currency it is to be paid. One would have, for instance, to balance the long-term benefit of integrated housing in the village against the possible ill effects of complementary benefits to families of the dominant caste, through whom this might be implemented. Because village leaders do not value the currency of liberalism and communal uplift, this does not mean that they are immune to all inducements. It means simply that the planners have proposed a desirable end, and not at all considered the ground upon which it can be achieved.

To sum up at this point: India's élite is committed to the creation of a state of affairs that does not adapt to—indeed would run entirely counter to—the established order of the mass of the population. This gulf between ideals finds demographic expression in the fact that this élite is of its nature urban in background and outlook. Entry to the Indian intellectual and governing élite is still, except in rare cases, through the town or city. But in the Draft Fourth Plan we find no such awareness of this difference, which is nothing less than a difference in world-view. On the contrary, on the grounds that planner and planned alike are all Indians, there is an *assumption* of continuity: some, many, are behind-hand; but the ideal is common to all. The sad truth is that the ideal is not common to all, and the planners should take this into account by making specific proposals aimed at creating the desired continuity.

3. POSSIBLE CHANGES IN THE PLANNERS' CONCEPTUAL STRUCTURE

Three interconnected intellectual operations seem necessary. Firstly, the members of the Planning Commission should conceive it possible that they are themselves the products of a certain social milieu with its specific values, ideals, assumptions, and blind spots. Such a self-consciousness should be made rationally objective in a formal ideal type. Secondly, this could then be the better compared with a similarly formal construct of the traditional situation based on the findings of social anthropology. Finally, resulting from this confrontation, a model, or rather a series of models of varying degrees of complexity, could be projected as guides to planning. These models would not be planning proposals themselves, however much closer to social realities they might be than much of the Draft Fourth Plan. They would be artificial, ideal constructs derived from the confrontation of the two former models. Thus if the planners realized that they were committed to demolishing not only the branches but also the roots of the caste system, they might, for example, consider the implications of the single-caste village, served from outside by specialist castes, secular and religious, on contractual terms. An important implication is that contractual relationships are encouraged in such a situation while, conversely, common residence subordinates contract and contractual interests to status relationships. When the encouragement of small-scale industry is being considered, the social value of such development can be assessed together with its economic value. It is socially valuable to the extent that it creates a landless villager free from dependence on a status-tied occupation. A few such people in any village have exemplary value, and their presence is corrosive to the traditional system. The ideal situation is that in which the families of the dominant caste in a village are reduced to the position of the single-caste villagers, obliged to contract with their fellow villagers who are now 'outsiders', or with others who in fact are residentially outside.

If such a model is erected in formal terms, then the contradictions between it and similar models emerge with clarity for more detailed consideration. For instance, when sociologists use the term 'dominant caste', they know that this refers to a condition of graduality on the ground. By this I mean that within the area of dominance of one caste there will be many villages in which the families of that village can be said to be 'dominant' only by association with their richer and more powerful caste-fellows in other villages. And at the fringes of the area equivocal situations are to be found.[4] Now it might be that the planners had erected, as a counter to caste stratification, an ideal of stratification by class. Clearly such a structural ideal would turn the mind more to a consideration of the possibility of exploiting the potentiality for fission in the economic disparity of the dominant caste, strengthening economic ties and equivalencies running across castes, and concentrating on village solidarities and inter-village rivalries.

It is perfectly possible that, in the making of practical decisions on the ground, the logical contradictions of models can appear to be ignored. It would, for instance, be clearly impossible (under Indian conditions of rapid population growth and scarce land) to draw off so much landless labour into local industry as to turn the village into a dormitory for the bulk of its population, leaving the cultivation of

[4] See for example D. Pocock, 'Inclusion and Exclusion', *Southwestern J. of Anthropology*, xiii, no. 1 (1957).

the land in the hands of relatively few farmers, as was the economic implication of the model of the single-caste village on p. 277. But such an 'ideal type' enables one the better to appreciate the more-than-economic advantages of an increase in local industries. Again, awareness of potentialities for class stratification in the rural areas could be related to the most general normative theme of the Planning Commission's charter: the socialist commitment. The controlled encouragement of a class society could be operated through the existing psychology of hierarchy. At the same time it would contradict the principles of the traditional hierarchy by substituting achieved for ascribed status. To the extent that this controlled development operated against caste, class could be used in the transition to a socialist society.

4. THE USE OF LOCAL INDUSTRY IN MOVING FROM CASTE TO ACHIEVEMENT AS THE BASIS OF HIERARCHY

I have so far been concerned chiefly with the planners themselves, since they appear to have ignored the social actualities of their own situation even more than those of the countryside. In this section I propose to describe a situation of social changes in the Okhamandal district of western Gujarat. The purpose of the description is to draw attention to likelihoods, and to suggest possibilities, for planned social action on a wider scale.

The traditional fame of the Okhamandal district derives from the temple of Dwaraka, which draws pilgrims from all over India. The area is bleak and chronically short of water. The availability of salt led to the establishment of the Tata Chemical Works, some twelve miles from Dwaraka town, and their privately-owned industrial colony, Mithapur. There are four major communities in Okhamandal. The Brahmans of Dwaraka traditionally serve in the temple and attend to the needs of pilgrims. The Lohana have been known for centuries as a trading community. These two are centered on Dwaraka town. In the surrounding district the Vagher are the dominant caste who, by their own admission, relied a great deal in the past upon brigandage, both locally on pilgrims and by making forays into the heart of Gujarat. Such cultivation as was possible in Okhamandal was carried on by the untouchable Meghwa. When Mithapur was first established, the great need was for unskilled labour and simple clerical labour. For the first, both Vagher and

Meghwa appear to have been employed in equal quantities. For the latter, Brahmans and Lohana were available. As the construction period drew to a close, and the industry became diversified, the need for unskilled labour decreased. The Vagher pride themselves on lordly traditions and are not suited to service, and (rightly or wrongly) personnel officers of the factory claimed that the Meghwa were more submissive and trainable. There has therefore been a decline in Vagher employment, and today a second generation of Meghwa is moving into the semi-skilled and skilled ranges of the daily rated workers.

What has happened to untouchability in the colony, and in the district as a whole? The formal policy of the management at Mithapur is more than non-discriminatory; it is not even permissive to caste prejudice. Details as to caste are no longer collected by the time-office. Restaurants in the colony, which operate on licence from the company, carry large notices announcing availability of service to all regardless of caste or religion. With the exception of a small chapel for the nuns connected with the hospital, the management has not allowed the construction of any temple or mosque on its property. In the factory no concession is made to caste prejudice either in the canteen or in nature of employment. A newly employed Brahman or Lohana, for instance, may well find himself appointed 'mate' to a man of lower caste, even an untouchable. This means that he has not only to work in close proximity with him, but even to fetch his tea and remove the dirty cup when it is finished. The latter act is traditionally regarded as particularly abhorrent.

The residential area of the colony is divided into named sections according to the type of housing and accompanying facilities available. There is no correlation between housing area and caste; the correlation is rather with wage grade. Nor does there appear to be any 'natural' tendency towards caste segregation. My samples do not suggest it, and the company's town officers state that requests for alternative housing are usually based on a desire for improved facilities rather than on objections to the caste of neighbours. They point out that the acute housing shortage militates against any 'natural' tendency there might be.

The housing shortage is important. The company's rents are low and, with some exceptions dating from the earlier period, the accommodation is satisfactory. Alternative accommodation exists in the surrounding villages at a price, and in Dwaraka and at Okha

Port, from which some workers in fact do commute. In such alternative accommodations, especially in Dwaraka, caste rules are often observed. It is clear, however, from Mithapur's long waiting list that even locally-born workers who have ancestral accommodation in their villages prefer the relative privacy, the running water, and the main drainage of the colony to the value of caste segregation in the village.[5]

Much of the above account may appear banal to the English reader. I therefore contrast it briefly with the situation in another Gujarati industrial colony which, for obvious reasons, I shall not name. There the formal charter of company policy was as at Mithapur. Caste was not officially tolerated. It was the experience of workers, however, that management, through foremen, was permissive to caste regulations; in assigning kinds of work and working partners, it took caste into account. In the residential area there was as clear a segregation of the untouchables' quarter as I have ever seen in a traditional village. The apparent contradiction between this and the official policy of the company (not to speak of the Government) was explained to me by the senior personnel officer. It was not that people were forced to live *apart* from others, but that people preferred to live *with* their own caste fellows. Even if we accept his statement as a faithful representation, we have here, nevertheless, an instance of wanton permissiveness. However, I observed a small shrine to Hanumān in the factory compound and asked why it should be Hanumān in particular. I was told that to move a Hanumān image required no elaborate deinstallation or reinstallation ceremony, and that therefore, if untouchables exercized their right to enter the shrine, the image could conveniently be removed into a private house.

To return to Mithapur, closer examination revealed that apart from housing, the belief in untouchability survived to a certain extent. Despite the notices in company-licensed restaurants, some restaurant-keepers were known to have given in to Vagher intimidation and discouraged Meghwa custom. The Vagher were said to shun the works canteen where the Meghwa were sure of service. This is the

---

[5] The housing shortage also means that it is difficult to entertain relatives for lengthy periods in the traditional manner. Some lament this, others significantly use it as an excuse for avoiding expenses associated with kinship. I suspect that there are many vulnerable spots in the body social at which people would gladly spend more on education, for instance, if they can be given a good excuse for avoiding traditional demands.

negative side of the affair. On the positive side we can point to what Mithapur expresses in almost pure form—the inevitable caste neutrality of a modern urban setting.[6] The Vagher are not concerned to discriminate against untouchables in general, indeed they scarcely have any such concept. They are concerned with their 'own' untouchables, the Meghwa. They do not care about people who may be regarded as untouchable from other people's point of view and who come from other areas. In general, all immigrant situations involving Indians are bound to affect caste hierarchy, whether the migration is to an industrial colony, to a city, or to a foreign country. A family, or a group of families can take hierarchical notions with it, but these notions can only be socially operative in the particular social surround of origin. Wherever migration situations have been described, there is no recorded example of a new hierarchy having been established between newcomers.[7] Castes continue to exist as endogamous blocs but the caste *system* has gone. We have to distinguish here between the caste system and 'casteism', by which we describe the phenomena of castes operating as interest groups in modern political situations. The latter is possibly the price to be paid temporarily for the destruction of the former.

In the surrounding villages the reversal of economic conditions between the Vagher and the Meghwa is striking. The Meghwa quarter is immediately identifiable by the altogether superior condition of its cottages and by the cleanliness and quality of the inhabitants' clothing which reflect the benefit of regular wages. The Vagher have taken to the plough and have developed the skills of intensive horticulture in response to a predominantly vegetarian market in Mithapur.

As regards relations between the two communities, the untouchability of the Meghwa in Vagher eyes remains unchanged. It is, however, no longer supported by specialization in religiously impure occupations or politico-economic dependence. For the majority of the Meghwa their villages have become dormitories and, as they are increasingly imbued with the secular values of the factory, they appear quite unconcerned to challenge their traditional ranking.

[6] The emphasis here is upon 'modern'. The modern urban situation co-exists very often with the traditional urban caste situation and is all too often ignored by social anthropologists. See D. Pocock, 'Sociologies: Urban and Rural', in *Contributions to Indian Sociology* (the Hague, 1960), iv.

[7] For a simple example see D. Pocock, 'Difference in East Africa', *Southwestern J. of Anthropology*, xiii, 4 (Albuquerque, New Mexico, 1957).

The Vagher have taken to horticulture, but largely preserve a subsistence psychology. A separate Tata organization, the Dorabji Tata Trust, has been working for their economic betterment. This has largely been achieved through one man who (and this seems an essential qualification) has been working among the Vagher for several years. The guiding policy of the Trust appears to be that assistance should be given in the first place to those who have, rather than to the have-nots. In accordance with Tata philosophy, assistance is in the form of interest-free loans, leniently collected, rather than grants. A Vagher farmer who already has a viable homestead and appears to be developing its resources as best he can, is loaned not only cash, but also improved grains, and is generally used as the inlet for more efficient farming techniques of all kinds. A few such selected farmers provide an experimental ground for the trust. Some years ago it was decided that the Vagher would benefit by the improvement of their poultry; White Leghorns and Rhode Island Reds were introduced. This innovation came up against Vagher traditions of hospitality, and after repeated attempts it became clear that no Vagher was willing to sacrifice the demands of hospitality or greed for the sake of a regular supply of eggs. The Trust's worker then set up in the egg and poultry business in his own compound, hoping by example to demonstrate the economic possibilities of the situation.

In agriculture the Trust had been, at the time of my visit, altogether more successful. There is little extreme disparity in income among the Vagher, and therefore the farmer used as a model to invite imitation was not already so far ahead of his fellows as to nullify the tactic. Neighbouring farmers could see the improved grain ripening on one side of the lane and the traditional grain on the other. They could see that there was no element of stakhanovism in the situation. In potentially more prosperous areas a farmer of middle-range income would serve this end better than one from the wealthiest families.

When the evident advantage of the improved grain had been established, there was no question of a paternalistic hand-out, but of a repetition of the pattern. That is to say, those who were sufficiently convinced, and were in a position to make the relatively small sacrifice, were encouraged to buy the seed-grain for the following year.

Michael Lipton has made the point elsewhere (pp. 113–17), here strongly endorsed, that it is probably erroneous to look out for the 'progressive farmer' whose value as a model for emulation is limited to the tiny minority of the rich. He points out that among the small farmers there are progressive ploughmen, composters, &c., but 'these are not the same people'. This may well be so, and we look forward to a detailed spelling out of what he has called the algorithms of particular families.[8] The issue is not, however, between wealthy 'progressive' farmers on the one hand and the utter specificity of a particular family with its peculiar algorithm on the other. The wealthy farmer is useless as a model precisely because his fellow villagers are all too aware of what they do not share with him— resources of all sorts. The middle-range farmer *is* useful as such a model because his fellow villagers are aware of what they share. Any one of them may be a better rice cultivator, or a better ploughman, but all cultivate rice, and all plough.

The Dorabji Trust's tactics suggest that the choice of an overall successful farmer in the middle range for the introduction of improved techniques works. An obvious reason is that the wealthiest farmers seem to lie outside the range of possible emulation. Here, attention will be drawn to three less obvious reasons for success—social reasons, pointing to the useful links that could be developed between planners and social anthropologists. The reasons are that the social respectability of agricultural experiment was guaranteed, that the diffuse associations of traditional social hierarchies were exploited to transform them, and that a sharp traditional distinction between two castes, each largely undifferentiated internally, can itself be a powerful source of rapid social and economic change.

First of all, the middle range farmer is chosen, for help and improvement, by a helping authority which may or may not guarantee the *economics* of the situation but which, by its intervening act of choice, guarantees its *social respectability*. This need seems to be well met in the overall Tata action. The Dorabji Tata Trust is separate from Tata Chemicals but derives moral support from its association with the company. The chosen farmers, by being chosen, are invested with a certain prestige. To this extent the operation depends upon the paternalistic principle, still very active in rural society. But by making loans and not grants, by keeping up a gentle pressure for collection of phased repayments—in general

---

[8] 'The Institutions of Uncertainty', Lipton's study of differences in efficiency among farmers in a Maharashtra millet village, is to be published in 1969.

by refusing to have any part of the 'something for nothing' mentality that can be, and in India often has been, the corrupt accompaniment of paternalism—the Dorabji Tata Trust seems to be successfully using a traditional principle for a revolutionary end.

A second reason for success in Okhamandal is that the tactic rests on the knowledge that status in Indian rural society is not differentiated as much as it is amongst ourselves. Once the religious qualifications are met, good economic standing connotes a diffuse prestige. This was and still is the way in which the Hinduism of the literary Brahmans and the philosophy of the sects percolate to the masses: through the assumption by wealthier families of religious practices which, because superior, are more in accordance with their economic standing. In the same way the economically advantaged family becomes, or can be made to become, the trend-setter for non-economic patterns of behaviour in the matter of hygiene, education, social morality, and so on.[9]

This modernization of a traditional hierarchy is not confined to Okhamandal. It was dramatically brought home to me in the Kaira district of Gujarat in 1964. Twelve years earlier the obsession with white-collar professions had dominated the minds of fathers thinking about their sons' education. Subsequently, in response to the opportunities open in industry for the technically trained, technical high schools had been privately founded in several of the wealthier villages. I could not have thought it possible in 1952 that the sons of men whom I then knew would be encouraged to work manually in all those trades traditionally associated with low castes like those of the ironsmith, mason, potter, and carpenter. This development has had a liberating effect upon poorer sections who now find a whole range of occupations open to them, the respectability of which is sanctioned by families whose superiority on all other matters is unquestioned.[10] I should make it clear that this development does

[9] A similar and related point is made by A. H. Hanson, *The Process of Planning* (OUP for RIIA, 1966). Speaking of caste and community groups he says: 'could it be that these much-maligned groups which appear to press so hard against the democratic frontier are in fact one of the forces that preserve it from violation?' (p. 255). I would add the proviso that the overall strategy accepts this view as inevitable and temporary. The tactical use of caste interests is quite a different thing from the encouragement of uneconomical caste occupations under the guise of fostering village industries. (See p. 273 above.)

[10] Similarly among the Patidar, a large Gujarati caste with members at many different economic levels, the custom of widow-remarriage is despised at the lower levels but admired, if not yet practised, at higher levels because yet more sophisticated kinsmen in Baroda and Ahmedabad have allowed it.

not raise the status of the traditional artisan castes. They, if anything, suffer by the loss of a traditional monopoly.

The third reason for success in Okhamandal points towards
further research. The degree of graduality among the Vagher is
slight (i.e. most of them are similar in socio-economic status and
function). The relevance and economic feasibility of any particular
demonstration of superior technique is therefore likely to be
appreciated on a relatively wide scale, and quickly. Where the degree
of graduality is greater (as it must almost inevitably be in a larger
caste), it is clear that the social area within which such improvements
will be appreciated as relevant and feasible has to be discovered by
the social worker.[11] The question of graduality has wider relevance
for social planning, as I have suggested above (n. 10). The Vagher/
Meghwa situation, like so many so-called 'tribal' situations, gives
simple expression to the basic purity/impurity formula of the caste
system.[12] In such essentially two-caste situations, unaccompanied by
graduality, untouchability may (for practical purposes if not in
appearance) be drawn off, as to a large extent it has been in Okhamandal. There are already signs that the Vagher are not only
obliged to cultivate their fields themselves, but also to take up
leather work which Meghwa are no longer available to carry out for
them. Where there is a two-caste situation with graduality within
the dominant caste, we may hypothesize that the neat Okhamandal
solution will be less likely in proportion to the degree of graduality.
Usually, but not always, a dominant caste will exhibit more
graduality where it comprises a high proportion of the local population.

5. VILLAGE POWER AND PLANNERS' ATTITUDES

As the Okhamandal story should have made it clear it is hardly
possible yet for the social anthropologist to supply 'variables' with
which the planning economist can adjust his models. Such relatively
sophisticated collaboration is premature in relation to the Draft
Fourth Plan. Only great faith in large-scale planning from which

[11] This is neither novel nor difficult. Adrian Mayer has distinguished the 'kindred
of co-operation' from the 'kindred of recognition' within caste. See his *Caste
and Kinship in Central India* (London, 1960), ch. 8. The kindred of co-operation
will be, formally or informally, an area of affinal ties which will correspond
roughly to economic parity.
[12] Compare the Kond/Pan situation in F. G. Bailey, *Tribe, Caste and Nation*
(Manchester, 1960), ch. 6.

localized benefits are expected to flow, or else inexcusable ignorance, can account for the naivety of the rural picture as presented by the Commission. The social anthropologist, trying to help the planner, must begin by recommending the monographs and theoretical studies that constitute a basic training in the subject. More creative co-operation can occur only when plans for social change are presented from a common body of shared knowledge.

If this sounds extreme, let us look at a final example of planthink. Michael Lipton has drawn attention (p. 135) to the failure to discuss the balance of power within the village. We could strengthen this observation and say that there appears to be no awareness that there is a balance of power. The Draft Outline's view of *panchayati raj* is an example of idealism so far departed from reality that it meets its opposite and is indistinguishable from cynical indifference. 'With the emergence of *panchayati raj* institutions as partners of the Centre and the States in the task of national development, it is necessary that these institutions should be induced in every way to step up their resource mobilization' (p. 213). 'Through *panchayati raj*, a system of rural democracy is being built up at the village, block and district level. It is essential that *panchayati raj* institutions should be fully involved in undertaking welfare programmes in these areas' (p. 364). Elsewhere (p. 382) it is recommended that such local communities and institutions should be induced to provide housing sites for untouchables, and in such a manner that the latter are not, even when adequately housed, still segregated.

The idealism springs, we may suppose, from the ideology of the nation-state. To wish that the integrated, harmonious intermeshing system suggested in the word 'partners' were the established state of affairs is idealistic, but wholesome enough. To ignore all the facts presenting an alternative picture, and the factors maintaining that alternative, suggests indifference.

The relation between the Centre and the parts at federal and at State level is a relation of conflict. This is most acute when we confront the two extremes, the Central Government and the village *panchayat*. It is by now commonplace that the political adaptability of the caste system has enabled powerful landowning castes, or factions of such castes, to turn local potentialities for power to their own gain (see pp. 136–41). One of the earliest discussions of this, which at the same time brings out the problem most simply, is Cohn's account of the attempts made by a depressed caste to enjoy those powers to which the constitution entitled them. The land-owners, with considerable political cunning, withdrew their opposition and allowed the untouchables to take over the forms of power and to learn for themselves that without control of the traditional underpinnings—wealth, influence, contacts—the mere assurances of constitutional rights were not enough.[13] More recently an Indian author, Dr Béteille, writing in 1965, observes in relation to his village study in Tanjore:

The image of the village *panchayat* as it has been visualized by the leaders of the country, is that it works through consensus and unanimity.[14]

He goes on to show how, in the village of his study, the *panchayat* is characterized more by domination and unequal participation. He describes how the formerly politically-dominant Brahmans have largely withdrawn from participation, while:

The Adi-Dravidas (Untouchables) by and large find themselves excluded because of their low economic, social and ritual position. When they do attend meetings of the *panchayat*, they are required to sit separately. Often they are informed about a meeting only after it has been held, and their thumb impressions are later secured on the relevant documents.[15]

These and similar facts are known not only to the social anthropologists, Indian and foreign, but also to local politicians. The latter, however high their ideals, know that what limited good they can achieve depends on conceding these realities. This is not to say that changes will not come, or indeed, are not already in process. But such changes are only impeded by what appears to be an idealistic disregard for the present reality on the part of those whose business it is to draw up the blueprint for them.

This extended comment on the first of the three passages from the Draft Outline, cited on p. 286, sufficiently places the quality of the two following ones. They are unimpeachable as exhortations, but as recommendations they fail for lack of a realistic assessment of the social facts.

I should here qualify the rather negative view of *panchayati raj* that the preoccupations of the chapter oblige me to take. The more balanced view is given by V. M. Sirsikar who, while recognizing the

---

[13] Bernard S. Cohn, 'The Changing Status of a Depressed Caste', in *Village India* (American Anthropological Association, Memoir no. 83 (1955)).
[14] André Béteille, *Caste, Class and Power* (Univ. Calif. Press, 1965), p. 151.
[15] Ibid. p. 153.

present gulf between ideal and actuality, stresses the educative function of the ideal and describes the gradual evolution of rural political leaders able to communicate both with the westernized élite and the peasantry.[16] Professor Adrian Mayer has suggested how the institution of *panchayati raj* has obliged power seekers to accommodate to new political forms.[17] This is not a dramatic success, but it is an encouraging beginning of a new political orientation.

6. WHAT ANTHROPOLOGISTS CAN DO

The literature that would furnish an altogether more informed and realistic view of likelihoods is there, but the planners have not used it at all. Nevertheless, the situation is not entirely satisfactory on the sociological side. This is not the place to spell out the criticisms in detail. The fact is that Indian sociologists have inherited, for the most part uncritically, an intellectual position built up in circumstances which differed markedly from their own. It was no part of the academic British social anthropologist's vocation to advise the colonial government how it might the better implement its notion of the colonial state. Social anthropology developed in an ambience that was at best neutral to colonial governmental interests. The contrast between the colonial and post-colonial periods could not be more marked than in the way it effects the moral stance of the social anthropologist in India. By and large, however, there is little sign that academic social anthropologists have recognized that their place is with the planners. By a greater consciousness and commitment they might have prevented much of the naivety that has been criticized. The kind of commitment sought would result in a significant shift in the emphasis in the work done. Local organizations would no longer be studied only to discover their self-maintaining mechanisms and their interaction with other organizations, but rather from the point of view of their vulnerability to change and their discontinuity from other institutions. It is by no means required of the academic anthropologist that he approve the Plan or even planning as such. His precise opposition may well be as

---

[16] V. M. Sirsikar, 'Political Role of Panchayati Raj', *Economic and Political Weekly*, 19 Nov. 1966 (Bombay). See also George Rosen, *Democracy and Economic Change in India* (Univ. Calif. Press, 1966), ch. 5.

[17] Adrian C. Mayer, 'Some Political Implications of Community Development in India', *Archiv. European Sociology*, iv (1963), pp. 86–106.

valuable as his collaboration; in my sense it *is* collaboration. Academic social anthropology in India is not expected to work for this or that particular end of the Plan, but it can be expected to take cognizance of it and to realize that planning is as much a part of Indian society as caste.

I would propose that apart from this moral commitment on the part of academics, they can also assist in a special way. The Draft Fourth Plan draws attention to the 'gap between planning and implementation' (p. 154), and the burden of this essay has been the need for sociological knowledge at the village level. One notes with approval the allocation in the Draft Fourth Plan of Rs 40 mn to the Commission's Committee for Social Science Research. We must hope that this committee, with the co-operation of academic social anthropology, will develop a distinctive cadre of constructive anthropologists who would be government employees working at village level.[18] Such workers would be committed to the implementation of plan policies far more than the academics. We might hope that the latter would have assisted in the formulation of realistic propositions at the planning stage. The work of the constructive anthropologist would be the implementation of these propositions in the particularities of each rural situation. In effect this is a proposal for a new kind of extension worker, altogether better trained than his predecessor, and fully conscious of his mediate role between national and local plan.

[18] I prefer the term 'constructive' to 'applied' as in 'applied anthropology' because there is no simple application of social anthropology. The training of a constructive anthropologist would be directed towards problems and tactics; it would emphasize economics, agriculture, dietary problems, health, and methods of education.

External Constraints

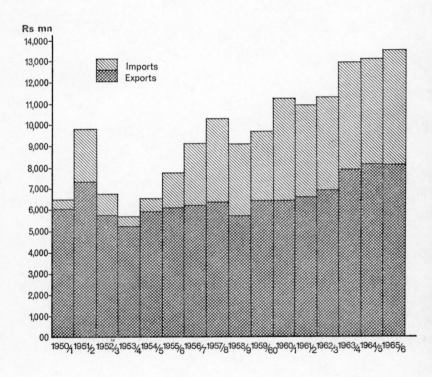

10

Foreign Trade:
A Commodity Study*

SIDNEY WELLS

A STUDY of the successive development plans shows that a change
has occurred in attitude in India towards foreign trade. The first two
development plans, drafted when the external position of India was,
superficially at least, relatively strong, paid scant attention to the
need deliberately to expand exports.

In these plans, rising imports were seen as a justification for
increased aid requests, rather than as a spur to export effort. Although trade figured more largely in the Third Plan, the emphasis
was on import substitution, rather than on export expansion. It is
only in the Fourth Plan period that an increase in exports is clearly
seen as fulfilling a vital role in progress towards external equilibrium.

1. THE BACKGROUND

Throughout the period of the plans, imports have in general grown
more rapidly than exports, with the resultant widening of the trade
gap, as shown in the chart opposite. Imports rose markedly from the
beginning of the Second Plan, partly as the consequence of industrialization, and partly as the result of more liberal import licensing
in the early years of the plan. During the first two plans exports
hardly rose at all.

When the Third Plan was formulated it was expected that imports
would rise by about 16 per cent. By then, production of essential
products and improvements in the infrastructure of the economy

* I am grateful to a large number of Government of India officials, industrialists,
and others, too numerous to mention by name, with whom I have had most helpful discussions while on a recent visit to India.

were such that it was reasonable to expect a reduction in the direct foreign exchange component of investment from 30 per cent in the Second Plan to 20 per cent in the Third.[1]

In the event, total imports were some 6 per cent less than anticipated, although food imports under PL 480[2] (Rs 8,500 mn) were higher than expected. Unfortunately, the shortfall in imports did not reflect increased self-sufficiency or efficiency in the Indian economy, but simply the drastic reductions in various import quotas in 1962–3, made imperative by the serious state of the current balance of payments.

Although exports rose only marginally during the First and Second Plans, it was hoped that under the Third Plan they would surge forward and reach between Rs 37,000 mn and Rs 38,000 mn— an increase of over 20 per cent—as compared with the Second Plan. In fact, total exports exceeded the Plan target and reached Rs 38,120 mn. As Tables 1 and 2 show, however, the performance of exports over the period was erratic—the reassuring rates of increase recorded between 1961–2 and 1963–4 were not maintained into the last years of the Plan, and in 1965–6 exports actually fell. There are, however, grounds for believing that the disappointing export performance in 1965–6 was due to temporary factors—famine and war.

In spite of setbacks, there were encouraging developments in the pattern of India's export trade during the Third Plan. For example, India's exports were slightly less concentrated in traditional products. The share of the three traditional export commodities, tea, cotton textiles, and jute manufactures in India's export trade declined from 48 per cent in 1960–1 to 43 per cent in 1965–6. Exports of engineering and chemical products still accounted for less than 4 per cent of all exports in 1965–6, but this was over twice as large as their share in 1960–1. The share of iron ore and of iron and steel products had also risen. A number of products in the light engineering sector appeared for the first time as exports; by the end

---

[1] For a detailed discussion of the anticipated external implications of the 3rd Plan, see GATT, Committee Three, Special Report, *Development Plans: Study of the Third Five-Year Plan of India* (Geneva, 1962).

[2] 'Public Law 480' is shorthand for the US Agricultural Trade Development and Assistance Act of 1954, which provides among other things for the sale of agricultural commodities against payment in the currency of the recipient country. During the first nine years of its operation, shipments under PL 480 accounted for 28 per cent of all US exports of agricultural products.

TABLE 1

The Indian Economy—Selected External Indicators 1950/1–1965/6

	Unit	1950/1	1951/2	1952/3	1953/4	1954/5	1955/6	1956/7	1957/8
1. Value of Imports	Rs mn	6,500	9,790	6,700	5,720	6,560	7,740	9,030	10,360
2. Value of Exports	Rs mn	6,010	7,330	5,780	5,310	5,940	6,090	6,200	6,350
3. Balance of Visible Trade	Rs mn	−490	−2,460	−920	−410	−620	−1,650	−2,830	−4,010
4. Balance of Payments	Rs mn	+389	−1,622	+602	+474	+60	+67	−3,128	−4,314

	Unit	1958/9	1959/60	1960/1	1961/2	1962/3	1963/4	1964/5	1965/6
1. Value of Imports	Rs mn	9,040	9,610	11,220	10,920	11,310	12,900	13,140	13,500 (a)
2. Value of Exports	Rs mn	5,730	6,400	6,420	6,610	6,850	7,930	8,160	8,050 (a)
3. Balance of Visible Trade	Rs mn	−3,310	−3,210	−4,800	−4,310	−4,460	−4,970	−4,980	−5,450
4. Balance of Payments	Rs mn	−3,270	−1,856	−3,924	−3,064	−3,455	−3,353	−4,367 (a)	−3,198 (ab)

a = provisional   *b* = Apr. to Sept. 1965.

Source: 4DO, p. 419.

TABLE 2

Growth of Indian Exports During The Third Plan
Rs mn (pre-devaluation)

	1960/1	1961/2	1962/3	1963/4	1964/5	1965/6	3rd Plan Total
Vegetable oils (non essential)	85	58	132	199	71	41	501
Oilcakes	143	173	311	354	398	346	158,2
Tobacco (unmanufactured)	146	140	180	211	244	196	971
Spices	166	175	138	160	167	231	871
Sugar	24	146	169	260	212	113	900
Fruit & vegetables	260	255	267	301	367	348	1,538
Fish	46	39	40	57	68	68	272
Tea	1,236	1,226	1,298	1,234	1,246	1,148	6,165
Iron ore	340	354	353	364	373	421	1,865
Cotton piece goods	576	483	482	543	576	552	2,636
(a) mill products	528	433	415	475	480	469	2,272
(b) hand loom products	48	50	67	68	96	83	364
Jute manufactures	1,352	1,459	1,495	1,542	1,682	1,829	8,007
Engineering products	56	69	80	149	143	200	641
Iron and steel	55	40	10	19	44	83	196
Chemical and allied products	34	37	39	40	68	91	275
Other exports	2,083	2,143	2,142	2,499	2,504	2,429	11,717
Total (including re-exports)	6,602	6,797	7,136	7,932	8,163	8,096	38,124
Index (1960/1 = 1,000)	1,000	1,029	1,080	1,202	1,235	1,225	

Source: 4DO, p. 93.

of the period India was exporting a wide range of 'light' manufactured goods, such as typewriters, plastic goods, and fountain pens.

As regards the geographical pattern of trade, Table 3 shows that the United Kingdom accounts for a steadily diminishing share of Indian exports: 18·1 per cent in 1965–6 as against 26·8 per cent in 1960–1. In view of Britain's possible entry into the EEC, this decreased dependence upon the UK market is a healthy sign. The United States' share in India's exports, on the other hand, rose, and in 1965–6 was 18·3 per cent. The most dramatic change in the pattern of Indian trade has been the growing importance of the East European market. Table 3 shows the trend since 1960–1. In 1960–1 the countries of Eastern Europe accounted for 7·7 per cent of India's exports; by 1965–6 the share of these countries was 19·3 per cent.

TABLE 3

Change in Direction of Indian Exports During The Third Plan
(Percentages)

	1960/1	1961/2	1962/3	1963/4	1964/5	1965/6	3rd Plan Total
Western Europe	37·3	34·3	34·4	31·7	29·6	27·2	31·3
of which EEC	8·1	8·2	7·9	7·8	7·0	6·8	7·5
of which UK	26·8	23·7	23·1	20·6	20·5	18·1	21·1
Asia and Oceania	25·8	25·9	23·5	27·1	25·0	23·2	24·9
Africa	7·6	8·3	7·0	5·8	5·7	7·6	6·8
America	21·5	22·0	22·1	21·7	22·1	22·3	22·0
of which Canada	2·8	2·6	3·1	2·7	2·1	2·5	2·6
of which USA	16·0	17·0	16·2	16·4	18·0	18·3	17·2
Eastern Europe	7·7	9·5	13·0	13·7	17·6	19·3	14·9
of which USSR	4·5	4·7	5·4	6·6	9·5	11·5	7·7
Total Value of Exports (a) Rs mn	6,428	6,797	7,136	7,932	8,163	8,096	38,124

(a) Includes exports from Goa, estimated at Rs 180 mn for each of the two financial years 1960/1 and 1961/2.
Source: 4DO, p. 94.

In the year 1965/6 exports to the USSR alone accounted for 11·5 per cent of all Indian exports. If, as seems likely, there is a substantial increase over the next decade in India's output of light engineering and miscellaneous manufactured goods, the cultivation of the East European market might become of fundamental importance for some of India's newer export industries.

It should be noted that there is considerable disquiet in India at the way in which trade with Communist (rupee account) countries operates. In return for much needed imports, India undertakes to supply exports to these countries in given quantities. But the Foreign Trade Corporations in the importing countries are often alleged to re-export Indian goods to the West at lower prices in order to obtain convertible currencies. Often these goods undercut similar products exported to Western countries directly from India and sold in these countries at economic prices. The practice appears to be particularly widespread in engineering products.

2. HOPES FOR THE FOURTH PLAN

Imports for the Fourth Plan period are expected to amount to some Rs 76,500 mn (at pre-devaluation exchange rates excluding

PL 480 food imports). Appreciable increases in imports of iron and steel, non-ferrous metals, components, and spares for machinery and transport equipment are expected. Imports of petroleum and vegetable oils are not expected to increase appreciably, while some decrease is anticipated in imports of chemicals, pharmaceuticals, textile fibres, paperboard, and newsprint.

The estimate for import requirements is surely optimistic. It assumes that domestic production targets will be reached; for example, any shortfall in output of fertilizers or steel will necessitate higher imports of these goods if the rest of the Plan is to be fulfilled.

In their estimates, the planners assumed that restrictions on the importation of raw materials and of durable and non-durable consumer goods will continue, unless these are specifically required for the manufacture of export commodities. The authors inform the reader that the estimates of import requirements have been made 'in terms of the major commodities, in the light of expected domestic requirements and domestic production' (p. 104). Unfortunately, no detailed breakdown is given of the likely impact of these factors upon imports at the level of commodities—or even commodity groups.

As regards exports, the planners hope that by 1970–1 these will be running at a level about 50 per cent above that achieved over the Third Plan period. Thus considerable progress should be made in reducing the trade gap by the end of the Plan.

Table 4 shows that if the import and export forecasts are correct then, taking into account the heavy burden of external debt servicing, the gap to be covered by external credit is some Rs 63,000 mn (in post-devaluation rupees). This is the measure of the loans and grants which India will require from developed countries and from international institutions in order to carry out the objectives of the Plan.

As Table 5 shows, the Government is hoping that exports will increase over a wide front; in particular, substantial increases are hoped for in tea, iron ore, engineering goods, jute manufactures, fruits and nuts, oil cakes, tobacco, clothing, iron and steel, and chemicals. Similar increases are expected for sugar, coffee, spices, coir yarn and manufactures, and handicrafts.

In recent years the authorities have taken a number of institutional measures to help expand exports.[3] Such measures, although useful, can be only peripheral to solving the real problem of India's foreign

[3] See below p. 320.

TABLE **4**

Draft Fourth Plan
Foreign Exchange Requirements

	Rs mn	
Payments	Pre-Dev. Rs	Post-Dev. Rs
Imports		
(*a*) Maintenance imports	52,000	81,900
(*b*) Project imports	24,500	38,590
Debt servicing	14,500	22,840
	91,000	143,330
Receipts		
1. Exports	51,000	80,330
Gap to be covered by external credit	40,000	63,000

Source: 4DO, p. 91.

trade, which is basically one of securing adequate domestic supply, both of import substitutes and exportables, and of selling abroad at competitive prices.

The authors of the Draft Fourth Plan are well aware of the crucial importance of supply factors in making possible import substitution and export availability. Indeed they go so far as to suggest (p. 98) that '*The most important* pre-condition for the fulfilment of the export programme is the realization of the production targets set for exportable commodities in the agricultural, mineral and industrial sectors' (my italics). Accordingly, the plan promises that the authorities will take account of export requirements in licensing additional industrial capacity, and in allowing freer importation of raw materials necessary for an expanded output of exportables.

Other contributors to this symposium have considered the problems of growth in the manufacturing and agricultural sectors. Table 6A, however, gives some idea of the progress of, and targets for, various sectors of Indian industry, in so far as imports and exports are likely to be affected. Up to 1965–6 there were dramatic increases in output of a wide range of industrial products. Output of cotton textiles increased much less markedly. As for the future, Tables 6A and 6B show that in the Fourth Plan period an eightfold increase

TABLE 5

Exports: Achievements and Targets

Commodity	Unit	1961/2 Quantity	1961/2 Value*	1964/5 Quantity	1964/5 Value*	1970/1 Target Quantity	1970/1 Target Value*
1 Agriculture and allied crops (including plantation crops)			2,611		3,173		4,540
2 Tobacco unmanufactured	mn kgs	44·4	140	78·6	244	100	330
3 Spices	mn kgs.	64·2	175	53·3	167		290
4 Sugar	thou. tonnes	372	146	271	212	600	190
5 Fruits and vegetables	thou. tonnes		255		368		580
6 Raw cotton	thou. tonnes	62	143	47	106	52	140
7 Raw wool	mn kgs	14·5	84	12	77	11·4	60
8 Tea	mn kgs	207	1,226	212	1,246	300	1,640
9 Coffee	mn kgs	29·7	90	31	134	40	190
10 Hides and skins (raw)	mn kgs	11·7	82	12·4	83	13·5	100
11 Minerals			558		600		1,060
12 Iron ore	mn tonnes	9·8	354	10·5	372	22	770
13 Manganese ore	thou. tonnes	995	107	1,552	131	1,800	150
14 Mica	mn kgs	28	97	31	97	55	140
15 Manufactures			2,805		3,342		5,000
16 Cotton fabrics	mn metres	513	482	523	576	665	670
17 Jute goods	thou. tonnes	803	1,459	960	1,683	1,150	2,110
18 Artificial silk fabrics	mn metres	81·3	76	57·4	65	100	100
19 Clothing			07		46		190
20 Coir yarn and manufactures	thou. tonnes	74·6	112	74·7	113	106	160
21 Footwear	mn pairs	4·6	24	7·6	42	25	140
22 Leather and leather manufactures			254		274		380
23 Engineering goods			69		143		480
24 Handicrafts			193		253		320
25 Iron and steel	thou. tonnes		40		44	500	200
26 Chemicals and allied products			37		68		190
27 Other exports			823		1,048		1,640
28 Total exports			6,797		8,163		12,240

1 tonne = 1,000 kg. = 2,204·6 lb.

Note * Value is in Rs mn (pre-devaluation)

TABLE 6A

India—Industrial Output

Progress and Targets

1950/1–1970/1

Product	Unit	1950/1	1955/6	1964/5	1965/6 Likely	1970/1	% Increase 1965/6 to 1970/1
Finished steel	mn tonnes	1·04	1·3	4·43	4·6	8·8	91·3
Steel ingots	mn tonnes	1·47	1·74	6·1	6·2	11·7	88·7
Cement making machinery	Rs 100,000	—	40	220	350	2,000	471·4
Sugar refining machinery	Rs 100,000	—	20	910	800	1,600	100·0
Machine tools	Rs 100,000	30	80	2,000	2,300	10,500	356·5
Ball and roller bearings	mn	0·1	0·9	5·9	9·0	30·0	233·3
Diesel engines (stationary)	thou.	5·5	10·4	74·1	85·0	200·0	135·3
Agricultural tractors	thou.	—	—	3·2	5·6	35·0	525·0
Electric transformers 33 kv	thou. kv.	178	625	3,000	3,300	5,000	51·5
Electric cables	thou. tonnes	1·7	9·4	48·8	55·0	120·0	118·2
Nitrogenous fertilizers	thou. tonnes	9	80	234	233	2,000	785·4
Phosphatic fertilizers	thou. tonnes	9	12	131	111	1,000	800·9
Sewing machines	thou.	33	111	330	450	900	100·0
Bicycles	thou.	99	513	1,442	1,700	3,500	105·9
Automobiles	thou.	16·5	25·3	70·8	68·5	170·0	148·2
Cotton textiles mill made	mn metres	3,401	4,665	4,676	4,434	5,486	23·7
Sugar	thou. tonnes	1,134	1,890	3,260	3,550	4,500	26·8
Electric fans	mn	0·2	0·29	1·27	1·5	3·5	133·3

kv = kilovolt.

Source: 4DO, p. 62.

TABLE 6B

*India—Agricultural Output
Progress and Targets, 1950/1–1970/1*

Product	Unit	1950/1	1955/6	1964/5	1965/6 likely	1970/1	Percentage increase 1965/6 to 1970/1
Foodgrains	mn tonnes	54·92	69·22	88·95	72·29	120·0	66·0
Cotton	mn bales	2·62	4·03	5·41	4·73	8·6	81·8
Sugar cane	mn tonnes	6·92	7·29	12·32	12·12	13·5	11·4
Oilseeds	mn tonnes	5·09	5·63	8·30	6·14	10·7	74·3
Jute	mn bales	3·51	4·48	6·02	4·48	9·0	100·9
Tea	thou. tonnes	273	285	n.a.	376	n.f.	—
Tobacco	thou. tonnes	261	303	370	400	475	18·7

1 bale = 180 kg.   n.a. = not available.   n.f = not fixed.
Source: 4DO, p. 62.

is hoped for in output of phosphatic fertilizers, a sixfold increase in the production of farm tractors, and a three to fourfold increase in the output of machine tools. Output of cars and bicycles is expected to more than double.

As regards traditional products, increases are expected to be more modest. For example, output of mill-made textiles is expected to grow by only 25 per cent.

The Draft Fourth Plan pays more attention to the agricultural sector than its predecessors.[4] The anticipated two-thirds increase in the output of foodgrains would reduce the need for imported food-stuffs. Only a small increase is anticipated in the production of sugar.

The prospects of success for India's export effort depends upon many factors; but they can be analysed as those concerned with supply factors in the Indian economy and demand conditions in world markets. The former will depend upon climatic considerations as well as the skill with which economic policy is fashioned and the plan implemented. The latter will depend upon the extent to which competing products are available from other sources, and upon the toughness or otherwise of tariffs and other import restrictions. Clearly it is impossible to examine this question in terms of Indian exports as a whole; much more can be learned of the foreign trade problems which are likely to arise by looking at the prospects for

[4] But see ch. 4.

certain important commodities in some detail. Accordingly, we shall examine briefly prospects for trade in those products which are of importance for the Indian balance of payments over the next five years; in the case of these goods we shall consider factors which bear upon either import saving or export promotion. First, however, we shall look briefly at some of the changes which have occurred in the very recent past in Indian economic policy, in so far as they are likely to affect foreign trade prospects.

3. 1966: POLICY REAPPRAISAL

The main outlines of the Draft Fourth Plan were determined before the devaluation was announced, and in assessing the prospects for the fulfilment of the plan, some account must be taken of the possible consequences of the devaluation (and the associated measures) for the plan.

In the months preceding devaluation the Indian economy was increasingly a siege economy. Import restrictions had been tightened. In August 1965 the duty on most consumption goods was raised to 100 per cent; on machinery it was doubled, bringing the nominal rate up to 40 per cent (although the effective import duty on most of these products was 30 per cent). The duty on basic raw materials was raised to 40 per cent; on processed materials it was as high as 60 per cent. Direct trade controls were stiffened, partly to safeguard the reserves and partly to accelerate the longer-term policy of import substitution. For example, imports of copper and zinc for the manufacture of pressure stoves and lamps were forbidden in order to encourage the use of home-produced aluminium. No longer was it possible to import nickel for the bicycle and sewing machine industries. Imports of wind-shield curved glass were forbidden. Mr B. R. Bhagat, Minister for Planning, told parliament that it would be necessary to give greater priority to import substitution and export promotion,[5] and the Directorate General of Technical Development was asked to produce reports on import substitution possibilities. It was in this situation that the serious economic crisis of 1966 occurred—or perhaps it would be better to describe what was happening as the culmination of a series of crises.

The war with Pakistan had greatly weakened India's external

[5] *The Hindu*, 6 Nov. 1965.

position; the temporary suspension of aid which followed the flaring up of hostilities was a further blow. The failure of the monsoon and famine conditions made substantially increased food imports necessary; at one time it was uncertain whether American food aid would come in time to avert a major catastrophe. There was a steep rise in retail prices, particularly of foodstuffs. Increasingly, the Indian economy became isolated from the rest of the world, with domestic prices well above those of competing imports. In this situation, and in spite of stringent restrictions, there was constant pressure for imports to be sucked in as substitutes for home-produced goods. Any trader able to get hold of imports could make substantial profits. Such goods were said to fetch prices which were anything between 50 and 300 per cent above their landed price.[6] The official exchange rate appeared quite unrealistic. A week before the June devaluation, the black market rupee rate was Rs 30 = £1, as against the official rate of Rs 13·3 = £1.

Devaluation as a policy was vigorously argued by the International Bank for Reconstruction and Development Mission of 1965 under Mr Bernard Bell, in its unpublished study of the Indian economic development effort.

The Bell Mission urged on the Indian Government a policy of greater flexibility, in particular in regard to import liberalization and the opening up of further export opportunities by devaluation. They believed that devaluation would choke off unnecessary imports more effectively than the existing battery of controls, which was complex in its operation and uncertain in its results. Accordingly they advocated import liberalization of a wide range of materials, which would, they believed, damp down domestic inflation and ease the supply problem of export industries. A devalued rupee would encourage industries to divert output from the home market to overseas outlets.

The Bell Mission had some hard things to say about what its authors regarded as the mismanagement of foreign exchange allocations during the Third Plan. The Indian plans divide imports into two categories—maintenance imports and project imports. The former are intended, as their description suggests, to maintain the level of output in industry already established, including replacement machinery and spares; the latter are imports which result from the starting of new projects and the completion of old

[6] *Financial Times*, 20 Aug. 1965.

ones. It was argued that fuller utilization of plant and equipment would be possible if foreign exchange earmarked for specific projects were available for maintenance imports.

The Mission deplored the amount of foreign exchange which had been used up to pay for food imports, arguing that more attention to agriculture in earlier plans would have ensured more adequate domestic supplies. Since 1950–1 imports of foodgrains have been growing at an average compound rate of about 3 per cent per annum. Only emergency imports under PL 480 had saved millions of Indians from starvation. In 1964–5 India consumed one-fifth of US current wheat production.

The policy changes which took place in the summer of 1966 went some way towards meeting the suggestions of the IBRD, acting on the Bell Report. But their importance should not be exaggerated; there was no question of India abandoning all import and export controls.

4. THE DEVALUATION

The policy measures announced in June 1966 were in the nature of a package deal rather than a simple currency adjustment. The rupee was devalued by 36·5 per cent, but export duties were imposed on twelve traditional export items.[7] On the import side, liberalization was announced in the case of some fifty-nine groups of products, selected on the basis of their contribution to exports. Import controls on other products, including virtually all consumer goods, were in no way relaxed; neither were tariffs lowered. Efforts were made to prevent the higher import prices resulting from devaluation from raising domestic costs and export prices. Importers of items of mass consumption were requested to fix wholesale and retail prices, and the Government took powers to fix maximum prices where necessary.

The immediate result of the devaluation was hardly dramatic. The black market rate remained unchanged; although there was a slight rise in share prices on the Stock Exchange, these soon fell back. A month after devaluation, tea and jute share prices were lower than

---

[7] Such duties were imposed on jute hessian and sacking, black pepper, oil cakes other than copra, raw cotton and cotton waste, raw wool, mica, hides and skins, coffee, tea, and unmanufactured tobacco. It seems that on average these duties offset about 30–40 per cent of the price change resulting from the devaluation.

they had been before the event. As for inflation, Government officials spent much effort in urging traders not to raise their prices, but by the end of the year some increase had taken place.

Although the devaluation was a substantial one, its likely effect upon exports can easily be exaggerated, for it should be remembered that the export subsidies which have largely been abolished applied to as much as one-fifth of India's total export earnings; the *duties* which replaced the subsidies affected over half of exports, and rates were fairly high, ranging between 25 per cent and 33½ per cent. The removal of the subsidies and the imposition of the duties thus offset to some extent the price effects of the devaluation.

In the case of traditional products, some 40 per cent of the price effect of devaluation has been washed away by export duties. Even in newer manufactured goods, where superficially the devaluation will be able to exert its full effect, the advantage to the producer is not a clear one, for the discount which exporters used to receive on raw materials to be worked up into exports no longer applies.

Nevertheless, the devaluation will result in some lowering (in terms of foreign currency) of Indian export prices; it would be surprising if there were no net gain on the export side of the balance of trade. Although India is a substantial supplier of jute products, tea, and cotton textiles, and the effect of devaluation is therefore likely to be less than in the case of commodities where India is a peripheral world supplier, in each of these staple products India has in recent years had difficulty in maintaining its share of the world market. Devaluation is likely to give it an edge over its competitors.

India is in effect operating a differential devaluation. By means of export duties it is trying to maintain unit values of exports in terms of foreign currency where it is a dominant or strongly placed supplier. It should also be noted that the policy secures substantial revenue for the Government.

In spite of the rising rupee price of imports, these are likely to increase in volume following devaluation. The import elasticity of demand for the raw material content of Indian exports is relatively low, because most such products cannot be produced in adequate quantities internally, at least in the foreseeable future.

Thus the expansion of imports made necessary by the increase of exports—and made possible by the liberalization of imports—is likely to be considerable. Since the Draft Outline of the Plan was prepared before devaluation, it seems that inadequate account has been taken of the effect of this liberalization upon the balance of payments.

It is arguable that the Indian devaluation is little more than an administrative device a way to get rid of import restrictions and other controls, rather than a means of directly improving the balance of payments. No doubt the IBRD advisers urged the importance of the package deal as a means of loosening up the Indian economy. But it is untrue to suggest that the deal is little more than a bonfire of controls. Apart from the fact that governing circles in India are far from being convinced of the virtues of a free economy, there can be little doubt that they (and Indian businessmen) regard the devaluation as primarily a means to the selective encouragement of exports. In any case most businessmen do not regard the 'bonfire of controls' as being nearly big enough, and in New Delhi one still gets the strong impression of being in a control-ridden society.

At this point it is worth noting that devaluation will have important effects upon the invisible and capital accounts. For example the rupee burden of servicing and repaying debt will increase by some 57·5 per cent. There is also the problem of the remission of funds by foreign enterprises in India. Foreign investment in India will now have to earn over 50 per cent more in rupees in order to produce as much foreign exchange as before the devaluation. It has been argued that this could eventually result in a marked reduction in the volume of direct investment of British and foreign firms in India, with a slowing down of the growth prospects of many industries.[8]

During the Third Plan direct investment was approximately Rs 1,500 mn; the planners hoped that this inflow would be greater during the period 1966–70 but a large question mark must rest over this. It is arguable that devaluation will attract more private capital, since it will make Indian industries more profitable. So far, there is no sign whatever of this happening, largely because devaluation appears so far to be ineffective in terms of increasing exports, and because the anticipated higher profits have not appeared. Finally, potential foreign investors still show a chronic lack of confidence in the ability of the Indian economy to lift itself out of the morass in which it is bogged down. In this respect political developments in India since devaluation have been far from helpful in instilling a

[8] On the whole question see, 'The Purpose of Rupee Devaluation', *National and Grindlays Review* (London, July 1966).

sense of confidence. Until confidence returns it seems unlikely that foreigners will be induced to invest more in India, whatever may be the theoretical benefits of the devaluation.

In analysing the likely impact of the devaluation upon the Indian balance of payments in the years ahead, it is wiser to examine prospects for particular industries than to assess the overall impact. Even this analysis is not easy, for it is clearly impossible to assess the likely consequences of devaluation in terms of prices alone. Much also depends upon supply conditions, not only in India but also in countries which are close competitors, notably Pakistan. Also important are attitudes of foreign Governments towards imports from India, a matter quite outside the ability of India to influence. Accordingly, all we can hope to do is to outline the considerations to be taken into account in looking at the overall export objectives of the Plan in relation to those products upon which success or failure is likely to depend.

5. AGRICULTURAL EXPORTS

Tea

Although the Draft Fourth Plan has little to say about the expected export achievements of the tea industry, the importance of this, one of India's oldest export industries, is such that its prospects are worth examining in detail. The export problems of this industry highlight those of the economy in general—a heavy dependence upon a relatively narrow range of products, many of which are now being produced more cheaply in other developing countries. These products, too, are often in areas where world demand is growing only slowly, or where restrictions are placed on imports into many countries.

About two-thirds of the Indian tea crop is exported, and in 1965 the Indian tea plantations supplied about 36 per cent of world exports. The other main suppliers were Ceylon, Africa and Latin America.

The high-income countries of Western Europe and North America absorb over 75 per cent of world tea imports; of these countries, the United Kingdom imports more than the rest put together.

India has been at a competitive disadvantage *vis-à-vis* other tea growing countries. In part this has been the result of a more rapid rise in costs, particularly wage costs (estimated in 1956 to account for between 38 and 45 per cent of total production costs).[9] Wage costs in Ceylon are higher than those in Indian plantations, but since the plucking season there is a longer one, labour can be used more efficiently. Wage costs have been rising considerably more rapidly in India than in Ceylon, and in both countries wage and production costs are higher than in Africa. According to the FAO, in the mid-1950s costs in Africa were estimated at some 14 to 21 pence per lb, compared with 27 to 31 pence per lb for comparable Indian teas.[10]

It is arguable that Indian Government policy has militated against increased tea exports. Until 1963, when the export duty on tea was abandoned, duties raised the price by about 10 to 15 per cent above the auction price. Moreover, exports were controlled by means of quota, and although actual exports have always tended to fall behind total quota allocations, the system created some market distortions which added to the costs of certain exporters. Export quotas were granted on the basis of production rather than exports, so that those who wished to export more than their quota were forced to purchase additional export rights from growers who held licences but did not wish to use them. There was a regular market in these trading rights.[11]

Presumably the authorities believed that, since consumers' demand for tea is generally agreed to be unresponsive to price, the burden of the export duty could well be passed on to the consumer in the importing country. Similarly, they thought that physical restrictions on exports from a country like India, which had such a large share of world trade, would help to maintain world prices. It may have been that the Indian Government underrated the strength of price competition from other supplying countries, notably in Africa. But perhaps a more relevant criticism is that too little attention has been given to the modernization and the development of quality teas. The Plantation Enquiry of 1956 noted that in Darjeeling, for example, 79 per cent of the area was in need of immediate replanting.[12] Modern methods of tea planting and gathering can, however, have markedly adverse effects upon employment. By using cuttings instead of seeds, large increases in yield are obtainable. Moreover, operating costs—and the number of workers employed—can be

[9] Plantation Enquiry Commission, *Report* (1956), i, p. 99.
[10] FAO, 'Tea Trends and Prospects', *Commodity B.* no. 30 (Rome, 1960), p. 44.
[11] See Manmohan Singh, *India's Export Trends and the Prospect for Self-sustained Growth* (London, 1964), p. 68.
[12] Plantation Enquiry, *Report*, p. 62.

considerably reduced by the cultivation of barks which grow to an equal height, making machine cutting possible. Replanting and modernization will accordingly create an employment problem, at least in the short run. On the other hand, a refusal to adopt modern cost-reducing methods will make it increasingly difficult for Indian tea exports to compete against those of other producing countries where such methods are adopted.

As for the future, it is clear that the Indian planners will have to pay more careful attention to supply factors. Quality is also an important factor; consumers' incomes are rising and lately the price of plain teas on the world market has fallen more than that of quality teas.[13]

So far, devaluation has not had a dramatically favourable effect upon tea exports. Indeed the reverse was the case in the weeks immediately following devaluation when countries, notably the USSR and the UAR, ceased to operate in Calcutta auctions for a short time, as the result of uncertainties regarding the rate of exchange at which rupees would be available to finance barter deals agreed before devaluation.

It would be optimistic to expect a great deal of improvement in tea exports resulting from price factors alone. Tea interests in India do not anticipate any dramatic upsurge in exports, although rupee devaluation will certainly improve the prospects of Indian tea *vis-à-vis* those of Africa. The measure of competition from East African teas can be seen by the fact that while India's share of the London tea market declined from 52·4 per cent in the calendar year 1965 to 48 per cent in 1966, that of Africa (and other countries excluding Ceylon) increased from 13·7 per cent to 20 per cent.

Devaluation might well be of assistance in encouraging growers to export, rather than to supply the home market.[14] Fundamentally, however, export availabilities will depend also upon supplies of adequate quality becoming available.

It seems unlikely that world consumption of tea will rise very

---

[13] For example, in 1962 average tea prices were roughly equivalent to those in 1961, but in some months plain teas were selling at prices which were only one third of those of quality teas. See G. K. Sarkar, 'Some Thoughts on the World Tea Economy', *Indian J. of Economics*, July 1965.

[14] It is difficult to assess the immediate consequences of devaluation on tea exports, since in both 1966 and 1967 shipments of teas were adversely affected by widespread labour difficulties, notably strikes in the plantations themselves, and disputes in the road transport industry.

rapidly. The FAO has made a number of estimates of future consumption, suggesting that by 1970–2 consumption of tea in industrial countries will be between 7 per cent and 16 per cent above the 1958–60 level.[15] In the less developed world, demand is likely to grow faster, but the total consumption of the less developed countries is only one-third of that of high-income countries.

A study by Dr Maizels and his colleagues at the National Institute of Economic and Social Research, London, suggests that to 1975, the consumption of tea in the United States and western Europe is likely to grow more slowly than that of coffee and cocoa.[16] In the United Kingdom the annual increase in consumption is estimated at 0·7 per cent compound, as compared with 3·5 per cent for coffee.

The more immediate prospects of increasing export sales of Indian tea are in the Eastern bloc countries, and in poor countries not growing tea. Both price and income elasticities of demand are likely to be higher in developing countries than in high-income industrialized countries.

Is it possible that increased tea supplies will become available only to meet with the refusal of overseas Governments to allow their citizens freely to import or consume the product? In developing countries there is a danger that Governments might restrict tea as a 'luxury' import when faced with balance-of-payments difficulties. Some of these countries already impose high tariffs on tea imports. The Brazilian duty on leaf tea for example is 50 per cent; on tea in bags it is 100 per cent.

In the more developed countries duties are not exceptionally high. The EEC common external tariff is nominally 18–23 per cent, depending upon the weight of the package, but the Community agreed to the suspension of this duty from the beginning of January 1964. The Netherlands is the only country which imports Indian tea in significant quantities. Moderate duties (usually specific) are imposed by EFTA countries. The USA and the UK import tea duty-free from all sources. Accordingly, import barriers in industrialized countries are unlikely to prove an obstacle to increased tea exports from India. Perhaps a slightly more serious problem is posed by the relatively high internal fiscal charges which are levied in a number of

[15] FAO, *Agricultural Commodities–Projections for 1970, Commodity Review,* Special Suppl. (Rome, 1962).
[16] A. Maizels and others, 'Exports and Economic Growth in the Overseas Sterling Area 1960–1 to 1975', *Economic Rev.* (National Inst. London, Nov. 1966).

countries, particularly in Western Europe. For example, in Western Germany revenue and turnover taxes on tea together add nearly 60 per cent to the import price. Although it is difficult to find people in India who believe that these duties are having a *marked* adverse effect upon exports, their reduction must surely help in expansion of exports.

The problem of increasing Indian tea exports seems to be twofold. In the first place, it is necessary for plantations to become more efficient and to concentrate on producing quality teas. Secondly, faced with a relatively slow rise in world demand, exporters should pay more attention to propaganda and 'drink more tea' campaigns in countries which are at present relatively small consumers.

Cashew nuts, tobacco, and spices

Tea has been selected for detailed discussion as one of the staple export crops of the Indian economy. No other primary product approaches it in quantitative importance as an exportable commodity; but there are a number of primary products in which India almost certainly has some comparative cost advantage and which might well make an important contribution to higher exports in the late 1960s. India is almost the only world exporter of *cashew nut kernels*; about 60 per cent of total exports of this crop are sold in the US. Considering its monopoly, one might conclude that devaluation would make little difference to exports; but these nuts are fairly close substitutes for a wide range of other types of nut, and a lowering of their price in overseas markets might cause a substantial switch in demand. Following devaluation the export prospects of cashew nuts are probably improved. Cashew nuts are regularly imported from Africa to augment the rather limited supplies of home-grown nuts for the Indian crushing industry. An expansion of domestic output of cashew nuts would not only add to export receipts; it would also save imports.

As regards *tobacco*, India and Rhodesia are the leading exporters, outside North America, of the Virginian-type tobacco. Devaluation might enable India to obtain a larger share of the world market at the expense of Rhodesia, but mandatory UN sanctions against Rhodesia, even if only partially effective, are likely temporarily to give to India a bigger slice of this market than would otherwise have been the case. The EEC arrangement with Greece and Turkey gives the tobacco industries of those countries wider opportunities in the EEC market, but this is not of immediate consequence to India, since the types of tobacco involved are not close substitutes.

Before the Second World War India was the largest producer and exporter of *groundnuts* in the world and accounted for almost half the world exports of groundnut seed and oil. In many respects India is well suited to production of oils and oilseeds. Unfortunately, even if trading conditions in these products were more favourable than they are at present, domestic supply conditions in India would inhibit any substantial expansion of exports. At the present time, exports of groundnut oil and groundnuts are forbidden.

Sugar is a product of which exportable surpluses are from time to time available, and could be increased. India sells part of its sugar exports to the UK at an agreed price of about £35 per ton; the rest it disposes of at the 'free' world price. As the result of extremely restrictive import barriers, coupled with elaborate domestic support policies, (especially in Western Europe), the industrialized countries are increasingly self-sufficient in sugar. Domestic producers in the EEC receive a price of £60 a ton—almost double the present (1967) world price of sugar. Here, perhaps, is a crop which could make a substantial contribution to India's foreign exchange earnings in the period to 1971, if freer entry into the markets of high income countries were possible—although it should not be forgotten that other sugar-producing countries more favourably placed than India might obtain the lion's share of the gains resulting from more liberal access.

6. TRADITIONAL MANUFACTURES
Jute

One of the greatest losses which India sustained following partition in 1947 was the cutting off of the jute mills, mainly in India, from their source of raw material, mainly in Pakistan. Although present-day India produces large quantities of raw jute, periodic shortages result in idle capacity and a shortfall in Indian exports. It is a serious weakness of the Indian external economic position that such a high proportion of the country's exports are dependent upon the vagaries of the monsoon and upon imports from Pakistan, a country which is a neighbour but not a friend. For example, in 1964–5 the Indian jute crop amounted to 6,500,000 bales. To enable the Indian mills to work at full capacity it was estimated that some 8,400,000 bales a year of raw jute were required. A little jute is exported from the

United States under PL 480 arrangements, and it is often possible to make increased emergency imports of lower quality jute from Thailand, but there can be little doubt that supply is the main factor limiting availabilities.[17] Accordingly, in the short run it is unlikely that devaluation will greatly influence export earning from jute manufactures.

Nevertheless, the price advantage which Indian jute manufacturers will—potentially—enjoy over their Pakistani rivals could well provide a much-needed stimulus, not only to fuller working of the manufacturing side of the industry, but also to greater attention being paid to increasing investment in the industry. Thus the long-term effects of the devaluation might be significant. In order to help the industry, the Government grants an import subsidy of Rs 500 a metric ton on imports from Pakistan and one of Rs 250 on imports from Thailand. Since devaluation, the Government has imposed an export duty of Rs 900 a metric ton on hessian and Rs 600 a ton on sacking. This export duty almost certainly creates serious difficulties for the jute exporters. While it continues, any advantage *vis-à-vis* Pakistan which might have been gained from the devaluation is greatly reduced, if not nullified.

The world demand for many jute products is likely to show a declining trend over the next five years. The increased use of mechanical balers in agriculture, of plastic bags rather than sacking for the transportation of commodities, and the tendency of manufacturers to supply goods to the retailer in pre-sacked units, have brought about a fundamental change in the demand for jute products. In part the motive for this change has been technological and social— but it may, to some extent, be due also to the relatively high cost of jute goods in the early 1950s, resulting from the extreme inelasticity of supply of raw jute at that time.[18] To a lesser extent the imposition of export duties by the Indian Government in the period 1949/52 also helped to raise world prices. Unfortunately, it is extremely unlikely that a moderate fall in the price of jute products would cause much substitution of, say, jute sacks for paper bags, now that users have become accustomed to the latter.

Although demand for traditional jute bags and hessian in Western countries has either stagnated or fallen, there has been a marked

---

[17] In 1966 the members of the Indian Jute Mills Association voluntarily agreed to reduce jute consumption by 15 per cent in order to conserve supplies.
[18] M. Singh, *India's Export Trends*, p. 48.

expansion in the sale of Indian carpet-backing cloth in the United States market. Imports of this type of jute cloth into the USA rose from 25 mn yards in 1960 to 83 mn yards in 1964. When it is remembered that sales of jute manufactures as a whole in the US market have increased by some 63 per cent over five years, the dramatic nature of what is happening becomes clearer. It should also be remembered that yard for yard the value of this backing cloth is much higher than that of ordinary hessian—85 cents a yard as against 9 cents a yard.[19]

Another reassuring trend is the tendency of other less developed countries to increase their demand for jute goods. It will be many years before a substantial number of such countries can employ bulk-handling equipment, and in any case many tropical crops (cocoa for example) are likely to continue to be packed in jute bags.

But while prospects for the world jute industry may not be as gloomy as is sometimes suggested, it by no means follows that India will be the main beneficiary of increased demand. The Pakistan industry has some advantage over the Indian, both in terms of access to the raw material (in 1960 the yield per hectare in Pakistan was estimated to be about 50 per cent higher than in India),[20] and in the efficiency of its mills. The Pakistan jute manufacturing industry is more modern than that of its Indian neighbour, all Pakistan jute mills having been built after 1950.[21] Labour costs are also higher in India.

Even if the full potential of the Indian jute industry is realized, it is not certain that markets will be open, for in most high income countries restrictions on imports of jute products are fairly stringent. Tariffs are high and a number of countries impose quantitative restrictions. The UK limits imports of quality jute products through the Jute Control. Although this arrangement has been partially liberalized, the effect of the control is to give protection to Britain's jute industry. The EEC common external tariff on jute yarn is 10 per cent, on sacks it is 23 per cent. France and Western Germany also impose direct controls as protective measures. The United States imposes fairly high duties, but no quantitative restrictions.

Although it has sometimes been claimed that restrictive policies

---

[19] 'Export Trade with USA', *Foreign Trade of India* (1966).
[20] See FAO, *Production Year Book, 1961*.
[21] See J. A. Rosario, *Productivity in Indian Export Industries*, (Indian Economic Association, Bombay Univ. Press, 1964) p. 25.

in high-income countries have had the effect of directly limiting India's exports of jute manufactures, this is only part of the story. Supply problems must also be taken into account.[22] Of course, if the supply difficulty were overcome, and if devaluation made India's jute exports competitive *vis-à-vis* those of other countries over a wide front, it might then be found that importers' barriers prevent a full exploitation of export opportunities. Even today such measures are indirectly harmful in that they are likely to inhibit supply by discouraging the massive investment necessary for the Indian jute-growing industry to reach its full potential.

Cotton and leather

In the early post-war years, India found a ready market for its manufactured cotton exports in the United Kindom. It was only in the late 1950s that serious difficulties arose as the result of the establishment of mills in a number of competing underdeveloped countries, and of growing demands for protection in the UK market itself. The increase in spindleage of newer producing countries in these years was quite startling. One development was the increasing number of countries, which in terms of installed spindles were relatively small producers in 1953, but by 1964 had established quite significant industries.

Especially in Western Europe, countries have for many years imposed very stringent restrictions on imports of cotton textiles from low-cost sources. Thus, as output from the underdeveloped world expanded rapidly after 1957, the pressure of imports became particularly acute in the United Kingdom, which as the result of the Indo-British Trade Agreement of 1939 had renounced the right to impose restrictions on imports of Indian cotton goods. In the absence of power to limit imports from Commonwealth countries, the UK negotiated 'voluntary' agreements with Hong-Kong, India, and Pakistan; these agreements placed ceilings on imports of cotton goods into the U.K. The United States, which like the United Kingdom, had a relatively liberal import policy, was also a target for cheap exports from underdeveloped countries, and accordingly negotiated a 'voluntary' import ceiling agreement with Japan.

[22] See M. Singh, 'India and the Common Market', *J. Common Market Studies* (Oxford) vol. 1, 3, 266. Dr Singh quotes the Report of the Import and Export Policy Committee which states that about 15–20 per cent of the industrial capacity of the jute industry was idle in 1960–1, for want of an adequate supply of imported components and raw materials.

In 1961 the United States proposed a more general agreement on world trade in textiles, which would apply to most of the leading importers and exporters. A temporary arrangement was negotiated for the year 1961–2, and in 1962 this was replaced by the Five Year Long Term Agreement which covered almost all exporting and importing countries outside the Eastern trading bloc. The agreement, renewed in October 1967, provides for an agreed expansion of imports into high-income participating countries, but permits these countries to restrain imports if, as the result of liberalization, they suffer 'market disruption'.

Under the agreement, the EEC agreed to increase its imports of cotton textiles over the five-year period by some 88 per cent; this rate of increase sounds dramatic, but at the base date cotton goods imports from developing countries were very small and accounted for only 4 per cent of world imports of these products. Unfortunately for India, the UK did not agree to increase its imports at all, in view of its already relatively liberal policy. This was a severe blow to the Indian mills which were dispatching about 20 per cent of their exports to Britain.

The Indians have been severely critical of the way in which the 'market disruption' escape clause of the agreement had been invoked. In this they are not alone, for Mr E. Wyndham White, Director General of GATT and Chairman of the Cotton Textiles Committee, has himself stated that 'restrictions have not been used as sparingly as was envisaged when the agreement was negotiated'.[23]

There can be little doubt that exports of cotton goods from developing countries have suffered from the way in which restrictive measures have been operated. Unfortunately, there is little evidence that even if these restrictions were removed, Indian textiles would be able to hold their own successfully against exports from other developing countries, most of whose mills are more modern than those of India.[24] If Indian textile exports are to compete successfully against the products of the rapidly growing industries of other Asiatic (and even African) countries, and also of a rationalized European industry, a substantial investment programme is called for. The textile planning group for the Draft Fourth Plan estimates that

[23] 1965 Annual Session of the participants of the Long Term Agreement, *New York Times*, 7 Dec. 1965.

[24] It is salutary to remember that the 1962–3 import quota granted by Western Germany could be only partially realized because Indian textile prices were said to be uncompetitive.

almost as much expenditure is required for the modernization of mills as for the building of new ones—Rs 1,590 mn as against 1,780 mn. It has been estimated that about one-third of India's spindles are fifty years old or more.[25] Whereas 70 per cent of Hong Kong and 60 per cent of Pakistan mills are automatic, the proportion in India is a mere 9 per cent.[26]

A serious problem has also arisen in regard to the diversion of exportable output to the home market. Domestic consumption has benefited from increased output, to the detriment of exports. The rupee devaluation should help in correcting this state of affairs.

Our general conclusion on the subject of cotton textiles is that more liberal import policies in high-income countries might create wider opportunities for Indian cotton manufactures. Whether or not these opportunities can be taken depends upon the extent to which Indian textiles are competitive *vis-à-vis* products, not only of potential importing countries, but also of competing developing countries. So far, there is little evidence that this is likely to be so. The role of the planners must be to ensure that adequate resources are channelled into the cotton industry, at both plantation and factory levels. For too long the textile industry has been the Cinderella of the Plans.

There are a number of other old established manufacturing industries—leather, for example—which might make a valuable contribution to the achievement of the export targets envisaged by the planners for 1970–1. However, more attention is required in the leather industry to new and more hygenic techniques of tanning and processing materials.[27] There would also be greater scope for the expansion of processed leather products if the tariff structure of high-income countries did not discriminate so sharply between raw leather imports and imports of processed leather products. For example the EEC duty on imported skins ranges between zero and 10 per cent, depending upon the products, while the duty on leather handbags, gloves, and purses is between 14 and 20 per cent.[28]

[25] *Economic Weekly*, July 1963 (Bombay), p. 1299.
[26] See R. L. Sabarwal, *Productivity in Export Industries with Special Reference to the Indian Cotton Textile Mill Industry* (Indian Economic Association, Bombay University Press, 1964).
[27] India is easily the largest exporter of leather and tanned hides among the developing countries.
[28] For a Table showing the marked degree of progression in duties on imports as they have a higher processing content, see the author's Table 5 in The EEC and Trade with Developing Countries, *J. Common Market Studies*, Dec. 1965.

Although these duties will be reduced as the result of the Kennedy Round, the reductions will be phased over a four-year period, commencing on either 1 January or 1 July 1968. Thus for most of the period of the Fourth Plan the Kennedy Round reductions will be only partially implemented.

7. NEWER PRODUCTS

For the period from 1966–7 to 1970–1 the Indian export effort will have to depend largely upon the staple products which we have discussed. But looking to the future, an increasing contribution will be made by exports of products which have only in recent years become feasible export propositions. Exports of engineering goods have grown rapidly. Table 2 shows that in 1960–1 engineering products accounted for 0·8 per cent; by 1965–6 they accounted for 2·4 per cent of exports.

Since India accounts for only a small proportion of world trade in engineering and allied goods, the price elasticity of demand for *Indian* engineering products is likely to be considerably greater than for engineering products of a major industrial country like Britain. Accordingly the rupee devaluation is likely to have a favourable effect upon their competitive performance in world markets. Dr Singh has quoted Tariff Commission Reports which suggest that in the late 1950s ex-works prices in India were less than 10 per cent higher than c.i.f. import prices (excluding duty) in the case of electric motors between 3 and 10 h.p., certain electrical conductors, and plywood tea chests. They were less than 30 per cent higher in 50 h.p. electric motors, many transformers, automatic looms, grinding wheels, copper sheets, plastic buttons, and dry cells.[29] This wide-ranging list of products gives some idea of the type of goods in which post-devaluation India could conceivably become competitive. Well over 10 per cent of the output of the Indian sewing machine industry is exported—mostly to South-East Asia. A general extension of tariff preferences in industrialized countries, along the lines proposed at the first UNCTAD Conference and now being worked out within the United Nations, would considerably widen the scope for these exports. This is particularly true of the United States market, where tariffs on imports of interest to India are substantially higher than the average US tariff.

[29] *India's Export Trends*, p. 331.

For the period of the Fourth Plan, however, the contribution which such goods can make to the balance of payments is marginal.

8. OUTLOOK

In recent years a number of developments have resulted in a greater export consciousness on the part of Indian producers. A Board of Trade advises the Government on export promotion; the Indian Institute of Foreign Trade is developing programmes of training, research, and market assessment. Export Promotion Councils, in part financed by the Government, have been set up. A Minerals and Metals Trading Corporation promotes the export of these products. Attention has been paid to quality inspection; by the end of the Third Plan some 80 per cent of the country's export goods had been brought under the Government Quality Control Inspection Scheme.

Considerable progress has been made in improving the image of Indian exports. But much more needs to be done. Too often one hears that certain products are saleable in Asia and the Middle East, where quality conditions are not so exacting, but are not saleable in the West. Perhaps too the Indian export effort would be strengthened if the Government were less doctrinaire in its insistence on the virtues of small scale industry and tiny trading units in the private sector. The experience of Japan suggests that India needs an organization akin to Zaibatsu in order to capture world markets. In Japan, by far the greater part of the export effort comes from a relatively few producing units. So far India's rulers have been determined to learn little from the free enterprise economies of Japan or Hong Kong. Perhaps the time has come for this attitude to change. At least, a more conscious effort could be made to mobilize small firms' export potential by the Government giving its blessing to the establishment of large private trading corporations. This could indeed be a legitimate use to which aid from the West might be put.

The Indian export problem is likely to become more acute, at least in the short run, if the United Kingdom joins the EEC. India will lose the tariff advantage which it at present enjoys in the United Kingdom. The most serious loss would be in the case of manufactures. At the 1962/3 Brussels negotiations it was decided that the United Kingdom would apply the common external tariff only gradually. For example, the then tariff of 18 per cent on textiles would not be imposed fully for at least three years after Britain joined the Community. At the same time the EEC agreed to reduce the duty on sports goods to zero; for other manufactured goods it was agreed that there would be a delay between Britain's accession and the full implementation of the common external tariff throughout the enlarged Community. But when the concessions were made it was crystal clear that the United Kingdom would ultimately have to raise the tariff against imports from India; there would be no permanent let-out for the developing countries of the Commonwealth. As for a second round of negotiations between Britain and the EEC, it seems extremely unlikely that the EEC would be prepared to make greater concessions today than in 1963. It is not even certain whether the concessions agreed to earlier would be applicable if a future application were successful.

In view of the many forces which are at present at work, it is impossible to forecast whether the foreign trade targets for the period 1966/7–1970/1 will be achieved. We can, however, summarize the conclusions which emerge from this chapter as suggesting that a period of greater flexibility in import policy is opening up, and that this will remove some of the distortions which till now have discouraged exporting. There is likely to be a certain supply problem in many sectors, particularly in jute and cotton (and as regards quality, in tea). Only if in its operation the Plan pays much more attention to supply in these key sectors than has been the case in the past, will adequate exports become available to take advantage of the devaluation.

In regard to the development of newer industries, it is desirable that the industries selected for development be those which have reasonably bright export prospects. Perhaps the time has come for some further shift of emphasis from import-saving to export-gaining. The industrialized countries can help forward this change by reducing their barriers to the import of Indian goods, but the immediate gains from freer access are likely to be slight. Nevertheless, the removal of restrictions will give greater confidence to the Indian business community and Indian planners as they face the almost heroic task of modernizing the traditional agricultural and industrial sectors, while at the same time developing newer export industries.

11

Aid to India

PAUL STREETEN AND ROGER HILL

1. THE TERMINOLOGY OF AID

AN important distinction is that between *project aid* and *non-project aid*. The former is a specific sum of money which is intended to cover the foreign exchange cost of an identifiable project within the total aid allocation. Such aid need not cover the whole foreign exchange component of the project, though it normally does. Donors provide aid to the Government of India, which makes the funds available, on its own terms, to the authority responsible for the project. Conditions may be attached by the donor to consultancy, supervision, bidding for contracts, shipping arrangements, &c. These 'strings' are of a different nature from the more general 'conditions' relating to performance in the economy at large, although they too can give rise to disagreements between donors and recipients.

Non-project aid refers to all other goods provided under the aid programme: primary products, semi-finished products, spare parts, components, machine tools, equipment, &c., which are needed to keep existing firms going or to start new projects and generally to support the balance of payments. Most of UK non-project aid consists of general purpose loans, which the Indians are free to spend on a wide range of imports from the donor country. The rest is devoted to purposes agreed on with the Indians. For example, the so-called 'Kipping aid'[1] is used to supply components and spares to metal-using industries which look to Britain as their source of supply. Similarly, a loan in 1963 was made for the procurement of steel plate in this country. Other donors, particularly the US, tie their non-project aid to specific commodities, though the range of these may be very wide.

In addition to being tied to projects, aid may be tied to purchases in the donor country. This is *procurement-tying*. At present nearly

[1] Named after Sir Norman Kipping who led a mission which recommended it.

323

all bilateral US aid and over half of bilateral UK aid is wholly or partially tied in this manner. Only a small proportion of German aid is formally tied, though in effect the proportion is much higher, for the Germans tend to avoid making commitments for projects in sectors in which German firms are not competitive. Donors tie their aid to protect their balances of payments. For the recipient country the main disadvantage is that it cannot buy its imports in the cheapest market, although a certain amount of 'switching', i.e. using aid to buy products on which 'free' foreign exchange would otherwise have been spent, is usually possible. The opportunity to switch will be greater, the larger are the commercial imports from the donor country and the more diversified the tied aid, while the desire to switch will depend on competitiveness of the products of the supplier. Mahbub ul Haq has estimated for Pakistan that aid-tying has raised the average price of all commodities imported under aid arrangements by 15 per cent.[2] In addition, aid-tying complicates the administration of aid.

Double-tying occurs when aid is both project- and procurement-tied. Donors double-tie to make it more certain that aid will produce extra demand for their goods. With procurement-tied aid for programmes, a recipient can select those commodities he would buy from the donor in any case. Double-tying makes such selection more difficult, since it is unlikely that a single donor will be the cheapest supplier of all the goods required for a project.

There are three stages in the process of aid-giving and aid-receiving: pledging, committing, and disbursing. First, each donor *pledges* a total amount at the annual meetings of the Aid India Consortium.[3] Pledges of one donor influence pledges of others, and Britain (giving about 10 per cent of Consortium aid to India) can therefore exercise some leverage on total aid contributions. Non-Consortium aid to India is largely Soviet aid. Not all aid provided by members of the Consortium has been pledged. Thus PL 480 aid was independent of the US pledge until 1967. Pledges are considered binding, although the Americans did not in fact commit aid pledged in 1965 after the Kashmir hostilities.

---

[2] Mahbub ul Haq, 'Tied Credits—A Quantitative Analysis', in *Capital Movements and Economic Development*, ed. J. Adler for the International Economic Association (London, 1967).

[3] It was set up by the World Bank in 1958 and consists of the US, Britain, Canada, Japan, West Germany, France, Italy, Netherlands, Belgium, Austria, the World Bank and, since 1959, IDA.

At the next stage, the pledged aid is *committed, allocated,* or *authorized.* At this stage aid is divided between project and non-project aid. The initiative for suggesting projects lies with the Indians, though representations from industrial and commercial interests are made to the donor country's authorities. The result is a compromise between Indian wishes and British commercial and prestige interests. The process of committing can take some time. For the UK, after the 1963 pledge it took nine months; after the 1964 pledge only three. Lags have also been reduced for other countries.

The final stage is that of *disbursements* or *utilization.* The rate of disbursement is clearly faster for non-project aid than for project aid, because the range of imports is wider, and for soft loans than for hard loans, because higher interest rates, payable when goods have been ordered, induce greater caution in giving orders. It is in the nature of a project that it takes time to negotiate, prepare, and execute, and disbursements are bound to be less than commitments. This shortfall rises as commitments increase. But slow disbursements can also be due to inadequate or inefficient administration by the Indians. Most of UK non-project aid is normally spent within the financial year of the pledge, though delays in the disbursements of Kipping aid beyond that have been known. Delays are longer in the disbursement of non-project aid from other donors, including IDA. The lag of disbursements behind commitments creates the *pipeline* which consists of unspent claims arising from past authorized loans. The pipeline permits the continuation of expenditure for a time when new commitments are run down. It creates problems for British economic policy, for it can give rise to unplanned claims on British resources. The size of the pipeline can be reduced by spreading commitments over the period of construction of projects. The lag of disbursements behind commitments, which can also be reduced by raising the proportion of general purpose aid to the total, and by softening the terms of aid, has the added drawback for India that commitments are made in terms of money, and rising prices wipe out part of the real value of the aid.

Gross aid disbursed in a year exceeds net aid by payments of interest on past loans and repayment of capital. *Debt relief* is perhaps the most urgent need. To avoid default, debt can be *rescheduled* or *refinanced.* Rescheduling means lengthening the period of the loan. Refinancing means making new loans to meet obligations on outstanding loans. Loans may be advanced with *grace periods* before interest falls due. This is another way of easing the terms of loans.

The provision of a *bisque*, advocated by some, is modelled on the waiver clause in the American loan to Britain of 1946, which allows Britain to opt out of capital re-payments (though not interest), in an agreed number of years.

In tackling the debt problem, one has to distinguish between *new* debt—the problem of the *terms of aid*—and *old* debt, which may be rescheduled or refinanced. The link between the two is that the attitude to accepting and servicing new debt will be influenced by the manner in which old debts are settled.

2. REVIEW OF PAST AID TO INDIA

Up to the end of March 1966 aid authorizations from all sources amounted to Rs 58,015 mn, of which 77 per cent (Rs 44,818 mn) had been utilized. Only Rs 290 mn, of the authorized aid and Rs 220 mn of the utilized aid were received prior to the First Plan.

Table 1 shows external assistance by sources. The donors' list

TABLE 1

(*Rs mn*)

Sources of Aid	Aggregate External Assistance Since Independence			
	Authorized up to March 1966		Utilized up to March 1966	
	Amount	% of Total	Amount	% of Total
IBRD/IDA	7,415	12·8	5,815	13·0
US	30,487	52·5	26,052	58·1
USSR	4,855	8·4	2,833	6·3
W. Germany	4,444	7·7	3,417	7·6
UK	3,660	6·3	2,931	6·6
Others	7,154	12·3	3,770	8·4
Total	58,015	100·0	44,818	100·0

Source: Reserve Bank of India, *Report on Currency and Finance 1965–6* (1966), p. 28, Table 28.

is dominated by the US, which provided over half the authorized aid, and a little under three-fifths of the utilized aid. Aid authorizations under PL 480 accounted for 51 per cent (Rs 13,860 mn) of US aid. IBRD and IDA, the main multilateral donors, have been responsible for just over 12 per cent of the aid received by India. Table 2 provides a more detailed breakdown of the sources of aid.

Table 3 breaks down external assistance by form. The outstanding feature here is the decline in grants: from 36 per cent of authorizations in the First Plan to 3 per cent in the Third Plan. Loans amounted to Rs 22,690 mn during the First Plan, but the 1951 US Wheat Loan accounted for Rs 9,030 mn (40 per cent) of this figure. Over two-thirds of the aid utilized in the Third Plan has been in loan form. Authorizations of PL 480 aid reached very high levels during the Second Plan and provided a large 'carry-over' into the Third Plan. For this reason utilization of PL 480 aid between 1961–6 was nearly double the authorization during the same period.

3. EXTERNAL DEBT

External debt servicing charges rose from $250 mn in the Second Plan (just under 4 per cent of export earnings) to $1,150 mn during the Third Plan (about 14 per cent of merchandise export earnings) and to 22 per cent in 1966. During the period 1966–70 these charges are estimated as $3,050 mn—28 per cent of estimated export earnings and 36 per cent of aid requirements. The total outstanding external public debt has risen from $400 mn in 1955 to $6,900 mn in June 1966.[4] The problem of external debt is a major one in the late 1960's. While debt servicing obligations rose by 84 per cent between 1962 and 1966, exports increased by only 14 per cent. This is the legacy of past loans. However, a marked softening of aid terms has taken place recently. The average rate of interest on new external debt contracted during 1960 was 4·19 per cent, the average grace period 4·0 years and the average term to maturity 16·7 years.[5] In 1965 the corresponding figures were 3·18 per cent interest rate, 7·4 years grace period, and 31·3 years to maturity.[6] This reflects an even greater improvement if account is taken of the general rise in commercial interest rates. Nevertheless, further renegotiations, rescheduling, consolidations and waivers of loans must be expected

---

[4] IBRD, *Ann. Rep.*, *1965–6* (1967), p. 33, Table 5, and *1966–7*, p. 31, Table 6.
[5] Ibid. p. 36, Tables 7 and 8.   [6] Ibid. p. 35, Table 9.

TABLE 2

Sources of External Assistance

(Rs mn)

	Aid Authorized up to end of 1st Plan	Aid Authorized during 2nd Plan	Aid Authorized during 3rd Plan
I. Loans			
(1) Repayable in foreign currencies			
i) International institutions	572	2,612	4,231
ii) US	903	1,085	7,917
iii) Canada	—	157	310
iv) UK	—	1,226	2,420
v) W. Germany	—	1,342	3,081
vi) Japan	—	268	1,381
vii) USSR	648	3,190	1,005
viii) Switzerland	—	65	180
ix) France	—	—	571
x) Italy	—	—	813
xi) Poland	—	143	270
xii) Yugoslavia	—	190	24
xiii) Czechoslovakia	—	231	400
xiv) Austria	—	—	85
xv) Belgium	—	—	114
xvi) Netherlands	—	—	219
xvii) Sweden	—	—	22
xviii) Denmark	—	—	14
Total	2,123	10,509	23,057
(2) Repayable in Rupees			
i) Denmark	—	—	10
ii) US	146	2,304	486
Total	146	2,304	496
II. Grants			
i) US	918	546	200
ii) Canada	323	571	551
iii) Australia	111	22	22
iv) New Zealand	17	17	7
v) UK	4	4	6
vi) W. Germany	—	21	—
vii) Norway	7	19	20
viii) USSR	—	12	—
Total	1,380	1,212	806
III. PL 480, 665, and Third Country Currency Assistance	169	11,307	4,506
Grand Total	3,818	25,335	28,865

Source: Reserve Bank of India, *Report on Currency and Finance 1965–6* (1966), Statement 82.

TABLE 3

External Assistance by Form

(Rs mn)

	Authorizations			Utilization		
Form	Up to end of 1st Plan	During 2nd Plan	During 3rd Plan	Up to end of 1st Plan	During 2nd Plan	During 3rd Plan
1. Loans	2,269	12,813	23,553	1,264	7,247	19,094
(i) Repayable in foreign currencies	2,123	10,509	23,057	1,241	6,079	17,530
(ii) Repayable in rupees	146	2,304	496	23	1,168	1,564
2. Grants	1,380	1,212	806	702	1,603	877
3. PL 480 and PL 665 aid and Third Country Assistance (gross),	169	11,280	4,506	51	5,423	8,532
4. Total	3,818	25,305	28,865	2,017	14,273	28,503
Debt Servicing Payments	n.a.	n.a.	n.a.	n.a.	1,192	5,470
Net Aid					13,081	23,033
Net Aid at 1965–6 import prices					13,769	25,403
5. IMF	476	952			476	952
Percentage Distribution						
1. Loans	59·5	50·7	81·6	62·7	50·7	67·0
2. Grants	36·2	4·8	2·8	34·8	11·2	3·0
3. PL 480 and 664 aid and Third Country Assistance (gross)	4·3	44·5	15·6	2·5	38·1	30·0
4. Total	100·0	100·0	100·0	100·0	100·0	100·0

n.a. = not available.

Source: Reserve Bank of India, *Report on Currency and Finance 1965–6* (1966), Statement 82.

during the Fourth Plan period, for servicing charges are likely to account for 28 per cent of a very optimistic export projection of Rs 80,330 mn (Rs 51,000 mn in pre-devaluation rupees).

The problem of debt service has several aspects.

  (i) In the 1970s the debt servicing problem will become even more serious. From 1966–7 to 1980–1 India will require some $18,000 mn of foreign aid but her debt servicing liability will come to $14,000 mn. After 1975 the planners expect repayments to outstrip inflows of capital.

  (ii) Next, there are the terms on which loans are incurred and renewed. India herself has in the past declared that she does not wish to receive grants. Some donors believe that soft terms discourage economic use and encourage waste. There cannot be much in this argument because the Government of India can lend on at appropriate interest rates, and can require these rates of return for its own projects. Soft terms are intended to get over the foreign exchange difficulty, and do not reduce the need to calculate adequate domestic returns on expenditure. Whether local currency counterpart funds for interest receipts should be accumulated by the creditor country is another question.

(iii) Most bilateral aid is tied to procurement from the donor and often tied to projects as well. Repayment, on the other hand, is demanded in convertible currency, and the use of such funds is not tied to Indian exports. This asymmetry introduces an additional element of hardness. The exception is aid from Russia and certain European countries which is usually repaid in the recipient's traditional exports; thus, in effect, repayment is in the borrower's own currency.

(iv) It is not sufficient to give debt relief when the time for debt repayment arrives. Foreign exchange has to be accumulated in the form of extra reserves, and hence diverted from development imports well in advance of the date when debt payments are due, and debt relief promised in advance is worth more than relief that comes later.

(v) From the point of view of any one creditor, debt relief should be given by all creditors. Otherwise the relief given by one can be regarded as being used to pay the obligations to others. (The same applies to giving aid on soft terms.) The World Bank, because of its need to raise money in the capital markets of the West, is in a special position and may not be able to give relief without impairing its impeccable credit standing. But bilateral Consortium donors normally consider that they must act in consort.

4. THE SLOW UTILIZATION OF AID

Until recently, a characteristic of Indian aid was the large proportion authorized but not disbursed. To help remedy this slow disbursement of aid, the Rao Report recommended in 1964 that a larger proportion of aid should be non-project.[7] In the years 1963–4 India received considerable quantities of non-project assistance (apart from PL 480) for the first time. In the years 1965–6 about half the aid pledged was non-project, while for 1967 Consortium members have agreed to about $900 mn (Rs 6,800 mn) of non-project aid.

However, the causes of slow disbursements are to be found on both sides. In India, slow disbursements may occur because of (*a*) inadequate project planning, i.e. faulty project preparation, programming, and scheduling, (*b*) faults in complementary actions, e.g. failure of supplies of raw materials and components, and services like electricity and transport, and (*c*) failures in aggregate planning, e.g. non-availability of rupee resources, inadequate aggregate demand, wrong choice of top personnel, and other wrong decisions. Even forms of aid which are avowedly the most useful, because they are not tied to projects, have been slowly disbursed. Thus 'Kipping loans' have, astonishingly, suffered from slow disbursements.

But the main reason for slow disbursement is found, the Rao Committee suggested, in the fact of project aid. Aid geared to the creation of capacity, it is said, is of little use and can be an obstacle if the main bottleneck is imports of raw materials and components, especially fertilizers, and spare parts. The superiority of general-purpose aid over project, and even non-project but specific-purpose aid, has been increasingly recognized, and the change in the composition has contributed to speedier disbursements. The need for non-project aid grows as development progresses. A final reason for delays has been the terms of aid. The harder the terms, the more reluctant the borrower will be to draw quickly on a loan, because interest is charged from the date of drawing, not from the date of commitment. Thus the share of loans tends to be higher in the aid pipeline than in total aid commitments.

However, more non-project aid and softening of terms, together with changes in the administrative machinery, especially in the vetting of import requirements, have produced in 1964 and 1965 a marked improvement in the rate of aid utilization. This is borne out by Table 4.

5. THE IMPACT OF AID

There is a widespread impression that India receives large sums of aid. This is, of course, true in the sense that India is a large

[7] Cte on the Utilization of External Assistance, *Report* (Min. of Finance, 1964.)

TABLE 4

Utilization of Loans

(Rs mn)

	Authorized and Undisbursed *(1)*	Used in Following Year *(2)*	2/1 per cent
March 1961	6,571	2,296	34·9
1962	8,378	3,058	36·5
1963	11,292	3,918	34·7
1964	11,755	4,831	41·1
1965	11,886	4,991	42·0

Source: Reserve Bank of India, *Report on Currency and Finance 1965–6*, Part I, Table 2.

country, containing 30 per cent of the population of the under-developed world. But it is not true if the relevant measure, viz. aid per head, is used. India received in 1961 $1·5, in 1962 $1·7, and in 1963 $2·1 from OECD countries and multilateral agencies, compared with Pakistan's massive doses: $2·8 excluding Indus Waters Scheme, $4·0 including it (some of this should, however, be credited to India) in 1962; $4·2 excluding, $4·9 including it (1963), and a further rise to about $6·0 in 1964. Stepping up gross aid to $10,000 mn for the period 1966–70 would mean raising aid per head to $4 a year, still considerably below the level of Pakistan and of many other aid recipients. Whatever aid criteria one wishes to choose, India should be given much higher priority than it receives now.[8] India is one of the poorest countries. Its development potential is high. It has an efficient administration, a high level of education and skills, and a reserve of potential entrepreneurship. Its plans are well conceived and it has applied stringent import controls and high levels of domestic taxation. There can be no doubt that it has a structural balance of payments problem and considerable absorptive capacity. It enjoys constitutional democracy and has been the victim of an attack by China. What India does will serve as an example to others. Whether one's criteria are cold war, the encouragement of democratic government, the promotion of self-help, good performance, the relief of the needy, or the activation of development potential, India should qualify for massive aid. In fact it is grossly under-aided.

[8] This is powerfully argued in I. M. D. Little and J. M. Clifford, *International Aid* (London, 1965), pp. 226, 231, 234.

Both the Right and the Left have attacked India's reliance on foreign aid, which both tend to exaggerate. The Right argues that aid, by encouraging central planning and public prestige projects, discourages the growth of private savings and private initiative, frightens away foreign enterprise, discourages economy in the use of capital, and generally destroys the basis of decentralized decision-taking which, on this view, is the prerequisite of development. Aid thus is thought to perpetuate the system which makes aid necessary; some go further and say that it pauperizes the country, making it increasingly dependent on external assistance.

The Left attacks aid on the ground that, by supporting reactionary groups in power, it retards the introduction of the institutional and political reforms, particularly effective land reform, which are necessary for development. Aid, on this view, props up reform-resisting oligarchies and conservative and feudal social systems, and again perpetuates the system which makes it necessary.

These arguments, which fit in well with the general disenchantment with aid among donors, are difficult to quantify and to assess. We shall discuss the argument in the context of food aid below. In order to bring out the costs and benefits of aid, and also in order to present clear political choices, it might be possible to draw up two simultaneous plans: one with a somewhat smaller reliance on aid, the other with somewhat more aid and with possible concessions to the donors. The cost of aid in the widest sense, including policies adopted or sacrificed, would thus be brought out clearly.

Table 5 shows the uses to which aid has been allocated. It adds to the total resources available to the community. It may be used to raise consumption, private investment, or government expenditure. In this general case, the value of aid to India is equal to the value of these additions. But if it helps to break a bottleneck—foreign exchange, particular items of equipment, or particular skills—the value of aid to India exceeds the nominal value of aid given. It makes fuller utilization of capacities in other sectors of the economy possible. Against this, it is possible that an aid-financed project imposes a burden of recurrent or other contributory expenditure on the domestic economy, and that these resources could have been used more productively in other lines. In such conditions the value of aid to India falls short of its nominal value. In so far as aid is available in freely-spendable foreign exchange, its value is likely to exceed its nominal value. The more it is tied to projects and donor procurement, the less likely will this be.

TABLE 5

Distribution of Foreign Loans/Credits by Purposes
(Figures in brackets show percentage distribution)
(Rs mn)

Loans/Credits	Authorized				Utilized			
	(1) Up to end of 1st Plan	(2) During 2nd Plan	(3) During 3rd Plan	Total 1 to 3	(1) Up to end of 1st Plan	(2) During 2nd Plan	(3) During 3rd Plan	Total 1 to 3
1. Railway Development	156 (6·9)	1,952 (15·1)	1,392 (6·1)	3,500 (9·2)	156 (12·3)	1,432 (20·1)	1,850 (10·1)	3,438 (12·8)
2. Power Projects	196 (8·6)	623 (4·8)	2,414 (10·5)	3,233 (8·5)	121 (9·6)	293 (4·1)	1,529 (8·3)	1,943 (7·2)
3. Iron and Steel Projects*	786 (34·7)	2,242 (17·4)	2,078 (9·1)	5,106 (13·4)	27 (2·1)	2,541 (35·6)	1,049 (5·7)	3,617 (13·5)
4. Ports and Development	—	205 (1·6)	186 (0·8)	391 (1·0)	—	68 (0·9)	180 (1·0)	248 (0·9)
5. Transport and Communication	—	148 (1·2)	930 (4·1)	1,078 (2·9)	—	90 (1·3)	759 (4·1)	849 (3·2)
6. Industrial Development	193 (8·5)	7,555 (58·7)	15,266 (66·7)	23,014 (60·5)	23 (1·8)	2,554 (35·8)	12,836 (69·6)	15,413 (57·5)
7. Agricultural Development	34 (1·5)	—	621 (2·7)	655 (1·7)	34 (2·7)	—	225 (1·2)	259 (1·0)
8. Wheat Loans	903 (39·8)	157 (1·2)	—	1,060 (2·8)	903 (71·5)	157 (2·2)	—	1,060 (3·9)
Total	2,268 (100·0)	12,882 (100·0)	22,887 (100·0)	38,037 (100·0)	1,264 (100·0)	7,135 (100·0)	18,428 (100·0)	26,827 (100·0)

* Includes Orissa Iron Ore Project.
Source: Reserve Bank of India, *Report on Currency and Finance 1965–6* (1966), Statement 83.

The conventional approach to analysing the impact of aid is to regard it as filling either of two gaps, depending upon which is larger. If growth is seen as a function of the ratio of investment to national income, aid is seen as filling the gap between target investment and domestic savings. Alternatively, if growth is regarded as constrained by foreign exchange, aid fills the gap between the foreign exchange required to achieve a given growth target, and the foreign exchange earned by visible and invisible exports plus private capital flows.

The weakness of the double gap approach is that it makes assumptions, sometimes justified in advanced economies, which are unwarranted for India. The savings gap approach assumes that the relationship between investment and additional output is fairly stable, that consumption makes no contribution to output, and that home and foreign savings are interchangeable. But in the diagnosis of India it is normal to assume that the dominant bottleneck is not savings, but foreign exchange. And we have certainly witnessed situations in which potential domestic savings have run to waste for lack of foreign exchange. Aid requirements therefore tend to be approached through the trade gap. This analysis assumes that growth of domestic production could be accelerated with more foreign exchange.

We see from Table 6 that the contribution of external finance to public plan outlay is large. However, the apparently greater dependence on external assistance in the Draft Fourth Plan is due to the rise in the rupee figure resulting from devaluation; in fact, if corrected for devaluation, the proportion of aid-financed public outlay is less in the Fourth than in the Third Plan. It may be that without aid India would have increased its already strong tax efforts even more, but it is impossible to dispute that the Second and Third Plans would have been smaller without aid.

Consider aid as a provider of foreign exchange, assuming that domestic savings are not the dominant constraint. The withdrawal of aid would then have necessitated a combination of four courses of action: non-development import retardation, development import substitution, export expansion, and a shift of plan outlay into areas with low foreign exchange requirements. Since the foreign exchange crisis of 1957–8 India has imposed the most stringent controls on imports of consumer goods. Table 7 shows that if foodgrains, 82 per cent of which consist of PL 480 imports, are excluded, the total

TABLE 6

Financing of Public Outlay
(Rs mn)

Sources	1st Plan	2nd Plan	3rd Plan	4th Plan
1. Balance from Current Revenues	3,820	110	−4,730	33,450
2. Surpluses of Public Enterprises	1,150	1,670	6,960	13,450
3. Capital Receipts	6,860	14,390	21,390	38,800
4. Deficit Financing	3,330	9,540	11,510	—
5. Additional Taxation	2,550	10,520	26,600	27,300
6. Budgetary Receipts corresponding to External Assistance	1,890	10,490	24,550	47,000 (a)
7. Total Resources	19,600	46,720	86,280	160,000
Row 6/Row 7 per cent	9·6	22·5	28·5	29·4 (b)

(a) Post devaluation.
(b) This figure is not comparable with the previous figures because of devaluation (see text).
Source: MFB, pp. 117–18, Table FR 2.

TABLE 7

Imports of Consumer Goods
(Rs mn)

	1st Plan	2nd Plan	3rd Plan
Consumer Goods	8,878	10,742	12,786
Foodgrains	6,015	8,046	10,330
Non-foodgrains	2,863	2,696	2,456
PL 480	51	5,448	8,800
PL 480 as percentage of total foodgrains	1·8	68·0	85·0

Source: 4DO, pp. 100–02.

value of consumer goods imports was lower in the Third Plan than in the First. Little foreign exchange can be gained by further restrictions of consumption imports. As for the second course, development-import substitution, raw materials, and equipment are closely scrutinized for possible indigenous replacement. In any case, import substitution of equipment requires, in the initial stages, larger, not smaller, imports. It is the strenuous attempt to set up domestic import-substituting capital goods industries which is responsible for the growth of raw material and capital imports.

There has been considerable unused capacity in Indian industry, largely as a result of inadequate imports of raw materials, components, and spare parts. A change in the composition of imports— a higher proportion of maintenance imports and a lower proportion of imports tied to new industrial capacity—would indeed lead to higher capacity utilization. But there is little scope for substituting domestic production for imports in such a way as to reduce import requirements substantially in the near future.

Export expansion, unaccompanied by an equivalent fall in unit prices of exports, is the third way of reducing dependence on aid. Indian exports stagnated during the First and Second Plans. They rose between 1960 and 1964–5, but seem to have run out of steam since. Traditional exports (tea, jute, cotton) run into limitations of demand, and non-traditional exports, though they showed impressive increases, are still a small proportion of the total. Exports of engineering goods, iron ore and steel, and chemicals are still less than 10 per cent of total exports. No doubt it is in the expansion of these exports that future earnings prospects lie, but foreign exchange will be needed in order to build up this export potential.

The fourth method of saving foreign exchange is to change the composition of plan outlay in the direction of economizing in foreign exchange. This means more for agriculture, less for industry. In the Third Plan public outlay in agriculture and irrigation was Rs 14,600 mn, exclusive of industries producing agricultural inputs such as fertilizers, and in medium and large industries Rs 25,700 mn. If aid reductions had forced a substantial switch of investment from industry to agriculture, some foreign exchange could have been saved, though limitations of absorptive capacity may have retarded growth. An increase in agricultural inputs such as fertilizers does require foreign exchange, directly if these are imported, and indirectly if domestic fertilizer plants are to be put up.

We conclude that added foreign exchange shortages would have led to even more severe cuts in the Second and Third Plans, even if domestic savings had been available. In addition, it is most unlikely that the Government of India could have raised enough resources to maintain the size of the plans even if structural balance of payments problems had not constituted an obstacle. These considerations suggest that the Second and Third Plans would have been reduced by an amount greater than the aid provided, if aid had been reduced. Or, to put the same point the other way round, in spite of some waste in the preparation, execution, and management of some projects, additional aid enables India to mobilize a multiple of the resources provided by aid.

6. AID AND THE DRAFT FOURTH PLAN

In the Draft Fourth Plan aid plays a crucial role. Economic planning aims ultimately at a 'steady and satisfactory rate of growth, without inflation and without dependence on foreign aid'.[9] It is planned to bring about a sharp fall in imports in the Fifth Plan coupled with a continued increase in exports, so that by 1977 the balance of payments gap will be closed even after providing for debt repayments, and no more aid will be needed. To do this, the Indians estimate that they will require gross external assistance of between $8,500 and $9,000 mn exclusive of PL 480 aid during the 1966–71 period. About $2,000 mn was in the pipeline at the end of the Third Plan, so that disbursements of new aid will have to be about $7,000 mn. To provide this volume of disbursement, commitments of between $8,000 and $10,000 mn will have to be made for the plan period. Since debt servicing during the period 1966–70 is likely to absorb around $3,000 mn of gross aid, net aid should amount to about $6,000 mn or Rs 45,000 mn. This is over 20 per cent of total estimated investment. In addition, external finance is to be the main source of public outlay during the Fourth Plan, accounting for 30 per cent of total planned development expenditure.[10]

But aid needs may be even greater than indicated by these figures. The aid requirements calculations are based on very optimistic

---

[9] It is envisaged that in the course of the Sixth Plan the stage will be reached when 'further economic growth will no longer require any net increase in our foreign indebtedness' (*4DO*, p. 28).

[10] These ratios are based on post-devaluation figures and cannot be compared with the same ratios for previous plans.

assumptions about domestic production, exports, and savings. Already, domestic production of fertilizers and steel shows shortfalls, and higher imports will be required to make up for them. The export earning projections seem over-optimistic, particularly the projected increase in jute and tea exports (see pp. 308–12, 313–16).

These are India's aid needs, but how much it will actually receive is another question. Germany has indicated that its aid to India will remain at its existing level during the period to 1970. America and Britain both have balance of payments problems, and until these are solved India cannot expect large increases of aid from these countries, unless there are major changes in the distribution of their aid. So far Aid India Consortium members have pledged sums of $900 mn of non-project financial aid each year for 1966–7 and 1967–8. To meet the aid requirements of the Draft Fourth Plan, India must receive in addition to the promised Russian aid ($1,000 mn for the Draft Plan, or more) about $1,600 mn of gross aid per year from the Consortium. The amount of aid India is receiving is therefore well below the aid requirements of the Plan. However, the virtual moratorium on Indian debt repayments during 1967–8 will save it some $400 mn of foreign exchange. How much the debt burden will be reduced in the later years of the Plan depends upon the outcome of the bilateral rescheduling negotiations.

In spite of errors and some faulty management, there is no doubt that India could absorb substantially more aid than it receives now. But the solution is more complex than simply changing the composition of aid in the direction of more maintenance imports. The contrast between project- and non-project aid over-simplifies the real issues. Not all capacity which has been created in India is equally valuable from a development point of view, and to underwrite maintenance imports for all existing capacity may lead to fuller utilization of capacity that should not be more fully used and may encourage the creation of undesirable capacity. On the other hand, economic progress, the unequal degree of capacity underutilization, and the fact that fuller utilization of the capital goods industries is possible only if new projects are started, imply that *some* new projects will have to be started, say some new fertilizer plants, while there is still under-utilization in less important sectors. It is then essential that these projects should be well selected, well prepared, and well executed. Donors should offer assistance in sector and project selection, execution, and planning, as well as raising the proportion of non-project aid. These measures would not only raise the productivity of aid directly, but would also lead to fuller utilization of existing capacity, thereby raising output indirectly. They would reduce the need for detailed physical controls, economize in scarce administrative talent, and thus contribute to higher productivity and better morale.

But all this is relevant largely for the urban industrial sector. The most serious constraint on development, apart from population growth, is the relative stagnation until recently in many rural areas.

TABLE 8

	Percentage of net domestic product at factor cost 1964–5	Annual growth rates 1961–5	Weighted growth
Agriculture	51	2·7	1·4
Industry	18	7·4 (assume 10)	1·3 (1·8)
Services	31	6·7	2·1
All sectors	100	4·8 (5·3)	4·8 (5·3)

Even a substantial speeding up of the already high industrial growth rate is bound to be halted unless food production is raised by much more than it has been in the past. Project the figures for 1961–5 into the future. Industrial output increased annually by 7·4 per cent, services by 6·7 per cent, and agricultural output by 2·7 per cent.[11] Weighting these growth rates by their respective shares in 1964–5 in net domestic product at factor cost, the total growth rate is 4·8 per cent, which is 0·8 per cent per annum less than the projected rate of growth 1964–5 to 1970–1 (See Table 8). Even if we assume that industrial output is raised by the planned 10 per cent per annum, the aggregate growth rate is raised, initially, to only 5·3 per cent. The lag of agricultural production constitutes a serious brake on the power of foreign aid to speed up development. Slow growth in agriculture limits essential supplies to industry, demand for mass-produced industrial products, and the savings ratio. And can, of course, also contribute to the growth of agricultural output and to

[11] Calculated from *4DO*, pp. 62–63.

rural development, particularly through higher fertilizer imports, but its efficacy there is more limited than in urban manufacturing industry. It can do relatively little to promote land reform or effective agricultural extension services on the spot. But more recently there have been promising signs that farmers, encouraged by high prices and responding to new techniques, have in some areas substantially increased production.

7. FOOD AID FROM AMERICA

Over half the aid India has received from the US and slightly less than a third of the total aid it has utilized has been in the form of commodities. (Part of the non-project aid also takes the form of commodities.) A small amount of this was received under the US Mutual Security Act (PL 665), but by far the greater part has come under the US Agricultural Trade Development and Assistance Act (PL 480), particularly under Title I which authorizes the sale of US agricultural commodities for foreign currencies. Between India's first PL 480 agreement with the US in 1956 and the end of the Third Plan, the total sales proceeds of PL 480 imports amounted to Rs 156,730 mn. Four-fifths of these counterpart funds were lent or granted to India; 7 per cent were loaned to US private enterprises,[12] the remaining funds (13 per cent) have been retained by the US Government for its own use.

Though self-sufficiency in foodgrains received top priority in the Third Plan, imports of PL 480 foodgrains have increased markedly since 1961–2. And this rise is not solely the result of large imports in 1965–6 following the disastrous harvest; year by year throughout the Plan, cereals imports have increased. Table 9 shows that nearly all the increase in imports during the Third Plan can be accounted for by larger quantities of PL 480 imports. Domestic production of foodgrains stagnated during the first three years of the Plan and fell severely in the fifth year, so that dependence on imported food has increased: in 1961 net imports of cereals were just over 5·2 per cent of net production; by 1963 this figure had risen to 7·8 per cent, and by 1964 to over 11 per cent.[13]

But the growing size of US food shipments is entirely contrary

---

[12] Under the Cooley Amendment, Cooley rupees have, according to AID, attracted over fifty American investors to India.

[13] Min. of Finance, *Economic Survey of India 1965–6* (1966), Table 1:4.

to American aid philosophy. US aid, perhaps more than that of other donors, is intended to promote self-reliance, not to undermine it. America has expressed its dissatisfaction with India. The most obvious expression of this dissatisfaction was President Johnson's four-month delay at the end of 1966 in sanctioning new PL 480 agreements with India, but another sign was the American stipulation in 1965 that India must pay in foreign currencies the whole cost of PL 480 freight, not just 50 per cent as previously. This has been followed by the US Food for Freedom Act which is intended to move countries receiving American food aid from soft currency payments to a system of dollar payments on long terms, but the Act is unlikely to be applied in its full rigour to India for some time. The US has in effect indicated to India its reluctance to continue food shipments at the present high levels. For one thing, the Americans feel that others should share the burden of feeding India. It is for this reason that the US has been the major force in getting food and food-related aid co-ordinated through the World Bank Consortium. Also, US Government wheat stocks have in recent years fallen dramatically, largely because of increased food aid, especially to India. This has led to the removal of area limits in order to stimulate US grain production.

There is, however, a deeper reason for the American reluctance to continue large-scale commodity shipments to India. The Americans fear that dependence on PL 480 food will breed ever greater dependence. It is felt by some Indians as well as Americans that US surplus food, available almost for the asking in years of good harvests as well as bad, has undermined India's determination to tackle its agricultural problem seriously. In particular, food management, and especially efforts to draw out the marketable surplus, may have suffered as a result of PL 480 aid. True, self-sufficiency in foodgrains received top priority in the Third Plan. But this was not achieved and has now been carried over to become a major target in the Fourth Plan. Though weather played its part in this failure, it is not yet clear that India has yet hit upon a combination of policies which will ensure a high and sustained rate of growth in agriculture. India has cut the share of investment in agriculture and has not a sufficiently strong policy to get trained personnel into rural areas. Such policies will involve difficult and unpopular choices and changes, and the Indians may prefer to postpone making them as long as possible. Certainly such postponement will be easier the more India can rely upon the US to bail it out of its worst consequences.

But US commodity aid may have had a more direct impact on agricultural production via its effect on cultivator incentives. PL 480 funds have been a major source of aid to the public sector. It is estimated that during the Third Plan funds arising from PL 480 aid financed over 10 per cent of public developmental outlay. PL 480 aid accounted for 56 per cent of the external assistance to public outlay. Because of the dangers of too much deficit financing and of the unpopularity of higher taxes, the Indian Government

TABLE 9

(*Rs mn*)

	1961–2	*1962–3*	*1963–4*	*1964–5*	*1965–6*
Total imports	11,071	11,356	12,229	13,490	13,490
PL 480 foodgrains	710	1,120	1,730	2,250	2,680
Net total imports	10,361	10,236	10,499	11,240	10,810

Source: *4DO*, p. 102.

has had an interest in making PL 480 imports and sales as large as possible, to raise funds to finance its plans. Larger PL 480 sales exert a downward pressure on food prices, and thus may reduce incentives for cultivators. They also divert limited sources of credit away from agriculture. A difficult choice has therefore faced the Indian Government: to acquire a non-inflationary source of finance for its plans, or to provide incentives for agriculture. The critics argue that the Government has favoured the former too much.

There are two ways for the Government to control the net availability of cereals directly. It can vary PL 480 imports, or it can vary the level of its cereal stocks. Table 10 shows increases over the previous year of net production of cereals and of net availability, i.e. net production plus imports less additions to stocks. It will be seen that Government imports and stocks policy has in most years had a stabilizing effect on the supply of cereals. However, this stabilizing effect has been very slight; in 1958–9, for example, the Government did very little to offset the large increase in the supply of cereals following the excellent harvest. In Table 11, column 4 shows the contribution to net availability of imports of cereals and changes in stocks. The trend of imports less additions to stocks has clearly been upwards. Only in two years since 1956—when the first PL 480 agreement was made with the US—has this trend been halted: 1958-9 and 1960-1, both years of bumper harvests. But the fall in imports less stock additions in these two years has been very small. The pattern is now clear: in years when agricultural production has fallen or risen only slightly, imports less stock additions have increased; in years of good harvests, they have remained stable. In years of bad harvests, therefore, the Government has used imports and stocks to put downward pressure on cereal prices, but in good years it has not lowered imports and added to stocks to offset the downward pressure on prices exerted by domestic production, but has simply kept cereal imports less stock additions at their former levels.

Turning now to the actual prices of cereals, it can be seen from Table 11 that cereal prices rose from 1956 to 1958. Also the cultivators' terms of trade, i.e. the ratio of the wholesale price index of cereals to the general wholesale price index, improved. But in 1959 production was 8 mn tons higher, while imports and stock withdrawals were still at the same level as in 1958—the net result was a fall in cereal prices from 107 to 104, and in the cultivators' terms of trade from 95 to 90.

In 1960 net availability of cereals was just below that of 1959, since the small fall in net production was offset by a large increase in imports, most of which was used to build up Government stocks. The quantity of cereals available was not sufficient to push cereal prices down, but it was sufficient to prevent them from sharing in the general price rise; as a result the cultivators' terms of trade fell from 90 to 83. In 1961 net output increased by 6·7 per cent; imports and stock withdrawals fell only slightly; net availability increased by 6·3 per cent; cereal prices and cultivators' terms of trade again fell. There followed three years of stagnation in agriculture.

TABLE 10

Percentage Changes in Net Production and Net Availability

	1956–7	1957–8	1958–9	1959–60	1960–1	1961–2	1962–3	1963–4	1964–5
Net production	+4·7	−6·3	+16·1	−0·9	+6·7	+2·4	−5·6	+4·7	+8·3
Net availability	+4·0	−4·7	+14·8	−0·3	+6·3	+2·8	−4·7	+9·1	+5·7

Source: Ministry of Finance, *Economic Survey of India 1965–6* (1966).

TABLE 11

	1 Net Production of Cereals (a)	2 Imports of Cereals	3 Change in Govt. Stocks	4 Imports Plus Stock Reductions	5 Net Availability of Cereals	6 Index No. of Cereals Prices (b)	7 Cultivators' Terms of Trade
1956	50·34	1·04	−0·60	1·64	52·34	96	91
1957	52·68	3·63	+0·86	2·77	55·45	101	93
1958	49·36	3·22	−0·27	3·49	52·85	107	95
1959	57·30	3·86	+0·49	3·37	60·67	104	90
1960	56·77	5·13	+1·40	3·73	60·50	104	83
1961	60·65	3·49	−0·17	3·66	64·31	102	82
1962	62·08	3·64	−0·36	4·00	66·08	106	83
1963	58·63*	4·55*	−0·02	4·57	63·20	116	86
1964	61·41*	6·26*	−1·26	7·52	68·93	139	91
1965	66·52*	7·45*	+1·12	6·33	72·85	148	—

* Provisional.
Cols. 1 2 3 4 and 5 units: mill. tonnes.
(a) Refers to agricultural year July–June: 1956 figure refers to net production in 1955–6. Net production is 8·75 per cent of total production, 12·5 per cent being provided for feed, seed requirements, and wastage.
(b) Refers to financial year March to February: 1956 figure for example refers to 1956–7. The base year of the Index is 1952–3 (= 100), as for col. 7.
Sources: Economic Survey of India 1965–6. Reserve Bank of India, *Report on Currency and Finance 1965–6* (1966), statements 12 and 13.

The evidence linking PL 480 imports and lower levels of cereal production is strong but circumstantial. There are a number of possible objections. Firstly, while PL 480 imports are mostly in the form of wheat, a high proportion of cereal consumption is in the form of rice. The two are not perfect substitutes. Secondly, the ratio of the wholesale price index of cereals to the general wholesale price index may be a poor indication of the actual terms of trade of agriculturalists.[14] Thirdly, though the agricultural stagnation of the early 60s came after large imports of PL 480 cereals, the weather and shortages of agricultural inputs were probably more important contributing factors. Fourthly, change in area cultivated is possibly a more accurate indication of producers' decisions than output. The impact of PL 480 on crop areas is less clear—in 1964, for example, the area under cereals was slightly higher than in 1961, and the area under wheat, the commodity most affected by PL 480, was only slightly lower. However, a recent econometric study of PL 480 in India by J. S. Mann lends support to the view that PL 480 has had a

[14] See in this connexion V. G. Mutalik-Desai, 'Terms of Trade and Food Surplus', *Indian J. Agric. Econ.*, Jan.–Mar. 1966 (Bombay).

23

depressing effect on cereal prices and production.[15] In this study Mann estimates that an increase in per capita imports of cereals under PL 480 of one pound (219,995 metric tons with the estimated 1962 population of 485 mn) has resulted in a 0·54 per cent drop in wholesale cereal prices in the same year and a decline in output in the second year of about 0·5 pounds of cereals per capita (about 109,997 tons with the same population). Output tends to rise in later years so that the depressing impact on output is trimmed to about 0·3 pounds per capita in the long run. This study measures only the direct impact of PL 480 imports; the indirect impact via the effect of readily available food aid on planners' attitudes to agriculture is not estimated.

The conclusion is not that ending PL 480 imports is an urgent matter deserving a higher priority. Indeed, Mann uses his analysis to argue the opposite: that since PL 480 cereal imports are only partially offset by the decline in domestic supply, they can make a positive contribution to filling the food gap. The inescapable fact is that for the time being India simply cannot do without food from abroad. In the two years 1965–6 India will have received about 19 million tons of food aid, which is equal to the Dradt Outline estimate for the whole Plan period. As late as 1975/6, minimum likely average import requirements for foodgrains will still be as high as 7 million metric tons per year.[16] This continuing need for foreign food is reflected in the special Consortium arrangements for co-ordinating food aid to India; they amount in essence to a method which enables the US to share with other donors the task— one it considers far from finished—of feeding India. Given a still sizeable flow of food aid to India over the next decade, the important lesson from past experience is the need to control the amount reaching the consumer, in particular to limit it when domestic harvests are good. In years of good harvests PL 480 cereals should be stockpiled.

8. NEW INITIATIVES

UK Policy and the Fourth Indian Five-Year Plan

Apart from trying to clear away the obstacles to the traditional methods of raising aid to India, it is worth exploring new methods.

[15] J. S. Mann, 'The Impact of P.L. 480 Imports', *J. of Farm Economics*, Feb. 1967, vol. 49, 1, pt 1.
[16] US Dept of Agriculture, *Supply of and Demand for Selected Agricultural Products in India, Projections to 1975–6*, ERS For. 100.

There are a number of ways in which modernization in the UK could be geared to assist India. In these sketchy remarks no clear distinction will be drawn between aid and trade reforms.

Matching Markets

The late John Strachey proposed a scheme by which Britain and India would agree to identify specific markets in each country to be supplied by the other. The intention was to treat such markets separately from aid arrangements through the Consortium. Britain would reduce barriers to specified Indian exports. Particular areas hit thereby, such as Lancashire or Dundee, would erect factories producing goods for which a ready, guaranteed market in India would be found. Thus the problem of raising Indian exports, of transferring workers from declining industries, and of finding new export markets would be solved simultaneously.

It may be asked whether the best location for these new factories would necessarily be the areas hit by the additional imports. Furthermore, there would be the question whether the new British export industries would supply the desired products at competitive prices to India. It is not, on the face of it, obvious that a bilateral arrangement is necessarily better than some more indirect way of substitution. But it is worth exploring methods of shifting resources in Britain so as to permit better access to Indian exports.

Aid from Surplus Capacity

The problem of aid from surplus capacity, additional to existing aid, is also worth exploring. There are three main objections: (a) delays in getting orders so that the surplus capacity has disappeared by the time the process is completed; (b) uncompetitively high prices and undesired products; (c) the difficulty of avoiding underwriting malinvestment in the UK. The Indians are confident that they could give an answer to the question whether specific types of goods would be required within fifteen days. In any case, a glance at the list of Indian imports should make it fairly clear what types of goods are required. The problem of uncompetitive prices, which has been made a lot of in Britain, does not seem to worry the Indians. To the problem of preventing desirable adjustments in Britain, the answer is that aid from surplus capacity should be found for those sectors in which demand has *temporarily* receded, and resources are not intended to be redeployed. It is important that aid from surplus capacity would have to be additional to other aid.

Second-hand Equipment

Since modernization often involves the replacement of physically workable but technologically obsolete machinery, it would be worth looking into the question whether, subject to arrangements about transport costs, such second-hand machinery could be used by India. It may, however, be true that breakdowns may occur more frequently, that maintenance costs are higher and that for export industries only modern equipment can be used.

Long-term Planning

Our own five-year and fifteen-year projections should accommodate not only increased trade with India, but also the flow and composition of aid. Debt servicing has to be reflected in admitting more Indian exports into the UK.

The value of aid to India could be greatly increased if the quantum, pattern, and terms were pledged over five or ten years, and committed, not annually, but for several years ahead. Not only the Indian Perspective Planning Division, but also such commissions as the Energy Commission (with Prof. E. A. G. Robinson) aim at projections for 1975, and a longer-term view, which embraces at least two plans, would give a more rational and effective pattern of aid.

Joint Enterprises

Another idea worth exploring is that of joint UK-Indian enterprises, whose aim it would be to promote exports to Europe and other developed countries. They would join UK private firms to either Indian private or public enterprises. What appears to be lacking in India is know-how of export promotion, and in particular of styling, design, &c., suited for selling light labour-intensive goods. An increase in export earnings must have a very high priority in Indian development. To provide not only export know-how but also easier entry into European markets would make it possible for Indian industry to earn foreign exchange. In addition to consumer goods such as dresses, shoes, ties, &c., there should be emphasis on light engineering goods.

Aid for Population Control

One area where the UK can take a major initiative is aid for population control. In the next five years India will add to its population a number of people roughly equal to the present population of this country. It is this rapid rate of population growth rather than the modest though not unsatisfactory increase in incomes which makes the outlook for India disturbing. However, India is one of the few countries which has taken up family planning as a national programme—Rs 950 mn are to be spent in this field between 1960 and 1970, while Britain is the major donor with few religious and other objections to giving aid for population control. But British policy has been to wait until asked for assistance. The result is that British aid for population control has been very small—£11,000 in 1965–6 and possibly £40,000 in 1966–7. Since there is a willingness on both sides, Britain should prompt India to ask for more assistance for population control. This should be in addition to the aid India is already receiving.

But all the initiatives discussed in this section are of comparatively minor importance. It is important to recognize that India is grossly under-aided by whatever criteria one may wish to apply, and to break through the crust of pessimism, cynicism, and disenchantment which has weakened effective co-operation on both sides.

12

Planning and Defence

K. SUBRAHMANYAM*

DURING 1967, as a result of the strains in the Indian economy from the extraordinary drought of 1965–6 and of the interruption in US aid following the Indo-Pakistani conflict of September 1965, it has been suggested that the level of Indian defence expenditure might be reduced. While those suggestions have mostly originated outside India, there have also been some from responsible quarters within India. Even though the Draft Fourth Plan itself had envisaged an average annual outlay of Rs 10,000 mn,[1] the adverse economic developments of the last two years might, it is argued, warrant further efforts to divert whatever can be spared from defence to economic development. There will always be the criticism that the defence planners make a fetish of the size of the outlay, to the exclusion of considerations of effectiveness in relation to the military objectives and of the urgent need to save resources for development. This particular criticism is difficult to answer; no defence planner can confidently assert that in an expenditure of Rs 10,000 mn there is no scope for economizing by better administration and efficiency. It is not our purpose here to examine such possible economies, but to ask whether total expenditure of this order is inescapable, given the security situation in which India is placed, and to outline the basic policy considerations which underlie India's defence planning.

1. HISTORICAL PERSPECTIVE OF DEFENCE OUTLAY IN INDIA

2. India's yearly defence expenditure was below Rs 2,000 mn throughout the 1950s. It was 1·8 per cent of the national income in 1950, 1·9 per cent in 1955, 2 per cent in 1960, and 2·1 per cent in 1961.

* Ministry of Defence, Government of India. Unlike most of the topics covered in this symposium, the place of defence in Indian development planning is little understood outside India. This chapter therefore departs from the pattern of the book, being an exposition from an Indian point of view rather than a critique. The views expressed in it are the author's own and are not to be attributed to the Government of India.

[1] *4DO*, p. 81, applying the 5 per cent yearly rise in non-plan outlays to 1965–6 (base) defence outlay of Rs 8,850 mn.

This was in spite of the fact that Pakistan, whose army at the time of partition was about a third of the size of the Indian army, entered into military alliances, expanded its armed forces to reach 70 per cent of the strength of the Indian armed forces, and had a steady inflow of arms technologically superior to India's. Pakistan was spending 3·7 per cent of a much smaller GNP on defence in 1950, 4·1 per cent in 1955, 4·3 per cent in 1960, and above 4 per cent thereafter.[2] India did not enter into an arms race with Pakistan, despite the armed clash over Kashmir in 1947, when a year of hostilities followed.

3. India became aware of a new threat developing from across the northern border in 1959, following the rapid deterioration in its relations with China and the Chinese attack on the Indian Police Patrol in October 1959. A number of measures were undertaken to meet this threat. A limited programme of modernization of the defence production base was undertaken. A Border Roads Development Board was formed and construction of roads in the Himalayan region was begun. Supply-dropping aircraft were acquired to maintain the forward outposts. A high altitude warfare school was started. But India still exercised considerable restraint in its defence expenditure, hoping that large-scale hostilities would not occur in the Himalayan terrain.

2. DEFENCE PLAN 1964–9

4. This hope was dashed in October–November 1962. After a period of shock and confusion it was realized that China intended to use its force in Tibet for a politico-military confrontation with India. Since this was going to be a long drawn-out affair, India decided to expand its armed forces to ensure adequate capability for this confrontation. A defence plan 1964–9 was prepared, and India sought assistance in weapons, equipment, plant, and machinery for defence production from friendly powers. The plan envisaged an army of about 825,000 men and an air force of 45 squadrons.[3] The outlay involved was about Rs 50,000 mn[4] over five years, about

---

[2] Ministry of Finance, *India–Pocketbook of Economic Information* (1965), p. 156. Of course Pakistan's GNP is much smaller than India's; however, India's defence budget includes all defence outlays and some others (NCC defence accounts, border-roads), while some of Pakistan's outlays *may* be classified under non-defence (airports, military housing, &c.). US defence aid was not, and Chinese aid may not have been, included in Pakistan's defence budget.

[3] 'The present state of defence production', *Economic Weekly*, 23 Oct. 1965 (Bombay), p. 1640.

[4] Min. of Defence, *Annual Report, 1965–6* (1966) (hereafter *RD*), p. 6.

11 per cent in foreign exchange.[5] It was expected that half of this foreign exchange cost would be covered by credit sales and equipment grants from the friendly powers.

5. The defence plan had hardly gone through eighteen months when the assistance promised by the US was suspended in the wake of the Indo-Pakistani hostilities of September 1965. Since then this defence assistance has been wound up. Between November 1962 and September 1965 India had received from the US less than Rs 400 mn worth of equipment—4 to 5 per cent of one year's defence budget.[6] US military aid to India in about thirty-three months was thus roughly one-twentieth of US military aid to Pakistan in the preceding ten years.[7]

3. NEW DEFENCE PLAN

6. India had to reformulate its defence plan and take into account the new situation that confronted it. The collusion between China and Pakistan, which India had suspected since 1961, seemed confirmed in September 1965, when the Chinese, shortly after Marshal Chen Yi's visit to Rawalpindi, delivered an ultimatum to India during the Indo-Pakistani hostilities. Collusion was further suggested by the arrival of Chinese tanks and MIG 19 aircraft in Pakistan.

7. During the 1965 hostilities India sought to convey to Pakistan by deliberate restraint in the conduct of war that it had no intention of changing the *status quo* or modifying the territorial integrity of Pakistan, even though Pakistan was infiltrating and later occupying Kashmir. India's aim was solely to frustrate the Pakistani drive to cut off Jammu and Kashmir from India by its attack in the Chaamb sector. India thus absorbed the air raids on Bagdogra, Kalai Kunda, and Barrackpore without retaliation on the East Bengal airfields from which they were launched. It did not retaliate against the naval attack on Dwaraka. Nor did the Indian army bombard the cities of Lahore or Sialkot which were well within the range of its artillery. But this message does not appear to have got through, and Pakistan is expanding its armed forces further by raising five more divisions.

8. China has been maintaining fourteen to fifteen divisions in Tibet. All along the Indian border it has built a network of roads which connect all the passes on the Indo-Tibetan border with the

[5] *India 1965—Annual Review* (London, 1966), p. 13.
[6] *Hindu Weekly Review*, 12 Dec. 1966 (Madras) p. 16.
[7] *Statesman Weekly*, 15 Apr. 1967 (Calcutta), p. 3.

main arterial road running parallel to the Indian border. There has been very little Indo-Tibetan trade or traffic since 1959, and consequently the purpose of this roadwork is unmistakeable. It enables the Chinese army in Tibet to concentrate its forces rapidly on any of the passes.

4. THE THREAT POTENTIAL

9. It is a sound strategic principle that a country has to prepare itself to meet the capabilities of hostile neighbours rather than to accept their current intentions, since capabilities are more durable than intentions. India has therefore to be prepared to meet a combined challenge of 13 Pakistani divisions (including 2 armoured divisions) and 14 to 15 Chinese divisions in Tibet which can be further increased temporarily. It is difficult to argue at the present stage, six years after forcible Chinese occupation of the area under the Indian posts in Ladakh, and only three years after Indian withdrawal from the areas occupied in the 1965 conflict with Pakistan, that this continuing confrontation is based on genuine but mistaken fears of Indian intentions towards China and Pakistan.

10. The magnitude of the task makes some Indians wonder whether this challenge can be met by India alone without allies. It has also caused the credibility of the Indian defence posture to be questioned in Western countries where, in spite of the happenings of 1965, a strong presumption exists that India will be forced to fall back on Western aid to contain serious Chinese pressure. Concerning Pakistani pressure on India there is a continuing ambivalence. This Western viewpoint finds sympathetic response in some Indian circles.

5. FEASIBILITY OF FOREIGN INTERVENTION

11. The above view overlooks certain basic factors in the Sino-Indian confrontation. The Indo-Tibetan border runs along one of the most difficult terrains in the world. If fighting were to break out, operations would be conducted at altitudes at which forces of other nations have not been accustomed to operate. Foreign troops are useless unless they have been acclimatized to this terrain. They are not likely to have the equipment and clothing required, nor to be familiar with the tactical, physiological, and other problems of this specialized warfare.

12. It may be argued that foreign forces should be stationed there to get acclimatized and to develop the necessary skill to operate.

But India is not short of manpower. In terms of wage-costs, the Indian soldier is cheaper than others. In other sectors of the world where collective defence arrangements operate, the main complaint has been that countries receiving defence support fail to find the necessary manpower. Therefore, it is hardly sensible to consider introduction of foreign manpower on the Himalayan borders when local manpower is available and is able and willing to defend the territory. A further argument in favour of foreign troops in India is that they would commit their country to the defence of India, especially if the Chinese were to break through the mountainous terrain. India is reluctant to accept such foreign commitment since it is likely to turn local conflicts into a major world conflict, and will not be in keeping with India's continued advocacy of reduction in tension. The Indian policy of keeping its disputes localized, though presenting considerable difficulties, has on the whole proved beneficial to its interests, and there are no indications that a departure from it would give greater benefits in terms of security or stability, economic or political. Events in other parts of the world, where major powers did become directly involved in local disputes, have not shown beneficial results following from such a policy.

13. If the Chinese were to break through into the plains—which is not very likely at present, in view of India's preparedness—they would meet the main body of the Indian army near its bases, fully supported by artillery and armour, and would thus find themselves at a considerable disadvantage. The stocking and provisioning policy of other nations is not such as to give them considerable matériel reserves to spare. In any case, if these nations are willing to assist India in case of a Chinese attack, there is no reason why such assistance should not be rendered to the Indian defence forces during the preparatory stage. This, as has been explained, has not happened in the case of the Western powers. It is reasonable to presume that the capability of outside forces to intervene on the side of India, once an Indo-Chinese confrontation has started, is low. During the thirty-three months when India was receiving military aid from the US, the latter equipped the Indian mountain divisions to only 6 to 8 per cent of their requirements.[8] These factors do not receive

---

[8] From defence aid, Rs 400 mn (see n. 6), we deduct sums for equipment specific to border roads, radar and defence production, and divide the balance by 9 (the number of mountain divisions receiving aid equipment). The dividend is 6–8 per cent of the equipment needed by a typical mountain division.

adequate attention in the Western world, when it is argued that India can rely on outside help in case of a Chinese attack.

6. NEED FOR TECHNICAL ASSISTANCE

14. This does not mean that India will be able to do without assistance by way of technical know-how, equipment, and weapons systems in its efforts to reach optimum preparedness. However, the arms market is not a free market, and definitely not a buyer's market. Sale or grant of arms, weapon and equipment systems, and plant and machinery for production of weapons and equipment, are governed by the political decisions of the supplier. Even though a squadron of C130s, using US pilots, operated from Delhi for some months in 1963, dropping supplies to the Indian troops in Ladakh, India was not allowed to buy the aircraft. Similarly, India could not buy US interceptor aircraft and air defence systems. Therefore, India has been compelled to look for weapons systems and capital equipment where they are more readily available, and where favourable financing arrangements can be concluded. This is an additional argument in support of the policy of nonalignment that India has been pursuing. In addition, India has to take into account the ambivalent attitude of the US in regard to its relation with Pakistan. Pakistan's intentions in joining CENTO and SEATO and in expanding its armed forces out of all proportion to the balance of power on the subcontinent were evident. Its tanks and heavy artillery could not have been meant for use anywhere except in the plains of the Punjab. Its air defence radar chain was along the Indian border. The supply of a submarine cannot have been intended to counter any Communist threat. Arms supplies on this scale cannot be explained purely in terms of defence; they enabled Pakistan, for example, to raise a second armoured division when India had only one. This tipping of the balance of power on the subcontinent in favour of Pakistan, together with India's difficulty in obtaining significant aid in its defence efforts against the Chinese threat, cannot but raise serious reservations in the Indian mind on the nature of the interests and intentions behind Western policy. India has therefore concluded that there is no alternative but to rely on its own efforts to defend its territorial integrity against the combined challenge of Pakistan and China. India has had to develop a self-sufficient defence production base, with such assistance as it has been able to obtain.

7. LIMITATIONS ON THE THREAT POTENTIAL

15. It is therefore fortunate that there are limitations on the threat potential, which bring it within the range of Indian defence capability. There are some severe constraints on the logistic capability of the Chinese on the Indo-Tibetan border. Though the Chinese armed forces are considerably larger than the Indian, China has longer (and also sensitive) frontiers to guard elsewhere. The Chinese army, in its operation in the Himalayan terrain, does not today have the superiority of weapons and manpower it possessed in 1962. The campaigning season is limited, and China has some real basis to fear the escalation of hostilities into an intervention against it by the super powers. Therefore, China is more likely to indulge in a long, sophisticated confrontation, applying pressures along different sectors of the long border. It is unlikely, however, that India will allow China to win this war of nerves and thus permit its encroachments on Indian territory—small at any one time, but progressively increasing, and ultimately establishing Chinese armed forces on the southern slopes of the Himalayas. Therefore, this long confrontation has to be contained by the necessary forces all along the border. The Chinese have certain tactical advantages of terrain. The high Tibetan plateau and the network of roads enable them better to deploy and redeploy forces at different points of the border. On the Indian side lifts are needed and lateral movement is restricted. This requires India to deploy a larger force and to maintain larger stockpiles. It will also have to maintain a force sufficient to frustrate any attempt on Pakistan's part, in collusion with China, to force a military decision on it on any issue. The Indian strategy is essentially one of minimum deterrence in a situation of possible conventional war of limited duration. Its aim is to raise the political and military risks of potential aggressors.

8. INDIAN FORCE LEVEL DETERMINED BY THREAT POTENTIAL

16. The size of the Indian forces is therefore to be related to the threat potential of Pakistan, and of the Chinese in Tibet. It also has to take into account the long communication lines to the different sensitive sectors, the restricted capability for lateral movement in the high altitudes, and the capacity of the Chinese to reinforce their

troops in Tibet. In the light of these considerations it is difficult to argue that the size of the Indian army is disporportionate to the threat it has to face. The Indian defence expenditure of 4 per cent of GNP in 1966 compares favourably with Sweden's 4·6 per cent, Yugoslavia's 4·7 per cent, and the UAR's 8·6 per cent.[9] It cannot be argued that India faces a smaller threat than any of these three non-aligned countries.

9. ALTERNATIVE POLICY OPTIONS

17. There have been critics of Indian defence policy who accept the existence of threat, but feel that India has not examined alternative policy options. These are (i) alliances, (ii) alternative strategies of defence preparedness which can bring down the cost, and (iii) policy initiatives to settle the disputes with China or Pakistan or both. India's unsatisfactory experience of obtaining aid in its defence efforts against China has already been mentioned. The assumption of outside intervention therefore lacks credibility in the Indian context. Added to this is the Indian anxiety not to allow local disputes in which it is involved to escalate or add to the tensions of the major conflict areas of the world. It is furthermore extremely improbable that other countries will incur expenditure in support of Indian defence with a view solely to reducing its burden of defence expenditure. The common complaint heard from countries giving defence aid is that the recipients are not making the maximum effort possible. The alliance option is therefore not a real one.

18. Four main alternative strategies have been suggested:

   (i) A more equipment-intensive strategy leading to reduction in manpower and recurring costs.

   (ii) Less emphasis on autarchy in defence production.

   (iii) Less expenditure on certain sophisticated weapons systems which cannot be strictly related to the nature and quantum of the threat.

   (iv) Reduction of the burden of a given defence expenditure by putting the armed forces to some productive use.

The Indian army's teeth-to-tail ratio is 62:38 and is said to compare favourably with what is obtained elsewhere in other armies. Although the army is man-intensive, pay and allowances form only

[9] Inst. of Strategic Studies, *The Military Balance 1966–7* (London, 1967), p. 46.

38 per cent of the 1967–8 defence budget, which is lower than the corresponding percentage in other armies, because of the comparatively lower rates of pay. It has not been established that an equipment-intensive army, with a consequently higher foreign exchange outlay, and in keener competition with other sectors of the economy for scarce resources, will be more cost-effective. For a situation such as the one prevailing on the long borders, a more man-intensive and less equipment-intensive confrontation is better suited to a controlled, flexible, and graduated response.

19. India has been compelled to resort to autarchic policies in its defence production for political, economic, and strategic considerations. India was warned by events in 1965 that reliance on foreign sources of supply can seriously hamper its defence effort by stoppage of spare parts and components at the crucial moment. Understandably, India does not want to undergo such an experience again. It has already been mentioned that the arms market is not a free market, and supply of arms is dictated by political considerations. In the supply of sophisticated weapons systems there is a noticeable reluctance on the part of established supplier countries to part with sophisticated systems unless the armed forces of the recipient countries are integrated with their own command, control, and logistic systems, and the supplier countries are confident of the influence they have on the armed forces of the recipient countries. Today's complexes of weapons systems are highly specialized to meet the needs (and likely wars) of the country concerned. India has its own highly-specialized type of operation to support: two fronts, high altitudes, long borders, non-alignment, and graduated response. So it must develop an inter-related and integrated weapons—and equipment-system complex which will meet those requirements. No single supplier is likely to suffice. Thus India's defence system has included British carbines, Belgian machine guns, French mortars, Japanese jeeps and trucks, US wireless equipment, and French helicopters—*plus* Indian rifles and mountain guns. However, the large size of the Indian armed forces renders it economically unwise to import equipment on a very large scale. It is cheaper to produce it locally, in view of the economies of scale. The arms factories exist in India already; its balance of payments is a powerful argument for rapid import substitution in this sector.

20. Some critics feel that India could cut down its defence expenditure by dropping what they regard as prestige weapons systems.

They usually refer to the expenditure on the purchase of submarines, construction of frigates, and development of a supersonic Mach 2 fighter. But this criticism tends to overlook the political realities of the present international defence system. India, in opting for these measures, was compelled by the realities of the situation which confronted it, in spite of its own persistent efforts to prevent their development. Other powers introduced sophisticated weapons systems (e.g. Pakistani submarine capacity) into the Indian Ocean area. This had an adverse effect on Indian maritime security, and thus forced its hand. The impact of asymmetric great power intervention in a localized conflict situation of low tension potential also resulted in the creation of sophisticated aircraft systems on the subcontinent. This influenced India to opt for an expensive aircraft development project at a time when available foreign supply of such aircraft with a feasible financing arrangement looked less likely than it in fact turned out to be. The subsequent continuation of the project has been mainly as a learning process and to derive the optimum benefit from the outlay already incurred. For the future, it is felt that sophisticated weapons systems can be locally designed and developed on the foundations of the weapons industry already laid; both the skills acquired and relevant industrial bases are expanding and getting diversified. The underlying hope is that even if the weapons system locally developed is not as sophisticated as a comparable one developed by either of the two super powers, it will be adequate to deter those powers likely to be hostile to India. Here the example before India is neither the super powers nor their allies, but Sweden.

21. The suggestion that armed forces should be put to some productive use had been examined in India in the mid-1950s and even then was considered unfeasible. It is claimed that in the Chinese Peoples' Liberation Army productive work is stressed; but there is also evidence that several Chinese military leaders have expressed their grave doubts on the usefulness of this. Moreoever, much of the Indian Army is deployed in uninhabited or sparsely inhabited areas. The Indian army lays considerable emphasis on continuous intensive training of the soldier, to keep him ready for combat at all times. It is difficult to combine both training and productive project work unless there is sufficient manpower to spare. If there is not, the result may be a greater deployment of manpower than necessary—in other words, a less favourable teeth-to-tail ratio—or

a less operationally efficient army which has to make up for this by accepting higher rates of casualties. The suggestion is therefore not really cost-effective. However, the Indian army, wherever it is deployed, uses its resources in support of the local population, purely as a public relations measure. In sparsely-populated border areas the army has also started assisting and advising on local development. But the impact of this as a cost-reduction measure should not be exaggerated.

22. The last of the policy options generally advocated is a direct Indian approach to either or both of the two hostile neighbours, with a view to settling their disputes. There are small but articulate groups in India who advocate this. Outside India, especially in the West, there are many who advocate a settlement with Pakistan. In India, the overwhelming majority would welcome a settlement with Pakistan or China or both. There is no analogy between the situation existing between India, China, and Pakistan, and those conflicts, familiar elsewhere in the world, where conscious and well-directed antagonisms, once whipped up, have proved difficult to control, and national policy formulation has to contend, mostly unsuccessfully, with misplaced moral fervour and misconceived perceptions. The Indian leadership has consciously avoided portraying the threat from China as a Communist threat, or a clash of national interests. It has been portrayed only as a temporary, chauvinistic aberration on the part of the present Chinese leadership, complicated further by the strains and stresses through which the Chinese revolution has to pass. The long-term nature of this confrontation is recognized mostly as a factor reflecting the likely continuity of this phase in Chinese leadership. It is the Chinese approach to the dispute, rather than the content of the dispute itself, which produced the present confrontation. Chinese readiness to resort to force to settle border disputes, in areas where hardly any people or resources exist, lends credence to the belief that their actions are motivated by other considerations. In any case it is difficult to conceive of this dispute coming up for a negotiated settlement till China successfully tackles its leadership issue and agrees on a set of well-formulated national policies. The unsettled nature of the Chinese revolution itself, the difficult confrontation it has voluntarily adopted with the Soviet Union, and the pressure put on it by the United States, may tempt China to try for what may appear to it easy local victories on the Indian border to offset its frustrations elsewhere. Therefore,

while continuing its present policy of not contributing to containment of China, and insisting on measures to bring it into the international community, India has to be vigilant on its long borders. At the same time, every effort should be made to look for an opening for settlement of the dispute. However, between such a settlement and the beginning of a *détente*, and before the establishment of a degree of mutual confidence which will lead to reduction of force levels on the Indian side, there will be a time lag of years rather than months.

23. As regards Pakistan and the Kashmir problem, the long years of oversimplified perception by the advocates of settlement with Pakistan tend to encourage them to believe that once this is settled—on Pakistan's terms at that—all will be well between India and Pakistan. The people of India do not share this view. They feel that Kashmir is only a symptom of a deeper source of conflict—the religious-state theory advocated by the leaders of Pakistan. India, with over 60 mn Muslims, cannot accept this theory without endangering its unity, and a nation's unity is not negotiable. Therefore, whatever disputes there are relating to Kashmir, they will have to be solved on a secular basis. Since this aspect, which has been pleaded by India for the last twenty years, has not received adequate recognition. the solution to the problem has been made difficult. It is India's hope that with the modernization of Pakistan secularism will gain ground there. Then, such issues as remain between the two countries can be settled on a secular basis. This will necessarily be a long-term process.

24. Critics have occasionally indulged in quantifying India's supposed policy options. They have concluded that it ought to settle the Kashmir problem and thereby reduce defence expenditure, instead of keeping a large force against Pakistan. Since this argument is put forward with an air of sophisticated rationality, it deserves to be examined in detail. As explained in paragraph 2, while between 1954 and 1961 Indian defence expenditure rose from 1·8 per cent to 2·1 per cent of its national income, the defence expenditure of Pakistan went up to 4·3 per cent.[10] The further expansion of Indian defence expenditure to 4 per cent was unrelated to the Pakistan threat. If there were no Pakistan threat one could argue that Indian defence expenditure would come down to about 3 per cent. The expenditure on basic installations such as training centres, navy, and air force would not come down proportionally. To reduce the hardship

[10] See above, nn. 1 and 2.

of the troops deployed at high altitudes and to maintain their morale, they would have to be rotated, and consequently a proportion of troops deployed at high altitudes would be in the plains. Today this is offset against the forces required against Pakistan. Even if there is no threat from Pakistan, this proportion will continue to be maintained. Out of 2 per cent of pre-Chinese attack defence expenditure, 1 per cent can be counted as likely savings, and 1 per cent as basic defence expenditure. If we accept Pakistan's contention that Kashmir alone is the problem between India and Pakistan, then, if that were settled, Pakistan would have no security problem. Thus, allowing for the minimum forces for internal security &c., Pakistan's defence expenditure should come down from 4 per cent to 1 per cent of its GNP. In other words, by settling the Kashmir problem, India would save 1 per cent of its GNP, but Pakistan would save 3 per cent of its GNP. Therefore, Pakistan should have a greater incentive to settle the Kashmir issue and work for a mutual reduction of forces. Since India does not subscribe to the view that Kashmir alone is the cause of Indo-Pakistani tension, it has less incentive than Pakistan to opt for an alternative policy based on this questionable premise.

10. IMPLEMENTATION OF DEFENCE PLAN

Manpower

25. In the following paragraphs the achievements and difficulties in different sectors of the Indian defence effort in the last five years are examined. As regards manpower, the armed forces in India have not experienced any difficulty in obtaining the required numbers, except in the categories of engineers, doctors, and skilled craftsmen. To remedy the shortage of engineer officers, a compulsory service liability scheme has been introduced, through which recruits to engineering services in the Central and State Governments and in public sector undertakings are liable to serve in defence services or defence undertakings for a period of four years. In March 1966 one observer[11] estimated that the armed forces and defence sector would have an initial non-recurring requirement of 1,000 engineers, 3,700 other technical personnel, 500 doctors, and 70,000 skilled

---

[11] Dr S. Paul, Inst. of Management Studies, Ahmedabad, in a contribution to a Delhi seminar in Mar.–Apr. 1966 on 'Defence and Economic Development—Implications of Self-Sufficiency' (mimeo).

workers in 1966–7. With an annual outturn of 10,300 engineers, 18,000 diploma holders, and 9,000 doctors, the manpower problem in these categories is not likely to persist. But in respect of skilled workers there is a problem. India's annual outturn[12] of craftsmen was only 116,570 at the end of the Third Plan, and in addition the apprenticeship training programme covered about 26,000. By 1970–1 the annual outturn of craftsmen is planned to increase by 100,000 and apprenticeship training will expand threefold. Can the armed forces absorb the personnel they require? Their training facilities, expanded in 1962–3, are available at short notice. The armed forces (army and air force) doubled in less than three years, and in future it will be possible to expand them even faster. However, for most of the rest of the 1960s, the technical manpower shortage is a real constraint on expansion of the armed forces; but in view of the difficulties confronting the civil sector industrial expansion in 1965–6 and 1966–7, the problem may turn out to be less acute than was anticipated.

Logistics

26. As regards rations, no special problem is involved except over milk supply. Since many Indian soldiers are vegetarians and thus need milk and milk products as protective foods at high altitudes, these are essential requirements. There is, therefore, competition between the supplies of tinned baby food and tinned milk to the troops at high altitudes. A further problem is the supply of tin plate which is also scarce in India. An accelerated freeze-drying plant to produce pre-cooked, dehyrated meat for supply to troops at high altitudes is being established, and it is expected to go into production in 1967–8. Its capacity will be adequate to meet the requirements of 100,000 troops per day.

27. Since a substantial portion of the troops are deployed at high altitudes on the northern borders, development programmes to bring fresh rations to the rear areas immediately adjacent to the areas of deployment will serve to lessen the load on the logistic effort, and ultimately bring down the cost of supplies and ensure provisions at short lead distances. This will also forge additional bonds between the armed forces and the population in the border areas of the north. Recently there have been reports of the army assisting the border populations in their development programmes.

[12] Annual outturns from *4DO*, pp. 116, 118, 122.

28. As regards petroleum products, India has now by and large sufficient capacity. The standard fuel for military jet aircraft, JP4, is now produced locally. The total military requirements of fuel form only a small proportion of the country's production, and the further expansion of the petroleum industry in India envisaged in the Draft Fourth Plan is likely to make this proportion still smaller. There may be a few special categories of lubricants which are at present being imported. Complete import substitution should be part of the development programme for the petroleum industry.[13]

29. Wool tops, artificial fibres, and natural fibres such as sisal and flax are some of the items which need special attention in development programmes from the point of view of defence. It is desirable to ensure that the targets for 1970–1 take into account not only defence requirements in general, but also some of their special item-by-item requirements. Improving the wool-bearing sheep is an urgent need. Another animal husbandry scheme of special defence interest is mule breeding.

Vehicle Requirements

30. The Draft Fourth Plan envisages stepping up of the production of commercial vehicles from 34,000 to 80,000 per annum, jeeps and station wagons from 10,000 to 20,000 per annum, and motor cycles, scooters, and mopeds from 50,000 to 120,000 per annum.[14] No difficulty is therefore anticipated in regard to availability of transport vehicles. A vehicle factory which is part of the ordnance factories organization is being set up at Jabalpur, and this factory will concentrate on production of 4 × 4 vehicles. Bharat Earth Movers in Bangalore is to produce crawler tractors and wheeled earth-moving equipment to meet the needs of the armed forces and of civilians. In addition, the Draft Fourth Plan envisages two units in the private sector to produce different kinds of crawler tractors. Besides this, production of some specialist vehicles like mobile cranes and lorry-mounted cranes, trailers, &c., will need special attention.

Communications Support

31. One of the most important aspects of defence support is a developed communication network of road, rail, and telecommunications. The Border Roads Development Board has been constituted

---

[13] A programme for establishing capacities for various lubricants has already been started. It has been found on investigation that complete import substitution is possible with very marginal additional effort.
[14] *4DO*, p. 289.

to develop road communications in border areas—especially in the hilly areas. But the 1965 events revealed the need to develop road communications on the border areas of Rajasthan and Gujerat. In addition, the logistic capacities of the rear highways also need to be augmented. The Draft Fourth Plan provides Rs 4,000 mn for the central road schemes. The Border Roads Development Organization incurs an expenditure of the order of Rs 200 mn a year on laying new roads and about Rs 20 to 25 mn on maintenance of roads already completed.[15] The impact of the defence effort on the railways programme is likely to be only marginal, and the demands on the railways are normally limited to certain contingency plans.

32. The Draft Fourth Plan provides for an additional 8,500 kilometers of coaxial cables and 8,500 microwave links. A reliable telecommunications network is absolutely essential for effective command and control over the forces and for maintaining adequate operational efficiency. Hindustan Teleprinters has planned an expansion of capacity from 3,000 to 8,500 machines.[16] Production of telecommunication equipment has also been included in the Draft Fourth Plan.

11. DEFENCE PRODUCTION—GENERAL CONSIDERATION

33. According to the annual report of the Ministry of Defence 1965–6,[17] the following major factors govern defence production in India:

(a) The demands for stores and equipment are not uniform over long periods. During the period of combat, consumption rates are very high, and in peace time they are very low, comprising training consumption only.

(b) The ideal situation would be to have sufficient stockpiles for two or three years of combat, or to have sufficient production capacity in the country to meet the demands of the services for consumption on a war-time scale. Neither alternative, however, is feasible or economically justifiable, because both

---

[15] Min. of Finance, *Explanatory Memorandum: General Budget 1967–8* (1967), pp. 45, 75.

[16] *4DO*, p. 306.

[17] Submitted to Parliament at the time of the budget debate, *RD*, pp. 32–33.

involve locking up enormous amounts of capital, as well as losses due to obsolescence or in storage.

(*c*) To develop a proper product-mix of weapons, every country has to take into account its own tactical and strategic position, and the type of war which it may have to fight.

(*d*) The defence sector can use civil industry only to the extent that special skills and capacities to work to the close tolerances required in the manufacture of armament components are available. While it is generally recognized that the capacity for filling ammunition or for the manufacture of special propellants and explosives has to be in the defence sector, it is not often appreciated that the capacity for forging and the high standard of machinery required for ammunition shells has also to be in the defence sector, as the civil industry does not ordinarily need or have such capacity.

34. The following are listed as the guidelines for production of defence equipment and for storing:

(i) The defence services must be equipped with modern and efficient weapons and equipment capable of performing well under all conditions.

(ii) The aim must be to strive to establish an indigenous capacity as far as possible, especially of those items of which the quantities required are large.

(iii) Adequate quantities of critical items should be stockpiled, particularly where there is no risk of obsolescence or of deterioration in storage.

(iv) To fill gaps in the quantity of end items or of components, the civil sector should be utilized.

(v) To permit rapid switching from peace-time level to peak rates of production, it is necessary to conserve trained manpower and techniques in the defence industries. This means that some lines of production, for which there is no peace-time demand, must be kept going, as it is easier and quicker to extend an existing line of production than to establish new capacity.

(vi) Once the stockpile objectives of the services are met, the capacity available in defence production establishments will become surplus even after setting aside some capacity to maintain production to keep the techniques alive. It will then be necessary to use such capacity to make products which will strengthen the economy of the country, but in such a manner that the capacity can be switched back to defence needs when necessary.

(vii) To decrease the dependence on foreign countries, greater emphasis should be laid on research and development of modern equipment to suit India's requirements.[18]

12. CIVIL SECTOR CONTRIBUTION TO DEFENCE PRODUCTION

35. It may be seen from the foregoing paragraphs that the Government had been placing reliance on civil industry supplementing the efforts of the ordnance establishments. The report of the Defence Ministry for 1965-6 gives the following data on assistance sought and received by the ordnance factories from the civil industries over a period of three years.

Rs mn

Type of Store	Value of Items for which Civil Assistance was Sought	Value of Items for which Civil Sector Committed Supply	Value of Items Supplied
Tools	1·9	1·5	0·7
Armaments/ammunition/ components	92·9	56·4	25·4
Ammunition packages	115·9	86·7	54·0
Roller ferrous	0·2	0·2	0·1
Ferrous and non-ferrous/ fabricated items	3·3	3·1	2·4
Tractor components	5·9	1·3	0·8
Truck components	137·9	124·3	83·3
Total	358·0	273·5	166·7

Source: RD, p. 39.

Against more than Rs 3,100 mn of issues from the ordnance factories, the civil sector supplied Rs 167 mn worth of intermediate products and goods. After excluding clothing supplies, it would

[18]There is no discussion about India's nuclear capabilities in this chapter, since the Government of India has so far resisted pressure to undertake nuclear weapons development, which is consequently not a factor in Indian defence planning. Arguments regarding costs of India taking the nuclear option may be relevant to a debate on the advisability of India exercising the option but do not appear to be relevant to planning based on India's current strategic posture.

appear that the civil sector contribution to ordnance factories production would hardly exceed 10 per cent of its value. It is worthwhile going into the reasons for such a small contribution from civil industry to the defence effort, as a widespread impression exists of the convertibility of civil industrial capacity to defence purposes, and very often the experience of the Western countries during the Second World War is cited in support. Galbraith has dealt with this myth in *The Affluent Society*, and has pointed out that the US war effort was not based on conversion of the existing capacity but on addition of new capacity.[19] In the current Indian situation, the following factors have contributed to the inadequate response from the civil sector.

(i) A lack of knowledge of the processes required for the manufacture of defence products.

(ii) The specifications and tolerances applied to defence products are very much more rigid. Very often the opportunity cost of manufacturing defence products is many times that of civil products.

(iii) Since defence orders are limited by authorized stockpiles, they are not likely to recur, and civil industry prefers regular customers.

(iv) The government procedures requiring the acceptance of the lowest bid make the continuance of orders, even for a limited period, uncertain.

Therefore, according to one observer,[20] the scope for private industry's participation seems limited, though much has been said about defence-orientation of industry and close participation of civilian industry in defence production. Consequently the expansion required for defence production is likely to continue to be in the ordnance factories.

13. RE-EQUIPMENT PROGRAMME IN PROGRESS

36. India is now manufacturing all its infantry requirements—namely self-loading rifles, carbines, machine guns, mortars, and recoilless guns. All these weapons are post-1960 models, and are the current weapons in the armies of the advanced countries. India has developed its own mountain gun, and is manufacturing L70

[19] J. K. Galbraith, *The Affluent Society* (Mass., 1958), ch. 12, sect. iv.
[20] S. Paul.

anti-aircraft guns under licence from Bofors. The first Indian-produced tanks, designed by Vickers, are going into regimental service at present. In the field of artillery, however, two Second World War vintage weapons, the 25-pounder field gun and 5·5" medium gun, need to be replaced. Reference has already been made to the production of transport vehicles and engineering equipment. In signal equipment, a new series of platoon sets, company sets, and long-distance communication sets are now being introduced, and all these are under production at Bharat Electronics.

37. Hindustan Aeronautics produces the piston-engined trainer aircraft, the jet trainer aircraft, the trans-sonic fighter aircraft, the supersonic ground attack fighter aircraft, and the medium transport aircraft. In addition, it has started assembling the Mach 2 fighter, and in the near future a full-scale manufacturing programme will be undertaken. At HAL, India is also manufacturing the Alouette helicopters under license from M/S Sud Aviation of France. The Mazagaon dock is to construct the Leander class frigates under licence from the UK.

38. Additional new capacities are also being created in the defence sector under the defence plan.[21]

(a) *New factories.* Out of the four new factories taken up after the Chinese aggression, the small arms ammunition factory, Varangaon, and the small arms factory, Tiruchirappalli, have been completed. The factories at Ambajhari and Chandrapur, which were to have been set up with military assistance from the USA and the UK respectively, and which were affected by suspension of aid, will be proceeded with, and alternative schemes for setting up are under implementation. It has been suggested that, consequent to the suspension of military assistance, the two projects earlier shelved because it was cheaper to stockpile imported high explosives and propellants (the explosives project at Burla and the propellants project at Panvel) might require to be revived.

(b) *A modernization programme of ordnance factories.* This has been drawn up and is under implementation. The programme covers the sectors of metal making and shaping, filling, production of explosives, material-handling, and special equipment for armaments production. In this connexion, the rapid strides made in the machine tools industry in India have to be taken note of. Similarly, indigenous manufacture has been established for furnaces and

[21] *RD*, p. 66.

material-handling equipment. This should enable modernization to be carried out without much foreign exchange outlay.

(*c*) *Other factories in the defence sector*. The annual report of the Ministry of Defence also mentions the proposed establishment of a 9,000 ton extrusion press[22] capable of extruding heavy sections of aluminium, the setting up of an alloy steels plant, and a grey iron foundry in the defence sector.

(*d*) *Alloy and special steels*. Also mentioned in the report are certain measures for substitution of materials, and for efforts to produce defence requirements of alloy steels in civil sector projects already engaged in production of steels and special steels. These highlight the need for co-ordinated material planning in the country, with special emphasis on meeting the needs of defence. The Fourth Draft Outline mentions a likely capacity of 460,000 tons of alloy and special steels,[23] and it is to be hoped that planning of the production requirements for defence of high yield special steels will be co-ordinated with the Plan targets.

(*e*) *Aluminium*. In the case of aluminium, the bottleneck is stated to be not the basic metal but the fabrication capacity arising from defence's special requirements for hard alloys. The opportunity-cost of manufacturing one ton of hard alloy is five tons of commercial grade alloy. It is expected that in planning the fabricating facilities at Koyna and Korba this aspect will receive due attention, and necessary capacities for the production of hard alloys and rolled products will be created.

(*f*) *Copper and Zinc*. The expansion in the production of copper from the present capacity of 9,800 tons to 37,500 tons and of zinc from the present 5,000 tons to 70,000 tons during the Fourth Plan will reduce the foreign exchange outlay on this in defence production.

14. ELECTRONICS AND DEFENCE

39. One of the fields in which a major effort is likely to be concentrated in the Fourth Plan period is electronics. A committee headed by the late Dr Bhabha carried out a comprehensive survey of electronics requirements over the next ten years, and made recommendations on the pattern of development. The committee estimated that the total requirements in electronic equipment over

[22] Ibid. p. 66.   [23] *4DO*, p. 289.

that period will be about Rs 16,500 mn, of which the existing facilities in India will be able to produce Rs 2,650 mn.[24] The committee proposed an investment of Rs 780 mn during the period 1966–70 as the first stage of development. The Draft Outline, however, mentions an investment of only Rs 64 mn[25] for electronics under the industries sector. In addition, a further investment of Rs 80 mn in Indian Telephone Industries is envisaged, and a second factory for production of long distance transmission equipment is proposed. Plan provision has also been made for broadcasting and television which includes strengthening of external services, effective coverage of border areas, and more intensive internal coverage. Electronics for the defence effort is not mentioned specifically in the Draft Fourth Plan, but experienced personnel in the field are concentrated in the Atomic Energy Commission and the defence production organization. There are already two electronics factories under the Ministry of Defence—at Bangalore and at Hyderabad, and recently the Minister for Defence Production announced that a third electronics factory, intended mainly for the production of air defence ground environment equipment, is to be established. Bharat Electronics is manufacturing mostly communication equipment for the army and, in addition, has also undertaken manufacture of components such as valves, transistors, capacitors, &c. In 1965–6 its production was Rs 90 mn, and it is planned to expand its production to Rs 190 mn in the next four years. The Hyderabad electronics factory is to produce avionics equipment. Recently the scientific adviser to the Defence Minister has pleaded for the manufacture of computers to be taken up.

40. The Hindustan Aeronautics Company has recently also given some indications of its future plans. Preliminary discussions have taken place on the design of a new combat aircraft for the air force. The company has an agricultural aircraft under design. It has recently completed the design of a turbojet engine to power the jet trainer, the KIRAN. Work on designing small engines, both jet and piston, is said to be progressing. The company is also setting up a components and accessories division. The chairman of the Hindustan Aeronautics has suggested a comprehensive inquiry into the

---

[24] Atomic Energy Commission, *Electronics in India* (Feb. 1966), pp. 11, 13, 32.
[25] *4DO*, p. 284. The discrepancy arises partly because the committee's report was not available until Feb. 1966, and partly because its proposed provisions were difficult to allocate between civil and military sectors.

future of the aeronautics industry in India along the lines of Bhabha's committee of inquiry into the development of electronics.

41. Other fields which are bound to have an impact on the defence effort are instrumentation and shipbuilding. The Draft Fourth Plan provides for two units to produce instruments at Kotah and Palghat. In addition, the atomic energy establishment at Hyderabad, Bharat Electronics, the National Instruments Company, and the Indian Telephone Industries are also likely to develop and expand their capacities in this field. In regard to shipping, the annual report of the Defence Ministry refers to investigations into the local construction of certain specialized types of ancillary naval craft. The Garden Reach Workshop is to set up a unit for the manufacture of marine diesel engines.

15. STANDARDIZATION AND R AND D

42. The above account presents a picture of the country on the threshold of a purposeful industrialization programme in support of the defence effort. India has come a long way since October–November 1962. However, there are two basic factors which should underlie the entire effort, and to which not enough attention has been paid. These two factors are not special to defence-oriented industrialization, but to industrialization in general. They are a crash programme of standardization and a R and D programme related to technological progress. Recently these two needs have been emphasized, and it is to be hoped that these programmes will be pursued with vigour. In this connexion, attention may be drawn to the efforts undertaken by the Directorate General of Supply Co-ordination in the UK to standardize the items in use in the different services in order to cut down unnecessary diversification in service store holdings, and to control the introduction of new non-standard items. Standardization and re-engineering are essential steps in import substitution. The Draft Fourth Plan provides for Rs 2,700 mn for research and development, and at the end of the plan the country is likely to spend 0·35 per cent of the GNP on R and D.[26] This highlights how far India has to go.

16. OUTLAYS INVOLVED

43. What is the cost of these measures? In 1966–7 the revised estimates provided for Rs 9,420 mn for defence expenditure, and

[26] *4DO*, p. 331.

Rs 200 mn for maintenance expenditure of border roads, and Rs 201·7 mn for capital expenditure on border roads—Rs 9,822 mn in all.[27] For 1967–8 the defence outlay is estimated at Rs 9,690 mn, the maintenance expenditure on border roads at Rs 219 mn, and capital expenditure at Rs 204·5 mn—Rs 10,120 mn in all. Assuming an annual increment in costs of 5 per cent as the effect of price increases, it may be estimated that the total defence expenditure during the Fourth Plan period will be about Rs 54,500 mn. It is not likely to exceed 4 per cent of the GNP.

17. FOREIGN EXCHANGE COSTS

44. It has been estimated that in 1965–6 11 per cent of the expenditure was on defence in foreign exchange.[28] Since then there has been an intensive drive towards self-reliance and self-sufficiency. India was spending about Rs 450–460 mn in foreign exchange for defence even before October 1962.[29] This will mean that India will have to spend annually an additional Rs 500–600 mn (at pre-devaluation rates) in foreign exchange for defence effort. But in view of the fact that Indian-manufactured equipment is replacing foreign equipment more and more, and is able to rely more on the supply of local plants and machinery, the foreign exchange requirements will lessen in future. India may try to distribute the burden of payments by seeking long-term credits from supplying countries. The additional burden on its balance of payments will depend on its success in getting long-term credits for its defence supplies. India's continued non-alignment will make a wider range of markets accessible and is thus likely to prove an asset.

45. It has been argued that whatever may have been the assumptions on defence expenditure at the time of formulation of the Draft Fourth Plan, the extraordinary economic strains that India had to undergo in 1965–6 and 1966–7 would justify a fresh look to see whether there can be a reduction in defence expenditure. It is argued that for every per cent of GNP saved from defence outlay and invested in economic development there will result an increase

[27] Defence service estimates presented to Parliament, March 1967. The total defence outlay has apparently been cut by Rs 60 mn in the May 1967 budget.
[28] As n. 2.
[29] Commitments to defence in foreign exchange, 1961–2 and 1962–3, from Public Accounts Committee, *33rd Report* (1963), p. 109.

in annual growth rate to the extent of 0·35 to 0·4 per cent. During the Third Plan period the plan targets of domestic savings could have been reached and even slightly exceeded if 1 per cent of GNP could have been diverted from defence to development. All this, however, presupposes that what Indians accepted as essential expenditure for national security, they would also have been prepared to incur on development, over and above the existing levels of expenditure. This is an arguable point.

18. CONSIDERATIONS IN DEFENCE PLANNING

46. However, in examining the size of the defence outlay, the following considerations have to be borne in mind. While the techniques of planning in defence and development have a good deal in common, the process of formulation of plan objectives and the constraints on planning are different in the two fields, and thus introduce certain special considerations. In planning for economic development, certain national objectives are assumed as the basis, a timed strategy to reach these objectives is worked out, and various steps to implement it are taken. In working out this development strategy, certain assumptions are made in regard to annual savings, foreign aid, capital/output ratios, the likely rates of growth, &c. During implementation some of these may turn out to be incorrect, or impeded by natural calamities. Nevertheless, the effort towards realization of the objectives can be maintained, at a slower or faster pace. There will be penalties for slower implementation, but they will be acceptable. On the other hand, in the case of defence planning, the objective of national preparedness and security is not merely determined by what a nation proposes to do by itself, but also by what its potential enemies do. Since long lead times are involved in reaching a state of preparedness, the objectives will be determined not only by the enemy's present capabilities, but by his likely capabilities at a future date. Planning for defence, therefore, must insure much more heavily against unfavourable contingencies than planning for economic development. Deterring a potential enemy from a hostile course of action necessarily involves being prepared with adequate capability to frustrate him, and therefore the timing of the build-up is vital.

47. In the case of economic development, the production pattern and output need not be so influenced by external considerations as

in the case of defence planning. For most of the goods in civil use, except where the industry is export-oriented and has to compete with foreign products, output need not systematically match rival products in sophistication. In the case of weaponry and equipment, however, an overall balance in weapon potential has to be maintained with the potential enemy, even though it may not be necessary to match weapon with weapon and equipment with equipment. Defence equipment and weaponry tend to become obsolescent faster than other goods, and one of the essential factors in maintaining the morale of fighting men is their confidence in their weapons and equipment. These factors require a defence planner to keep in step with potential enemies in foreseeing and designing weapons and equipment systems and planning for their production, keeping in view the technological breakthroughs likely in the next seven to ten years. Adequate attention has not always been given to the fact that this consideration is as applicable to the defence planning of a power like India, which plans for a conventional defence system, as to super powers planning for a nuclear war. The magnitude and range of the problem may be different, but it is common to all defence planners. An example of this was the Sino-Indian conflict of 1962 when the Chinese used the 120 mm. mortar, which outranged the World War Two vintage 4·2″ mortar used by the Indian troops.

48. Successful implementation of economic development plans will require a degree of internal stability. Preoccupation with an uncertain border situation, and lack of confidence that India can withstand the strain of confrontation, are likely to undermine considerably the efforts towards economic development. If so, there are political and economic costs, concealed but large, in skimping defence expenditure. This consideration is vital for a vast and diversified national community such as India, which is still in the process of national cohesion and integration.

49. The societies in east, south-east, south, and south-west Asia are in a state of flux, and the simultaneous pressures of social, political, and economic changes are subjecting them to enormous strains and stresses. Added to these are pressures from outside powers in a rapidly shrinking world. Interrelated pressures are applied in these different fields, and the degree of success with which a transitional Asian society can absorb them in an orderly way, preserve its territorial integrity and sovereignty, and do this with a

sense of national consensus depends on its ability to resist external pressures and carry out its own programme of change. This has been the experience of all those nations which have had to carry out a programme of rapid social and political transformation and economic development in this century. India cannot afford to lose sight of this valuable lesson of twentieth century history.

Statistical Appendix

ROGER HILL

TABLE 1

Selected Economic Indicators

	1950–1	1955–6	1960–1	1964–5 (Provisional)	1970–1 (Planned)
1. *National Income by Industrial Origin* (at 1948–9 prices) (Rs mn)					
Agriculture	43,400	50,200	59,000	65,000	93,400*
Mining, Manufacturing, and Small Enterprises	14,800	17,600	21,100	25,500	52,600*
Commerce, Transport and Communications	16,600	19,700	24,600	29,700	44,900*
Other Services	13,900	17,300	23,100	31,400	43,000*
Net Domestic Product at Factor Cost	88,700	104,800	127,800	151,600	233,900*
Net Income Earned from Abroad	–200	0	–500	–1,100	–2,900*
National Income	88,500	104,800	127,300	150,500	231,000*
2. *Percentage Distribution of Income by Industrial Origin*					
Agriculture	48·9	47·9	46·2	42·9	39·9
Mining, Manufacturing and Small Enterprises	16·7	16·8	16·5	16·8	22·5
Commerce, Transport and Communications	18·7	18·8	19·2	19·6	19·2
Other Services	15·7	16·5	18·1	20·7	18·4
	100·0	100·0	100·0	100·0	100·0

For sources of all tables, see pp. 393–4.

3. *National Income* (net, at factor cost)					
At Current Prices (Rs mn)	95,300	99,800	141,400	200,100	295,000 (b)
Annual Growth Rate (a)	—	0·9	7·2	9·1	6·7
At 1948–9 Prices (Rs mn)	88,500	104,800	127,300	150,500	n.a.
Annual Growth Rate (a)	—	3·4	4·0	4·3	5·5 (c)
Per head at Current Prices (Rs)	266·5	255·0	325·7	418·7	532·0
Annual Growth Rate (a)	—	—	5·0	6·5	4·1
Per head at 1948–9 Prices (Rs)	247·5	267·8	293·2	314·9	n.a.
Annual Growth Rate (a)	—	1·6	1·8	1·8	2·9 (c)
4. *Output*					
Index of Industrial Production (1956 = 100)	73·5	91·9	130·1	174·7	306·0
Annual Growth Rate (a)	—	4·6	7·2	7·7	9·8
Index of Agricultural Production (1949–50 = 100)	95·6	116·8	142·2	158·0	207·8
Annual Growth Rate (a)	—	4·1	4·0	2·7	4·7
5. *Prices*					
Wholesale Prices (1952–3 = 100)					
All Commodities	111·8 (d)	92·5	124·9	165·1 (e)	202·2 (f)
Percentage Increase	—	−17·3	+35·0	+32·2	—
Food Articles	112·5 (d)	86·6	120·0	168·9 (e)	228·8 (f)
Percentage Increase	—	−23·0	+38·6	+40·7	—
Consumer Prices (All-India) (1949 = 100)	101·0	96·0	124·0	169·0 (e)	—
Percentage Increase	—	−5·0	+29·2	+36·3	—

n.a. = not available; * = at 1960–1 prices.

(a) Compound yearly percentage of growth implied by increase *from* year in previous column *to* year in same column.
(b) Likely achievement at 1965–6 prices.
(c) Based on National Income figures for 1964–5 and for likely achievements 1970–1 both at 1965–6 prices, *4DO*, p. 61.
(d) Derived figures.
(e) 1965–6.
(f) Figures to May 1967.
Sources: For sources and other details for all tables see below.

TABLE 2

Selected Targets and Achievements
Annual Average Growth Rates

	Physical Indicator	Targets 1955-6 Over Actuals 1950-1	Actuals 1955-6 Over Actuals 1950-1	Targets 1960-1 Over Actuals 1955-6	Actuals 1960-1 Over Actuals 1955-6	Targets 1965-6 Over Actuals 1960-1	Actuals 1964-5 Over Actuals 1960-1	Targets 1970-1 Over Actuals 1964-5
Agriculture								
i) Agricultural Production								
Foodgrains	Weight	3·4	4·7	4·1	3·5	4·0	2·0	5·1
Cotton	Bales	7·7	6·6	10·2	0·5	5·8	0·6	8·0
Sugarcane—gur	Weight	2·4	1·4	5·4	9·0	(a)	2·4	1·6
Oilseeds	Weight	1·5	1·9	6·3	4·4	7·0	4·4	4·3
Jute	Bales	10·4	4·9	5·5	(b)	2·8	9·9	6·9
Tea	Weight	n.a.	0·7	1·9	2·4	4·6	3·2	3·8
ii) Agricultural Inputs								
Nitrogenous Fertilizers Consumed	Weight	—	13·8	n.a.	14·4	n.a.	2·0	23·8
Phosphatic Fertilizers Consumed	Weight	—	13·1	n.a.	40·0	n.a.	20·6	37·4
Power								
Electrical Capacity Installed	mn kw	9·4	8·1	14·9	10·5	17·8	11·3	15·1
Minerals								
Iron Ore	Weight	5·9	7·5	23·8	20·6	17·8	8·3	23·6
Coal	Weight	3·8	3·5	9·3	7·4	11·7	3·7	8·7

Industry								
Finished Steel	Weight	10·6	5·0	27·8	12·1	24·2	16·5	12·1
Machine Tools	Value	—	16·7	30·6	54·3	33·8	30·0	31·8
Aluminium	Weight	24·6	12·8	31·3	19·9	34·2	31·2	35·2
Nitrogenous Fertilizers	Weight	57·4	54·0	29·8	4·3	52·0	25·0	43·0
Phosphatic Fertilizers	Weight	27·2	5·9	57·4	35·1	49·4	24·0	40·3
Paper and Paperboard	Weight	11·9	10·4	13·3	13·0	14·9	9·0	10·5
Cement	Weight	12·2	11·2	23·1	11·3	10·3	5·3	12·4
Cotton Cloth (mill made)	Length	4·8	6·5	0·2	(b)	2·7	0·1	5·4
Sugar	Weight	6·0	10·7	3·9	9·4	3·1	1·8	5·5
Bicycles	No.	39·8	39·0	14·3	15·8	13·8	7·7	6·1
Electric Fans	No.	11·6	7·6	15·3	29·8	18·7	4·6	18·4
Transport and Communications								
i) Railways								
Passengers	Train Miles	—	2·7	2·8	4·5	n.a.	4·7	4·1
Freight	Tons Carried	—	4·5	7·3	6·1	9·8	5·6	8·1
ii) Roads Surfaced	Miles	—	4·6	3·1	5·1	3·0	4·0	3·6
iii) Shipping		—	4·2	13·4	12·4	7·8	12·9	13·5
iv) Posts								
Post Offices	No.	—	8·8	6·4	7·0	4·1	5·9	2·1
Telephones	No.	—	10·6	10·6	10·7	8·7	13·4	12·1
Social Services								
i) Education								
No. of Pupils								
Primary/Jnr. Basic	Pupils	—	5·6	5·5	6·8	8·9	8·1 (c)	6·2 (d)
Middle/Sen. Basic		—	6·6	5·5	3·3	5·5	10·4 (c)	11·5 (d)
Secondary/Higher		—	9·2	7·9	9·3	12·7	12·1 (c)	11·4 (d)
ii) Health								
Hospital Beds	No.	—	2·0	4·4	8·3	5·2	5·3	4·6
Doctors	No.	—	3·0	1·5	1·2	3·0	4·0	8·1
Family Planning Clinics	No.	—	n.a.	78·0	62·0	37·8	47·0	35·8

— = no target fixed.   n.a. = not available.
(a) Target for 1965–6 below 1960–1 actual figure.
(b) Fell during this period.
(c) For period 1960–1 to 1965–6 ('likely achievement').
(d) For five-year period 1965–6 to 1970–1.

TABLE 3

India's Balance of Payments
($ mn; minus signs indicate debits)

	1958	1961	1962	1963	1964	1965
1. Exports f.o.b.	1,185	1,388	1,412	1,623	1,714	1,678
2. Imports mainly c.i.f.	−2,219	−2,139	−2,228	−2,493	−2,946	−2,932
3. *Balance of trade* (2 + 3)	−1,034	−751	−876	−870	−1,232	−1,254
4. Net investment income	−32	−134	−171	−189	−214	−251
5. Other net invisibles	133	93	102	169	182	87
6. *Current balance of payments* (3 + 4 + 5)	−933	−792	−945	−890	−1,264	−1,418
7. Private transfer payments	88	58	47	73	58	52
8. Private capital movements	−47	−7	3	2	−10	−36
9. Repayments of loans (including aid loans)	−7	−134	−114	−121	−143	−199
10. Other capital movements	47	5	5	40	63	53
11. *Capital balance of payments* (7 + 8 + 9 + 10)	81	−78	−59	−81	−32	−130
12. Net errors and omissions	−45	8	8	−8	−150	98
13. *Balance of payments* (6 + 11 + 12)	−897	−862	−996	−979	−1,446	−1,450
14. Foreign grants received	70	76	147	174	299	128
15. Foreign loans drawn	573	682	674	883	1,078	1,295
16. *Foreign aid received* (14 + 15)	643	759	821	1,057	1,377	1,423
17. *Monetary movements* (−13 − 16)	254	104	175	−78	69	27

Source: IMF, *Balance of Payments Yearbook* (July 1967), India, p. 6. To convert to Rs mn, multiply by 4·78 (the rate until the 1966 devaluation).

TABLE 4

Merchandise Exports and Imports
1958 = 100

	1951	*1956*	*1961*	*1962*	*1963*	*1964*	*1965*
Volume of exports	96	101	105	112	126	134	124
Volume of imports	83	97	111	120	117	124	151
Export prices	143	101	111	106	106	106	112
Import prices	114	97	99	94	97	100	102

Source: IMF, *International Financial Statistics*, Suppl. 1966/67, p. 123.

TABLE 5

Investment Outlays as Proportions of National Income (a)
(per cent)

Form of outlay	*1st Plan Actuals*	*2nd Plan Actuals*	*3rd Plan Actuals*	*4th Plan (c) Draft Figures*
1. *Development Outlay*	3·9	7·5	9·9	12·9
2. *Public Sector Investment*	n.a.	6·0 (b)	8·5	11·0
3. *Estimated Private Investment*	3·6	5·0	4·7	6·3
4. *Estimated Total Investment*	n.a.	11·0	13·2	17·3

n.a. = not available.

(a) National Income—net national product at factor cost.

(b) Public investment estimated to be Rs 37,310 mn; see Table 9 n. b.

(c) Assumes that cumulative national income 1966–7 to 1970–1 will be Rs 1,237,250 mn at 1965–6 prices, given planned growth rate of 5·5 per annum.

TABLE 6

Developmental Outlay for Public Sector at Current Prices
(Rs mn)

	India				Pakistan
	1st Plan Actual Outlay	2nd Plan Actual Outlay	3rd Plan Actual Outlay	4th Plan Draft Pro-vision	3rd Plan Plan Pro-vision (d)
1. Agriculture & Community Development	2,900	5,490	11,030	24,100	8,210
i. Agricultural Programmes (including co-operation)	2,110	3,230	8,110	21,500	⎫ n.a.
ii. Community Development	790	2,260	2,920	2,600	⎭
2. Irrigation & Power	5,830	8,820	19,190	29,940	13,630
iii. Multipurpose Projects	2,370	(a)	(a)	(a)	
iv. Irrigation & Flood Control	1,970	4,300	6,570	9,640	⎫ n.a.
v. Power	1,490	4,520	12,620	20,300	⎭
3. Industries & Mining	970	11,250	19,850	43,710	8,920
vi. Large & Medium Industries & Mineral Development	550	9,380	17,650 (b)	40,010 (b)	⎫ n.a.
vii. Village & Small Industries	420	1,870	2,200	3,700	⎭
4. Transport & Communications	5,180	12,610	21,160	29,450 (c)	10,630
viii. Railways	2,600	8,140	13,230	14,100	⎫
ix. Roads & Road Transport	1,430	2,540	4,720	8,250	⎟ n.a.
x. Other Transport	740	1,360	1,890	4,050	⎬
xi. Broadcasting & Communications	410	570	1,320	3,050	⎭
5. Social Services	4,120	7,700	13,920	31,450	11,060
xii. Education	1,490	2,730	5,960	12,100	4,610
xiii. Health	980	2,280	3,570	9,600	3,580
xiv. Housing & Construction	330	850	1,100	2,800	2,180
xv. Rehabilitation	960	640	480	900	—
xvi. Other Social Programmes	360	1,200	2,810 (b)	6,050 (b)	690
6. Other Programmes	600	850	1,160	700	1,230 (e)
Total	19,600	46,720	86,310	15,935 (c)	53,680

n.a. = not available; — = not applicable.
(a) Allocation distributed between Irrigation and Power.
(b) Scientific Research Outlay distributed between Large and Medium Industries and Other Social Programmes.
(c) Excludes outlay on Farakka Barrage.
(d) Post-Devaluation Indian Rs.
(e) Outlay on Government Buildings and New Capitals.

TABLE 7

Developmental Outlay for Public Sector at 1960–1 Prices
(Rs mn)

	1st Plan Outlay (a)	2nd Plan Outlay (a)	3rd Plan Outlay (a)	4th Plan Draft Provision
1. Agriculture and Community Development	3,680	5,950	9,570	18,230
i. Agricultural Programmes (including co-operation)	2,640	3,490	6,920	16,260
ii. Community Development	1,040	2,460	2,650	1,970
2. Irrigation & Power	7,130	9,680	16,150	24,160
iii. Multipurpose Projects	2,920	n.a.	n.a.	n.a.
iv. Irrigation & Flood Control	2,390	4,720	4,730	7,290
v. Power	1,820	4,960	11,420	16,870
3. Industries & Mining	1,240	12,300	17,950	36,060
vi. Large & Medium Industries & Mineral Development	560	10,260	16,000	33,260
vii. Village & Small Industries	680	2,040	1,950	2,800
4. Transport & Communications	6,370	14,110	19,120	24,400
viii. Railways	3,170	9,210	12,090	11,720
ix. Road & Road Transport	1,790	2,780	4,160	6,240
x. Other Transport	900	1,500	1,730	3,370
xi. Broadcasting & Communications	510	620	1,140	3,070
5. Social Services	5,150	8,310	12,090	23,790
xii. Education	1,870	2,940	5,170	9,150
xiii. Health	1,230	2,460	3,130	7,260
xiv. Housing & Construction	430	920	970	2,120
xv. Rehabilitation	1,170	710	410	680
xvi. Other Social Programmes	450	1,280	2,410	4,580
6. Other Programmes	770	930	990	530
Total	24,340	51,280	75,870	127,170

n.a. = Figures not separately available but included partly under Irrigation and partly under Power.
(a) Sum of deflated actual annual outlays; for method see Sources and Methods.

TABLE 8

Percentage Distribution of Developmental Outlay for Public Sector

	India				Pakistan
	1st Plan (b)	2nd Plan (b)	3rd Plan (b)	Draft 4th Plan (c)	3rd Plan
A. At Current Prices					
1. Agriculture & Community Development	14·8	11·8	12·8	15·1	15·3
2. Major & Medium Irrigation	22·1 (a)	9·2	7·6	6·0	25·4
3. Power	7·6	9·7	14·6	12·8	16·6
4. Village & Small Industries	2·2	4·0	2·5	2·3	
5. Organized Industry & Minerals	2·8	20·1	20·5	25·1	
6. Transport & Communications	26·4	26·9	24·5	18·5	19·8
7. Social Services & Other Programmes	24·1	18·3	17·5	20·2	22·9
8. Total	100·0	100·0	100·0	100·0	100·0

	1st Plan (d)	2nd Plan (d)	3rd Plan (d)	Draft 4th Plan	3rd Plan
B. At 1960–1 Prices					
1. Agriculture & Community Development	15·1	11·6	12·6	14·2	
2. Major & Medium Irrigation	21·8 (a)	9·2	6·2	5·7	
3. Power	7·5	9·7	15·1	13·3	
4. Village & Small Industries	2·3	4·0	2·6	2·2	n.a.
5. Organized Industry & Minerals	2·8	20·0	21·1	26·2	
6. Transport & Communications	26·2	27·5	25·2	19·2	
7. Social Services & Other Programmes	24·3	18·0	17·2	19·2	
8. Total	100·0	100·0	100·0	100·0	

n.a. = not available.
(a) Including Multipurpose Projects
(b) Actual Outlays.
(c) Planned Outlays from 4DO.
(d) Sum of deflated actual annual outlays; for method, see Sources and Methods, pp. 393–4, Table 7.

TABLE 9

Public Sector Investment

(Rs mn)

	2nd Plan 1956–61 (Actual)	3rd Plan 1961–66 (Actual) (a)	4th Draft Plan 1966–71 (Planned)	Percentage increase 3rd over 2nd Plan	Percentage increase 4th Draft over 3rd Plan
A. At Current Prices					
1. Agriculture & Community Development	2,100	7,240	15,750	244·8	117·5
2. Major & Medium Irrigation	4,200	6,520	9,640	55·2	47·9
3. Power	4,450	12,620	20,300	183·6	60·9
4. Village & Small Industries	900	1,390	2,300	54·4	65·5
5. Organized Industry & Minerals	8,700	17,350	39,360	99·4	126·9
6. Transport & Communications	12,750	21,160	30,100	66·0	42·2
7. Social Services & Other Programmes	3,400	8,320	18,550	144·7	123·0
8. Total	36,500 (b)	74,600	136,000	104·4	82·3

	2nd Plan 1956–61 (Actual)	3rd Plan 1961–66 (Actual) (a)	4th Draft Plan 1966–71 (Planned)	Percentage Increase 3rd Over 2nd Plan	Percentage Increase 4th Draft Over 3rd Plan
B. At 1960–1 Prices					
1. Agriculture & Community Development	3,360	6,280	11,910	87·0	89·6
2. Major & Medium Irrigation	4,610	4,700	7,290	2·0	55·1
3. Power	4,960	11,420	16,870	130·2	47·7
4. Village & Small Industries	980	1,230	1,740	25·5	41·5
5. Organized Industry & Minerals	9,520	16,000	33,260	68·1	107·9
6. Transport & Communications	14,110	19,120	24,400	35·6	27·6
7. Social Services & Other Programmes	3,680	7,080	13,670	92·4	93·1
8. Total	41,220	65,830	109,140	59·7	65·8

(a) Calculations based on actual outlay figures and on the breakdown between current and capital public outlays provided in the Third Plan and in the Draft Fourth Plan.

(b) Later estimates suggest that public investment was nearer Rs 37,310 mn, breakdowns of which are not available.

TABLE 10

Private Investment (a)

(Rs mn)

	2nd Plan Actual	3rd Plan Proposed (d)	4th Plan Draft Provision
A. At Current Prices			
1. Agriculture & Community Development	6,250	8,000	9,000
2. Major & Medium Irrigation (b)			
3. Power	400	500	500
4. Village & Small Industries	1,750	2,750	3,200
5. Organized Industry & Minerals	6,750	10,500	23,500
6. Transport & Communications	1,350	2,500	6,300
7. Social Services & Other Programmes	9,500	10,750	16,000
8. Inventories	5,000	6,000	19,000
9. Total	31,000 (c)	41,000 (c)	77,500 (c)
	2nd Plan Actual	**3rd Plan Proposed (d)**	**4th Plan Draft Provision**
B. At 1960–1 Prices			
1. Agriculture & Community Development	6,830	6,440	6,810
2. Major & Medium Irrigation (b)			
3. Power	440	460	420
4. Village & Small Industries	1,910	2,440	2,420
5. Organized Industry & Minerals	7,390	9,600	19,520
6. Transport & Communications	1,480	2,250	5,220
7. Social Services & Other Programmes	10,270	9,330	12,110
8. Inventories	5,410	5,120	14,370
9. Total	33,730 (c)	35,640 (c)	60,870 (c)

(a) Private Investment in First Plan estimated to be Rs 18,000 mn (excluding transfer of Rs 2,000 mn from public to private sector)—breakdown not available.
(b) Included under Agriculture and Community Development.
(c) Excludes transfers from public to private sector.
(d) According to the Fourth Draft Outline, private investment in the Third Plan is likely to be higher than stated in this table, though no figures were given.

TABLE 11

Estimated Total Investment

(Rs mn)

	2nd Plan (b)	3rd Plan (c)	Draft 4th Plan
A. At Current Prices			
1. Agriculture & Community Development	8,350 (a)	15,240 (a)	24,750 (a)
2. Major & Medium Irrigation	4,200	6,520	9,640
3. Power	4,850	13,120	20,800
4. Village & Small Industries	2,650	4,140	5,500
5. Organized Industry & Minerals	15,450	27,850	62,860
6. Transport & Communications	14,100	23,660	36,400
7. Social Services & Other Programmes	12,900	19,070	34,550
8. Inventories	5,000	6,000	19,000
9. Total	67,500	115,600	213,500

	2nd Plan (b)	3rd Plan (c)	Draft 4th Plan
B. At 1960–1 Prices			
1. Agriculture & Community Development	10,190 (a)	12,720 (a)	18,720 (a)
2. Major & Medium Irrigation	4,610	4,700	7,290
3. Power	5,400	11,880	17,290
4. Village & Small Industries	2,890	3,670	4,160
5. Organized Industry & Minerals	16,910	25,600	52,780
6. Transport & Communications	15,590	21,370	29,620
7. Social Services & Other Programmes	13,950	16,410	25,780
8. Inventories	5,410	5,120	14,370
9. Total	74,950	101,470	170,010

(a) Includes private investment in Irrigation.
(b) Actual figures, but see Table 9, n. b.
(c) Estimated actual public investment plus proposed private investment.
Source: See notes on Tables 9 and 10 in Sources and Methods.

TABLE 12

Percentage Distribution of Planned and Actual Outlays

	1st Plan		2nd Plan		3rd Plan		4th Draft Plan Provision
	Report Figure	Actual	Report Figure	Actual	Report Figure (a)	Actual	
1. Agriculture and Community Development	17·4	14·8	11·8	11·8	13·4	12·8	15·1
2. Major and Medium Irrigation	21·0 (b)	22·1 (b)	10·1	9·2	8·1	7·6	6·0
3. Power	6·2	7·6	8·9	9·7	12·6	14·6	12·8
4. Village and Small Industries	1·3	2·2	4·1	4·0	3·4	2·5	2·3
5. Organized Industry and Minerals	7·0	2·8	14·4	20·1	23·6	20·5	25·1
6. Transport and Communications	24·0	26·4	28·9	26·9	20·4	24·5	18·5
7. Social Services and Other Programmes	23·1	24·1	21·8	18·3	18·5	17·5	20·2
8. Total	100·0	100·0	100·0	100·0	100·0	100·0	100·0

(a) Cost of Physical Programmes.
(b) Includes Multipurpose projects.

Sources and Methods

Table 1

The main source is Reserve Bank of India, *Report on Currency and Finance, 1965–6* (Bombay, 1966), Statement 1B. National income targets for 1970–1 are from *4DO*, p. 61. Distribution of income by sector: 1970–1 adjusted figure from *MFB*, p. 7.

Table 2

All target figures are taken from Planning Commission, *Selected Plan Statistics* (SPS) (1963), Table 2, with the exception of 1970–1 targets which are from *4DO*, Ann. I. Actuals for 1950–1 and 1955–6 are from SPS, 1963, Table 2; actuals for 1960–1, 1964–5, and 1970–1 from *4DO*, Ann. I.

Table 3

From IMF, *Balance of Payments Yearbook*, vol. 18, *1961–6* (Washington, 1967), India, p. 6.

Table 4

From IMF, *International Financial Statistics*, Ann. Suppl. (1966), p. 123.

Table 5

All figures derived from following tables.

Table 6

First and Second Plan actual outlay figures are from *Selected Plan Statistics*, Table 2. Third Plan actual and Fourth Plan provisional outlays are from *4DO*, pp. 72–74. Proposed public sector outlays during Pakistan's Third Plan are based on Table 1, p. 37, of Pakistan's *Third Five-Year Plan* (1965). Tables on pp. 196–7 and on p. 235 have been used to reallocate Pakistan Government expenditure on physical planning and on its works programme to provide greater comparability with Indian outlays. The Pakistan figures have been converted to Indian Rs using the current (post-devaluation) exchange rate.

Table 7

First, Second, and Third Plan constant price outlays are the sum of *annual* actual outlays which have been adjusted for price changes. Annual outlay figures for 1951–5 are published in *Progress Report for 1954–5* (1956), Statem. I. The 1955–6 outlay figure was found by subtraction of 1951–5 total from First Plan outlay. Annual outlay figures 1956–62 are published in *Selected Plan Statistics*, Table 2.   Annual figures for 1962–4 can be found in *Statistical Pocketbook of Indian Union* (1965), pp. 132–3. Annual figures for 1964–5 and 1965–6 were estimated by subtracting actual outlay figures for the first three years of the Plan from total Plan outlay and dividing by 2.   Wholesale price indices were then used to adjust for price changes.   The General Wholesale Price Index was then used for all outlays except those under heads v, vi, viii and x, for which the Wholesale Price Index of Manufacturers was used.   Price indices are financial year averages taken from *Report on Currency and Finance, 1965–6*, Statem. 12.   The base year of the indices is 1952–3, but the old 1949 = 100 indices are used until 1955 when they have been spliced to the 1952–3 = 100 indices.   The Wholesale Price Indices were then adjusted so that they equalled 100 in 1960–1.

Table 9

Public investment during the Second Plan is published in *Selected Plan Statistics*, Table 23.   Public investment during the Third Plan has been estimated by applying an average of the anticipated ratios of capital to total public outlay in the Third Plan and in the Fourth Plan (see *Third Plan Report* and *4DO*, Table 2, p. 41) to estimated public outlay during the Third Plan.

Table 10

Actual private investment during the Second Plan is published in *Selected Plan Statistics*, Table 23.   Proposed private investment during both the Third and Fourth Plans is published in *4DO*, Table 3, p. 42. Since annual figures of private investment are not available broken down by sectors, it was assumed in adjusting for price changes that private investment was distributed through time in each Plan in the same proportions as public development outlay.   The same price indices were used as for public outlay.

Table 12

Report figures are based on public development outlay figures given in Planning Commission, *First Five Year Plan Report* (1952), *Second Plan Report* (1956), and *Third Plan Report* (1961).   Fourth Plan provisional figures are based on *4DO*, p. 41.

Glossary

Ayacut	multi-purpose river basin
Dharma	spiritual and caste duty
Gherao	a 'lock-in'; workers barricade employers (or civil servants) in their office, and refuse to release them until wage demands are met
Gramsevaks	Village Level Workers (VLW)
Jajmani system	Craftsmen (e.g. carpenters, barbers) work free for landowners, who give them a set share of harvest
Panchayati raj	local self-government
Panchayat Samiti	joint council of 20–30 villages
Patwaris	local revenue collectors
Sadhus	wandering holy men
Swadeshi	Indian-made goods
Tagai	Government
Zilla Parishad	parliament of District (1–3 mn people)

INDEX

Adi-Dravidas, 287.

Administration: quality of, 53, 80, 120, 126, 134, 151, 332; agricultural 89, 103, 117, 120–3, 128, 134, 145, 342; rural, 94, 99, 103, 202; Block level, 103, 110, 120, 130, 203, 286; District level, 121, 203, 286; urban bias in, 130f., 134; State level, 161, 164, 202, 219; in irrigation, 161–2; salaries in, 223; employment expansion in, 230; health and, 239, 268; expenditure on, 262; of aid, 324–5, 331, 338–40; of defence, 351.

Administrative Reforms Commission (ARC), 48f., 55, 57.

Africa, 309; exports to, 287; tea exports of, 308; 310; cashew nut exports of, 312.

Agency for International Development (AID), 341n.

Agriculture, 6f., 10, 54n., 68, 77, 83–147, 176, 180, 191, 215, 305, 340f.; priority for, 10, 32, 77, 84f., 120, 123, 130, 144, 156, 337; debt in, 105, 126; implements in, 110f., 132; techniques in, 110, 115, 117, 132f., 165; efficiency of, 137, 233, 342; and industry, 245, 340; caste and, 274f., 282f.

Inputs, 37, 84, 95, 98–100, 105, 117, 132, 345; industrial, 100, 146, 337; prices of, 102f.; relocation of, 109–18; complementarities of, 110, 118, 163; traditional restrictions on the use of, 115, 117, 133; overhead sector and, 156f., 163–5.

Investment: public sector, 7f., 70, 85, 87f., 94, 99, 120, 128, 144, 242, 337; rate of return to, 63, 83, 93f., 101, 105, 107, 118f., 145, 241; share of planned investment, 77, 85f., 97, 107, 120, 142, 144, 342; private

Agriculture, *cont.*

sector, 85, 87, 101, 106, 112, 130f., 144f.; import content of, 87, 90, 144, 337; complementarity of, 91, 110, 244; absorptive capacity for, 94, 337.

Production: growth of, 3, 6f., 23, 25, 97–98, 119, 132–3, 239, 299, 340f.; 343–6; potential, 64, 110f., 119f.; *4DO* targets, 83, 97–100, 118, 120, 132, 146, 302; constraints on, 134, 225, 305, 340; for export, 299–300, 302, 308–13.

Research in, 7, 84, 103, 110f., 123, 205; research stations, 101, 117, 132, 135, 145.

Strategies, 5, 88, 117, 342f.

See also Cereals; Community development; Education; Farmers; Fertilizers; Foodgrains; Irrigation; Land; PL 480.

Agricultural Development Committees, 132.

Agricultural Prices Commission, 102.

Agricultural Production Officers, 120

Agro-Economic Research Centres, 132.

Aid, 5, 14, 60, 213, 219f., 323–49, 375; shortages of, 7, 35, 332, 339; strategies of, 10, 13, 92f., 333–8; debt, 10n., 13, 67, 307, 325, 330; rescheduling of, 13, 325–6, 327, 339; suspension of, 22, 304, 324, 351, 353, 370; dependence on, 31, 67, 81, 334, 338–9, 349; repayment of, 67, 328, 330, 338–9, 341; and industrial growth, 73, 75, 320, 334; and agriculture, 93, 144, 334; and overhead sector, 150, 174, 334; tied aid, 150, 323f.; non-project aid, 211, 323f., 325, 331, 339; attitudes to, 214, 333; and family

Aid, *cont.*
planning, 268f., 349; servicing of, 298f., 307, 325, 327, 329, 338, 348; in *4DO*, 298, 329, 332, 338–41; terminology of aid, 323–6; project aid, 323–5, 331f., imports and, 323, 331, 337, 339; balance of payments and, 324, 332, 338; refinancing of, 325–6; utilization of, 326f., 330, 332, 334, 339; terms of aid, 326f., 330–1; exports and, 327, 329–30, 335, 337; impact of aid, 331–8; military aid, 352f., 354–5, 358–9, 370, 374.
Aid India Consortium, 13, 34, 324, 330, 339, 346f.
Air force, 352f., 356, 359, 362; equipment, 360, 370, 372.
Almond, G., 53–54.
Aluminium, 371.
Andhra Pradesh, 29; dry-milch cow ratio in, 109; utilization of irrigation in, 161.
Animal husbandry, 83, 99, 147.
Annual Plans, 23, 27f., 49, 55; relationship to *4DO*, 4, 60; family planning in, 263–7; aid and, 339; military expenditure in, 374; *see also* Budgets; Current expenditure.
Apprenticeship schemes, 195, 209, 364.
Army, 355; use for development, 12, 358, 360–1, 364; size of, 352, 358; problems facing, 354, 357, 363; equipment, 355f., 358f., 369–73; teeth-to-tail ratio, 358–60; training of, 360, 362; manpower requirements, 360, 362; logistics, 364–5; *see also* Defence and armed forces.
Assam, 30, 52, 270, 309; household land-holdings in, 125; co-operative credit in, 127; family planning programme, 267n.
Atomic Energy Commission, 372.

Balance of payments, 25, 65, 295; exports and, 303, 320; imports and, 307; invisible and capital account, 307; effect of devaluation on, 308; aid and, 324, 332, 338; defence and, 359, 374; *see also* Exports; Imports.

Balance of trade, 66, 295, 298, 306.
Balvantray Mehta Committee, Report of, 36.
Barve, S. G., 43, 48.
Bell, Bernard, 304.
Béteille, André, 287.
Bhabha, Dr H., 371, 373.
Bhagat, B. R., 303.
Bhakra Nangal dam, 129.
Bhaktavatsalam, M., 27f., 31.
Bicycles, 301f.
Bihar, 154; famine in, 98; co-operative credit in, 127; coal fields, 181; water-rates in, 162n; family planning programme in, 267n.
Birla, G. D., 32–33, 34f.
Birth-control, 226, 268; economic argument for, 238; measures, 251; programme, 254, 261; returns to investment in, 255–63; cost per prevented birth, 259, 266; complementary factors in, 262; techniques, 264–7; *see also* Family Planning.
Birth-rate, 11, 236, 252, 269f.; economics of reducing, 252, 255–63; urban-rural differences in 252, 270; marriage age and, 253f.; relationship to death-rate, 253–4; *see also* Family Planning; Fecundity; Fertility; Marriage.
Block Development Officer (BDO): role of, 120, 122; training, 121; urban bias in, 131; manpower requirements of, 202–5; social anthropology and, 275.
Boad and Ganjam Caste, 136.
Bombay, 173f., 181; utilization of irrigation in, 161.
Border Roads Development Board, 352, 365–6.
Bose, S. P., 136.
Bottlenecks, 10, 15, 371; in overhead sector, 150; in family planning programmes, 265; aid as means to break, 331, 333, 335.
Brahmanandra Reddy, K., 29.
Brahmans, 132, 137, 272, 274, 278f., 284, 287.
Brahmanism, 132; *see also* Hinduism.
Budgets: Central, 32, 194–5, 247, 306; State, 32, 194–5, 222, 236, 244; *see also* Annual Plans; Current expenditure; Investment.

Business leaders, 32f., 141; urban status of, 131; views on devaluation, 307.
Cabinet, *see* Government of India.
Calcutta, 173f, 181, 310.
Capital, 7n., 166, 193; rates of return to, 5, 7, 14, 167, 216, 229, 233, 246–7; utilization of, 9, 70f., 211, 247; inflow of, 13, 329; formation of, 65f., 80; human capital, 187–249; social opportunity cost of, 194, 241f.; productivity of, 231, 233, 240; *see also* individual sectors; Investment.
Capital goods, 192, 212f., 267.
Capital-intensive production, 10, 33, 71n., 160n., 169, 231, 358.
Capital-output ratios, 9f., 15, 255, 258f., 260n., 335, 375; in industry, 70–73, 90; in agriculture, 83–89, 144; *see also* individual sectors.
Cash crops, 83, 123.
Cashew nuts, 312.
Caste, 38, 115, 124, 249; restrictions, 133, 141, 143; domination of *Panchayats*, 135; majority casteocracy, 135–6; cultivator castes, 136, 278; craftsmen castes, 136; organization of, 271, 273; *4DO* proposals on, 272–4; urban caste neutrality, 273, 281; dominant castes, 274, 276f.; and agricultural development, 274f., 282f.; caste versus economic class, 277–8; specialist castes, 277; community groups and, 284n.; artisan castes, 285; graduality in, 285.
Scheduled castes, 275; investment proposals for, 191, 196.
Untouchability, 135f., 281, 285f.; proposals in *4DO* on, 272, 275; rural, 272; in industry, 273, 279–80.
Casteism, 51, 281.
Cattle, 98, 115, 141, 147; milch cows, 108–9; cattle fodder, 108, 118; *see also* Animal husbandry.
Central Water and Power Commission, 174.
Centre-State relations, *see* States and Centre.
Cereals, 141; income elasticity of demand for, 96; production of, 100, 142; prices of, 106, 146; nutritional value of, 107.

Ceylon: tea exports, 308, 310; wage costs in, 309.
Chaliha, B. P., 30.
Chanda, A., 46.
Chemicals, 20, 68, 210; exports of, 294, 296, 298, 300, 337; imports, 298.
Chen Yi, Marshal, 353.
Chief Executive Officers (CEO), 131.
China, People's Republic of: Indian conflict with, 26, 332, 352f., 361–2, 370, 376; armed forces of, 353–4, 357, 360.
Cholera, 237f.
City Compensatory Allowance, 103.
Civil sector: and defence production, 366–9.
Civil servants, 103, 145.
Coal, 166, 177, 181; working group on, 20; coal freight, 154, 168, 169n., 173, 181; demand for, 175; coal equivalents, 175f.
Coarse grains, 101; income elasticity of demand for, 96; production of, 100, 142; prices of, 106, 146; nutritional value of, 107.
Cocoa, 311.
Coffee, 298, 300, 305n., 311.
Coir yarn, 298, 300.
Communalism, 51, 55n.
Communists, 52.
Community development and agricultural extension, 11, 14, 36f., 85n., 145, 341; investment in, 88, 107f., 191; administration of, 94, 106, 117, 121f., 204–5; *see also* Administration; Agriculture; Rural development; Village Level Workers
Compost, 116; techniques, 111, 115; urban, 100n., 109, 146.
Compulsory service scheme, 363–4.
Congress Party (Indian National Congress), 27, 47; election performance of, 3f., 34, 52, 58–60; strength at Centre, 5, 52; prospects, 51–53, 55; *see also* Politics; States; and States and Centre.
Consumer goods, 11, 133, 212; production of, 63f., 70, 76, 81; and income distribution, 76; imports of, 298, 336f.; duty on, 303; prices of, 305.

Consumption, 25, 40, 42, 66, 77, 237f., 333; income and, 8, 66, 76; public, 8, 65; conspicuous, 13, 138f.; productive, 15, 255, 257, 335; private, 65f., 78, 93, 127; distribution of in *4DO*, 66, 81; standards, 256, 263.

Contingency planning, 7, 14; *see also* Planning.

Cooley Amendment, 341n.

Co-operation, 38–9, 85n., 88, 108, 135, 191; co-operative credit, 38, 84, 126–8; farming co-operatives, 104, 136; co-operative services, 121; administration of, 128, 205; caste in, 136, 272; co-operative consumer loans, 139, 141, 147; co-operative road transport, 159.

Copper, 303, 371.

Corruption, 32, 121, 126, 284.

Cost-benefit approach, 8, 241; in defence, 12; in agriculture, 89–94, 109, 111; in overhead sectors, 152, 159, 171; in irrigation, 171–2; in education, 187–9, 191–2, 200, 217, 220, 225–6, 230, 241–9; in health, 187–9, 191–2, 235–6, 238–41: in family planning, 258, 261; in aid, 333–8.

Cotton, 88, 146, 168n., 275, 318; production of, 97, 101, 302; exports of, 300; export duties on, 305n.

Cotton textiles: production of, 63, 299, 301f.; textile mills, 88, 317–18; exports of, 294, 296, 298, 300, 306, 316–18, 337; spindleage, 316, 318; Five-Year Long Term Agreement on, 317; prices of, 317n.

Craftsmen, 191f., 195; outlays on, 190, 195; demand for, 202, 209, 212; military requirements of, 363–4.

Cropping patterns, 100, 105, 114f., 134f., 146f., 161.

Currency, 52; *see also* Devaluation; Foreign exchange; Prices; Exchange rates.

Current expenditure, 41, 191, 193f., 333; on education, 192, 194–5, 243–4; on health, 192f., 207, 236; in agriculture, 193; in community development, 193; in defence, 351, 358, 374.

Death-rate, 236f., 251; relationship with birth-rate, 253–4.

Decentralization: of planning process, 28f.; in decision making, 333.

Defence and armed forces, 34, 52, 351–77; planning of, 12, 352–4, 358, 363, 367, 375–7; requirements of, 22, 356, 363–5, 367; policy and strategy of, 351, 356–8, 362f., 368n.; cost-effectiveness of, 355, 359, 361; equipment, 356, 358, 376.

Defence production, 355f., 366–74; civil sector and, 366–7, 368f.; guide lines for, 367–8; and army re-equipment programme, 369.

Deficit financing, 32, 139, 219; public sector, 336, 343.

Demand elasticities, 96, 106–7, 146f., 180, 306, 309, 311, 319.

Depreciation, 8, 91, 167–8, 170, 259, 261.

Desai, H. K., 31f.

Devaluation (June 1966), 12, 30, 303–8; effect on plan formation, 23, 25, 193–4, 335; and exports, 66, 75, 232, 299, 306, 312f.; and agriculture, 87, 88n., 144; education and health allocations, 193–4; imports and, 306; and foreign investment, 307–8.

Development Councils, 24.

Development strategies, 144, 333; 'long-haul', 87, 92; 'self-sufficiency', 213, 335, 337.

Dharma, 140f., 275

Discount rates, 247f., 258, 261.

Diseases, 237f.; *see also* Cholera; Dysentery; Malaria; Smallpox; Tuberculosis.

Doctors, 92, 104, 131, 215, 241; rural, 95, 101, 103, 146, 206–7; urban, 103, 243; salaries of, 191f., 194, 227f., demand and supply of, 202, 227; population ratios of, 206–7; in family planning programme, 206–8, 265, 267n., 268; private practice, 227, 236; emigration of, 245; military requirements of, 363–4; *see also* Health sector; Medical sector.

Dorabji Tata Trust, 282–4.

Dravida Munetra Kazagan (DMK), 27.

Droughts, 7, 14, 85, 99, 146, 167, 351.
Dwaraka, 278f., 353.
Dysentery, 95n., 132, 138, 143, 237f.

Eastern Europe: imports from India, 296f., 311; aid to India, 328.
Economic and Political Weekly, 48.
Economic growth, 28, 36, 42, 54, 130, 188, 216f., 241, 338, 375; strategies for, 10, 87, 92, 144, 213–14, 231–35, 333, 335, 337; planned rates of, 14, 19–20, 175, 209, 340; role of education and health in, 187–235; population growth and, 255–6, 258–62, 340; aid strategies and, 335, 337.
Education, 42, 84, 90, 95, 101, 187f., 196–202, 214–226; rural, 103, 128–9; urban bias in, 104, 128, 132; in-plant training, 195, 210, 220–1, 243f., 249; social education, 196; girls' education, 198, 201–2; political pressures on, 198f., 215, 217f., 223–4, 244; quality of, 199–200, 217f., 223–4, 332; Constitutional Directive on, 200–1; 4DO objectives for, 200–217; enrolment policy, 200, 214f., 218–19, 225; wastage in, 200, 224–5, 244; caste and, 284.
Agricultural, 110, 117, 128f., 145, 147, 191, 203–6, 219f., 241; at primary level, 103, 128, 225; in universities, 103, 204, 216, 221; colleges, 117, 203; training centres, 122f.; polytechnics, 204.
Elementary, 103, 195, 197, 234; enrolment in, 133, 196, 201f., 214; political aim, 200f.; wastage in, 200f., 225; population in, 221.
Investment in, 7, 28, 190, 194–5, 196–9, 234, 244–9; priority of, 188, 193f., 248f.; import content of, 193, 219; States outlay on, 194–5, 219; in private sector, 195, 243; in elementary education, 196, 201; in secondary education, 196, 201; gestation lag in, 244.
Secondary, 197f.; enrolment in, 201f., 214f.; wastage in, 214; employment value of, 220.
Technical, 11, 20, 30, 218, 220; investment in, 190, 196; teachers in,

Education, *cont.*
221; language of instruction in, 224; high schools, 284; in armed forces, 364.
Vocational, 196f., 214, 219–20, 225; in agriculture, 205, 220; in industry, 220; in secondary schools, 220; teachers needs in, 221.
See also Schools; Teachers; Universities.
Education Commission, 103, 128, 147, 194n., 204, 218, 222f.
Electricity and power, 28, 71, 90 130n., 150, 155–6, 166, 173–83; working group on, 20; rural, 27, 87, 134, 178–9; non-importable nature of, 63, 74, 150; targets in, 68, 175; capital-output ratios in, 70; supply failures of, 118, 173–4, 331; generation of, 155, 169–70, 174f., 179–82, 183; transmission and distribution, 155, 170, 173f., 178f., 181; demand for, 155, 173–4, 176, 177f., 183.
Investment in, 21, 27, 150f., 165, 183; in 4DO, 153, 155, 170, 177, 182.
See also Coal; Nuclear power; Power stations.
Electric Power Survey, 176.
Electronics, 69, 371–3.
Élites, 53f., 288; urban, 131, 142, 271, 276.
Employment, 5, 7n., 10, 72, 77, 240; policies, 10, 84; agricultural, 79, 120, 133, 143, 147, 203–6, 230, 309–10; seasonal, 91, 144, 234, 240–1; urban, 104, 143, 230; rural, 137, 143f., 230; employment norms, 209; planning of, 229–35; profiles of, 247–8; caste and, 278–80, 284; *See also* Manpower planning; Underemployment; Unemployment.
Employment opportunities, 77, 144, 147, 200f., 214f., 245, 248; creation of, 10, 65, 77–9, 81, 229f., 231–5; creation in 4DO, 77–9, 81, 143–4, 229f.; in education, 215, 220.
Employee's State Insurance Scheme, 268.
Energy Survey Committee, 155, 173f., 179, 348.
Engineering Association of India, 32.

27

Engineering colleges and polytechnics, 192, 194, 209, 221, 224f., 244.
Engineering sector: working group on, 20; investment in, 69–74; capital-output ratios in, 70f., 90; excess capacity in, 71, 210; planning norms in, 209–214; output of, 209f., 297, 301; language of instruction in, 224; exports of, 294, 296, 298, 300, 319, 337, 348; prices in, 319.
Engineers, 91f., 101, 104, 216, 245; training of, 191–2, 196, 202, 364; graduate, 202, 209f., 216; requirements of, 202, 209, 212, 214, 363f.
English language, 224.
Enke, S., 258, 259n., 261.
European Economic Community (EEC): and the UK, 296, 320–1; imports from India by, 297; tariff on tea imports, 311; tobacco imports by, 312–13; sugar prices in, 313; tariffs on jute manufactures imports, 315; imports of cotton textiles, 317; import duty on leather and leather goods, 318–19.
European Free Trade Association (EFTA), 311.
Exchange-rates, 75, 304f., 310.
Exports, 42, 65f., 74, 81, 138, 167, 293f.; and industry, 10, 74, 376; promotion of, 12, 74, 298, 303, 320, 348; incentives for, 12, 307; opportunities for, 15, 64, 75, 304, 339; surplus, 40; and economic growth, 63, 348; traditional exports, 67, 294, 305–6, 337; past performance of, 74–5, 293f., 337; attitude to, 293, 308, 320; pattern and direction of, 294, 296–7; new and manufactured goods, 296–8, 300, 306, 319–21, 337, 347; of handicrafts, 298, 300; duties on, 305–6, 311–12, 314–15; subsidies for, 306; Government policy on, 309; quotas for, 309, 317n.; restrictions on, 312f., 321; diversion of, 318; aid and, 327, 329–30, 335; *see also* Five-Year Plans; Tariffs; and individual goods and sectors.
Export Promotion Councils, 320.
External Assistance, *see* Aid.

Family planning, 11, 32, 95n., 263, 266n.; investment in, 190f., 235–6, 241f., 262, 267n., 349; training and manpower requirements for, 196, 202, 207–8, 227f., 236, 265f., 268; doctors in, 207–8, 265, 267n., 268; nurses, 207–8; midwives in, 207, 265; IUCD's, 208, 263–7; sterilization, 208, 263–4, 266; medical auxiliaries, 208, 265, 268; in *4DO*, 263–7, 349; conventional contraceptives, 263–4, 266; cost and efficiency of techniques, 264–7; foreign assistance in, 268–9, 349; *see also* Birth-control; Birth rates; Fertility; Marriage.
Farmers, 98, 105, 108, 111f., 127f., 132f.; progressive farmers, 84, 135, 137, 140, 283; taxation of, 93, 116; Village level workers as, 122; literacy and, 226.
Incentives to, 13, 83, 102–3, 341; PL480 and, 343–6.
Big farmers, 83f., 122, 139f., 283.
bias to, 104–6, 131–2, 135, 142, 146; Small farmers, 117, 131, 133, 140; assets of, 105; credit and, 126f., 146–7.
Fecundity, 254.
Federalism, 5, 46, 119.
Fertilizers, 94, 101f., 142, 146, 161, 205; working groups on, 20; attitude of cultivators to, 54n., 141; production of, 63, 100, 298, 301–2, 339; manures, 100, 127, 146; prices of, 102; and IAAP, 110–12, 118, 145; use of, 117f., 156; imports of, 331, 339, 341.
Fertilizer industry, 68, 73, 214; *4DO* investment in, 70, 88, 337, 339; profitability of, 79.
Fertility, 251–3, 256, 262; marital, 252, 253n., 266, 270.
Finance Commission, 57.
Fishing and fisheries, 85n., 108.
Five-Year Plans, 35, 49, 55, 63, 120, 189, 196, 293.
1st Plan (1951–6), 32, 94: agriculture in, 98; exports in, 293f., 337; aid in, 327; imports in, 336f.
2nd Plan (1956–61), 19, 32, 74, 85n., 162; 'Plan Frame,' 8, 20, 25; strategy of, 11; and Perspective

Five-Year Plans, *cont.*
Planning Division, 25; price policies in, 102; employment generation in, 143; imports in, 293, 336, 345; exports in, 293f., 337; foreign exchange and, 294, 338; aid in, 327; agricultural production in, 345.
3rd Plan (1961–6), 21, 26, 74, 78, 189; performance of, 3, 5, 11, 19, 22, 32, 64, 67–68; agriculture in, 3, 6f., 37, 99f., 114, 125f., 340f., 345f.; aid in, 6n, 327, 335–6, 338; exports in, 12, 293f., 296f., 300, 320–1, 327; 'Dimensional Hypotheses' of, 20, 25; and Perspective Planning Division, 25; industry and, 67, 71, 76–77, 154, 340; foreign exchange in, 67, 294, 304, 338; employment generation in, 71–72, 78, 143, 230–31; imports in, 93n., 293, 336f., 341, 343, 345; irrigation in, 119, 161f.; overhead sector in, 153f., 161f., 170n., 178; national income in, 154; education in, 205, 364; savings in, 375.
4th Plan Draft Outline; 'Material and Financial Balances', 4, 7, 64n., 175; and Annual plans, 4, 60; strategies in, 5, 10–11, 20, 76, 87, 92, 213, 271–3, 335, 337; realism of, 5–7, 25, 32f., 40, 44–45, 64, 71–74, 95, 134, 188, 231; plan size, 11, 14–15, 21, 31, 45f.; growth-rate in, 14, 19–20, 175, 340; 'Perspectives of Development', 20; 'Notes on Perspectives, etc.', 20, 25; 'Size and Pattern of Investment in', 21; 'Resources, Outlays and Programmes, etc', 22; effect of devaluation on, 23, 25, 194, 335; agriculture in, 38–9, 83–149, 163–5, 302; national income in, 40, 73, 178, 260; industry in, 63–82, 132; consumption in, 66, 81; exports in, 66f., 75, 293f., 298f., 308, 320–1, 329, 339; imports, 67, 293, 297–300, 321; employment generation in, 77–9, 81, 143–4, 229–35; education in, 128, 196–226; overheads in, 149–72; energy in, 155, 169–70, 173–83; GNP in, 175; unemployment in, 230; social services sector

Five-Year Plans, *cont.*
in, 241; family planning and population in, 251–71, 349; social anthropology and, 271–89; caste proposals in, 272–4, 275f.; aid in, 298, 323–49.
5th Plan, 213, 247; income per capita by, 20; production in, 68; manpower requirements of, 200f.; employment generation in, 233; imports in, 338.
6th Plan: aid in, 67, 338; manpower requirements of, 200.
See also Investment; Planning; Planning Commission; Prices; and individual sectors.
Food, 106; *4DO* targets for, 8, 93, 97; production of, 76, 91n., 92, 101, 108, 122, 133, 179, 340; self-sufficiency aim in, 85; imports of, 91, 96, 219, 294, 302, 304–5, 341–6; demand for, 95, 101, 107; consumption per capita, 96; urban consumption of surplus, 104; processing industries, 232f.; *see also* Calories; Cereals; Milk and dairy products; Nutrition; Proteins.
Foodgrains, 11, 14, 101, 108, 117, 121, 144f., 335; *4DO* targets for, 95, 97, 144, 302; imports of, 95, 98, 102, 305, 335f., 341–6; income elasticity of demand for, 95–96, 106; production of, 96, 98f., 100, 102, 117, 123, 302, 341; demand for, 96, 98, 106, 346; stocks of, 112, 343–5; self-sufficiency aim in, 130, 144, 341–2; *see also* Cereals; Coarse grains; Rice; USA (PL480); Wheat.
Ford Foundation (Report), 37, 112.
Foreign exchange, 93, 100, 122, 144, 323f.; scarcities of, 7, 13, 89n, 130, 150, 166, 211; earnings and reserves, 10, 75, 303, 313; component in domestic investment, 12, 90, 169, 193–4, 219, 234, 294, 353, 359, 371, 374–5; development constraint of, 12, 67, 75, 81, 146; price of, 75, 193, 232; restricted access to, 151, 173, 181; *4DO* needs of, 299f.; allocation of available, 304f.; aid and, 323, 335, 337; minimization strategies of,

Foreign exchange, *cont.*
335, 337; and defence, 353, 359, 371, 374–5.
Foreign policy, 34, 52, 351, 356–8, 362f., 368n.
Foreign trade, *see* Balance of trade; Exports; Imports.
Forestry, 85n., 108; labour co-operatives, 39.
Forum for Free Enterprise, 33.
France, 324n., 328, 359, 370; *commissions de modernisation*, 24; tariff on jute manufactures, 315.
Freight, 153–5, 159; rail, 153–5, 158, 168–9; road, 155, 158, 160; rates, 168–9.
Fruits and vegetables, 296, 298, 300.
Fuels, commercial, 175.

Gadgil, D. R., 46–47, 50n, 60n.
Galbraith, J. K., 369.
Gandhi, Indira, 31, 50n.
Gandhi, Mahatma, 132.
General Agreement on Tariffs and Trade (GATT), 294n., 317; *see also* Kennedy Round.
General Election (1967), 34, 48; and effects on planning, 51–61; *see also* Congress Party; Politics.
Germany, Federal Republic: import tariffs, 312, 315, 317n.; aid to India, 324, 326, 328, 339.
Goa, 297.
Gokhale Institute (Poona), 117.
Gorwala, A. D., 36, 37n.
Government of India, 48, 55n., 194, 286; and *4DO* formulation, 3, 20f., 31, 45, 49, 51; revenue and budgets of, 32, 193; and foreign trade, 40, 309, 320; and Planning Commission, 47, 50f., 56; fiscal and social policies of, 76, 267; and agriculture, 91, 102–3, 137, 343–4; employment and manpower, 103, 228, 280, 363; overhead expenditure of, 158, 165; social and political objectives of, 188, 242; and free education, 200; medical services and policy of, 206, 227, 235f.; language policy of, 223–4; family planning policy, 253, 261, 267; aid and, 323, 330, 338, 343f.; nuclear defence policy of, 368.
Cabinet of, 19, 21, 45, 49.

Government of India, *cont.*
Parliament, 21f., 141, 267n., 303, 366n., 374n.
Prime Minister of, 4, 21f., 31, 46, 50; *see also* Administration; Lok Sabha; *Panchayat; Panchayat Samiti;* Planning Commission; Politics; States; States and Centre.
Graduates, 202, 218, 220; urban migration of, 142; agricultural, 202–5, 215, 228, 241, 243; engineering, 202, 209f., 216; unemployment of, 215, 216n., 217.
Gram Sevaks, see Village Level Workers.
Groundnuts, 312.
Gujerat, 31; co-operative credit in, 127; castes and co-operatives in, 272; Patidar castes in, 275; social change in, 278–85; roads in, 366.

Hanumān, 280.
Harayana, 55.
Harrison, Selig., 51, 53.
Health sector, 145, 187f., 215, 235–41; primary health centres in, 87, 228, 235, 239; capital-output ratio in, 90; and agricultural productivity, 129, 239; priority of, 188, 193f., 234; standards in, 188, 237; salaries in, 191f., 227f., 236; imports in, 194; manpower requirements in, 202, 205, 207, 214, 236; policy aims and conflicts, 236–41.
Investment in, 190f., 207, 221–2, 234, 247; current expenditure in, 27, 192f., 207, 236; in *4DO*, 95n., 188, 222, 236–41; capital in, 193; in private sector, 195; States' outlay on, 194–5.
See also Doctors; Family planning; Medical sector.
High Yielding Varieties Programme (HYVP), 203.
Hinduism, 109, 137, 284.
Hong Kong, 316, 318, 320.
Hopper, D., 112, 117.
Horticulture, 282.
Hospitals: investment in, 194, 235f., 242; district, 228.
Housing and construction sector, 68, 73, 76; annual plan allocations, 28,

Housing, *cont.*
63; in *4DO*, 73f., 191; village and rural housing, 88, 228; employment generation in, 230; costs in, 232; private investment in, 258; caste segregation in, 275, 279–80, 286.

Import and Export Policy Committee, 316n.
Imports, 40, 65f., 75, 150, 211, 293f., 313; bottlenecks, 10, 331; development imports, 12, 323; of raw materials, 12, 91, 298f., 306, 316n., 331, 337; maintenance imports, 13, 75, 211, 298–9, 304f., 316, 331; component in Centre-State expenditure, 30; projected in *4DO*, 67, 293, 297–300, 321; prices of, 87, 90, 304f., 319; of food and foodgrains, 91, 95f., 98, 102, 219, 294, 302, 304f., 335f., 341–6; industrial, 95; restrictions and controls on, 182, 302f., 307, 332; of capital goods, 193, 213; of foreign technology and knowhow, 213, 235; of manpower, 213; licences, 293; quotas, 294; project imports, 299, 304; subsidies for, 314; aid and, 323f., 330f.; of weapons and defence requirements, 359–60; *see also* Foreign exchange; USA (PL480).
Import substitution, 15, 74, 212, 293, 303, 321; policy of, 12, 67, 299, 337; of capital goods, 68, 72, 75, 337; aid and, 335f.; in defence production, 359, 365, 373.
Incentives: monetary and fiscal, 5, 12, 15, 104, 158–9, 162, 228; in agriculture, 15, 101–4, 107, 111, 127, 130f., 134, 144, 146, 343–6; in family planning programme, 267.
Income elasticity of demand: for foodgrains, 96, 106–7, 146f.; for milk, 146; for tea, 311.
Incomes, 25, 76, 106, 237f., 249; income-savings ratio, 3, 10, 92, 139; distribution of, 8, 13, 19, 76f., 104, 107, 117, 262; per capita, 20, 25, 96, 133, 154, 196, 222, 255f., 270; industrial generation of, 63, 65; urban, 101, 103, 106, 146; incomes

Incomes, *cont.*
policy, 241; *see also* National income; Wages and salaries.
India, Govt, *see* Government of India.
Indian Administration Service (IAS), 103.
Indo-British Trade Agreement (1939), 316.
Indo-Pakistan War (1965), *see* Pakistan.
Industrial Policy Resolution (1956), 35.
Industrial training institutes, 192, 195, 209.
Industrialization: policy of, 64, 80, 82, 212, 373; and castes, 272f.; imports and, 293.
Industrial sector: capacity utilization in, 7, 19, 23, 71f., 210, 212, 231, 337; bottlenecks in, 10, 74; prices in, 60, 72, 75, 90n.; in *4DO*, 63–82, 132, 340; in Third Plan, 67, 71, 73, 76, 154, 340; value-added in, 69, 71–2, 77, 90n.; capital-output ratios in, 70–73, 90, 92–93; wages and salaries in, 72, 78f., 92f., 223; profits in, 77, 79f., 93, 307; labour and labour force in, 84, 130, 143, 230, 238; priority and emphasis on, 92, 132; urban industry, 104, 340f.; and agriculture, 106, 146, 337; underemployment in, 210, 233–4; manpower planning in, 208–214; choice of techniques in, 231–5; export targets of, 299f.; civil sector and defence production, 366–73.
Production, 23, 63, 132, 154, 182, 299, 301, 339–40; of consumer goods, 63, 69f., 74, 76, 81; of capital goods, 68, 70, 74; of intermediate goods, 69–71; targets, 81, 231, 300, 365–6, 371–2; and defence needs, 366–7, 368f.
Village and small scale: (labour), capital-output ratios in, 10; Centre-State outlays on, 21, 30; *4DO* proposals on, 39, 320; electricity and, 179; caste and, 273f., 277–85.
Heavy industry, 11, 75, 81, 192f.
See also Engineering sector; Investment; Location of industry;

Industrial sector, *cont.*
Machine tools industry; Private sector; Public sector; Vehicle industry.
Indus Waters Scheme, 332.
Infant mortality, 237f., 253, 254n.
Inflation, 7, 32f., 80, 87, 219, 244, 304, 338.
Infrastructure, *see* Overhead sector.
Intensive Agricultural Areas Programme (IAAP), 99, 100f., 128, 132, 141, 144; success of, 37, 84, 117; selection and location of, 84, 105, 108, 110f., 118–20, 125, 136; implementation and administration of, 84, 110, 120–3, 145, 203; cultivators. use of, 106, 109–18, 127; spill-off from, 127.
Intensive Agricultural District Programme (IADP), 37, 113, 226; coverage and basis of, 110, 112, 118, 125; performance of, 118f., 125, 145; manning patterns of, 203.
Interest rates, 134, 139, 142; of aid, 67, 325f., 330f.; in rural sector, 126, 137; in overhead sector, 151, 170, 182.
Intermediate goods, 63, 71f.; prices of, 72f., 75; in agriculture, 100, 146, 337; in defence sector, 368.
International Bank for Reconstruction and Development (IBRD), 13, 324, 326, 330; Bell Mission of, 304–5, 307; International Development Association (IDA), 324n., 325f.; Consortium of, 342.
International Monetary Fund (IMF), 329.
Investment, 7f., 15, 20, 25, 76, 85, 130, 189, 213, 245, 249, 336; criteria for, 7, 9–10, 89, 152, 165, 242–3; balance of public and private, 8, 151, 213–14; foreign exchange component of, 12, 90, 169, 193–4, 219, 234, 294, 353, 359, 371, 374–5; in organized sector, 63, 67, 77, 79, 87, 142, 153; employment generating effects of, 65, 229–35; gestation lag of, 68f., 73, 92, 151, 156, 161, 183, 244, 246; absorptive capacity for, 89, 94, 337; company, 93; lumpiness of, 150; investment-employment

Investment, *cont.*
norms, 230–1; composition of, 257; Joint UK-Indian, 348.
1st Plan: agriculture, 86, 94; health, 190; education, 190, 197.
2nd Plan, 85; agriculture, 7f., 85f.; in overheads, 87n., 162; in housing, 88; in education, 197.
3rd Plan, 20, 28, 39n., 69, 73, 337, 343; in agriculture, 37, 39n., 85–87, 94, 99, 101, 104, 107f., 114, 342; in industry, 87n, 88; in education, 87, 122, 190, 194, 197, 204f., 364; in overheads, 87, 119, 152f., 156, 158, 161, 166, 170, 173–5, 178; in housing, 88; in health, 190, 194; foreign investment during, 307.
4th Draft Plan, 20, 23, 40, 64, 66, 69–70, 80, 153–5, 157, 166, 178–9, 190, 193, 231–42, 335; in industry, 63f., 70, 87n., 88; in agriculture, 70, 77, 83, 85f., 94, 97, 107f., 120, 128, 142, 144, 342; fertilizer industry, 70, 88, 337, 339, in overheads, 70, 119, 149, 152–4, 161f., 164, 166, 170, 177, 182, 336.; in housing, 88; in health, 95n., 187f., 191, 207, 234–5; in power, 153, 155, 170, 177, 182; in education, 189, 190, 191, 196, 198f., 225; in family planning, 191, 207–8, 235, 349.
Centre-State, 21, 28, 30, 114, 142, 165.
Foreign investment, 8, 10, 13, 21, 93, 213–4, 307–8, 320, 333, 335, 341.
Import content of, 75, 95, 150, 294; in agriculture, 87, 90, 144, 337; in education, 193, 219.
Rate of return on, 5, 7, 14, 167, 187f., 191f., 216, 228, 232f., 247f.; at village level, 8; to education, 9, 147, 187f., 198, 200f., 215f., 217, 223f., 229, 234f., 241–9; in overhead sector, 9, 151, 165–72; in family planning, 11, 238, 241, 251–63; in agriculture, 63, 83f., 93f., 101, 105, 107, 118, 120, 145, 241; in public sector, 80, 128, 165–72, 179; in private sector, 101, 167–8, 198, 202; in irrigation, 145, 162, 170–1, 233–4;

Investment, *cont.*
in health, 146, 187f., 229, 234, 236–41; criteria for raising, 165–6; targets for in *4DO*, 166; in railway sector, 166–8; in road transport, 167; in electricity and power, 169–70, 179–80, in human capital, 191f., 241; to literacy improvement, 226; and aid, 330.
See also Aid; Capital; Capital-output ratios; Current expenditure; Private & Public sectors; Savings.
Iron, 70, 168n.; *4DO* growth of, 68, 298.
Iron ore, 294, 296, 298, 300, 337.
Iron and Steel: investment in, 70–71; exports of, 294, 296, 300; imports of, 298; aid and, 334.
Irrigation, 14, 27, 70, 85n., 88, 105, 142, 145, 151, 179; utilization of capacity in, 23, 156, 160f., 170; charges for, 41, 162, 170–1; dams, 63, 91, 94, 134, 143n., 144; major irrigation, 85, 160f.; canals, 91; minor, 91, 108, 151, 156; area under, 100, 156, 161; IAAP & IADP and, 111f., 145, 171; need for co-ordination in, 157, 161f.; administration of, 160f.; medium irrigation, 160; field channels in, 161, 163, 233; electricity and, 180f.; tanks and, 234.
Investment in, 119, 145, 151, 153, 337; Centre-State outlays on, 21, 30; on major, 85, 153, 156, 160–3; rate of return to, 145, 162, 170–1, 234; on minor, 151, 153, 156, 161–3, 172, 234; on medium, 156.
See also Agriculture; Farmers; Fertilizers; IAAP; IADP; Wells, etc.

Jajmani system, 274.
Jammu and Kashmir, *see* Kashmir.
Japan, 317, 320, 324n., 359.
Johnson, Lyndon, 342.
Jute, 168n.; production of, 97, 302, 313f., 321; share prices of, 305; imports of, 313f.; jute control (UK), 315.
Manufactures: exports of, 337; effects of devaluation on, 12, 306, 313–16; in 3rd Plan, 294, 296, 300; proposed

Jute, *cont.*
in *4DO*, 298, 300, 339; duties levied on, 305n., 314.
Mills, 313f.

Kashmir, Jammu and, 270; social services in, 30; household land-holdings in, 125; hostilities in, 324, 351, 353; desired political settlement in, 362–3.
Kennedy Round, 319.
Kerala, 58, 132, 270; dry-milch cow ratio in, 109; seed prices in, 118; household land holdings in, 125–6; utilization of irrigation in, 161.
'Kipping aid', 323, 325, 331.
Krishnaswami, K. S., 48.

Labour, 105, 152, 210f.; industrial, 84, 130, 143, 237; unskilled, 91, 192, 211, 232f., 239f., 274, 278; skilled 91, 226, 238, 264; productivity of, 93, 104, 107, 129, 210–13, 229f., 237, 239, 255–6; agricultural, 99–100, 105f., 123, 125, 129, 146, 238, 274; surplus, 129, 143, 231, 280; seasonal, 144, 240, 275; shift-working of, 170, 180, 210; price of, 193, 232; direction of, 228; clerical, 233; castes and, 274;
See also Employment; Manpower planning; Unemployment; Wages & salaries.
Labour force, 143, 225, 262f.; industrial, 130, 237; quality of, 199; participation rates in, 202, 232; women in, 202, 256; education of, 210, 226, 248; urban, 229, 239f.; size of, 229, 240, 256, 258n., 261; health of, 239–41.
Labour-intensive production, 9, 39, 231–5, 358.
Labour-investment norms, 230, 248.
Labour market, 206, 226–9, 241, 245f., 248; *see also* Manpower planning.
Labour-output ratios, 10n., 211.
Land, 98f., 112f., 146; dry, 99; cultivated area, 99–100, 110, 115, 124, 345; labour per acre, 99, 105–6, 123, 125; irrigated, 100, 161–3; IAAP inputs to, 105–6, 110f.; ownership of, 106, 124, 126, 272, 286f.; productivity of, 123, 125;

Land, *cont.*
ceilings on ownership, 124, 135; caste ownership of, 275.
Landlords, 125f., 131, 135, 137, 142.
Land reform, 84, 110–11, 123–6, 134, 142, 145, 333, 341; fragmentation and, 115, 124–5, 136, 138; scope and objectives for, 123–4; evasion of, 124f.; consolidation, 125f., 131, 138, 146, 163.
Land tenancy, 123–6, 127, 131, 134f., 137; rents in, 105, 115, 123–5, 134f., 137, 141, 163; and rural credit, 127.
Language problem, 26, 223–4.
Latin America, 308.
Lawyers, 103, 131, 199.
Leather and leather goods, 300, 318–19.
Literacy, 188; rural, 120, 226; child, 200; adult, 225–6; investment in, 226.
Location of industry, 9, 30–31; input costs and, 166; transport charges and, 168; in UK, 347.
Locomotives and rolling stock, 155, 167–8, 173.
Lohana caste, 278f.
Lok Sabha, 43; Cabinet, 19, 21, 45, 49; Estimates Committee of, 47.

Machinery: *4DO* targets, 68; capital-output ratios in, 70, 72; investment in, 70, 242; excess capacity in, 71; production of, 74; import duty on, 303.
Machine-tools sector, 76, 192, 212, 323; production in, 69, 301f.; labour productivity in, 211.
Madhya Pradesh, 270; rents in, 106; Central Co-operative Bank of, 106.
Madras, 31, 58, 181; planning demands of, 27; rural credit in, 106; dry-milch cow ratio in, 109; household land holdings in, 125f.; abolition of land revenue in, 139; utilization of irrigation in, 161; water-rates in, 171.
Mahalanobis, P. C., 43, 47n., 50n., 92; 'Plan Frame' (1955), 8, 20, 25.
Maharashtra, 29f., 48, 132; Chief Minister's demands, 29–30; millet village experiences in, 116, 283n.;

Maharashtra, *cont.*
co-operative credit in, 127; cultivator castes in, 136; rural radio in, 165; family planning programme in, 267n.
Mahbub ul Haq, 324.
Malaria, 96, 133f., 237f., 254n.
Management, 9, 212, 234, 239; in public sector, 151, 165.
Manganese ore, 300.
Mann, J. S., 345–6.
Manning patterns, 202, 209f., 213.
Manpower, 83; demand for, 198, 234, 246; requirements of, 199, 202, 210–14, 215–17, 220, 231, 234f.; forecasting, 202, 210–14, 229, 241–9. Planning of, 8, 202–34, 241–9; in agriculture, 203–6, 214; in medical sector, 206–7, 214; in family planning, 207–8; in industry, 208–214; at State level, 219.
See also Employment opportunities; Labour.
Manure, 127; organic, 100; green, 100, 146.
Marketing: in agriculture, 161, 163; of tea, 312; disruptive, 317; of exports, 320; matching markets, 347; of arms, 356, 359.
Marriage: dowries, 135; ages at, 252f., 264f.; Government policies on, 253, 265, 268; birth-rates and, 253–4, 264f.; caste and, 273.
Meat, 108, 364.
Medical sector: students in, 95n., 216, 227; education and training in, 195–6, 198, 201, 206–7, 220, 227, 226, 241, 265; research in, 196, 207 236; planning norms in, 206–7; investment in, 207–8, 235; teaching staff for, 215, 221.
Mehta, Asoka, 47, 49, 85n.
Metal industries, 70, 323.
Migration: rural-urban, 104, 128, 131, 143, 232; caste and, 281.
Milk and dairy products, 96, 107n., 108f., 142, 146, 364.
Millet, 108.
Minerals: production, 299; exports, 300.
Minerals and Metals Trading Corporation, 320.
Minhas, B. S., 119.

Mining and mines, 68, 90, 153, 178.
Mithapur, 278f.
Moneylenders, 38, 126f., 131, 137, 141, 226; *see also* Rural credit.
Monsoons, 6, 89n., 94, 98, 102, 114, 118, 165, 304, 313.
Montagu-Chelmsford Reforms, 53.
Mysore, 27, 270; dry-milch cow ratio in, 109; utilization of irrigation in, 161.

Nagaland, 30.
Nag Chaudhuri, Dr B. D., 50n.
Nagpur Resolution, 38.
Naik, V. P., 29, 30.
Nanda, Gulzarilal: 47.
National Council for Applied Economic Research (NCAER), 163n., 171n.
National Development Council (NDC), 19, 21, 24, 32, 48f., 51; committees of, 21f., 48; State's claims at meetings, 27, 29f.; role in plan formulation, 55n., 56.
National income, 195, 335; past growth of, 6, 154, 178; proposed *4DO* growth of, 40, 73, 178, 260; sectoral origins of, 68.
Gross domestic product, 65–66.
GNP: *4DO* growth of, 175; defence expenditure and, 362–3, 374; research and development expenditure and, 373.
Net domestic product, 68, 340.
National Planning Council (NPC), 22, 24.
National Sample Survey, 107n.
Navy: submarines, 359; frigates, 360, 370; expenditure on, 362; equipment of, 373.
Nehru, Jawaharlal, 42, 92; death of, 26, 37.
Nickel, 303.
Night soil, 100.
Nijalingappa, S., 27, 30.
Non-ferrous metals, 298, 303.
Nuclear defence capability, 368n.
Nuclear power, 177, 180–2.
Nutrition, 89n., 96, 97, 104, 107–8, 135, 146; rates of return to improved, 9, 129, 145; policies, 84; *see also* Protein.
Nurses, 202, 206, 208; salaries of, 191.

Organization for Economic Co-operation & Development (OECD.), 7n., 259n., 332.
Oil, 166, 168; supply difficulties, 173; requirements, 175; foreign-exchange constraint on, 181.
Organized sector, *see* Industry.
Overhead sector, 33, 149–72, 173; efficiency in, 9; prices in, 9, 152, 165–72; nature of, 149–52; non-importable nature of, 150f.; capacity in, 151f.; cost-benefit analysis in, 152, 159, 171; Investment in: risk asymmetry of, 14, 150, 152, 182–3, 215–17; pattern of in *4DO*, 149, 152, 156; allocation within, 149, 257; criteria for, 152; and agricultural development, 156f., 163–5.
Private sector in, 149, 151, 158–9.
See also Electricity; Irrigation; Power; Railways; Roads; Transport.

Pakistan, 102, 308, 351f.; aid per capita, 6n., 332; 2nd Plan of, 15; tubewells in, 87, 152; partition, 98, 313; jute production in, 313; jute exports of, 314f.; cotton textile exports, 316; cotton mills in, 318; aid and import prices, 324; defence aid, 352n., 353; army of, 352, 354, 356; defence expenditure, 352, 363; navy of, 353, 356, 360.
War with India (1965), 26, 294, 303–4, 351f.; economics of settlement, 12, 361, 362–3; effects on 4th Indian Plan, 22, 25; suspension of aid following, 22, 304, 324, 351.
Panchayat, 35f.; and economic development, 36; political role of, 36f.; and Community Projects, 37, 286; in *4DO*, 39, 286; outlays on, 107–8; BDOs and, 121; caste domination in, 135–6, 275, 286–8; and village power-structure, 135, 286–8; and elementary education, 195; VLWs and, 204–5; *see also* Administration; Politics; Villages.
Panchayat Samiti, 37.
Pant, P., 48, 50; 'Dimensional Hypotheses' of, 20, 25.
Parliament, *see* Government of India.

Patidar caste, 275, 284n.
Peasants, 38, 84, 101, 112f., 141f., 275, 288; behaviour of, 112–16, 144; survival algorithms of, 116–17, 133–4, 140, 144, 283.
Perspective plans, 49, 203.
Pest control, 118.
Pesticides, 70, 100, 111, 205.
Petroleum, 298, 365.
Pipelines, 157.
PL 480, *see* USA.
Planners, 66, 108, 143, 271f., 321; questions facing, 19; nature of, 25, 40, 95, 271–3; pressures on, 26–35; criticism of, 83–4, 188; exhortations by, 40–43, 287; remoteness and urban bias of, 84, 130f., 134f., 142, 271, 276, 346; and IAAP, 112; ideology of, 271–3; changes in conceptual framework of, 276–8; social anthropology and, 283, 288; and exports, 321; *see also* Five-Year Plans; Planning; Planning Commission.
Planning in India, 3, 6f., 10, 84; philosophy and assumptions of, 5, 14, 19, 44, 271, 375; projections of, 5, 15, 44; politics and, 6, 40–44, 51–60; 'planning from below', 15, 20, 35; objectives of, 19, 338, 375; attitudes towards, 26, 44–45; pressures on, 26–29; bargaining processes in, 26–27, 54–59; machinery and implementation of, 32–33, 50f., 56, 120–3, 375; causes of crisis in, 35; orthodoxies of, 35–45; efficiency and realism of, 43, 52, 58; likely changes in, 55–60; targets in agricultural, 95–101; of manpower, 202–34, 241–9; for full employment, 229–35; village power and attitudes to planning, 285–8; UK planning and, 346; long-term planning, 348; and defence, 351–77.
Macro-economic planning, 7f., 120, 274f.; failures in, 331.
Micro-economic planning, 8, 14; need for, 8–9, 142; lack of, 9–12, 120, 134; *see also* Five-Year Plans; Planners; Planning Commission.
Planning Commission: power and prestige of, 4, 45–49; plan formula-

Planning Commission, *cont.*
tion, 19, 20f., 31–39, 46, 50n.; and NPC, 22; negotiation with States, 31f., 56–59; scepticism about, 34–44; political role of, 36, 46; Nehru and, 42–43, 47, 55; membership of, 43, 45–51; criticism of, 45f., 273–4, 286; and Government structure, 45–51; ARC report on, 48; proposed changes in, 48–51, 55–56; and industry, 64, 72, 81; and agriculture, 97, 120, 149; and overheads, 149, 154f., 159; and health, 189; and education, 189, 204, 222; and manpower planning, 202, 204, 209, 215f., 231; and social anthropology, 272f., 276, 278, 286.
Committee for Social Science Research, 289.
Perspective Planning Division (PPD), 4, 20, 348; 'Material and Financial Balances' of, 4, 7, 64n., 175; in plan formulation, 25, 41–42; suspicion of, 25; reputation of, 48; sectoral growth estimates of, 67; perspective plans of, 202.
Programme Evaluation Organization (PEO), 36.
Public Opinion Analysis Unit, 32.
Politics and politicians, 11, 19–60, 152, 226, 288, 307; fears of Union disintegration, 6, 51–53, 60, 376; leadership, 54; stability of non-Congress States, 58–60; pressure on pricing policies, 80, 171; and rural big-farmer bias, 104, 135–42; pressure in IAAP–IADP selection, 119–20; urban pressures on, 131, 134, 146; *4DO* objectives, 188; pressure on education from, 197f., 215, 218–19, 223f.; attacks on aid by, 333; and defence policy, 351–77; *see also* Administration; Government of India; *Panchayat*; States; State and Centre; Universities.
Population, 115f., 130, 154, 251f., 269, 332; growth of, 11, 96, 174, 251f., 268f., 277, 340; rural, 38, 95, 133, 136, 178, 206–7, 252; urban, 96, 103, 143, 232, 252; age-structure of, 96, 196, 256, 262, 269; sex-ratios of, 104, 143, 252; of working age, 188, 255f.; young people in, 196; child

Population, *cont.*
    population, 197, 255, 263; life
    expectation of, 236–8; control of,
    251, 349; dependency ratio, 257;
    Muslim, 262; *see also* Birth-control;
    Birth-rate; Death-rate; Family
    planning; Fecundity; Fertility.
Ports and harbours, 153, 160, 165,
    171, 334.
Power, *see* Electricity.
Power stations, 174; thermal, 167,
    180–1; hydro, 175, 177, 180–1;
    nuclear, 177, 180–2.
Power structure, 9; village level, 104,
    126, 135f., 286–8; urban, 131;
    rural, 135, 142.
Praja Socialist Party, 47.
Press: reactions to *4DO*, 32.
Price elasticity of demand: for
    electricity, 180; for tea, 309, 311;
    for engineering exports, 319.
Prices, 189, 193, 249, 308; food, 13, 91,
    93, 101f., 107, 123, 142, 304; rise
    in, 31, 34, 40, 244, 304, 306, 325,
    344; in industry, 60, 72, 75, 90n.;
    and marginal costs, 75; of elec-
    tricity, 75, 79–80, 156, 167, 169–70,
    179–80; shadow prices, 87, 89n,.
    90, 179, 232–5, 238, 243; whole-
    sale, 87n., 90n., 164n., 189, 305,
    344–6; farm prices, 87n., 101f.,
    145, 341; of manufactured goods,
    102f., 123, 131, 305; retail, 102,
    304f.; coarse grains, 106, 146;
    procurement prices, 123, 127; food-
    grain, 131; in public enterprises,
    167f.; share prices, 305; tea,
    309f.; cashew nuts, 312; sugar, 313;
    raw jute, 314; jute manufactures,
    315; cotton textiles, 317; cereals,
    343–6.
Pricing policies: in industry, 79–81;
    in agriculture, 102, 123, 127, 305;
    in overhead sectors, 152, 166; in
    electricity, 156, 179–80; in irriga-
    tion, 162, 170–1.
Private sector, 34; profits in, 9;
    exports of, 12; incentives in, 15;
    and 4th Plan formulation, 24;
    schools in, 42; consumption in,
    65f., 78, 93, 127; production of
    intermediate goods in, 72, 273;
    savings in, 93, 151, 333; road

Private sector, *cont.*
    transport in, 152, 158f., 166, 310n.;
    electricity in, 174; education in,
    195, 243; labour productivity in,
    213; medical practice in, 227;
    shadow prices in, 232; vehicle
    production in, 365.
Investment in, 15, 24, 85, 93; foreign
    inflows of, 8, 10, 13, 21, 213–14,
    320, 333, 335; in *4DO*, 70, 85, 87,
    258; in agriculture, 70, 85, 87, 101,
    106, 112, 130f., 144f.; in overheads,
    70, 149, 151, 158–9; in 3rd Plan, 85,
    101; rate of return to, 101, 167–8;
    in health, 195; in education, 195,
    213, 243–4; in housing and con-
    struction, 258.
Profits: private sector, 9; industrial,
    77, 79f., 93, 307; agricultural, 93,
    112, 139; in public sector, 166,
    336; in railways, 167f.
Profit-wage ratios, 10f., 93.
Programme Evaluation Organization
    (PEO), 36.
Proteins, 97, 101, 104, 107f., 138;
    cattle filtration of, 109, 141.
Public opinion: of *4DO*, 32, 34, 37,
    41–42, 44; of family planning
    programme, 265.
Public sector, 189, 229; consumption
    in, 8, 65; utilization of capacity in,
    40; costs in, 40, 80; savings in, 63;
    prices in, 79–80, 167f.; profits in,
    79, 166, 336; rate of return on
    investment in, 80, 128, 165–72, 179;
    labour productivity in, 213; salaries
    in, 223; shadow prices in, 232;
    wage and salary differentials in, 245;
    see also individual sectors; In-
    vestment &c.
Punjab, 30, 270; utilization of irriga-
    tion in, 161; use of tanks in, 356.

Quality Control Inspection Scheme,
    320.

Radio and broadcasting, 157, 171
    372; rural, 133, 165.
Rainfall, 111f., 123, 177.
Railways, 11, 63, 68, 71, 150; employ-
    ment and output in, 72; profit-
    ability of, 79, 166–8; freight
    carried by, 153–5; 158n., 168–9,

Railways, *cont.*
181; passengers on, 154, 168–9; modernization and equipment on, 154–5, 157n., 158, 169; operating efficiency of, 155, 157, 169; price policies of, 167–9; defence use of, 365–6.
Investment in; 70, 73, 165, 167f.; risk asymmetry in, 14; capital-output ratios in, 70, 72; in *4DO*, 153–5, 157, 166; aid and, 334.
Railways, Ministry of, 157, 159.
Rajasthan, 35, 52, 55, 270; *Panchayati raj* in, 36n., 135; irrigation utilization in, 161; water-rates in, 162n.; family planning programme in, 267n.; roads in, 366.
Rao, V. K. R. V., 48, 222.
Rao Committee on Utilization of External Assistance, 330–1.
Rates of return on investment, *see* Investment.
Raw materials: imports of, 12, 91, 298f., 306, 316, 331, 337.
Reddiar, V. V., 30.
Regions: development balance of, 5; pressure on planners from, 26f.; agricultural investment concentration in, 111f.; political tensions in, 152; electricity reorganization in, 155, 176–8; transport groupings in, 159; dispersal to, 168; Regional Engineering Colleges, 198; educational shortages in, 217; teachers' salaries in, 223; language problem in, 223–4; wage differences between, 245; social organization, 274.
Backward regions and Hill Areas, 12; NDC committee on, 21; transport and, 158; investment in, 191; use of army in, 361.
Research and development, 210, 213f.; in military sector, 368, 373.
Rice, 7n., 132, 142, 345; production of, 97, 107; income elasticity of demand for, 96, 146; price of, 106; yields of, 117; new varieties of, 118.
Roads, 11, 171; village approach roads, 27, 133, 156, 164; investment in, 156, 158, 336; rural roads, 163–5; per cultivated acre, 164; military, 352f., 365, 374.

Rural credit, 94, 122, 126–8, 146, 161, 163, 282f., 343; big farmer bias in, 104, 106, 146; agricultural debt, 105, 126; security for, 106, 127; crop loans for, 110, 137, 146; shortages of, 118; co-operative, 126–8; *see also* Moneylenders.
Rural development: water supplies, 27, 129, 228, 235, 237; housing and construction, 27, 233–5; rural decentralization, 36, 232, 273; rural-urban inequalities, 84, 104, 131, 142, 340; health, 92, 95, 227–8, 240; administration and services, 103, 131; rural institutions, 135–40; labour exchanges, 137; rural electrification, 156, 178–9; broadcasting, 133, 165; education, 201, 223, 243.
Rural insurance, 94; for crops, 110–11, 123, 127, 137, 140f.

Sadiq, G. M., 30.
Savings, 3, 14, 42; ratio, 3, 11, 259, 260n., 340; requirements, 8; domestic, 11, 13, 333, 335, 338f., 375; attitudes to, 42, 137f.; and economic growth, 45, 63, 77, 255; in public sector, 63; household, 79, 93, 257; propensity to save, 89n., 257–8; in private sector, 93, 151, 333; in agriculture, 104f.; and taxation, 139; and aid requirements, 335–8.
Schools, 171, 221; meals in, 27, 225; uniforms, 27; private, 42; investment in, 196, 243; population of, 200; agricultural, 204; and agricultural operations, 225; *see also* Education.
Schultz, T. W., 112.
Scientists, 213, 220, 245.
Seeds, 98f., 105, 116, 127, 161; improved seeds programme, 11, 54n., 94, 99f., 107, 110–12, 117, 128, 145, 282; planned expansion of, 100, 108, 118; criticisms of, 109, 117; prices, 119.
Sen, S. R., 43, 48.
Sewing machines, 301, 303, 319.
Shastri, Lal Bahadur, 21f.
Smallholders, 93, 104, 127, 142.

Smallpox, 237.
Social anthropology, 3, 271–89; and *4DO* 271–4, 289; village studies, 274, 289; models as planning guides, 276–7; links with planners, 283, 285–6, 288–9; Western orientation of, 288.
Social Science Research Committee, 289.
Social security, 140; and fertility, 253.
Social services sector, 84; States' demands in, 27f.; population basis for, 30; in rural areas, 128, 178, 201; investment in, 188, 190–1, 245; priority of in *4DO*, 242; and population growth, 257; *see also* Education; Family planning; Health; Rural development.
Socialist pattern of development, 34f., 278.
Society and social change, 8, 252, 273, 376; and agricultural development, 133, 283; cleavage in, 271; social organization, 274–5, 333; caste *v.* class in, 277–8; in Gujerat, 278–85; rural status and, 283–4.
Soil conservation, 108, 110, 153, 156.
South East Asia Treaty Organization (SEATO), 356.
Srinivas, M. N., 274.
States, 105, 131, 139, 141, 202; Governments of, 4, 20f., 26, 56–60, 157, 194, 236, 267n., 363; election results in, 4, 29, 34, 48, 51f., 58–60; political pressures from on planners, 26–31, 46, 56, 59, 219; Chief Ministers of, 27f., 48–49, 59f.; Centrally sponsored development in, 28–29; use of Central resources by, 28, 57, 126, 219, 236; State plans, 29, 56, 59; big farmer bias in politics of, 104; agricultural production targets in, 118; land reform in, 124–6; co-operative credit in, 126; Parliaments of, 131; crop insurance in, 141; transport groupings of, 159; irrigation administration and politics, 161f., 171, 178; Committee of State Ministers on Irrigation, 162; rural road expenditure by, 164; Electricity Boards of, 174, 176f., 179f.; non-plan expenditure

States, *cont.*
by, 194–5, 219, 222, 243, 267n.; medical services of, 195, 227, 236f., 263; agricultural services, 204; administrative employment in, 230; *see also* Administration; States-Centre; and individual States.
States and Centre: plan allocations between, 21, 30, 104, 142, 165, 236; relative political strengths of, 29, 31, 48, 52–60, 219, 286; plan bargaining between, 56–60; relative current expenditure of, 194–5, 219, 236, 242; and *Panchayat* administration, 286.
Steel, 8, 72, 89n., 168n.; working group on, 20; production of, 68, 298, 301, 339, 371; price of, 75; shortages of, 93; imports of, 323, 339.
Steel plants, 150, 181, 371; investment in, 11, 73f.; capital-output ratios in, 70, 72, 90f.; profitability of, 79, 167.
Steel products, 154; exports of, 294, 337.
Subramanian, C., 112.
Subsidies: to agriculture, 102, 123, 132, 142; to overhead sector, 152, 158; to exports, 167; to rural employees, 227f.; for industrial training, 244; to jute mills, 314; for imports, 314.
Sugar, 146, 168n., 302; production of, 97, 101, 301f.; exports of, 296, 298, 300, 313.
Sukhadia, Mohan Lal, 35.
Swadeshi, 42, 138f.
Swatantra Party, 59.

Tanjore District, 105, 125, 287.
Tariffs, 74, 302, 305; on tea exports, 311–12; and EEC, 311, 320–1; on jute manufactures, 315–16; on leather, 318; preferences, 319; UK level of, 320–21.
Tariff Commission, 319.
Tata, J. R. D., 24, 32f.
Taxation, 5, 27, 30f., 42, 76, 79f., 93, 343; evasion of, 40, 138f.; land taxes, 41, 123, 139; income taxes, 57; corporation taxes, 57; of agriculture, 80f., 142; of farmers,

Taxation, *cont.*
93, 116; taxation system, 140, 267–8, 336; irrigation, 163; Government revenue from, 193, 335–6; and child allowances, 332.
Tea, 97; devaluation and exports, 12, 306, 310; production of, 101, 302, 309–10, 312, 321; exports, 294, 296, 298, 300, 308–12, 337, 339; share prices of, 305; duties, tariffs, and quotas on, 305n., 309, 311–12; plantations, 308; export prices of, 309, 312; consumption of, 310–12.
Teachers, 101, 103, 215f.; salaries of, 191f., 194f., 222–3, 228, 244; investment in training, 198f., 221f.; women, 201; demand for, 202, 221f. shortages of, 221, 225; *see also* Education; Manpower planning.
Technical Development, Directorate General of, 303.
Technicians, 92, 202, 209, 234; rural, 95; training of, 191f.
Technological change, 211, 230–1, 246f., 314; indigenous, 233–5; in defence, 376.
Television, 76, 165, 372.
Textiles, *see* Cotton textiles.
Thorium, 182.
Tibet: Chinese in, 352f., 357; Indo-Tibetan trade, 354.
Tinplate, 364.
Tobacco, 97, 275; exports of, 296, 298, 300, 312; output and targets, 302; export duties on, 305n.
Tractors: production of, 88, 301f., 365; factories, 91, 365.
Trade unions, 131, 134, 141.
Transport and communications, 68, 150, 176, 182, 334; working group on, 20; Centre-State outlays on, 21; long distance, 52; costs of, 74, 167, 181, 348; prices in, 75, 157, 167; profitability of, 79; rural, 109, 228; investment in, 90, 94, 152, 334; co-ordination of, 156–9, 331; demand for, 157; defence and, 365–6.
Air: civil, 153, 157, 165; fares of, 169; military, 352f., 372; agricultural, 372.

Transport communications, *cont.*
Road, 151, 156f., 159; private sector, 152, 158f., 166, 310n.; freight, 155, 160, 167; flexibility of, 158; buses, 160; rate of return to, 167.
Rail, *see* Railways.
See also Roads, Railways.
Transport, Min. of, 157, 159.
Transport Policy and Co-ordination, Committee on, 157n., 158f.
Trone, Solomon, 43.
Tuberculosis, 239.
Turkey, 312.

Underdeveloped countries: import substitution by, 74; population problems of, 252; demand for jute goods, 315; cotton textile exports by, 316–18.
Underemployment, 129f., 229f., 234; in industry, 209–10, 232–4; of educated people, 216–17, 229; in agriculture, 233, 240.
Unemployment, 229f., 232f., 248; rural, 95, 143, 147, 233–4, 240–1; urban, 131, 143; voluntary, 143, 147; educated, 216–17, 229, 246; seasonal, 240–1; population and, 256, 262, in tea plantations, 310; *see also* Employment; Labour; Labour force; Manpower planning.
United Arab Republic (UAR), 310, 358.
United Kingdom (UK), 182, 222, 268, 311, 319; economic planning in, 6f.; Min. of Overseas Development, 251n.; aid to India, 268, 323, 325f., 339; imports from India, 296f., 308, 311, 313, 315f., 348; investment in, 307, 347; National Institute of Economic and Social Research, 311; and the EEC, 320–1; joint planning possibilities with India, 346–9; military aid to India, 359, 370; Directorate General of Supply Co-ordination in, 373.
United Nations Organization: Food and Agriculture Organization (FAO), 133n., 309, 311, 315n.; Department of Economic and Social Affairs, 251n., 252–4, 262, 264f.,

United Nations Organization, *cont.*
266n., 269n.; World Health Organization (WHO), 269; sanctions against Rhodesia, 312; Conference on Trade and Development (UNCTAD), 319; *see also* International Bank for Reconstruction and Development.

United States, 135n., 245; food aid from, 11, 304, 324, 341–6; Dept of Agriculture, 96n.; agricultural exports of, 294n.; imports of, 296f., 311–12, 315f.; wheat production in, 305; import tariffs in, 319; total aid from, 323f., 339; political pressure on India, 341n.; Food for Freedom Act, 342; military aid to India, 352n., 353, 355, 359, 370.

Public Law 480 (PL480), 294n., 297, 305, 324, 329, 331; and farmers' incentives, 13, 102, 342–6; as share of imports, 93n., 294, 336, 341; use of counterpart funds of, 219–20, 341; jute imports under, 314.

Public Law 665 (PL665), 328, 341.
See also Aid; Food; Foodgrains; Incentives.

Universities, 103, 134, 213, 220, 224; investment in, 197–8, 243; political pressure on, 197–8, 215, 217–18, 224, 244; places in, 197f., 214, 216, 244; enrolment in, 201, 214; wastage rates in, 215, 218; affiliated colleges of, 216, 218–19; staffing needs, 221–2; wages and salaries in, 222–3.

Uranium, 182.

Urban bias, 271; in agriculture, 84, 101, 103f., 108, 124, 130–5, 140–1, 145; in employment planning, 143; in irrigation pricing, 171; in health sector, 206, 227.

Urban sector: labour force in, 93, 230; political power in, 142, 179; caste neutrality in, 281.

Urbanization, 89n., 96, 107, 154, 252.

USSR, 43, 297, 310; aid from, 324, 326, 328, 330, 339; Sino-Soviet relations, 361.

Utilization of capacity, 7, 9, 160f., 247, 305, 339; in industry, 7, 19, 23, 71f., 210, 212, 231, 337; in power sector, 23, 155, 170, 180; in

Utilization of capacity, *cont.*
public sector, 40; prices and, 75, 167–72; in railways, 158, 166–7; in irrigation, 160–3, 170; in ports, 160, 166; in fertilizer industry, 169; in education, 208f., 218, 224–5, 244; of labour force, 211, 233; in jute mills, 313, 316n.; aid and, 331, 333, 337, 339–40, 347–8; in civil sector for defence production, 366–9.

Uttah Pradesh, 270; Congress Party in, 55; family planning programme in, 267n.

Value-added: in industry, 69, 71–72, 77, 90n.; in agriculture, 90n., 107, 134.

Vegetable oils, 296, 298.

Vehicle industry: production, 76, 160, 301–2, 365; military requirements, 365, 370.

Venkatappiah, B., 50n.

Venkataraman Committee, 80.

Veterinary graduates, 202.

Villages, 27, 84, 119, 121, 126, 133, 273; balance of power in, 84, 135–41, 142, 285–88; leadership loss in, 104, 276; village buses, 109; village level studies, 120, 129, 132, 142, 274, 289; land reform and village structure, 126; politics in, 131; caste-structures of, 135–6, 273, 277, 280; education and, 195, 228; medical needs of, 206–8; see also *Panchayat*.

Village Level Workers (VLWs), 106, 121, 140, 145; training of, 121f.; 145, 205.

Wages and salaries, 40, 129, 243; in industry, 72, 78f., 92f., 223; in agriculture, 92n.; rural, 103, 120f., 228; urban, 103, 131; in teaching, 191, 194f., 222–3; medical sector, 191f., 194, 227f., 236, 265; inter-occupational differences in, 245; inter-regional differences in, 245; of tea plantation workers, 308f.; in jute mills, 315; in army, 355, 358f.

Water supply and sanitation, 238, 242; investment in, 27, 30, 152, 191f., 195, 235; rural, 27, 129, 178, 228, 235, 237f.; IAAP and, 110f., 145;

Water supply and sanitation, *cont.*
import content of investment in,
193; scarcity of, 234, 278.
Waterways, 153, 157.
Wells, 99, 141, 163; tube wells, 87,
152, 163, 179, 234; *see also*
Irrigation.
West Bengal, 132, 136, 154; Chief
Minister's claims for, 30f.; price
incentives in, 60; dry-milch cow
ratio in, 109; household land
holdings in, 125; caste in, 136;
coal fields, 181.
Wheat, 96, 107, 118, 142, 345;
production of, 97, 101, 117; prices
of, 106f; *see also* Cereals; Foodgrains.

White-collar professions, 284.
Women: in labour force, 202, 256;
doctors, 206–8, 227; widowhood
and remarriage of, 254, 284n.
Wool, 300, 305n., 365.
Works: local and rural public,
143f.
World Bank, *see* International Bank
for Reconstruction and Development.
World Health Organization (WHO),
269.
Worm infestation, 8, 95n., 129, 131,
138, 143, 237, 239.

Zilla parishad, 37, 132.
Zinc, 303, 371.